W. R. Cooper

Chaldean magic

Its origin and development

W. R. Cooper

Chaldean magic
Its origin and development

ISBN/EAN: 9783741169250

Manufactured in Europe, USA, Canada, Australia, Japa

Cover: Foto ©Andreas Hilbeck / pixelio.de

Manufactured and distributed by brebook publishing software (www.brebook.com)

W. R. Cooper

Chaldean magic

ITS

ORIGIN AND DEVELOPMENT.

TRANSLATED FROM THE FRENCH.

WITH

CONSIDERABLE ADDITIONS BY THE AUTHOR,

AND NOTES BY THE EDITOR.

BY

FRANÇOIS LENORMANT.

Multæ terricolis linguæ, cœlestibus una.

À

M. SAMUEL BIRCH, LL.D., F.S.A., etc.,

en témoignage

d'une vieille et respectueuse

affection.

CONTENTS.

	PAGE
Author's Preface	vii
Editor's Preface	ix
Chap. I.—The Magic and Sorcery of the Chaldeans	1
Chap. II.—The Chaldean Demonology	23
Chap. III.—Chaldean Amulets and their Uses	39
Chap. IV.—Chaldean Sorcery and its Dual Nature	58
Chap. V.—Comparison of the Egyptian with the Chaldean Magic	70
Chap. VI.—Contrasts between Egyptian and Chaldean Magical Systems	78
Chap. VII.—The Magic of the Ritual of the Dead	89
Chap. VIII.—Contrasts between Accadian and Egyptian Magic	107
Chap. IX.—The Chaldaio-Babylonian religion and its doctrines	111
Chap. X.—Development of the Chaldean Mythology	127
Chap. XI.—The religious System of the Accadian Magic Books	136
Chap. XII.—The Origin of the Myth of the Zi	143
Chap. XIII.—The Mythology of the Underworld	177
Chap. XIV.—The Religions and the Magic of the Turanian Nations	210
Chap. XV.—The Early Median Mythology compared with that of the Chaldeans	216

CONTENTS.

	PAGE
CHAP. XVI.—Finno-Tartarian Magical Mythology	241
CHAP. XVII.—Further Analysis of Finnish Demonology	253
CHAP. XVIII.—The Accadian People and their Language	263
CHAP. XIX.—The Accadian Language	268
CHAP. XX.—Differentiation of the Accadian and its allied Languages	283
CHAP. XXI.—Altaic affinities of the Accadian Language	292
CHAP. XXII.—Accadian and Altaic affinities	299
CHAP. XXIII.—Phonology of the Accadian Language	309
CHAP. XXIV.—The origin of the Kushito-Semitic religion	318
CHAP. XXV.—The two Ethnic elements in the Babylonian nation	331
CHAP. XXVI.—The Origin of the Chaldaio-Babylonian Cosmogonies	336
CHAP. XXVII.—The Priority of the Accadian Population of Chaldea	350
CHAP. XXVIII.—The Sumirian Influence in Chaldean and Babylonian Civilization	356
CHAP. XXIX.—The Influence of the Kushite Mythology in Chaldean Faith	367
CHAP. XXX.—The Turanians in Chaldea and Ancient Asia	371
CHAP. XXXI.—The Archaic Legislation of the Accadians	378
APPENDIX.—Sumir and Accad	387
INDEX.	

THE AUTHOR'S PREFACE.

THIS book came out in France three years ago. Since that time science has been making rapid strides, and in prosecuting my studies I have found a confirmation of many of my opinions. I could not therefore allow a translation of my studies relating to "Chaldean Magic" to appear without making a new edition of it, subject to various corrections and additions. To this end I have carefully revised all the translations of Cuneiform texts contained in this volume, and in some cases slight modifications have been necessary to bring them into harmony with the latest discoveries. I have added a translation of several interesting fragments which were not comprised in the French edition, and entirely rewritten some of the chapters. The book which I now offer the English public may, therefore, be regarded as an almost entirely new work, which alone represents the present state of my opinions and studies.

EDITOR'S PREFACE

"LA MAGIE CHEZ LES CHALDEENS," of which this present volume is an enlarged edition, was issued by M. Lenormant in the autumn of 1874; it was preceded by *Les Premières Civilisations*, and closely followed in 1875 by *La Divination et la Science des Présages;* all these works possessing the same characteristic feature: the exposition of Assyrian thought, as evidenced by the language of the Cuneiform inscriptions themselves, compared with the traditions and usages of other contemporary and descended races, both Semitic and Turanian.

The interest excited in the philosophical world by these treatises was still further increased, by the publication in England, almost immediately afterwards, of the late George Smith's *Chaldean Genesis*, in which for the first time since the era of Assurbanipal, the myths of the ancient Accadians were read in the light of day. By the additional texts thus recovered for the use of students, the premises of M. Lenormant were to a great extent confirmed; and the interest of Biblical scholars in Assyrian mythology showing every sign of increasing, it was deemed advisable to present the general public with an English edition of *La Magie*. This task was at once undertaken by Messrs. Bagster and Sons, and on the MSS. being sent to the author, he in the most generous manner offered to recast the earlier Chapters of the work, and to rewrite some of the latter. While this was being done, the researches of Prof. Sayce and other Assyriologists elucidated new facts, and discovered fresh parallels between the Accadian and Ugro-Finnic theologies. These discoveries had all to be considered and incorporated with the original text of M. Lenormant, and the result was, in the end, an almost entire remodelling of the French edition. To the editor was assigned, with the consent of the author, the office of adding references from English authorities to the citations already given from Continental writers, especially as

La Magie was, in its new form, designed for a larger circulation than that of scholars alone. The various texts issued in the *Records of the Past*, and the *Transactions of the Society of Biblical Archæology*, had to be cited wherever it was possible to do so; and further, such various readings noted as had been adopted by English translators. These numerous emendations, while they increased the value of the work, delayed its progress through the press far longer than was anticipated, and even now, at the last moment, it has been judged expedient by M. Lenormant to add an Appendix bearing upon the ethnographical meaning of the term "Sumirian," in reply to a pamphlet by Dr. Oppert, which has become the centre of a controversy, the waves of which have begun to reach our shores.

These circumstances will account for one or two apparent discrepancies in the present translation: viz., the use of the syllable "dug" for "khi," in the ideograms composing the name of the god Marduk, from p. 19 to p. 64, and its subsequent abandonment by the author in favour of the older reading in p. 108, *et seq.* The expansion of the note from Berosus on p. 157, regarding the deity Oannes into an Appendix to Chapter XIII., at p. 201, is another example of the progressive revision which this translation has undergone.

These revisions and corrections, both of the original work and the present translation, as passed by M. Lenormant, are only such as from the nature of the theme, and the advancing condition of Assyrian philology might be expected. Of Assyriology it may truly be written, "day unto day uttereth knowledge." There is probably no section of the science of comparative mythology of which, till recently, less has been known, or of which, at present, more authentic materials remain, than the subject of "Chaldean Magic : its Origin and Development."

W. R. C.

VENTNOR,
  November, 1877.

ERRATA.

Page 83, line 2 of note.   *For* Osiris Baris *read* Osiris *Baris*.

Page 103, line 14.   *For* Schu *read* Shu.

Page 133, line 6.   *For* Chaldaic Babylonian *read* Chaldaio-Babylonian.

Page 134, line 24.   ,,   ,,   ,,

Page 172, line 20.   *For* Silik-mulu-dug *read* Silik-mulu-khi.

Page 244, line 2 of note.   *For* Asyekoks *read* Angekoks.

CHAPTER I.

The Magic and Sorcery of the Chaldeans.

A GENERAL, but tolerably complete idea of the magic conjuration of the Chaldeans, its processes and its principal applications, may be obtained from a document which Sir Henry Rawlinson and Mr. Edwin Norris published "in facsimile" in 1866, in the second volume of their collection of the *Cuneiform Inscriptions of Western Asia*. This document is a large tablet from the library of the royal palace at Nineveh, containing a succession of 28 formulæ of deprecatory incantations, unfortunately partly destroyed, against the action of evil spirits, the effects of sorcery, disease, and the principal misfortunes which may attack man in the course of his daily life. The whole forms a litany of some length, divided into paragraphs, which all finish with the same solemn invocation. It would seem, judging from the concluding paragraph, that the intention was not to use the detached formulæ of this litany on special occasions, but to recite the whole as a protection from all the fatal influences against which it provides. This tablet, however, like all the other works on magic from Assyria and Chaldea, is written in Accadian, that is, in the Turanian language, which was related to the Finnish and Tartaric dialects spoken by the primitive population of the marshy plains round the lower Euphrates. An Assyrian translation accompanies the ancient Accadian text, and is placed opposite to it. Centuries ago, when Assurbanipal, king of Assyria, of the VIIth century before our era, had the copy made which has been handed down to us, this kind of document could be understood only by aid of the Assyrian version, which may be traced to a much earlier date. The Accadian was already a dead language; but the Assyrians attributed so much the more mysterious power to the incantations expressed in this language, because the script had become unintelligible.

In order to place the reader at once in the midst of the strange world into which I ask him to follow me, I shall now reproduce in its entirety the formulæ of this tablet, those at least which it is possible to interpret, for there are still some phrases which defy explanation, and I shall accompany my translation with short notes. I have been preceded in this undertaking by M. Oppert, with whom in most cases I agree perfectly. Should anyone, however, wish to compare our two translations, he will find some differences, which almost all result from the fact, that the learned Professor of the College of France has translated from the Assyrian version, while I have preferred to adhere to the original Accadian text. The Assyrian version is by no means always a literal one; and of this the reader may judge for himself, as I have annotated all the passages in which it differs from the earlier original. The Accadian text appears to be divided into rhythmical verses, each of which forms a separate line upon the tablet; I have marked these divisions carefully.

INCANTATION.

1 'The wicked god, the wicked demon,
the demon of the desert, the demon of the mountain,
the demon of the sea, the demon of the marsh,
the evil genius,[2] the enormous *uruku*[3]
the bad wind by itself,
the wicked demon which seizes the body(?), which disturbs the body.
Spirit of the heavens, conjure it! Spirit of the earth, conjure it!

2 The demon who seizes man,[4] the demon who seizes man, the *Gigim*[5] who works evil, the production of a wicked demon,
Spirit of the heavens, conjure it! Spirit of the earth, conjure it!

3 [6]The consecrated prostitute with the rebellious heart, who abandons the place of prostitution,

[1] Another version of this tablet has been published by Mr. Sayce in *Records of the Past*, Vol. I., p. 130 (*second edition*).

[2] "Noxious cherub." Sayce.

[3] I shall presently examine more closely these names of the various Chaldean demons.

[4] The Assyrian version reads "the demon who takes possession of a man." This is analogous to the Egyptian doctrine of the interpenetration of the soul by an evil spirit. See an article by M. Chabas in *le Bulletin Archéologique*, June 1855, p. 44.—*Ed.*

[5] "Spirit of the neck." Sayce.

[6] This passage has not been translated by Mr. Sayce.

the prostitute of the god Anna,[1] who does not do his service,

to the evening of the beginning of the incomplete month,

the sacred slave[2] who fails to go to his place,

who does not lacerate his chest,[3]

who does not . . . . his hand,

making his chest resound, completing . . . .[4]

Spirit of the heavens, conjure it! Spirit of the earth, conjure it!

---

4   That which does not go away, that which is not propitious,

that which grows up,[5] ulcers of a bad kind,

poignant ulcers, enlarged ulcers, excoriated ulcers, ulcers . . . . ,[6]

ulcers which spread, malignant ulcers,

Spirit of the heavens, conjure it! Spirit of the earth, conjure it!

---

5   Disease of the bowels, the disease of the heart, the palpitation of the diseased heart,

disease of the vision, disease of the head, malignant dysentery,

the tumour which swells,

ulceration of the reins, the micturation which wastes,[7]

cruel agony which never ceases,

nightmare,

---

[1] This is the Accadian name of the god who is called in Assyrian Anu.
[2] That is, "the slave of the temple."
[3] Compare 1 Kings xviii. 28.
[4] Many explanations have already been given of the monstrous aberration of the spirit of heathen devotion, which had produced in the religions of ancient Asia the infamous rites of *qedeschim* and *qedeschoth*; I shall not dwell therefore on this repugnant subject, but refer the reader to what has already been said. I only wish to remark that our magical formula will henceforth be one of the most important texts on the subject.
[5] "Spreading quinsy of the gullet." Sayce.
[6] The Assyrian version does not repeat here each time "the ulcer."
[7] Query, an unclean disease, Lev. xv. 1, etc.—*Ed.*

Spirit of the heavens, conjure it! Spirit of the earth, conjure it!

6 He who forges images,[1] he who bewitches
the malevolent aspect, the evil eye,
the malevolent mouth, the malevolent tongue,
the malevolent lip, the finest sorcery,
Spirit of the heavens, conjure it! Spirit of the earth, conjure it!

7 [2] The nurse.
The nurse whose breast[3] withers,
the nurse whose breast is bitter,
the nurse whose breast becomes ulcerated,
the nurse who dies of the ulceration of her breast,
the woman with child who does not preserve her offspring,
the woman with child whose embryo splits,
the woman with child whose embryo grows rotten,
the woman with child whose embryo does not prosper,
Spirit of the heavens, conjure it! Spirit of the earth, conjure it!

8 Painful fever, violent fever,
the fever which never leaves man,
unremitting fever,
the lingering fever, malignant fever,
Spirit of the heavens, conjure it! Spirit of the earth, conjure it!

9 Painful plague, violent plague,
plague which never leaves man,
unremitting plague,
the lingering plague, malignant plague,

---

[1] Here we have the first reference to a custom well known in the Middle Ages. A waxen figure was made, and as it melted before the fire the person represented by it was supposed similarly to waste away. It will be remembered that Horace (*Sat.* i.'8, 30, *et seq.*) speaks of the waxen figure made by the witch Canida in order that the lover might consume away in the fires of love. Roman and Mediæval sorcery had its origin in that of ancient Accad.—*Ed.*

[2] Untranslated by Sayce.

[3] The words "whose breast," in this and the following verses, are a very happy explanatory addition to the Assyrian version.

Spirit of the heavens, conjure it! Spirit of the earth, conjure it!

10 ' Painful disease of the bowels,
the infirmity which makes gloomy and cuts,[2]
the never-ceasing infirmity, the infirmity of the veins,
the infirmity which does not go away, the malignant infirmity,
Spirit of the heavens, conjure it! Spirit of the earth, conjure it!

11 That which acts in the mouth, the poison noxious to the voice,[3]
the expectoration of the consumption which noxiously prostrates,[4]
scrofula, pustules, falling off of the nails,
purulent eruptions, inveterate tetters,
shingles causing pits and scars,[5]
leprosy covering the skin,
food which reduces the body of man to a skeleton,
food which eaten is returned again,
liquids which make the drinker swell,
fatal poison which does not . . . .[6] the earth,
the pestilential wind which comes from the desert and returns not,
Spirit of the heavens, conjure it! Spirit of the earth, conjure it!

12 The frost which makes the earth to shiver,
the excess of heat which makes the skin of man to crack,
evil destiny . . . .

---

[1] Untranslated by Sayce.

[2] In the Assyrian version: "the colic disease." Is this a form of cutaneous malady in which the skin is hardened and cracks into sores?—Ed.

[3] In the Assyrian version. "The poisonous consumption which in the mouth malignantly ascends."

[4] Literally, the *sputa* or effete matter cast off by the lungs in mucus in advanced stages of the disease.

[5] This qualification is added by the Assyrian version. Herpetic maladies. See the Eleventh Tablet of the Izdubar Series, *Trans. Soc. Bib. Arch.*, Vol. III. part ii. p. 576, and Vol. IV. part i. pp. 68, 69.—Ed.

[6] Here is a word still untranslateable.

which unexpectedly cuts off a man's career,
parching thirst which aids the Spirit of the plague,
Spirit of the heavens, conjure it! Spirit of the earth, conjure it!

The XIIIth formula is too much effaced for me to attempt to translate it; but, judging from what remains, it was destined to avert the action of a demon dwelling in the desert.

The XIVth is in the same condition; its object was to ward off a misfortune which might attack a man at any time, eating, drinking, sleeping, or standing at his own fireside; possibly sudden death. Only the Accadian text remains of the four following formulæ; the Assyrian Version is destroyed.

15 He who in the gaol dies of hunger,
he who in the gaol dies of thirst,
he who being hungry in a pit (?)
beseeching (is therefore reduced to eat) dust.
he who in the earth or in the river,
perishes and dies,
the female slave who possesses no master,
the free woman who has no husband,
he who leaves an infamous memory of his name,
he who leaves no memory of his name,
he who in his hunger cannot recover,
he who falls ill and cries at the beginning of an incomplete month,[1]
Spirit of the heavens, conjure it! Spirit of the earth, conjure it!

16 The protecting god of man,
who (guarantees) the prolongation of man's life,
may he fortify him to the sight of the Sun![2]

---

[1] Or an unlucky month. See a list of these in Sayce's *Astronomy of the Babylonians*, Trans. Soc. Bib. Arch., Vol. III. part i, pp. 158, 159.—*Ed.*

[2] Compare Eccles. xi. 7, "a pleasant thing for the eyes to behold the sun."—*Ed.*

> The genius, the favourable giant,
> may he penetrate into his head
> for the prolongation of his life!
> He will never depart from him!
> Spirit of the heavens, conjure it! Spirit of the earth, conjure it!

The XVIIth formula presents difficulties which cannot be explained in the present state of our acquaintance with the Accadian language; we can only discern that it was the prescription of a protective and conjuring rite.

18 Two double bands of white cloth[1]
> upon the bed on the platform[2]
> as a talisman if he binds on the (right) hand,
> two double bands of black cloth
> if he binds on the left hand,[3]
> the bad demon, the wicked *Alal*, the wicked *Gigim*,[4]
> the bad *Telal*, the wicked god, the wicked *Maskim*,
> the phantom, the spectre, the vampyre,
> incubus, succubus, nightmare,
> wicked sorcery, the philter, liquid poison,
> that which gives pain, that which hurts, that which is evil,
> their head upon his head,
> their foot upon his foot,
> they never seize him, they will never return.[5]
> Spirit of the heavens, conjure it! Spirit of the earth, conjure it![6]

A great gap occurs here, occasioned by a fracture

---

[1] Untranslated by Sayce.

[2] See in the plates of M. Place's great work (*Ninive et l'Assyrie*) the position of the platform of the bed in the bedrooms of the harem of the palace of Khorsabad.

[3] We must follow the inversions of the text in order to preserve the division of the verses.

[4] See note 3 page 3.

[5] Rather "they shall never seize him, they shall never return."

[6] See a partial rendering of this passage by Mr. Fox Talbot in *Records of the Past*, Vol. III. p. 140.—*Ed.*

of the tablet, in which at least two formulæ, and the beginning of a third, have disappeared. I discovered in the British Museum a small fragment, which is not in the published text, and which, finding here its proper place, shews the end of the XIXth formula.

> . . . . . .[1] May the wicked demon depart!
> May they seize one another!
> The propitious demon, the propitious giant,
> may they penetrate into his body!
> Spirit of the heavens, conjure it! Spirit of the earth, conjure it![2]

The first line of the XXth formula, which is found upon the same fragment, shows that its object was to cure some disease of the bowels.

The remainder of the XXIst contains an enumeration of all the parts of the house from which the magical words were to exclude demons. All this portion is extremely obscure, and its translation is rendered almost impossible by the multiplicity of the architectural terms employed, to which we have no key, particularly as the Assyrian version is here wanting.

> 22   The phantom, child of heaven,
>   which the gods remember,
>   the *Innin*,[3] prince
>   of the lords.
>   the . . . .[1]
>   which produces painful fever,
>   the vampyre which attacks man,

---
[1] Lacuna.
[2] Of these magical tablets there were at least 30,000 in the royal library of Assurbanipal. Smith's *Assyria*, p. 20.—*Ed.*
[3] A species of Lemur. A kind of hobgoblin.

> the *Uruku* multifold
> upon humanity,
> may they never seize him!
> Spirit of the heavens, conjure!
> Spirit of the earth, conjure!

The tablet, in its present state, gives only the beginnings of the lines of the XXIIIrd and XXIVth incantations in the Accadian version; it is therefore impossible to try and translate them. All that can be discovered is, that in the first the god Silik-mulu-khi[1] is invoked, to whom texts of the same kind generally attribute the *rôle* of a mediator, and who is compared further on to the Marduk of the official religion of the Assyrian period; the second is addressed to the god of fire, Izdubar, which we shall describe later with more precision.[2]

The XXVth formula only exists in the Accadian; and that only as far as the first fourteen lines. These show, however, that it begins with an invocation to the water god, Nin-a-zu; it then treats of diverse maladies, and ends thus:

> The sea,
> the sea,
> the desert without water,
> the waters of the Tigris, the waters of the Euphrates,
> the mountain of the west, the mountain of the east,
> the agitated mountain,[3]
> may they close their chasms,
> Spirit of the heavens, conjure!

---

[1] See *Nimrod et les Ecritures Cuneiformes*, par Joseph Grivel, in *Trans. Soc. Bib. Arch.*, III. p. 137, where Silikmulukhi is identified with the god Amarud or Marduk.—*Ed.*

[2] The mythical hero Izdubar, whose name is said to mean, "Mass of fire." Rawlinson *On the Deluge Tablet*, in a letter to the *Athenæum*, 1873.—*Ed.*

[3] Perhaps a volcano; those near the river Chaboras were always active.

Spirit of the earth, conjure!

26 Nin-ki-gal,[1] spouse of the god Nin-a-zu,
may she cause him to turn his face toward the place where she is!
May the wicked demons depart!
May they seize one another!
The favourable demon,[2] the favourable giant,
may they penetrate into his body![3]
Spirit of the heavens, conjure!
Spirit of the earth, conjure!

27 The god Ztak,[4] the great messenger, the supreme ensnarer
amongst the gods, like the god of the heights.[5]
May he penetrate his head
for the prolongation of his life!
He will never depart from him!
Spirit of the heavens, conjure!
Spirit of the earth, conjure!

28 The man passing (on the earth), who makes sacrifices,
may pardon and peace flow for him like molten brass!
May the sun enlighten the days of this man![6]
Silik-mulu-khi,[7] eldest son of the ocean,[8]
strengthen in him peace and happiness!
Spirit of the heavens, conjure!
Spirit of the earth, conjure!

But the rich and varied information contained in

---

[1] Ninkigal, called in the Assyrian Allat, was the sister of Ishtar and the wife of the Assyrian Pluto; she was called "the lady of the great region," i.e., Hades. See Talbot, "The descent of Ishtar into Hades," *Records of the Past*, Vol. I. p. 141.—*Ed.*

[2] The Assyrian version has "the genius."

[3] Into the body of the person on whose behalf the invocation is made.

[4] The god who presides specially over the river Tigris; he keeps his Accadian name until the Assyrian epoch. His wife is called Nin-muk.

[5] In the Assyrian version: "the god who has begotten him."

[6] The Assyrian version has only "this man."

[7] The Assyrian version replaces this name by that of Marduk.

[8] Eldest son of Hea, the god of the ocean.

this text, which has now been placed for many years at the disposal of scholars, is extended and confirmed in the most happy manner by some new documents, which are soon to be presented to the public. Amongst the many thousand fragments of clay tablets discovered by M. Layard in the hall of the library in the palace of Kouyunjik on the site of Nineveh itself, and which are preserved at present in the British Museum, are the fragments of a vast work on magic, which, in its perfect state, formed a series of not less than two hundred tablets, and which was for Chaldea what the Atharva-Veda was for ancient India. This was such a collection of the formulæ, incantations, and hymns of the Chaldean magi as the classical writers speak of, and of whom Diodorus Siculus says: "They try to avert evil and procure good, either by purifications, sacrifices, or enchantments."[1] The fragments of this work have been patiently collected from the chaos of rubbish of all kinds in which they were buried; and they have been prepared for publication as the IVth volume of *The Cuneiform Inscriptions of Western Asia*, by Sir Henry Rawlinson. This eminent Orientalist from the other side of the Channel has laboured more than any one else to decipher the Cuneiform Anarian text, in which work he has been assisted by his young colleague Mr. George Smith, who has since taken for himself a prominent place in science. To give an idea of the material extent of the fragments under consideration, suffice it to say, that they are more than fifty in number, and contain many perfect tablets covered with from three to

[1] Lib. ii. Cap. 29.

four hundred lines of writing, and that they fill almost the whole of thirty folio copper plates. With a scientific generosity seldom seen, of which I cannot better show my appreciation than by proclaiming it, Sir Henry Rawlinson kindly sent me the proofs of the fac-simile plates of this publication, before they were brought out. It is one of the most precious works which has ever enriched Assyriology; and from it I have taken greater part of the data of the present treatise.[1]

The great work on magic, many copies of which had been executed by the scribes of Assurbanipal, according to the pattern placed centuries since in the library of the famous school for priests at Erech in Chaldea, was composed of three different books. We know the title of one of the three, " The Wicked Spirits," for we find at the end of each of the tablets, which come from it and which have been preserved entire, " Tablet No. — of the Wicked Spirits."[2] As the title shows, it was filled exclusively with formulæ of conjurations and imprecations, which were designed to repulse demons and other wicked spirits, to avert their fatal action, and to shelter the invoker from their attacks. Portions of a second book exist, and, judging from what remains of it, it would seem to be formed of a collection of these incantations, to which was attributed the power of curing various

---

[1] I thought it both fitting and useful to give in a note the origin of all the quotations I have borrowed from the volume which will soon appear, and which I designate by the abbreviation, *W. A. I.*, IV. The volume was issued to the public on the 1st of August, 1875.—*Ed.*

[2] See Fox Talbot, "The War of the Seven Evil Spirits," in *Records of the Past*, Vol. V. p. 163.—*Ed.*

maladies.[1] Lastly, the third book contained Hymns to certain gods. A supernatural and mysterious power was attributed to the chanting of these hymns, which are, however, of a very different character from the regular liturgical prayers of the official religion, a few of which have been preserved to us. It is curious to notice that the three parts composing thus the great work on magic, of which Sir Henry Rawlinson has found the remains, correspond exactly to the three classes of Chaldean doctors, which Daniel[2] enumerates, together with the astrologers and divines (*Kasdim* and *Gazrim*), that is, the *Khartumim* or conjurors, the *Chakamim* or physicians, and the *Asaphim* or theosophists. The further we advance in the knowledge of the Cuneiform texts, the greater does the necessity appear of reversing the condemnation much too prematurely pronounced by the German exegetical school against the date of the writings of the fourth of the greater prophets. The language of the Book of Daniel, interspersed as it is in various places with Greek words, proves without doubt that the definitive translation[3] as we possess it, is posterior to the time of Alexander. But the foundation of the work dates much further back; it is tinged with a very decided Babylonian tint, and certain features of the life at the court of Nebuchadnezzar and his successors are there pictured with a truth and exactitude, to which a writer a few centuries later could hardly have attained.

---

[1] A similar text has been translated by Mr. Sayce in *Records of the Past*, Vol. III. p. 147, and by Mr. Smith in *History of Assyria*, p. 18.—*Ed.*

[2] Daniel ii. 2; v. 11.   [3] "Redaction" in the original.—*Ed.*

The formulæ, hymns, and incantations in this triple collection are in the Accadian language, but they are accompanied by an Assyrian translation, placed according to the usual interlinear method. There are, however, some rare hymns, the original of which was no doubt already lost, since such a long period had elapsed since the first collection was made; and of these an Assyrian version only is given, of which the style bears the mark of a remote antiquity, and the syntax, by certain constructions contrary to the genius of the Semitic dialects, indicates the real character of the entirely different language in which the original was drawn up, and which has been lost to us for so many centuries. The different sections are separated by a deep mark, upon the tablet, and the beginning of each is preceded by the word *ên*[1] "incantation," which indicates still more clearly the commencement of a new formula. All the hymns of the third book finish by the Accadian word *kakama*, which is translated in Assyrian by "amen" (*amanu*).

The style of the conjurations to be used against the malevolent spirits is very monotonous, as they are all cast in the same mould. They begin by enumerating the various kinds of demons whom the conjurations are to subdue by their power, and then describe the effects of the charm. The desire to see them repulsed, or to be delivered from them, follows; and this is often expressed in the

---

[1] The ideograph which expresses this word is a complex character formed of the sign *su*, which represents the idea of "gathering" and "cohibition," and the sign *an*, "god." It seems therefore that the formation of this character proceeds from an idea analogous to that of the θεῶν ἀνάγκαι of the Neoplatonic theurgy.

affirmative form. The formulæ finished by the mysterious invocation from which they derive their efficacy: "Spirit of the heavens, conjure! Spirit of the earth, conjure!" This part alone is necessary, and is never wanting, but sometimes similar invocations of other divine spirits are joined to it.

I shall as an example now quote one of these conjurations, which was intended to combat different demons, diseases, and fatal influences, such as the evil eye.[1]

> The plague and the fever which scourge a country,
> the disease which devastates a country,
> bad for the flesh, fatal for the entrails,
> the wicked demon, the wicked *Alal*, the wicked *Gigim*,
> the malevolent man, the malevolent eye, the malevolent mouth, the malevolent tongue
> —of the man, son of his god,[2] may they depart from his body, may they depart from his entrails.
> They shall never take possession of my body,[3]
> they shall never do any evil in my presence,
> they shall never walk in my train,
> they shall never enter my house,
> they shall never step over my timbers,
> they shall never enter into the habitation of my house.
> Spirit of the heavens, conjure!
> Spirit of the earth, conjure!
> Spirit of Mul-ge,[4] lord of countries, conjure!
> Spirit of Nin-gelal,[5] lady of countries, conjure!

---

[1] *W. A. I.*, IV. col. 3.   [2] I shall explain this expression afterwards.

[3] This sudden change of person is a common feature of all Oriental composition to the present day, the Egyptian papyri and the chapters of the Koran abound with instances of it.—*Ed.*   [4] This is the great god Bel of the Assyrians.

[5] In the Assyrian, the goddess Belit.

Spirit of Nin-dar,[1] powerful warrior of Mul-ge, conjure!
Spirit of Nusku, sublime messenger of Mul-ge, conjure!
Spirit of En-zuna,[2] eldest son of Mul-ge, conjure!
Spirit of Tiskhu,[3] mistress of the armies, conjure!
Spirit of Mermer,[4] king whose impetuosity is beneficent, conjure!
Spirit of Udu,[5] king of justice, conjure!
Spirits Anunna-ge,[6] great gods, conjure!

Here is another, in which the final enumeration is less detailed.

The day of mourning, the wind which brings misfortune,
the day of misfortune, the fatal wind which makes itself felt,
the day of misfortune, the fatal wind which precedes it,
the children of vengeance, the sons of vengeance,
the messengers of loss,
the ravagers of Nin-ki-gal,[7]
the lightning which ravages the country,
the seven gods of the vast heavens,
the seven gods of the great earth,
the seven gods of the igneous spheres,
the seven gods, these are the seven gods,[8]
the seven malevolent gods,
the seven malevolent phantoms,
the seven malevolent phantoms of the flames, in the heavens seven, on the earth seven,
the wicked demon, the wicked *Alal*, the wicked *Gigim*,
the wicked *Telal*, the wicked god, the wicked *Maskim*,

---

[1] In the Assyrian Adar, the Hercules of the religion of the borders of the Euphrates and Tigris, and the god of the planet Saturn.
[2] In the Assyrian Sin, the god of the Moon.
[3] In the Assyrian Ishtar, the goddess of the planet Venus.
[4] In the Assyrian Bin or Ramanu (the biblical Rimmon), the god of the luminous atmosphere and of the atmospheric phenomena.
[5] In the Assyrian Samas, god of the Sun. Compare the Assyrian title of the Sun god Diannisu, "judge of men." Whence, probably, the title of the Indian Bacchus Dionysus. Fox Talbot.—*Ed.*
[6] In the Assyrian Anunna-irtsiti, the spirits of the earth.
[7] The earth personified as a goddess. This is an allusion to earthquakes.
[8] The Assyrian text gives: "the seven gods of the (celestial) legions."

> Spirit of the heavens, conjure!
> Spirit of the earth, conjure!
> Spirit of Mul-ge, king of the countries, conjure!
> Spirit of Nin-gelal, lady of the countries, conjure!
> Spirit of Nin-dar, son of the zenith, conjure!
> Spirit of Tiskhu, lady of the countries, which shines in the night, conjure![1]

But more generally there is no mythological enumeration at the end. As a type of the most simple formulæ I shall quote a conjuration against the seven subterranean demons, called *Maskim*, which were considered to be amongst the most formidable of the spirits:[2]

> They are seven! they are seven!
> in the depths of the ocean, they are seven![3]
> in the brilliancy of the heavens, they are seven![4]
> They proceed from the ocean depths, from the hidden retreat.
> They are neither male nor female,
> those which stretch themselves out like chains.
> They have no spouse, they do not produce children;
> they are strangers to benevolence;
> they listen neither to prayers nor wishes.
> Vermin come forth from the mountain,
> enemies of the god Hea,
> they are the agents of the vengeance of the gods,
> raising up difficulties, obtaining power by violence.
> The enemies! the enemies!
> they are seven! they are seven! they are twice seven![5]
> Spirit of the heavens, may they be conjured!
> Spirit of the earth, may they be conjured![6]

---

[1] *W. A. I.*, IV. 1.   [2] *W. A. I.*, IV. 2.

[3] There is a beautiful mythological account of a rebellion by these same seven evil spirits against the greater deities, translated by Fox Talbot in *Records of the Past*, Vol. V., p. 161. A new translation of this valuable mythological document, by the author of this book, will be given in the Appendix.—*Ed.*

[4] "In the heights of heaven." Fox Talbot.

[5] "They are seven, they are seven! twice over they are seven." Fox Talbot.

[6] See another version by Fox Talbot in *Records of the Past*, Vol. III., p. 143.

CHALDEAN MAGIC AND SORCERY.

We see that the Chaldean exorcist did not spare the use of invective against the demons he wished to repulse. The poetical imagination of the authors of the Accadian conjurations indulged itself in these accumulations of withering epithets, in descriptions of the sinister effects produced by the spirits of evil and of darkness, and further by an assemblage of images of a varied character, possessing often great brilliancy and remarkable power.

Sometimes also the formula of exorcism is extended, and partakes of a dramatic character. After having described the ravages made by the demons, it supposes that the complaint has been heard by the benevolent god Silik-mulu-dug,[1] who watches over man, and acts as a mediator between him and the superior gods.[2] But his power and science are not sufficient to conquer the more powerful spirits whose action must be averted. Silik-mulu-dug then addresses himself to his father Hea,[3] the divine intelligence which penetrates the universe, the master of the eternal secrets, the god who presides over theurgical action; he it is who reveals to his son the mysterious rite, the formula, or the all-powerful hidden name, which shall thwart the efforts of the most formidable powers of the abyss.

The incantations against diseases describe a great variety of cases, as may easily be seen from the long litany which we translated at the beginning of this chapter. But the most numerous are those which

---

[1] While passing through the press M. Lenormant has found reason to prefer the reading *dug* for that of the last syllable of the name of the god who has hitherto been rendered Silik-mulu-khi.—*Ed.*
[2] See another version by Fox Talbot in *Records of the Past*, Vol. III., p. 143.
[3] The Assyrians afterwards identified him with their Marduk, the god of the planet Jupiter, but they were quite different in their origin. *Ed.*

aim at the cure of the plague, fever, and " disease of the head;" this latter, judging from the indications which are given of its symptoms and its effects, appears to have been a sort of erysipelas, or cutaneous disease. It would be interesting if a traveller who was also a physician could discover whether there is now an affection of this kind which is peculiar to the marshes of the Lower Euphrates, as the elephantiasis is to Damietta. These are the principal passages of a long incantation against "the disease of the head:" the tablet on which we find it bears six other long formulæ against the same evil.[1]

> The disease of the head exists on man,
> The disease of the head, the ulceration of the forehead exists on man.
> The disease of the head marks like a tiara,[2]
> the disease of the head from sunrise to sunset.
> In the sea and the vast earth
> a very small tiara is become the tiara,
> the very large tiara, his tiara.[3]
> The diseases of the head pierce like a bull,
> the diseases of the head shoot like the palpitation of the heart.
> . . . .[5]
> The diseases of the head, like doves to their dove-cotes,
> like grasshoppers into the sky,
> like birds into space may they fly away.
> May the invalid be replaced in the protecting hands of his god!

This specimen will give the reader an idea of the uniform composition of these incantations against

---

[1] *W. A. I.*, IV. 3, 4.

[2] Or, as we should call it, a crown or ring, a common result of scalp diseases.—*Ed.*

[3] Meaning, "his power over the earth and the waters is diminished."

[4] Throbbing of the temples, produced by the distention of the bloodvessels of the head, and indicating a tendency to internal cephalic disease, contrary to the preceding malady.—*Ed.*   [5] Lacuna.

diseases, which filled the second book of the work under consideration. They all follow the same plan throughout, beginning with the definition of the disease and its symptoms, which occupies the greater part of the formula; and ending with a desire for deliverance from it, and the order for it to depart. Sometimes, however, the incantation of the magician assumes a dramatic form at the end, as we have just pointed out in certain conjurations against the evil spirits. An example is that dialogue in which the god Hea points out the remedy to his son, who has consulted him about it.

I have found another very remarkable illustration of this characteristic in a long formula, which required a whole tablet to itself.[1] The beginning is unfortunately very much effaced, and the gaps, which occur continually, prevent my giving a connected translation of this part. The text begins thus:

> The disease of the forehead proceeds from the infernal regions,
> it is come from the dwelling of the lord of the abyss,

In what remains of the verses which described in the most precise manner the effects of this malady; it treats of "the tumour which swells;" of "the suppuration which begins;" of the violence of the pain which "makes the sides of the head crack like those of an old ship." The text then relates that the invalid has tried the effect of purifying rites, which have not succeeded in subduing the scourge of the infernal regions: "He has purified himself, and has not conquered the bull; he has purified himself, and has not brought the buffalo under the

[1] *W. A. I.*, IV., 22, 1.

yoke; the pain continues to gnaw him like swarms of crickets." Here therefore the gods intervene, and from that point the narrative is consecutive.

> Silik-mulu-dug has helped him;
> he has gone to his father Hea into his dwelling, and has called him:
> "My father, the disease of the head is gone forth from the infernal regions."
> Twice he speaks to him thus:
> "Prepare the remedy; this man is not acquainted with it; he submits to the remedy."
> Hea has replied to his son Silik-mulu-dug:
> "My son, thou dost not know the remedy; let me teach it to thee.
> Silik-mulu-dug, thou art not acquainted with the remedy; allow me to teach thee the remedy.
> What I know, thou knowest.
> Come my son, Silik-mulu-dug.
> Take a sieve;
> draw some water from the surface of the river.
> Place thy sublime lip upon this water;
> make it shine with purity from thy sublime breath. . . .[1]
> Help the man, son of his god; . .[1]
> cover his head. . . . .[1]
> Let the disease of his head depart.
> May the disease of his head be dissipated like a nocturnal dew." . . . .[1]
> May he be cured by the command of Hea!
> May Davkina[2] cure him!
> May Silik-mulu-dug, the eldest son of the ocean, form the relieving image!

It is evident that in uttering these words, the magician is understood to do the things prescribed by the god.

---

[1] Lacuna. [2] Wife of Hea.

CHAPTER II.

The Chaldean Demonology.

THE documents of which I have just spoken, and to which we must add the numerous talismanic inscriptions to be found in our museums, engraved upon all kinds of Babylonian and Assyrian objects, show that there existed amongst the Chaldeans a demonology as refined and rich as the imagination of Jacques Sprenger, Jean Bodin,[1] Wierus,[2] or Pierre de Lancre[3] ever pictured. There is a complete world of malevolent spirits, the distinguishing characteristics of which are strongly marked, and their attributes determined with precision; while the hierarchy to which they belong is classed in a most learned manner. At the top of the scale are placed two classes of beings, which partake more nearly than the others of the divine nature; and are genii or demi-gods, a sort of inferior deities. The first bear the

---

[1] A French lawyer, a native of Angers who died A.D. 1596. His chief work, *La Demonomanie et des Sorciers*, has been often reprinted, and is a curious collection of illustrations of witchcraft and demonology.—*Ed.*

[2] A German demonologist, surnamed Piscinarius. He wrote a great book on witchcraft, entitled, *De Prestigiis Dæmonum*. He died A.D. 1588.—*Ed.*

[3] A French writer on Demonology, who caused many persons to be burnt to death for sorcery in the XVIIth century. He died A.D. 1630. His chief work is *Le Livre des Princes*.—*Ed.*

Accadian name of *Mas* "soldier, warrior," which is substituted in the Assyrian by *Sed* "genius;" the second, the Accadian name of *Lamma* "giant," translated in Assyrian by *Lamas*. In the religious texts these names often designate propitious and protecting genii, under whose shelter people placed themselves;[1] but at other times, wicked and hurtful genii, whose power had to be charmed away. Whether the Chaldeans believed that there were opposing parties of good and bad *Mas* or *Alap*, of good and bad *Lamma*, or whether they supposed them to possess, like certain gods, a double character, and to show themselves according to circumstances, now beneficent, now malevolent, sometimes protectors, and sometimes adversaries; is a question which must be left undecided until new researches have thrown more light on the subject.

We are better acquainted with all that relates to the spirits of an inferior and decidedly malevolent order, the demons properly so called. Their generic name is *Utuq*, which has passed from the Turanian Accadian into the Semitic Assyrian. This term comprises all demons, and may also sometimes be well employed as a general appellation for all spirits of an inferior rank to those of which we have just spoken. The name *Utuq*, however, further takes the more limited and special signification of a particular kind of demons. The other species are the *Alal* or destroyer, called in the Assyrian *Alu;* the *Gigim*, in the Assyrian *Ekim*, the meaning of which is not known; the *Telal* or

---

[1] The winged bull which guards the gates of the Assyrian palaces is a beneficent genius or *Sed;* hence this class of spirits receives also the name of *Alap* "bull," a term adopted even in the Accadian. The winged lion or *Nirgallu*, which sometimes takes the place of the bull in the same position, belongs also to the category of the *Lamas*.

"warrior," in the Assyrian *Gallu;* and lastly the *Maskim* or "layer of ambushes," in the Assyrian *Rabits.* As a general rule each class is divided into groups of seven, that most important magical and mysterious number.

We have at present no light on the respective hierarchical rank of the five classes of demons which have just been enumerated, the only faint ray upon this subject comes from the following fact, that speculations upon the value of numbers held a very important place in the Chaldaic ideas of religious philosophy.[1] In consequence of these speculations, each god was designated by a whole number of the series between one and sixty, corresponding to his rank in the celestial hierarchy. One of the tablets in the library of Nineveh gives the list of the principal gods, each with his mystic number. Now it seems that in connection with this scale of whole numbers applied to the gods, there was a scale of fractional numbers applied to the demons, and corresponding in the same way to their reciprocal ranks.

The *Utuq,* the *Gigim,* and the *Maskim,* were all three designated in writing by a complex group of ideographic signs, in which only the alteration of the first element effects a distinction, the others remaining the same; this variable element is always one of those signs which serve to note one of the most important divisions of unity in the sexagesimal

---

[1] There is an excellent tablet of these roots in *W. A. I.,* IV., Pl. 40. See also a special treatise on the mathematical values of the Chaldeans, by the author of this work. *Essai sur un Monument Mathématique Chaldéen, et sur le Système Métrique de Babylon,* Paris, 1868.—*Ed.*

system of numerations of fractions, one of the essential bases of Chaldean arithmetic. For the *Utuq* it is ⅓ or 20/60, for the *Gigim* ⅔ or 40/60, and lastly, for the *Maskim* ⅚ or 50/60.[1] I state this fact without undertaking to explain the odd speculations which gave birth to it, and I shall only remark that the hierarchical classification corresponding to the indication of these fractional numbers, placed each order of demons in a rank so much the more elevated, according as its numbers had a greater numerator. Of the three classes whose figures are known to us, the *Maskim* belonged to the highest, and the *Utuq* to the lowest.

The demons of the Babylonians were of two kinds. The most powerful and formidable were those which had a cosmical character, whose action was exercised upon the general order of nature, and whose wickedness had power to trouble it. In one of the formulæ which we quoted earlier, we saw that seven bad spirits were placed in the heavens: "seven phantoms of flame;" seven demons "of the ignited spheres;" forming an exact counterpart to the seven gods of the planets who were invested with the government of the universe.[2] Unfortunately the

---

[1] May not the mystical use of certain numbers by the writers of the Jewish Cabala have had their origin from these Babylonian theories?—*Ed.*

[2] It may be of interest to some readers to add the names of the angels, spirits, and intelligences of the planets. According to the Cabbala, they are as follows:—

Planet.	Angel.	Intelligence.	Spirit.
Sun	Raphael	Nagiel	Smeliel
Venus	Hamiel	Hagiel	Noguel
Mercury	Michael	Tiriel	Cochabiel
Moon	Gabriel	Elimiel	Lemanael
Saturn	Zapkiel	Agiel	Sabathiel
Jupiter	Zadykiel	Sophiel	Zadakiel
Mars	Chamael	Graphael	Modiniel

Kircher, *Ædipus Judiacus* II., pars i., p. 210.—*Ed.*

conjuration which speaks of these spirits does not give their name, we do not know whether they belonged to one of the different classes of demons whose appellations we have seen, or whether they constituted a seventh group of genii distinct from the others.

We have more information about the seven spirits of the abyss, which are mentioned in the same way without giving their names, in another formula, which has been already quoted. These were certainly the seven *Maskim* or "ensnarers:" demons which dwelt in the bowels of the earth, and which surpassed all the others in power and in terror. I have found a long incantation in six verses,[1] which depicts their ravages, and was to be pronounced in order to stop a great convulsion in the economy of the world which was attributed to their action, probably in the case of an earthquake. It is in fact directed against the Seven, the malevolent *Maskim*, who ravage heaven and earth, who trouble the stars of the sky and interrupt their movements.

> They, the Seven, proceeding from the western mountain,
> they, the Seven, increasing the eastern mountain.

Acting thus contrary to the normal course of nature, and the regular movement of the stars, these spirits inhabited the depths of the earth, they caused its tremblings, "they are the terror of its mass;" "they are without glory in heaven and earth." Their antagonist was "The god Fire*" who elevates himself,

---

[1] *W. A. I.*, IV., 15.

* There is a beautiful hymn to this potent deity, the analogue of the Agni of the Aryans, in 4 R. 14, l. 6. It is translated by Talbot in *Records of the Past*, Vol. III., p. 137, and a revised translation of the same will appear further on in the work.

the great chief who extends the supreme power of the god of heaven, who exalts the earth, its possessions, its delights," and who tried vainly to oppose their ravages. Having stated this, the incantation directs the god Fire to address himself to Silik-mulu-dug, the mediator before Hea.

> Approach Silik-mulu-dug, explain this prayer to him,
> to him, the command of whose mouth is propitious, the sublime judge of heaven.
> The god Fire has approached Silik-mulu-dug and explained the prayer to him;
> the latter in the dead of night has heard the prayer.
> He has gone into the house to his father Hea, and has called him:
> "Father, the god Fire has come and explained his prayer to me.
> Thou that understandest the movements of the Seven tell us in what places they dwell.
> Listen, son of Eridu!"[1]
> Hea has replied to his son Silik-mulu-dug; "My son, the Seven dwelling in the earth,
> they, the Seven, proceeding from the earth;
> They, the Seven going from the earth,
> they, the Seven which are born in the earth,
> they, the Seven which unfold themselves in the earth,
> shaking the walls of the watery abyss.
> Come, my son Silik-mulu-khi."

The indications given by Hea as to the means of conquering the terrible Seven follow, and are again also very obscure. He mentions some coniferous tree, cypress or cedar,[2] which is to break the power

---

[1] A town near the junction of the Euphrates and Tigris, the Rata of Ptolemy, actually called Abu-Shahrein. This was the earliest seat of the worship of Hea.

[2] The deity Marduk is often represented as holding a fir cone in his hand. See Bonomi, *Nineveh and its Palaces*, figs. 151, 152; and Smith, *Chaldean Account of Genesis.—Ed.*

of these *Maskim;* and also the supreme and magic name,[1] "the memory of which Hea keeps in his heart." The god reveals this name, before which all the powers of hell must bend, to his son. Other divine personages guided by the orders of Hea, Nin-kigal, goddess of the earth, Nin-akha-quddu, a goddess whose attributes are not well known, alternate with the god Fire to finish conquering and binding the *Maskim.* The whole inscription concludes by an invocation to Hea, master of the abyss of waters and lord of Eridu.

These demons had a general cosmical power, attacking mankind, and producing "the evil command which comes from the midst of heaven; the evil destiny which issues from the depths of the abyss;" fatal spells against which the following conjuration is directed in which their effects are described:[2]

> From the four cardinal points the impetuosity of their invasion burns like fire.
> They violently attack the dwellings of man,
> They wither everything in the town or in the country.
> They oppress the free man and the slave.
> They pour down like a violent tempest in heaven and earth.

The malevolent spirits were however pretty closely related to certain elementary spirits which do not belong to the order of demons, but which were considered, to quote the text, as "bad in themselves." Such were the spirits of particular winds, whose burning and unhealthy breath in the original state of

---

[1] This terrible name of the supreme Being, like the tetragrammaton of the Cabalists, was probably never uttered at full length. By the possession of this name the early Jewish opponents of Christianity declared that the miracles of Christ were performed. The mystical word *Om,* of the Budhists of India and Tibet is supposed to possess similar virtues to the present day.—*Ed.*

[2] *W. A. I.,* IV., 19, 1.

the climate of Chaldea favoured the development of diseases. The other demons were more directly connected with the ordinary incidents of terrestrial life; but these operated habitually upon man, spread snares incessantly for him, and were the cause of all his evils.

They, the productions of the infernal regions, says a conjuration,[1]

> On high they bring trouble, and below they bring confusion.
> Falling in rain from the sky, issuing from the earth, they penetrate the strong timbers, the thick timbers; they pass from house to house.
> Doors do not stop them,
> Bolts do not stop them,
> they glide in at the doors like serpents,
> they enter by the windows like the wind.
> They hinder the wife from conceiving by her husband;[2]
> they take the child from the knees of the man;
> they make the free woman leave the house, where she has borne a child.
> They, they are the voices which cry and which pursue mankind.

And in another:[3]

> They assail country after country.
> They take away the slave from his place.
> They make the free woman to leave her house and desert her child;
> they make the son quit his father's house.
> they make the dove from his dove-cote to fly away;
> they force the bird to lift himself up on his wings;[4]

---

[1] *W. A. I.*, IV., 1, 1.
[2] See Tobit vi. 13. There is probably no Biblical book which has received more illustration from the researches of students into Babylonian demonology than this Hebræo-Chaldaic History, and the *Book of Enoch*, especially caps. vii., sec. 2, and viii.—*Ed.*
[3] *W. A. I.*, IV., 27, 5.   [4] Thus causing it to fall out of its nest and be killed.—*Ed*

they make the swallow fly from his nest into space;
they cause the ox to run away; and the lamb to escape,
the wicked demons, who lay snares.

The habitual residence of these evil beings was in uncultivated wilds and deserts, from whence they wandered into inhabited places to torment mankind. This long litany, which I have already cited, enumerates the demons according to the places where they dwelt, as the desert, the bleak summits of mountains, the pestilential marshes, and the sea. In another place it is said that[1] "the *Utuq* inhabits the desert, the *Mas* dwells on the heights, the *Gigim* wanders in the desert, the *Telal* steals into towns." But their principal home was the desert, we read constantly in the magical texts of demons which watch man from the depths of the desert: and the object of the exorcisms was to send them back to those dreary solitudes. It was the general belief in Syria, as well as in Chaldea, and Mesopotamia, that demons inhabited the desert, and the Israelitish prophets appear to have countenanced the popular opinion. Isaiah, in describing the destruction of Edom says:

And thorns shall come up in her palaces,
nettles and brambles in the fortresses thereof;
and it shall be an habitation of dragons,
and a court for owls.[2]
The wild beasts of the desert[3] shall also meet with
    the wild beasts[4] of the island,
and the satyr shall cry to his fellow;
the screech owl[5] also shall rest there,
and find for herself a place of rest.[6]

[1] *W. A. I.*, IV, 16, 2. [2] Or "Ostriches," A. V. [3] Heb. *Ziim*.
[4] Heb. *Ijim*. [5] Or "Night Monster," A. V. [6] Isa. xxxiv. 13, 14.

Among the fatal effects exercised by these demons upon mankind, one of the most formidable was possession. There exist some special formulæ for exorcising those who were thus afflicted, and many passages in other incantations also allude to it. For example, the demons which might attempt to possess themselves of the body of the king, were repulsed by an incantation which finished with these words:[1]

> They shall not enter into the palace,
> they shall not seize upon the king.

This singular belief, common to the Egyptians, and all people to whom the influence of the Chaldaio-Assyrian civilisation extended, gave rise to one of the most curious episodes in the relations of Egypt with the nations on the borders of the Euphrates. This event happened at the commencement of the 12th century B.C., when the Egyptian suzerainty founded by the great conquests of the XVIIIth and XIXth dynasties still extended to the eastern part of Mesopotamia and it is related upon a famous Egyptian stele which is now preserved in the National Library of Paris. The Theban king, Rameses XII,[2] made a journey throughout his domain to receive tributes, and on the borders of Egypt met the daughter of the chief of the country of Bakhtan,[3] who pleased him so much that he married her. Some years later, when Rameses was at Thebes, he was told that a messenger from his father-in-law was waiting to beg the king to send a physician, chosen

---

[1] *W. A. I.*, IV., 6, 6.   [2] See *Records of the Past*, Vol. IV., p. 53.
[3] This lady was re-named by her husband, Raneferu, "most beautiful sun," as a mark of his affection. See Birch *Egypt*, p. 150.—*Ed.*

by himself, to the queen's sister, the princess Bint-reschit,[1] who was attacked by some unknown malady and was possessed with a demon.[2] So a renowned Egyptian physician,[3] belonging to the sacerdotal class, departed with the messenger. He tried in vain all the resources of his art; "the spirit refused to obey," says the obelisk, and the physician was obliged to return to Thebes without having cured the king's sister-in-law. This happened in the 15th year of Rameses' reign. Eleven years later, in the year 26, another messenger arrived. The chief of Bakhtan did not desire a physician this time, as it was his opinion that only the direct intervention of one of the gods of Egypt could cure the princess. As on the first occasion, Rameses consented to the request of his father-in-law, and the sacred ark of one of the great Theban gods, Khonsu, departed to work the required miracle.[4] The journey was long, lasting one year and six months. At last the Theban deity arrived in Mesopotamia, and the conquered spirit was expelled from the body of the young princess, who recovered immediately. A god whose presence alone was sufficient to work such miraculous cures was indeed precious, and at the risk of quarrelling with his powerful ally, the chief of Bakhtan resolved to keep him in his palace. So during three years and nine months the ark of Khons was detained in

---

[1] Or Bent-rash.
[2] The report was, "a malady has penetrated her limbs," literally, "there is an evil movement in her limbs," query, a kind of nervous paralysis.—*Ed.*
[3] He was a royal scribe also; his name was Tetemhebi.—*Ed.*
[4] The assent of the deity was given by a nod, or inclination of the head of the statue, "he moved the head very much." Khonsu was also a Fire deity; he was the third member of the great triad of Elephantine.—*Ed.*

Mesopotamia. But at the end of this time the Asiatic chief had a dream. He thought he saw the captive god flying away to Egypt under the form of a golden sparrow-hawk, and at the same time he was attacked with sudden pains. The father-in-law of the Theban king accepted the dream as a heavenly warning; and immediately gave orders for the ark to be sent back, and the god returned to his temple at Thebes in the 33rd year of the reign of Rameses XII.[1]

When once these possessing demons were expelled from the body, the only guarantee against their return was to obtain by the power of incantations, an opposite possession by a favourable demon. A good spirit must take their place in the body of the man; we have already had an instance of this in the XIXth and XXVth formulæ of the long litany translated in Chapter I.

> May the bad demons depart! May they seize upon one another!
> The propitious demon
> The propitious giant,
> may they penetrate into his body!

This beneficial possession was sometimes desired as the most happy of the supernatural effects of magic, even when it was not required to prevent the return of possessing demons. Such is the idea in a hymn for the prosperity of the king, which asks that he may be like the gods, and become the dwelling of good spirits.[2] This hymn is so curious that it is worth

---

[1] Dr. Birch, in the IVth volume of the new series of the *Transactions of the Royal Society of Literature*, and at full in *Records of the Past*, Vol. IV., p. 53. See also De Rougé, *Etude sur une stèle égyptienne appartenant a la Bibliothèque impériale*, Paris, 1858.—*Ed.*   [2] *W. A. I.*, IV, 18. 3.

while for us to translate what remains of it, in spite of the deplorable state of mutilation in which it is found: we must fill up the gaps to the best of our ability, so as to give a general idea of the meaning.[1]

> The crowns ....[2]
> distinguished shepherd ....[2]
> upon the thrones and the altars ....[2]
> The marble sceptre ....[2]
> Distinguished pastor ....[2]
> May the network of canals ....[2] (be in his possession);
> may the mountain, which produces tributes, (be in his possession);
> may the pasturage of the desert, which produces tributes, (be in his possession);
> may the orchards of fruit trees, which produce tributes, (be in his possession).
> The king, the shepherd of his people, may he (hold) the sun in his right hand,
> may he (hold) the moon in his left hand.
> May the favourable demon, the favourable giant, which governs the lordship and the crown, penetrate into his body!
> Amen.

In the creed of the Chaldean all diseases were the work of demons. Hence the fact, which attracted the attention of Herodotus, that in Babylon and Assyria there were, correctly speaking, no physicians. Medicine was not with them a rational science as with the Greeks; it was simply a branch of magic, and was practised by incantations, exorcisms, the use of philters and enchanted drinks. Nevertheless, in the composition of these drinks certain ingredients

---

[1] Compare another beautiful hymn on behalf of the king in *Records of the Past*, Vol. III. p. 133.—*Ed.* [2] Lacuna.

were employed, which experience had shown to possess a healing power. But their ideas upon the nature and origin of diseases were not very different from the medical incantations which we possess. Sometimes the disease was treated as an effect of the wickedness of different demons, and sometimes it seems to have been considered as a personal and distinct being, which exercised its power upon man. This personal character is particularly attributed to the two gravest and most fatal diseases with which the Chaldeans were acquainted,[1] the plague and fever, the *Namtar* and the *Idpa*.[2] They were represented as two demons, which were always distinguished from the other evil beings. They possessed very marked personal characteristics, and were considered as two of the strongest and most formidable of the demons who afflict mankind.[3]

The execrable *Idpa*,
says one fragment,[4]
    acts upon the head of man,
    the malevolent *Namtar* upon the life of man,
    the malevolent *Utuq* upon the forehead of man,
    the malevolent *Alal* upon the chest of man,
    the malevolent *Gigim* upon the bowels of man,
    the malevolent *Telal* upon the hand of man.[5]

---

[1] The Hindus of Dacca being visited with the small-pox, which proved very fatal to them, invented a goddess of the malady, whom they represented as a white woman covered with spots, and whom they besought to turn away the affliction from them.—*Ed.*   [2] In the Assyrian *Asakku*.

[3] In the story of the descent of Ishtar into Hades, Namtar is the servant of Allat, the goddess of those gloomy regions.   [4] *W. A. I.*, IV., 29, 2.

[5] In Egyptian mythology a nearly similar theory prevailed, every part of the body having its specific deity, who was invoked to protect it both in this life and after death. It was written of the deceased, "there is not a limb of him without a god," *Ritual of the Dead*, cap. xlii., "The chapter of turning away all injury, and turning back the blows made in Hades."—*Ed.*

In the train of these active demons, to whose agency all evil was attributed, were those other beings which, without having so direct an influence, manifested themselves by frightful apparitions, and bore a close resemblance to the shades of the dead, who were confined under the earth in the sombre dwellings of the infernal country, which corresponded exactly to the *sheol* of the ancient Hebrews. Such were the *Innin* and "the enormous *Uruku*," a species of hobgoblins and larvæ. But the three principal beings of this class were the Phantom,[1] the Spectre,[2] and the Vampire.[3] The two first alarmed by their appearance only, but the vampire "attacked man." The belief that the dead rose from the tomb under the form of vampires existed in Chaldea and Babylon. In a fragment of the mythological *epopée* which is traced upon a tablet in the British Museum,[4] and relates the descent of the goddess Ishtar into Hades, we are told that the goddess when she arrived at the doors of the infernal regions, called to the porter whose duty it was to open them, saying:

> Porter, open thy door;
> open thy door, that I may enter.
> If thou dost not open the door, and if I cannot enter,
> I will attack the door, I will break down its bars,
> I will attack the inclosure, I will leap over its fences by force;
> I will cause the dead to rise and devour the living;[5]
> I will give to the dead power over the living.

---

[1] In the Accadian *Rapganme*, in the Assyrian *Labartu*.
[2] In the Accadian *Rapganmea*, in the Assryrian *Labassu*.
[3] In the Accadian *Rapganmekhab*, in the Assyrian *Akhkharu*.
[4] *Records of the Past*, Vol. I., p. 143.
[5] "I will raise up the dead to be the devourers of the living." Fox Talbot.

The enumerations of the conjuring formulæ mention afterwards, as a distinct class, the demons who induced nocturnal pollution, and who abused sleep to bring men and women into their embraces, the Incubus, and the Succubus or the Lilith.[1] This Lilith plays a great part in the Talmudic demonology; the cabalistic rabbis forged a whole legend in which this spirit is stated to have taken a feminine form to deceive Adam and to have united herself to him. As we saw just now in the quotation from Isaiah the prophets even counted the Lilith amongst the number of demons. To the Incubus and Succubus was joined the Nightmare, in the Accadian *Kiel-udda-karra*, in the Assyrian *Ardat*. I know of no text which defines exactly its nature and its action; but it is probable, judging from its name, that it was one of those familiar spirits which make the stables and the houses the scene of their malicious tricks; spirits whose existence has been admitted by so many people, and which are still believed in by the peasants in many parts of Europe.

To this picture of the superstitions which alarmed the minds of the Chaldees must be added their firm belief in the evil eye, which is often mentioned in the magical conjurations, and in the fatal effects produced by certain unlucky words pronounced even involuntarily, and without any intention to injure; this last accidental augury was called "the malevolent mouth," "the malevolent word," and it is mentioned almost always in conjunction with "the evil eye."

---

[1] In the Accadian *Gelal* and *Kiel-Gelal*, in the Assyrian *Lil* and *Lilit*.

CHAPTER III.

Chaldean Amulets and their Uses.

"THE Hindoos have to do with so many demons, gods, and demigods, that it is no wonder they live in constant dread of their power. There is not a hamlet without a tree, or some secret place, in which evil spirits are not believed to dwell. Hence the people live in constant fear of those spirits of darkness, and nothing but the most pressing necessity will induce a man to go abroad after the sun has gone down. See the unhappy wight who is obliged to go out in the dark; he repeats his incantations, and *touches* his amulets; he seizes a firebrand to keep off his foes, and begins his journey. He goes on with gentle steps; he listens, and again repeats his prayers. Should he hear the rustling of a leaf, or the moaning of some living animal, he gives himself up for lost. Has he worked himself up to a state of artificial courage, he begins to sing and bawl aloud 'to keep his spirits up.' But, after all his efforts, his heart will not beat with its wonted ease till he shall have gained a place of safety.'"

[1] Blair, *The grave.*
[2] Roberts, *Oriental Illustrations of Scripture*, p. 542.

This description of the modern Hindoo is in every way applicable to the ancient Chaldees, and may give a good idea of the state of superstitious terror in which they were kept by the beliefs which have been mentioned in the foregoing Chapter. We will now inquire what was the aid offered to them by the arts of sacred magic against the demons and evil influences of all kinds, by which they believed themselves continually surrounded. There were first of all incantations like those we have already quoted. These incantations dated from the most remote antiquity, and were placed in collections like those of which we possess the remains. The complete knowledge of them could only belong to the priests of magic, who made of it a regular science. But every man had to know a few relating to the most common occurrences of life, and the most frequent dangers, in the same way that every Hindoo learns by heart a certain number of precatory *mantras*.

Acts of purification and mysterious rites also lent their aid to augment the power of the incantations. In one formula,[1] we read of a man who is to be preserved from injury:

> He has purified his hand; he has done the work for his hand;
> he has purified his foot, he has done the work for his foot;
> he has purified his head, he has done the work for his head,

and with this the evil spirits were supposed to have been put to flight.

[1] *W. A. I.* IV., 6.

We must add to the number of those mysterious rites, the use of certain enchanted drinks, which, doubtless, really contained medicinal drugs, as a cure for diseases, and also of magic knots, the efficacy of which was so firmly believed in, even up to the middle ages. Here is a remedy which one of the formulæ supposes to have been prescribed by Hea against a disease of the head:[1]

> Knot on the right and arrange flat in regular bands, on the left a woman's diadem;[2]
> divide it twice in seven little bands; . . .[3]
> gird the head of the invalid with it;
> gird the forehead of the invalid with it;
> gird the seat of life with it;[4]
> gird his hands and his feet;
> seat him on his bed;
> pour on him enchanted waters.
> Let the disease of his head be carried away into the heavens like a violent wind; . . .[3]
> may the earth swallow it up like passing waters![5]

Still more powerful than the incantations were conjurations wrought by the power of numbers. In this way, the supreme secret which Hea taught to his son, Silik-mulu-khi, when he consulted him in his distress, was always called "the number."[6] In a collection of metrical proverbs, and old popular Accadian songs,[7] we have these two couplets, which were to be sung

---

[1] *W. A. I.* IV, 3, 2.
[2] The diadem proper was simply an embroidered fillet, sometimes decorated with artificial leaves and flowers in gold and gems, it was tied in a knot behind the head, the two ends falling upon the shoulders; this was the Egyptian, Etruscan, and Assyrian form of the ornament. The later Greeks and early Romans converted it into a double or triple bandage for the hair, and the Byzantine princesses changed it into a thin circlet of solid gold.—*Ed.*
[3] Lacuna. [4] Qy., an euphemism for the virile members?—*Ed.*
[5] *Records of the Past*, Vol. III., p. 141, also *Trans Soc. Bib. Arch.*, Vol. II., p. 54.—*Ed.*
[6] In the Accadian *ana*, in Assyrian *minu*. [7] *W. A. I.* II., 16.

at some rustic fête, that was considered to exercise a happy influence upon the growth of the crops.

> The corn which stands upright
> shall come to the end of its prosperous growth ;
> the number (to produce that)
> we know it.
> The corn of abundance
> shall come to the end of its prosperous growth ;
> the number (to produce that)
> we know it.

Unhappily, although in the magic documents which we possess, frequent mention is made of conjuration by numbers ; and, although we know that the number seven had its particular functions, no single formula of these conjurations has been handed down to us, and the indications which remain upon this subject are not sufficiently precise.

But the highest and most irresistible of all the powers dwells in the divine and mysterious name, "the supreme name," with which Hea alone is acquainted. Before this name everything bows in heaven and in earth, and in Hades, and it alone can conquer the *Maskim* and stop their ravages. The gods themselves are enthralled by this name, and render it obedience. In the story of the descent of Ishtar into Hades, the celestial goddess is taken captive by the infernal goddess Allat.[1] The gods of heaven are much agitated about her fate, and try to deliver her ; the Sun goes to find Nuah (the Assyrian equivalent for Hea), to whom they always had recourse when spells were to be broken, and relates to him what has happened to Ishtar :

---

[1] Or "Ninkigal" in Fox Talbot's translation.—*Ed.*

CHALDEAN MAGIC AND SORCERY.

Nuah in the mysterious sublimity of his heart, has made a resolution:
he has formed the phantom of a black man,[1] in order to deliver her.
Go to her deliverance phantom; at the door of the immutable country present thyself.
Let the seven doors of the immutable country open before thee!
May the great Lady of the earth (Allat) see thee and rejoice before thee!
She will calm herself from the bottom of her heart, and her anger will be appeased.
Utter the name of the great gods.[2]
Bearing thy head high, attract her attention by miracles;
for the principal miracle produce the fishes of the waters in the midst of dry land.

And, in fact, Ishtar was immediately delivered. The great name remains the secret of Hea; if any man succeeded in divining it, that alone would invest him with a power superior to that of the gods. Sometimes also in that part of the incantation before us which takes a dramatic character, it is supposed that Hea is teaching it to his son Silik-mulu-khi. But, even then it is not uttered, it is not written in the formula, and they think that the mention of it alone is sufficient to produce a decisive effect when the incantation is recited.[3]

Everyone knows to what a pitch the belief in the all-powerful and hidden name of God has grown amongst the talmudical and cabalistic Jews, and how

---
[1] "He formed, for her escape, the figure of a man of clay." The original has *Assinnu*, which I have derived from the Chaldee word *Sin*, clay. But this is a mere conjecture." Fox Talbot, *Records of the Past*, Vol. I., p. 147.—*Ed.*

[2] "Awe her (Ninkigal) with the names of the great gods." Fox Talbot.—*Ed.*

[3] Our readers will at once recollect the reserve of Herodotus in mentioning the name of Osiris.—*Ed.*

general it still is amongst the Arabs. We now see clearly that it came from Chaldea. After all, such a notion ought to have taken rise in a country where they considered the divine name, the *Sehem*,[1] as endowed with properties so special and individual that they succeeded in making of it a distinct person. We can but quote the celebrated axiom of Varro, "*nomen numen.*"

Side by side with the incantations, the Chaldeans, and later, the Assyrians following their example, made great use of talismans.[2] A formula which was to be recited over one of these talismans for preventing the demons from stealing into the different parts of the house, and which was supposed to give to it its efficacy,[3] extols the power of it in magnificent terms, and shows the gods themselves as subject to it.

> Talisman, talisman, boundary that cannot be taken away,
> boundary that the gods cannot pass,
> boundary of heaven and earth, which cannot be displaced,
> which no god has fathomed,
> which neither god nor man can explain,
> barrier that cannot be taken away, disposed against malevolence,
> barrier immoveable, which is opposed to malevolence!
> Whether it be a wicked *Utuq*, a wicked *Alal*, a wicked *Gigim*, a wicked god, a wicked *Maskim*,
> a Phantom, a Spectre, a Vampire,
> an Incubus, a Succubus, a Nightmare,
> or else the bad plague, the painful fever, or a bad disease;
> he who raises his head against the propitious waters of the god Hea,

---

[1] Cf. the *Memra* of the Cabalistic Jews.
[2] In the Accadian *Sagba*, in the Assyrian *Mamit*.
[3] *W. A. I.* IV., 16.

may the barrier of the god Hea (stop him) !
He who attacks the barns of the god Serakh,[1]
may the barrier of the god Serakh hold him imprisoned !
He who crosses the boundary (of property,) the (talisman) of the gods, boundary of heaven and earth, will never let him go again ! He who does not fear the . . . . .[2] may the (talisman) retake him a prisoner !
He who lays ambushes against the house,
may they imprison him in the dungeon of the house !
Those who hold each other in an embrace, may he repulse them together into desert places !
He who works mischief at the door of the house,
may he be imprisoned in the house, in a place from which there is no outlet !
He who endeavours to injure the columns and the capitals,
may the column and the capital stop his way !
He who slides into the young oak and under the roofing,
he who attacks the sides of the door and the grates,
may he (the talisman) make him weak like water ! may he make him tremble like leaves ;
may he grind him like paint ![3]
May he leap over the timber, may he cut his wings !

The talismans were of different kinds. First of all there were those which consisted of bands of cloth, covered with certain written formulæ, and were fastened to the furniture or the garments like the phylacteries of the Jews.[4] There were also the amulets in different materials, which were worn round the neck, as a safeguard against diseases, demons, and misfortunes. Amulets of this sort, in

---

[1] In the Assyrian Nirba, the god of harvests.   [2] Lacuna.

[3] That is, "grind him to powder," "come du fard quil le broie."

[4] The preparation of one of these talismans is prescribed in the XVIIIth formula of the long litany translated above. See also *Records of the Past*, Vol. III., p. 142, note.—*Ed.*

hard stones,¹ occur frequently in museums. They are often engraved with images of divinities or genii, and always have a talismanic formula. Here is one which was to be worn by a woman with child. There are two such specimens in the collections of the British Museum. It is quite an exceptional case that it should be written in the Semitic-Assyrian language.

> I am Bit-nur, the servant of Adar, the champion of the gods, the favourite of Bel.
> Incantation. O Bit-nur, remove far from us all pains; strengthen the germ, develop the head of man.²

The greater number of the formulæ which are inscribed in this manner upon amulets are in the Accadian language. I shall now quote one of them, which was evidently intended to preserve a man who was already cured of the plague, from experiencing any relapse.

> Incantation. Wicked demon, malignant plague, the Spirit of the earth has made you leave his body. May the favourable genius, the good giant, the favourable demon, come with the Spirit of the earth.
> Incantation of the powerful, powerful, powerful,³ god. Amen.⁴

The legends in which the Mussulman writers delight each time that they speak of the heathen antiquity, and of the ancient Asiatic empires, whose

---

¹ It must be noted that the oldest Egyptian scarabei and amulets were wrought in steatite and soft materials, it was not till the revived empire that they obtained the power of engraving in hard stones, indeed the finest amulets wrought in lapis lazuli belong to the Greco-Egyptian period.—*Ed.*

² Lenormant, *Choix de textes Cunéiformes*, No. 24.

³ This iteration is a common form of concluding the magical texts on Assyrian divination or talisman cups. Many are engraved and translated in Layard's *Nineveh*, and an exceptionally fine, albeit, late example, is published by Rev. J. M. Rodwell in *Trans. Soc. Bib. Arch.*, Vol. II., p. 118.—*Ed.*

⁴ Lenormant, *Choix de textes Cunéiformes*, No. 26.

history they have forgotten, but the monuments of which still strike them with astonishment, and seem to them the work of a supernatural power; these legends, I say, are filled with stories of talismanic statues, composed according to the rules of magic, to which are attached the destinies of empires, cities, or individuals. The narratives are only worthy of the *Arabian Nights;* nevertheless, they often contain a confused tradition of a true fact, for, at the present time, we can prove by texts and original monuments that the Chaldeans, and their disciples the Babylonians and Assyrians, believed in these talismanic images, and used them frequently.

When M. Botta searched the palace of Khorsabad, he discovered under the pavement of the threshold, a number of statuettes in biscuit pottery, which may be seen in the Louvre.[1] They are some rather rough images of the gods: Bel with a tiara ornamented with many rows of bulls' horns; Nergal with a lion's head; Nebo bearing a sceptre. In the inscription preserved at Cambridge, Nergalsarossor, the Neriglissor of the Canon of Ptolemy, one of the Babylonian successors of Nabuchodorossor, speaking of his restoration of the doors of the sacred pyramid of Babylon, says that he had had placed there "eight talismanic figures in solid bronze, which were to keep all wicked and antagonistic people at a distance by the fear of death."[2] The use of these images, and the power attributed to them, are minutely explained by a mutilated magic formula, which orders that a

---

[1] For engravings of these, see Bonomi, *Nineveh and its Palaces,* p. 179.
[2] See *Records of the Past,* Vol. V., p. 138.

number of such little figures shall be placed in the house in order to protect it.

> Place the image of the god Nergal, who is without an equal, in the enclosure of the house.
> (Place) the image of the god, showing courage, which is without an equal,
> and the image of the god Narudi, lord of the great gods, on the ground near the bed.
> In order that no evil may happen, (place) the god N . . .[1]
> That his god . . . .[2] N[3]   that his goddess . . . .[2]
> and the god Latarak at the door.
> In order to repulse all evil (place) as a scarecrow at the door . . . .[2]
> the fighting hero (Nergal) who cuts in pieces, inside the door.
> (Place) the fighting hero who cuts in pieces, who rules the hand of rebels on the threshold of the door,
> right and left.
> Place the guardian image of the god Hea and the god Silik-mulu-khi, inside the door,
> right and left.
> the lip of the god Silik-mulu-khi, who inhabits the image . . . .[4]
> That his lips may grant to him a (joyous) regeneration like the coming in and going forth of young animals.[5]
> O ye, offspring of the ocean, sublime children of Hea . . .
> eat well, drink freely in order to be on your guard; that no harm (may penetrate)
> . . . .[2] before the face of seven images
> who bear . . . .[2] who bear arms.[6]

The last paragraph seems to indicate very clearly

---

[1] Here follows a name which has not yet been deciphered.   [2] Lacuna.
[3] This space for a proper name has been left blank for the insertion of that of the man in whose favour the incantation was to be used.
[4] See also *Records of the Past*, Vol. III., p. 142.
[5] In Assyrian, "He has confirmed his spell of agreement upon him."
[6] *W. A. I.* IV., 2, 1.

that it was the custom to place in some part of the house, food and vessels of drink for the gods and genii whom people called upon to guard their houses by covering themselves with their images, as protecting talismans. I think amongst no people do we find the idea that the gods obtained material sustenance and new strength from the offerings made to them, expressed in more set terms than in the Accadian magical documents. Thus I read in an incantation to the Sun :[1]

> Make a ray of peace shine upon him, cure the disease.
> The man, son of his god,[2] is burdened with the load of his shortcomings and his transgressions,
> his limbs are diseased, his disease pollutes him painfully.
> Sun, at the lifting up of my hands, come at my call,
> eat his food, absorb his sacrifice, strengthen his hand!
> By thy command, may his iniquities be pardoned, may his transgressions be put away!

A formula which Sir Henry Rawlinson has not inserted in his collection, and which I have copied from an unpublished tablet in the British Museum, bearing the number K 142, relating to the enumeration of the demons, and the diseases from which it was to preserve the possessor; ends with these words:

> Feast, sacrifice, and draw near all of you.
> May your incense ascend to heaven,
> may the Sun absorb the meat of your sacrifice,
> may the son of Hea, the warrior (who combats) witchcraft and sorcery, prolong your life!

---
[1] W. A. I. IV., 17.
[2] The pious man; I shall explain this expression later.

And, lastly, in a small fragment of a magical hymn,[1] it is said to a god:

> In sublime dishes eat sublime food.
> From sublime cups drink sublime waters.
> May thine ear be disposed to judge favourably of the king, son of his god.

Talismanic figures of quite another kind, but inspired by a much more original idea, were also employed. The Chaldeans represented the demons under such hideous forms that they believed that it was sufficient for them to be shown their own image, to cause them to flee away alarmed. The application of this principle is illustrated in an incantation against the plague, followed by a prescription for curing it, which is not in Sir Henry Rawlinson's collection.[2]

> The malevolent *Namtar*[3] burns the country like fire;
> *Namtar* attacks man like fever;
> *Namtar* spreads over the plain like a chain;
> *Namtar* like an enemy takes man captive;
> *Namtar* burns man like a flame;
> *Namtar* has no hand, no foot, he comes upon man like a snare;
> *Namtar* bends the invalid like a bundle;
> he pollutes his . . . .[4]
> he shuts his . . . .[4]
> he seizes . . . .[4]
> . . . .[4]
> His god . . . .[4] oppresses him (the invalid)
> His goddess (expels) the good from his body.
> Silik-mulu-dug (has accorded to him) his (propitious) favour;

---

[1] *W. A. I.* IV. 13, 2.

[2] British Museum, Tablet K 1284. Edited in my *Études Accadiennes*, II., 1, No. 18.

[3] The plague.   [4] Lacunæ.

CHALDEAN MAGIC AND SORCERY. 51

to his father, the Lord of the earth,[1] into the dwelling he entered and said to him:

"My father, the malevolent *Namtar* is burning the country like fire."

For the second time he said to him:

"He has tried the remedy; he does not know the remedy; he is submissive to the remedy."

The Lord of the earth made answer to his son Silik-mulu-dug:

"My son, thou dost not know the remedy; let me prepare the remedy. Silik-mulu-dug, thou dost not know the remedy, let me prepare the remedy for thee.

"What' (I know, (now) thou knowest it also).

Come, my son,[2] (Silik-mulu-dug).

Mould the . . . .[3] of the ocean,

make of it an image in his likeness (*Namtar*).

Lay the man . . . .[3]

Apply (the image) to the living flesh of his body;[4]

instil into him the regenerative grace of Eridu;

turn his face towards the setting sun.[5]

May the malevolent *Namtar* who possesses him pass into the image!"

Amen.

The image in his likeness is all powerful.

The museum of the Louvre has lately bought a very curious bronze statuette of Assyrian workmanship. It is the figure of a horrible demon in an

---

[1] Hea.

[2] These dialogues which occur very frequently in the incantations are only briefly indicated here by the first words of their principal parts.   [3] Lacunæ.

[4] The Buddhists of Ceylon still apply to the diseased part of the body the image of the demon, who is considered to have propagated the disease, thinking to cure it thus. J. Roberts, *Oriental Illustrations of Scripture*, p. 171.

[5] It is curious that in Egypt all good and healing and life proceeded from the West, the land of the setting sun, and all evil from the East, the land of its rising. See *Ritual of the Dead*, Caps. xv., and xciii., "The Chapter of not causing a Person to go to the East from Hades."—*Ed.*

upright posture, with the body of a dog, the feet of an eagle, the claws of a lion, the tail of a scorpion, the head of a skeleton but half decayed, and adorned with goats' horns, and the eyes still remaining, and lastly four great expanded wings.' This figure was originally suspended by a ring behind the head. On the back there is an Accadian inscription, which informs us that this hideous creature was the demon of the south-west wind, and by placing this image at the door or the window, its fatal influence might be averted. In Chaldea, the south-west wind comes from the deserts of Arabia, and its burning breath which dries up everything causes the same havoc as the *Khamsin* in Syria, and the *Simoon* in Africa. This particular talisman was an example of one of the most numerous species of amulets. The British Museum alone possesses two specimens of the repulsive head of this demon of the south-west wind, one in a yellow, and the other in a red, stone, each bearing the same magical formula as the bronze one of the Louvre; there is also a third specimen in bronze but without any inscription.

The collections of the various museums contain many similar images of demons, which were made in order to serve as talismans, and to keep at a distance the wicked spirits which they were supposed to represent. Some have the head of a ram upon a neck of immense length, others the head of a hyæna with an enormous open mouth, the body of a bear, and

---

' Many nearly similar monstrous combinations are found on the Gnostic gems, especially those from the East. A very large collection of them is contained in Montfaucon, *L'Antiquité Expliquée.—Ed.*

the claws of a lion. The imagination of the sculptors of the middle ages was not more fertile than that of the Babylonians and Assyrians in forming, by means of odd combinations, horrible types of demons. Unhappily, as a rule, we do not know the exact name to give to these singular representations.

The monstrous forms thus assigned to the demons, which were composed of parts borrowed from the most different animals, were also, according to Berosus, characteristic features of the first rudimentary beings born in the darkness of chaos, before Bel-Marduk the demiurgus began his work. The Assyrian and Babylonian artists, as Mr. Smith lately proved,[1] even represented by a figure of this sort the mother and queen of these monstrous beings, Tihamat, the personification of the primordial sea, the source of all things, the Tauthe of Damascius, the Thavath-Omoroca of Berosus. In fact certain legends, like the one of which Mr. Smith has discovered the fragments, described the labours of Bel-Marduk, as organizing the still chaotic mass under the figure of a struggle between the god and the mystical Tihamat, who is represented by a monster in whom all the disorder of the primitive creation was reflected. This struggle is depicted upon some cylinders and in a large bas-relief of Nimrod (at present in the British Museum); on which Tihamat has the body the head and the fore-paws of a lion, the wings the tail and the hind claws of an eagle, while the neck and

---

[1] In *Babylonian Account of Genesis*. See also *Trans. Soc. Bib. Arch.*, Vol. IV., p. 287.

upper part of the body are covered with feathers or scales.

The magical documents however throw much light, which we might elsewhere seek in vain, upon the interpretation of these figures.

There are in the sculptures of the Assyrian palaces, side by side with historic scenes and religious representations, many bas-reliefs incontestably of a talismanic character, which were intended to avert fatal influences on the principle that an image has the same value as an incantation, and like it, acts in a direct manner upon the wicked spirits.

The winged bulls with human heads, which flanked the entrance gates, were genii which kept real guard, and were tied to the post all the time that their image dwelt there without being disturbed. This is expressed as follows by the king Esarhaddon in one of his inscriptions:

> May the guardian bull, the guardian genius, who protects the strength of my throne, always preserve my name in joy and honour until his feet move themselves from their place![1]

At Koyunjik, in the magnificent residence which Assurbanipal had constructed in the heart of Nineveh itself, there were represented in many of the chambers numbers of monstrous figures having the body of a man, the head of a lion, and the feet of an eagle.

---

[1] See Fox Talbot, "Inscription of Esarhaddon" in *Records of the Past*, Vol. III., p. 121.

> "Bulls and lions carved in stone,
> which with their majestic mien
> deter wicked enemies from approaching.
> The guardians of the footsteps, the saviours
> of the path of the king who constructed them,
> right and left I placed them
> at the gates."

These were arranged in groups of two figures fighting with daggers and clubs. There were other demons also, and the sculptures were only a pictorial translation of the formula which we have already met with in many incantations.

> May the bad demons depart, may they seize (upon) each other!

Evidently therefore the Chaldeans believed that to sketch upon the walls of the palaces the combats of these demons was one way of repeating for ever under another form the imprecation which condemned them to conflict and defeat.

Nothing is more common than to see upon the small cylinders of hard stone, which were used as seals by the Babylonians and Assyrians, representations of combats of monsters of various singular forms, with one of the two gods Adar or Nergal,[1] the Hercules and Mars of the religion of the countries bordering the Euphrates and the Tigris. In the monsters which are being attacked we recognize the evil demons, and indeed according to the magical texts the two gods in question were specially charged with a mission to struggle against malevolent spirits. A whole hymn of the magical collection is dedicated to the celebration of the warlike exploits of Nin-dar,[2] and in an incantation against numerous demons one of the final wishes is, " may they come before Nergal, the powerful warrior of Mul-ge."

Sometimes instead of wrestling with fantastic monsters, the gods we have just mentioned struggle with one or many bulls or bull-headed men whom they

---

[1] In the Accadian *Nin-dar* and *Nirgal*.   [2] *W. A. I.* IV., 13, 1.

assail with their swords. In the earlier days of Assyriology some students sought in this subject to find some astronomical significance in connection with the presence of the sun in the sign of Taurus, and a very estimable scholar has even discovered in these conflicts an indication of the Babylonian origin of the Mithriac mysteries, as also the connecting link of a complete theory of the Asiatic religion. These theories were however vain attempts to discover many mysteries where really there was nothing so sublime. Subjects of this kind never represented anything but Adar or Nergal as warlike gods triumphing over demons of the kind called by the Accadians *Telal*, and the Assyrians *Gallu*, demons in the form of a bull, which, as we learn by this fragment of conjuration, were particularly hurtful to man:[1]

> Devastator of heaven and earth, devastator of the earth,
> the genius who devastates countries.
> the genius who devastates countries and whose power is very great,
> whose power is very great, whose trampling is formidable,
> *Telal*, the bull which pierces, the very strong bull, the bull which passes through dwellings,
> (it is) the indomitable *Telal*, there are seven of them.[2]
> They obey no commands,
> they devastate the country like . . . . ;[3]
> they know no order,
> they watch men,
> they devour flesh; they make blood flow; they drink blood;

---

[1] *W. A. I.* IV., 2, 4.

[2] So also the Egyptians had seven mystical cows, or Hathors, and seven bulls. The cows were mysteriously connected with life and death. See *Ritual of the Dead*, Cap. cxlix.—*Ed.*

[3] Here is the name, which is still however doubtful, of a kind of gnawing and destructive animal.

they (injure) the images of the gods;
they are the *Telal* which multiply hostile lies,
which feed on blood, which are immovable.

The figure of the celestial gods conquering the demons could nowhere find a better place than upon the cylinders. By the mysterious and protecting virtue attributed to it, this representation made them into talismans for those who wore them, and preserved the secrets or treasures which bore its imprint from diabolical encroachments.

The discovery by Mr. Smith of the epic legend of Izdubar, suggests a new and probable interpretation of some of the representations on the cylinders, in which the gods and heroes are fighting against a bull. It signifies the struggle of Izdubar and his companion Heabani against the bull created by Anu at the request of Ishtar, who desires to revenge herself upon the hero of Erech for his disdain, and this struggle is related in the VIth tablet of the poem. But we must not, I think, generalize this application too much. The representation of the episode which occurs in the legend of Izdubar seems to me particularly distinguished by the fact that the heroes combating the bull are two in number; one, Heabani, who is holding the animal by the head and tail, while the other, Izdubar, is piercing it with his sword, in accordance with the details of the epic recital. But when, as often happens, two persons are combating two bulls, or creatures which are half men half bulls, I consider it quite a different subject, and I think the interpretation here proposed must be adopted.

CHAPTER IV.

Chaldean Sorcery and its Dual Nature.

AMONGST all nations the belief in that magical power, which, by means of certain words and rites, commands the evil spirits and constrains the gods themselves to obey him who knows all their powerful secrets, has produced in the natural order of things a dual system corresponding to that of the good and bad spirits. The supernatural power by which man succeeds in conquering the spirits may be in its nature either divine or diabolical, celestial or infernal.[1] In the first case it is confounded with the power that the priest derives from the superior gods; it is exercised in a beneficent manner to avert misfortunes, to conjure diseases, and to combat demoniacal influences. In the second case it becomes perverse and impious, constituting sorcery or witchcraft with all their criminal aberrations. This distinction was made by the Chaldeans, and it exists

---

[1] Those who are interested in these distinctions may read with profit the works of Dr. John Dee, as transcribed by his assistant, John Kelly, and edited with ample notes by Meric Casaubon, the son of the famous reformer. It contains perhaps the finest and latest examples of the peculiar rites of the Chaldao-Mediæval sorcerers.—*Ed.*

everywhere, except perhaps amongst some positively barbarous tribes, by whom the priest of magic is more feared for his sorcery than blessed for his beneficent conjurations.[1] Of course the sacred books, the remains of which we possess, only contain the formulæ and incantations of the divine magic, of the conjuring and propitious art; the diabolical and malevolent magic is excluded with horror, and its practices are energetically condemned.

Nevertheless, the Chaldean tablets do not leave us without any insight into witchcraft, as their formulæ were destined to counteract the effects of the sorceries of this impious art, as well as the spontaneous action of demons. Witches and wizards figure largely in them, and we see that they were numerous in ancient Chaldea, amongst the Accadian people. Sometimes the spells were mentioned together with demons and diseases in the enumeration of the plagues to be averted; sometimes they were attacked by special incantations. Of the latter class was one which cursed the sorcerer by calling him " the malevolent evil-doer, this malevolent man, this man, malevolent amongst men, this bad man ;" and which spoke of "the terror which he spreads," of the " place of his violent aggressions and of his wickedness," of "his spells which are driven away from men." In these tablets Hea, as the chief protector against all infernal powers, and with him the Sun, were the gods invoked for protection from the sorcerer.[2] For as the evil magi

---

[1] See Tylor, *Primitive Culture*, and *Researches into the Early History of Mankind*, for numerous illustrations of these superstitions gathered from all parts of the world, and of all religions.—*Ed.*

[2] *W. A. I.* IV., 6, 6.

prepared their sorceries in the dark, the Sun was their great enemy. A hymn in the magical collection[1] addresses Hea in these terms:

> Thou that dispellest lies, thou that destroyest the evil influence
> of the prodigies, auguries, vexatious prognostications, dreams, evil apparitions,
> thou that frustratest wicked plots, thou that condemnest men and countries to perdition
> which abandon themselves to witchcraft and sorcery.

As a rule the sorcerer was called "the evil-doer, and the malevolent man" in the old Accadian conjurations. The expressions describing his practices had always a mysterious character impressed with the terror which he inspired; they did not dare to describe his secrets explicitly, and the Assyrian translations alone gave a more exact meaning to these expressions. The spells were generally indicated by the words "that which acts, that which is bad, that which is violent;" the rites of sorcery were called "the work," the incantations "the word," and the poisonous philters "the mortal thing." M. Pictet has recorded exactly parallel facts in the language of the different Aryan nations.[2]

There was no evil which the sorcerer could not work. He ordered at will the fascination of the evil eye or of unlucky words; his rites and formulæ for enchantment subjected the demons to his orders; he let them loose upon the person he wished to injure, and made them torment him in every way; he sent ill-luck alike to countries or individuals, and caused

---

[1] *W. A. I.* IV., 17.

[2] In *Les Origines Indo-Européenes, ou les Aryas Primitifs*, 1859.

demoniacal possession and other terrible diseases. He could even take away life with his spells and imprecations, or else by the poisons of which he had learnt the use, and which he mixed in his fatal potations. In this latter case, the conjuration by which his intended victim opposed his acts was designed to turn upon the sorcerer or sorceress the effects they tried to produce. "May she die and may I live!" is the phrase which terminates an unpublished formula against the enchantments of a sorceress, who had undertaken to cause the death of an unknown person by her spells.[1]

An incantation, of which we only possess the Assyrian version,[2] enumerates divers kinds of operations used by the Chaldean sorcerers.

> The wizard has charmed me with the charm, has charmed me with his charm;
> the witch has charmed me with the charm, has charmed me with her charm;
> the sorcerer has bewitched me with the spell, has bewitched me with his spell;
> the sorceress has bewitched me with the spell, has bewitched me with her spell;
> He who enchants images has charmed away my life by image;
> he has taken the enchanted philter, and has soiled my garment with it,
> he has torn my garment and dragged it in the dust of my feet.[3]
> may the god Fire, the hero, dispel their enchantments.

Another formula[4] averted the effect of "the image

---
[1] British Museum, K 43.   [2] *W. A. I.*, IV., 56, 2.
[3] The translation of these two verses is still very doubtful, and rests mostly upon conjecture. Our interpretation is a mere guess.
[4] *W. A. I.* IV., 16, 2.

which holds up its head," and which was resisted by the use of purified and enchanted waters; of him "who by the strength of his plans causes disease," of the philter which spreads in the body (desiring that it may run off like clear water) of "the charm concealed in the philter," and lastly " of the lip which utters the enchantments."

We have here then a spell, which by means of the words recited by the sorcerer,[1] by the use of "works" of mysterious rites, and of enchanted objects, had an irresistible effect; amongst those rites may be noticed the charming away of a person's life by means of a wax figure,[2] and the casting of spells, and lastly of the concoction of philters from certain herbs known to the magician, who increased their power still more by pronouncing incantations over the potions.

The Chaldeans, however, like the ancient Greeks, made no distinction between the enchanted philter and poison, designating both by the same name; this may throw some light upon the character of these drinks, the effect of which was so much feared.

The VIth formula of the long litany is directed against him "who makes the image," and indeed charming away life by means of a wax figure seems to have been one of the most frequent practices of Chaldean sorcerers. The magical documents often allude to it. It is the more curious because, according to the Arabian writer Ibn Khaldun, who lived in the XIVth century of our era, and writes as an

---

[1] Called by the Latins *carmen*, whence the English word charm.
[2] As the Lapland witches are traditionally said to do.

eye-witness, this practice was still very common amongst the Nabathean sorcerers of the Lower Euphrates, who have inherited many traditions, more or less corrupted, from the ancient inhabitants.

"We saw with our own eyes one of these individuals making the image of a person he wished to bewitch. These images are composed of things, the qualities of which bear a certain relation to the intentions and the projects of the operator, and which represent by means of symbols the names and the qualities of the unfortunate victim, in order to unite and disunite them. The magician afterwards pronounces some words over the image which he has just placed before him, and which is a real or symbolical representation of the person whom he wishes to bewitch; then he blows and emits from his mouth a little saliva which had collected there, and at the same time makes those organs vibrate which are used in the utterance of this malevolent formula; next he holds over this symbolical image a cord which he has prepared with this intention, making a knot in it to signify that he is acting with resolution and persistence, that at the moment when he spat he made a compact with the demon who acted as his associate in the operation, and to show that he is acting with a determined resolution to consolidate the charm. To these processes and malevolent words a wicked spirit is united, which comes forth from the operator's mouth covered with saliva. Many evil spirits then descend, and the result of all is that the magician causes the victim to be attacked by the desired evil."[1]

But the most powerful of all the means which "the malevolent man," who seeks to injure, can employ, were imprecations. The formula of imprecation not only unloosed the demons, but it acted upon the celestial gods themselves, and, by binding their

[1] "*Prolégomènes d'Ibn Khaldoun*," translation by Slane, Vol. I., p. 177.

action to its words, turned them to evil purposes; it also commanded the gods attached to each man according to the Chaldaic ideas, and changed him from a protector into a malevolent enemy. This belief is indicated in set terms by a long conjuration, which describes by means of truly poetical images, the effects of the imprecation it is to avert.[1]

> The malicious imprecation acts on man like a wicked demon,[2]
> the voice which curses has power over him;
> the voice which curses has power over him;
> the malicious imprecation is the spell (which produces) the disease of his head.
> The malicious imprecation slaughters this man like a lamb;
> his god oppresses him in his body;
> his goddess creates anguish in him by a reciprocal influence,
> the voice which curses covers him and loads him like a veil.
> Silik-mulu-dug has accorded to him his protecting favour;
> to his father, the Lord of the earth,[3] into the dwelling, he entered and said to him:
> "My father, the malicious imprecation acts upon man like a wicked demon."
> For the second time he said to him:
> "He has tried the remedy; he does not know the remedy; he is submissive to the remedy."
> The Lord of the earth has made answer to his son Silik-mulu-dug:
> "My son, thou dost not know the remedy; let me prepare the remedy for thee.
> Silik-mulu-dug, thou dost not know the remedy; let me prepare the remedy for thee.

---

[1] *W. A. I.* IV., 7.
[2] See also *Records of the Past*, Vol. III., p. 147.
[3] Hea.

What I know (now) thou knowest it wholly.
Come, my son Silik-mulu-dug.
. . . . from the high dwellings stretch out thy hand to him.
Avert the evil fate, deliver him from the evil fate,
may the evil which upsets his body
be an imprecation from his father,[1]
an imprecation from his mother
an imprecation from his eldest brother,
or else an imprecation from an unknown person."
The evil fate, by the command from the lips of Hea,
may it be destroyed like a plant,
may it be divided into pieces like a fruit!
may it be torn and plucked up like a twig!
The evil fate, Spirit of the heavens, conjure it!
Spirit of the earth conjure it!

The latter expressions of this formula are explained by the following portion of the same document. It contains a series of conjurations which were supposed to be uttered by the person who was anxious to be delivered from the effects of the spells. Whilst he was pronouncing these conjurations, he had to perform certain rites strongly resembling those described in the *Pharmaceutria* of Theocritus, and in Virgil's VIIIth *Eclogue*.

1. As this plant withers, so shall also the spell.
   The burning fire shall devour it.
   It shall not be arranged on the lines of a vine-arbour;
   It shall not be trained into an arch and an . . . . ;
   the earth shall not receive its root;
   its fruit shall not grow, and the sun shall not smile upon it;
   it shall not be offered at the festivals of kings and gods.
   The man (who has cast) the evil fate, his wife,

[1] " From the curse of his father,
    From the curse of his mother."—Smith.

the violent operation, the indigitation,[1] the written spell, the curses, the sins

the evil that is in my body, in my flesh, in my bruises,

may (all that) be withered like this plant!

May the burning fire devour it this day!

May the evil fate depart, and may I behold the light again!

2 As this fruit is divided into pieces, so shall also the spell be.

The burning fire shall devour it;

it shall not return to the supporting branch from which it is cut off;

it shall not be offered at the festivals of kings or gods.

The man (who has cast) the evil fate, his wife,

the violent operation,[2] the indigitation, the written spell, the curses, the sins,

the evil that is in my body, in my flesh, in my bruises,

may (all that) be divided in pieces like this fruit!

May the burning fire devour it this day!

May the evil fate depart, and may I behold the light again!

3 As this twig is plucked up and broken to pieces, so shall also the spell be.

The burning fire shall devour it;

its fibres shall not again unite themselves to the trunk;

it shall not arrive at a perfect state of splendour.

The man (who has cast) the evil fate, his wife,

the violent operation, the indigitation, the written spell, the curses, the sins,

the evil which is in my body, in my flesh, in my bruises,

may (all that) be broken in pieces and plucked up like this twig!

May the burning fire devour it this day!

May the evil fate depart, and may I behold the light again!

---

[1] "The finger pointing."—Smith. [2] "The evil invocation."—Smith.

4 As this wool is rent, so shall also the spell be.
The burning fire shall devour it;
it shall not return to (the back of) its sheep;
it shall not be offered for the garments of kings and gods.
The man (who has cast) the evil fate, his wife,
the violent operation, the indigitation, the written spells, the curses, the sins,
the evil which is in my body, in my flesh, in my bruises,
may (all that) be rent like this wool!
May the burning fire devour it this day!
May the evil fate depart and may I behold the light again!

5 As this banner is rent, so shall also the spell be.
The burning fire shall devour it;
it shall not return to the top of its staff;
it shall not float in its splendour.
The man (who has cast) the evil fate, his wife,
the violent operation, the indigitation, the written spells, the curses, the sins,
the evil which is in my body, in my flesh, in my bruises,
may (all that) be rent like this banner!
May the burning fire devour it this day!
May the evil fate depart, and may I behold the light again!

6 As this fulled stuff is rent, so shall also the spell be.
The burning fire shall devour it;
the fulling mill shall not dye it (to make it into) a covering;
it shall not be offered for the garments of kings and gods.
The man (who has cast) the evil fate, his wife,
the violent operation, the indigitation, the written spell, the curses, the sins,
the evil which is in my body, in my flesh, in my bruises,
may (all that) be rent like this fulled stuff!
May the burning fire devour it this day!

> May the evil fate depart, and may I behold the light again!

The formulæ of imprecation were really terrible. They called upon all the gods of heaven and of the abyss to display their power by overwhelming with misfortunes the person against whom they were directed. I shall quote as an example those upon the celebrated monument of our national library, which is known by the name of Caillou Michaux, after the traveller who brought it from the suburbs of Bagdad. It is an ovoid boulder of black basalt, fifty centimetres[1] high, upon the lower part of which are sculptured some sacred symbols; the rest of the stone is covered with a long inscription in the Assyrian tongue, containing the law concerning landed property as a dowry for a woman on her marriage, and giving the whole measurement of the land to which the stone served as a boundary. After the copy of the act passed in an authentic manner, come the imprecations against any one who displaced the boundary, or troubled in any way the peaceable possessor of the lands.

> They (the imprecations) shall precipitate this man into the water; they shall bury him in the ground; they shall cause him to be overwhelmed with stones; they shall burn him with fire; they shall drive him into exile into places where he cannot live.
>
> May Anu, Bel, Nouah, and the Supreme Lady[2] the great gods, cover him with absolute confusion, may they root up his stability, may they efface his posterity!
>
> May Marduk, the great lord, the eternal chief, fasten him up with unbreakable chains!

---

[1] Or 19.685 inches English.

[2] Belit, the wife of the god Bel, of which she was more literally the feminine form. Bilat or Beltis, as she is sometimes called, was the Assyrian goddess of war.—*Ed.*

May the Sun, the great judge of heaven and earth, pronounce his condemnation, and take him in his snares!

May Sin, the illuminator, who inhabits the elevated regions,[1] catch him in a net like a wild ram captured in the chase; like a buffalo whom he throws to the ground by taking him in a noose!

May Iṣhtar, queen of heaven and earth, strike him in the presence of gods and men, and entice his servants to perdition!

May Adar the son of the zenith, the child of Bel, the supreme, destroy the limits and the boundary of his property!

May Gula, the great lady, the spouse of the winter Sun, pour inside him a deadly poison; may she cause his blood and sweat to flow like water!

May Bin, the captain of heaven and earth, the son of Anu, the hero, inundate his field!

May Serakh destroy the firstfruits of his harvest . . . .[2] may he enervate his animals!

May Nebo, the supreme intelligence[3] overwhelm him with affliction and terror, and lastly may he hurry him into incurable despair!

And may all the great gods whose names are mentioned in this inscription curse him with a curse from which he can never be released! may they scatter his race until the end of time!

It will be easily understood that nothing short of the direct intervention of the god Hea could deliver a man from the weight of imprecations such as these.

---

[1] The moon god, father of Ishtar of Arbela. See a beautiful Assyrian poem, "The Death of the Righteous Man," translated by Fox Talbot in *Records of the Past*, Vol. III., p. 135.   [2] Lacuna.

[3] Nabo or Nebo was the supreme intelligence considered as an abstract spiritual entity. He was the god of wisdom and of learning.

CHAPTER V.

Comparison of the Egyptian with the Chaldean magic.

ALL magic rests upon a system of religious belief, and upon a fixed conception of that supernatural world, the innate consciousness of which is experienced by every man, making him seek to pierce its secrets with his intellect, even in a state of utter barbarity. If we consider the elementary ideas of mankind with the magic superstition arising from them, and the religious beliefs of which the latter is the corruption, we must divide them into three classes, according as the diversity of their origin imparts to them different tendencies and different characters.

First of all comes primitive magic, connected with the worship of elementary spirits. " The religion of a savage or very barbarous man is," says M. Maury, " a superstitious naturalism, an incoherent fetichism, in which all phenomena of nature and all created beings become objects of adoration. Man places everywhere personal spirits made in his own image, sometimes representing the objects themselves, and sometimes having a different signification. Such is the religion of all the black nations, of the Altaic tribes, the colonies of Malacca, and the other primitive populations of Hindostan, of the red races of America, and the islanders of Polynesia; such was at first that of the Aryans, Mongols, Chinese, Celts, Germans, and Slavonians." In a system of this kind magic is at first of all only a part of the worship, or indeed the worship itself. The supreme end of magic was to conjure the spirits, for the savages feared their malevolent influence more than they expected benefit from their goodwill. As the worship amongst these people was reduced to little more than the conjuration of spirits and the veneration of animals, their priests were only sorcerers, whose mission it was to communicate with the demons they so much feared. In other words, their worship was almost entirely limited to magical ceremonies. Such is even now the character of the priesthood amongst many barbarous nations and demoralized tribes. The professors of magic are found in all countries where fetichism takes the place of religion. These priests combine the functions of diviners, prophets, exorcists, thaumaturgists, physicians, and makers of idols and amulets. They teach neither morals nor good works; they are not devoted to the practices of a regular worship, or to the service of a temple or an altar. They are only sought for in cases of necessity, but they exercised nevertheless a considerable sway over the populations with whom they take the place of more sacred ministers.

In the beginning, and in a state of complete

barbarity, there is no distinction between favourable and fatal magic, just as there is none between magic and worship, at least not more than the radical difference which exists between good and bad spirits. The priest of magic is the same as the sorcerer; following the caprices of his will, he exercises his mysterious power or good or evil, according as he has been made a friend or a foe. But the first result of progress towards a more regular social state, and of the development of the morals, is to bring to light in this coarse and primitive naturalism an idea of the dual system, which is more or less marked, and may become, as with the Persians, the foundation of a very lofty and entirely spiritual religion. These distinguish by contrasting them, the world of light from that of darkness, and good, from physical, if not yet from moral, evil. They then proceed to separate into two classes the spirits spread all over the universe, regarding some as good, and the others as bad, both essentially so and so by nature. All pleasant things are attributed to the action of the former, and all fatal and painful things to that of the latter. The priest is still a magician, but his power is exercised henceforth in an exclusively beneficent manner; he holds no communication with the bad demons, except to combat and repulse them; his rites and incantations are all powerful in expelling them, while, at the same time, they act upon the good spirits, and ensure their co-operation and protection. He is no longer to be confounded with the sorcerer, who keeps up an intercourse with bad spirits and demons, taking part in their wickedness, and subjecting them to his orders for evil purposes. The acts of the sorcerer are from that time cursed and condemned as impious, whilst the power of the favourable magician, or the thaumaturgic priest, is respected and considered as holy and divine.[1]

This is the second phase of the primitive magic, founded upon the belief in the elementary spirits. But in spite of this important modification, which somewhat purifies it, the principle remains essentially the same, and the dual system which is thus established is often more conspicuous than real. Magic built in this way upon the coarse naturalism of a state of barbarity, sometimes survives the adoption of a more noble and philosophic religion, with a higher conception of divinity and a perception of its fundamental unity. The new religion accepts and tolerates it, recognizing its existence, while excluding it from the official worship. The priests of magic still exist, but they form an inferior class of the priesthood. The elementary spirits, at first the only objects of worship, are not admitted into the supreme ranks of the pantheon, unless some of the more important are identified, purposely or by force, with certain gods of the official religion; but a place is found for them amongst the *dii minores*, the inferior personifications to whom no public worship is addressed. In this way they manage to legalize the use of the old magic formulæ which seem to take no notice of the great gods, and to preserve, still bearing intact the imprint

---

[1] This was exactly the distinction maintained in the Dark and Middle Ages of Europe, when a Pope Sylvester and a Saint Dunstan were both accredited with magical powers, while at the same time invoking the curses of the church upon the professors of the hellish or black art.—*Ed.*

of the ancient system from which they arose, its hierarchy of gods and demons concealed underneath the exterior and entirely different covering of the prevailing religion: we shall prove this fact in a very clear manner when we analyse the religious beliefs of Chaldea.

Entirely different from the preceding in principle, and consequently in the nature of its rites and incantations, although putting forth the same pretensions, is theurgical magic; the superstitious contortion of a philosophic religion, which would make to issue from an infinite and universal, but vaguely conceived god, by a peculiar system of emanation, a whole hierarchy of supernatural powers, each bearing a closer resemblance to nature than the last, and at the same time participating, though in different degrees, in the divine perfections and in human weaknesses. In a system such as this, man, by the power of purificatory rites, and above all by the possession of science, succeeds in rising towards divinity, approaching it indefinitely near, and becoming like it, so that in consequence he is enabled to govern the powers of the inferior emanations, and to make them obey his orders. Enchantment becomes again an important part of the worship; it is the holy and legitimate intercourse established by the sacred rites between man and the gods. Magic of this kind is essentially a divine work, as the name theurgy, given to it by the Neoplatonists, clearly shows. Its action is entirely beneficent, and if some perverse creatures abuse the power given them by divine science over the spirits and inferior gods in order to satisfy a guilty covetousness, and to do evil, it is an odious sacrilege, the effects of which are paralysed by certain invocations of the divine power.

The theurgical system attained perfection amongst the Neoplatonists of the Alexandrian school, particularly amongst those of the last epoch, and the propensity to demonological rites which is already marked in the time of Porphyry,[1] triumphs completely under Proclus.[2] From this time the worship of the Neoplatonists consists in the rendering of homage and thanks to the good deities, and the use of conjurations, exorcisms, and purifications against the wicked. In other words, their religion becomes exclusively a theurgy, in which all the magic rites of the different nations of antiquity have a place, those of the Chaldeans as well as those of the Egyptians. The magic of ancient Egypt was quite theurgic in origin and doctrine, and we cannot deny that the reveries of the later Neoplatonists are in a great

---

[1] "All these beings likewise, and those who possess a contrary power are invisible, and perfectly imperceptible by human senses, for they are not surrounded with a solid body, nor are all of them of one form, but they are fashioned in numerous figures. . . . Sometimes also those that are malefic change their forms. . . . Hence there is no evil which they do not attempt to effect, for in short, being violent and fraudulent in their manners, and being also deprived of the guardian care of more excellent demons, they make for the most part vehement and sudden attacks, sometimes endeavouring to conceal their incursions, but at other times assaulting openly. Hence the molestations which are produced by them are rapid; but the remedies and corrections which proceed from more excellent demons appear to be more slowly effected, for every thing which is good, being tractable and equable, proceeds in an orderly manner, and does not pass beyond what is fit." Porphyry, *De Abstinentia*, sec. 39.—*Ed.*

[2] See Proclus, *Elements of Theology*, props. cxi., cxliii., and clvii. But better still Iamblicus, *On the Mysteries*, lib. i., cap. xviii., "How some of the gods are beneficent, but others malefic," for which the subtle Platonist gives an astrological reason: and the answer of Abammon to Porphyry, cap. ii.—*Ed.*

measure due to its influence,¹ although it had not attained to such a degree of systematic development, as to take the place of all other worship; indeed it still retained its character of inferiority in relation to the official religion, and was not formally recognised as a rite.²

There is finally a third species of magic, thoroughly diabolical in character, and openly acknowledging itself as such. This kind helps to perpetuate, by still believing in their power and transforming them into dark practices, the rites of adoration of the ancient gods, considered as demons after the triumph of a new religion, the exclusive spirit of which repudiates all association with the remains of the old worship. The enchanter in this case, far from considering himself an inspired and divine personage, consents, provided he reaps all the benefit of his magic practices, to be nothing more than the tool of the bad and infernal powers. He himself sees devils in the ancient gods evoked by his spells, but he nevertheless remains confident of their protection; he engages himself in their service by compacts, and fancies himself going to a witch-dance in their company. The greater part of the magic of the middle ages bears this character, and perpetuates the popular and superstitious rites of paganism in the

---

[1] "Others who are conscious what they are doing in other respects are divinely inspired according to the phantastic part. Some indeed received darkness for a co-operator, others certain potions, but others incantations and compositions, and some energize according to the imagination through water, others in a wall *sic* (well ?), others in the open air, and others in the light of the sun, or some other celestial body." Iamblicus, *On the Mysteries*, lib. ii., cap. xiv.

[2] See a singular account of Moslem incantational magic in Lane's *Modern Egyptians*, Vol. II., the secret of which is still unexplained.

mysterious and diabolical operations of sorcery. It is the same with the magic of most Musulman countries. In Ceylon, since the complete conversion of the island to Buddhism, the ancient gods of Sivaism have become demons, and their worship a guilty sorcery, practised only by enchanters.[1]

We shall be obliged however to return to this last species of magic in another work[2] in order to find how much of the Chaldean traditions has been preserved in the rites and beliefs of the sorcerers of the middle ages. But as it possesses nothing ancient, and only appears long after both the others, we need here only mention it in passing without going into details.

[1] See Robert Hunter, *History of India*, cap. 4, where it is shown that an exactly similar process of political antagonism has converted the asuras of the Aryans from angels to become the devils of the Vedas.

[2] Since published as *La Divination et la Science des Presages chez les Chaldeens*, 1875.

CHAPTER VI.

Contrasts between Egyptian and Chaldean Magical Systems.

EGYPT and Chaldea are, as we have already said, the two sources of all learned magic for Greek and Latin antiquity, as well as for Jewish and Arabian tradition. But without exactly defining the doctrines of either, we must distinguish, as quite different in their principles and processes, the Egyptian from the Chaldean school. This is almost a truism, and the study of the original documents on either side confirms it. Chaldean magic, as we have explained it, and as it appears to us so closely united in every part, is like the last words and the most learned system of the ancient magic of the primitive ages founded upon the belief in the spirits of nature. Egyptian magic is a theurgy arising from the doctrines of a theological philosophy which had become already somewhat refined.[1] The one began by being the sole worship of a naturalistic and coarse

---

[1] "The art of divination in Egypt is confined to certain of their deities. There are in this country oracles of Hercules (*Onouris*), of Apollo (*Horus*), of Minerva and Diana (*Neith* and *Nepthys*?), of Mars (*Besa*), and of Jupiter (*Amen-Ra*). But the oracle of Latona at Butos (*Sekhet*) is held in greater estimation than any of the rest: the oracular communication is regulated by no fixed system, but is differently obtained in different places." Herod., *Euterpe*, lxxxii. This is a fair example of the inaccuracies blended with facts and disguised by false assimilations with which the writings of the Greek historian abound.—*Ed.*

religion, and preserved the imprint of it in spite of the learned appearance that it sought to give to its systematic development; the other is the superstitious conception of a religion higher and purer in its tendencies, and retaining in its subtleties the impress of a higher faith.

It is very important to define well this difference, and to make it more clear I think it will be best to glance at the Egyptian magic, giving an outline of its doctrines, and quoting some of its formulæ in order to compare them with the Accadian formulæ that we have already mentioned. This will require some explanation of the fundamental religious beliefs of Egypt out of which magic arose. But such a digression does not appear to me out of place in the study which I am pursuing, for it will make the character of Chaldean magic stand out more distinctly, without reference to the conceptions upon which it rests. These conceptions differ as much from the Chaldaic-Assyrian religion of the entirely historical centuries as from the religion of Egypt, and belong consequently to another heathen source.

However far we go back in the documents relating to the Egyptian religion, we find there, as a foundation, the grand idea of a divine unity. Herodotus affirms that the Egyptians of Thebes recognized a single god, who had no beginning, and was to have no end of days.[1] And this assertion of the father of history is confirmed by the reading of the sacred texts in hieroglyphic characters, in which it is said of this god "that he is the sole progenitor in heaven

[1] *Euterpe*, clxliv.

and earth, and that he himself is not begotten . . .' that he is the sole god existing in truth, begotten of himself . . . who exists from the beginning . . . who has made all things, and was not himself created."² But this sublime notion, if it was retained in the esoteric doctrine, soon became obscured and disfigured by the conceptions of the priests and the ignorance of the people. The idea of God became confounded with the manifestations of his power; his attributes and qualities were personified as a crowd of secondary agents arranged in a hierarchical order, co-operating in the general organisation of the world, and in the preservation of created beings. In this way that polytheism was formed which in the truth and peculiarity of its symbols, ended by embracing the whole of nature.

The Egyptians were interested above all in the fate which awaits man in another life. They fancied they could see in many natural phenomena images and symbols of this future existence; but it seemed to them more particularly announced by the daily course of the sun. According to them, that planet reproduced each day during its progress the transformations reserved for the human soul. It was not a strange idea, however, on the part of a people who had no knowledge of the true character of the heavenly bodies. The sun, or Ra, as the Egyptians

---

[1] The Ancient of Heaven, the Oldest of the earth,
Lord of all existences, the Support of things, the Support of all things,
The ONE in his works, *single* among the gods,
Lord of truth, Father of the gods,
Maker of men, Creator of beasts,
Lord of Existences. "Hymn to Amen," *Records of the Past*, Vol. II., p. 127.

[2] Lenormant, *Ancient History of the East*, Vol. I., p. 318. "The Egyptians are the first of mankind who have defended the immortality of the soul." Herod., *Euterpe*, cxxiii.

called it, passed alternately from the region of darkness or death into the region of light or life. Its beneficent fires give birth to, and nourish existence; the sun plays then in relation to the universe the part of a progenitor or father; it gives life, but is not itself begotten; existing by itself it is its own progenitor. This symbolism once accepted it increased more and more, and the imagination of the Egyptians sought in the succession of solar phenomena an indication of the divers phases of human existence. Each point in the course of this luminous planet was regarded as corresponding to the different stages of that existence.[1]

But Ra the sun was not considered merely as the celestial prototype of the man who is born, lives, and dies to be born again; the Egyptians, like all the other heathen people of antiquity, regarded it as a divinity, as the supreme divinity, because it was the most brilliant and the greatest of the planets, and its beneficent influence vivified the world. The theological conception of the Egyptians did not stop there, for it subdivided this one supreme divinity, so to speak, into many other divinities. Considered in its different positions and its diverse aspects the sun became in each phase a different god, having its peculiar name, attributes, and worship; this trait of Egyptian mythology is common to all other mythology. Thus the sun during its nocturnal existence was Tum, when it shone in the meridian it was Ra, when it produced and nourished life it was venerated as Kheper. Those were the three principal forms of the solar divinity, but there

[1] See *Ritual of the Dead*, caps. cxxx. to cxl., "The Adorations to the Sun."

were also many others. Since, according to the Egyptians, the night precedes the day, Tum was considered to have been born before Ra, and to have issued alone from the abyss of chaos.¹ Theology reunited the three manifestations of the solar power in a divine trinity, which became the prototype of many other trinities composed of divinities personifying the various relations of the sun with nature, and its varied influence upon the cosmic phenomena.

Anthropomorphism, from which no ancient religion was ever entirely free, gradually intruded itself into these first sabeistic data, and the Egyptians came to consider that the race of the gods was perpetuated in the same way as amongst human beings. They were therefore obliged to divide the divine existence into a male and active principle, and a female and passive principle, and they transported into their theogony their ideas about the respective office of the sexes in the mysterious act of nature by which the species is perpetuated. At the same time their ideas about the sun were extended also to the divinity, which was conceived in a vaguer and higher way; each of its acts was personified as a separate god, as a new divine personage. Of this origin are the deities of a more abstract and philosophic conception, and less closely allied to a fixed phenomenon of nature, as Amen, Nun, or Pthah.

Since navigation upon the Nile was the usual mode of transport in Egypt, the solar trinity, as also the trinity of the inferior hemisphere, the emblem of the other life, was always represented in its progress as

---

¹ See Pierret, *Dictionnaire d'Archeologie Egyptienne*, art. "Ra ou Phre."—*Ed.*

being carried in a bark.¹ The sun of the Lower Hemisphere took more especially the name of Osiris. Its companions and deputies were the twelve hours of the night personified as so many gods, at the head of which was placed Horus, the rising sun itself; and mythology stated that this god pierced with his dart the serpent Apophis or Apap, the personification of the crepuscular vapours which the rising planet dissipated with its fires. The struggle of Osiris, or Horus his son, with darkness, according to a symbolism found in all mythologies, naturally resembled that of good with evil. This gave rise to a very popular Egyptian fable which is alluded to by several monuments, and which was the starting point for a great religious development. Evil was personified in a particular god, Set or Sutekh, called also sometimes Baal, who was the supreme god of the neighbouring Asiatic populations, and at a later period of the shepherd kings; the Greeks considered him the same as their Typhon, and it was said that Osiris had succumbed to his blows.² Having been

---

¹ These barks had different names according to the deities which were in them. That of the sun Ra was called *Uaa*, of the god Pthah *Mafekh*, of Osiris Baris (?), and of Khonsu *Sekhu*. They were often carried in procession on the shoulders of the priests, the figure of the deity standing under a shrine covered with a transparent linen veil.—*Ed.*

² The worship of this god passed through two historical phases. At one time he was held in honour and accounted as one of the greater gods of Abydos. He appears to have had a position analogous to that of the Theban deity Mentu, in which he was the adversary of the serpent Apophis, the symbol of wickedness and darkness. Some time later on, in consequence of political changes, the worship of Set was abolished, and his statues destroyed. It is difficult to state at what period Set was introduced into the Osirian mythos as a personification of evil, and became the murderer of Osiris. The contests of Horus, the avenger of his father Osiris, are related at considerable detail in the inscriptions of the temple of Edfu which have been published by M. Ed. Naville in *Textes relatifs au Mythe d'Horus*, 1870. The treatise (by Plutarch) *De Iside et Osiride* makes Nephthys the companion of Set, and she is represented united with him in a group in the Musée du Louvre, Salle des Dieux. The animal symbolical of Set was a carnivorous quadruped having a long curved snout and upright square topped ears, which characters are often exaggerated to distinguish him from the jackal of Anubis. Pierret, *Dictionnaire d'Archeologie Egyptienne*.—*Ed.*

resuscitated by the prayers and invocations of his wife, the good god found an avenger in his son Horus. The death of Osiris, the grief of Isis, and the final defeat of Set furnished mythology with an inexhaustible fund of fables, which recall those of the various Eastern religions, particularly the history of Cybele and Atys, of Venus and Adonis.[1]

When once the course of the sun was regarded as the type of existence in the infernal regions, the reproduction of the same symbolism was all that was needed amongst the Egyptians to constitute the doctrine of the other life, according to which man descends into the tomb only to rise again, and after his resurrection he will lead a new life by the side or in the heart of the luminous planet.[2] The soul immortal like Ra accomplishes the same pilgrimage. We see upon the covers of certain sarcophagi the soul (*Ba*) figured as a sparrow-hawk with a human head, holding in its claws the two signet rings symbolising eternity, and also, as emblem of the new life reserved for the dead, the rising sun attended in his course by the goddesses Isis and Nephthys.[3] This explains why the solar period, represented as the bird bennu, the lapwing, which the Greeks called phœnix, was the symbol for the cycle of human life; the mysterious bird was reported to accompany man during his earthly race. The dead revived after their pilgrimage in Hades, and the soul re-entered into the body in

---

[1] See also Herod., *Euterpe*, cxliv., with Larcher's and Beloe's notes in *loco*.—*Ed.*

[2] See Deveria, *Le Livre de l'Hemisphere Inferieur*, in Cat. Manuscripts, etc., *Musée du Louvre.*—*Ed.*

[3] See De Horrack, "Lamentations of Isis and Nephthys" in *Records of the Past*, Vol. II., page 117.—*Ed.*

order to give it back movement and life, or, to use the language of Egyptian mythology, the deceased arrived finally at the bark of the Sun, where he was received by Kheper Ra, the scarabeus god, and became illuminated with the splendour which he bestowed upon him. The tombs and the coffins of mummies abound in paintings representing the various scenes of this invisible existence. A vignette of the Ritual of the Dead[1] represents the mummy lying upon a funeral couch, while the soul, or the sparrow-hawk with the human head, is flying towards it with the handled cross, the emblem of life.[2]

This doctrine may be traced in Egypt to the remotest antiquity; it conduced necessarily to the inspiration of a great respect for the remains of the dead, since they were some day to be recalled to life, and it was the origin of the custom of embalming corpses. The Egyptians made a point of preserving intact, and protecting against all destruction, this body which was destined to enjoy a more perfect existence. They thought also that the mummies thus enveloped were not entirely deprived of life, and the Ritual shows us that the deceased was supposed still to use his organs and members; but, in order better to insure the preservation of the vital warmth, they had recourse to the use of mystic formulæ, pronounced at the time of the funeral, and to certain amulets placed upon the mummy.[3] In general, most of the funeral ceremonies, the various envelopes, the

---

[1] Cap. lxxxix., "The Chapter of the Visit of the Soul to the Body in Hades."—*Ed.*
[2] A subject repeatedly figured. See Sharpe, *Bible Texts*, p. 185.—*Ed.*
[3] *Ritual*, "Preservation of the Body in Hades," caps. xxvii. to xlii.—*Ed.*

subjects painted inside and outside of the coffin bear reference to the different phases of the resurrection, such as the relaxing of muscles, the new function of the organs, the return of the soul.

The belief in immortality has never been separated from the idea of a future reward for the acts of the present, and this may be particularly observed in Egypt. Although the bodies of all men descended into the infernal regions, the Ker-neter[1] as it was called, they were nevertheless not all sure of the resurrection. To obtain it they must have committed no grave fault either in deed or thought. The deceased was to be judged by Osiris and his forty-two deputies; his heart was placed on one side of the scales held by Horus and Anubis; the representative scenes of psychology show the image of justice; the god Thoth registered the result of the weighing. Upon this judgment, given in the "hall of double justice," the irrevocable fate of the soul depended.[2] If the deceased was convicted of unpardonable faults, he became the prey of an infernal monster with the head of an hippopotamus,[3] and he was beheaded by Horus and by Smu, one of the forms of Set, upon the *nemma* or infernal scaffold. Final annihilation was received by the Egyptians as being the punishment of the most wicked. The just, purified from his venial sins by a fire, which was guarded by four

---

[1] Called also the "Amenti," "the place of the gods."

[2] *Ritual*, cap. cxxv., "The Book of Going to the Hall of the Two Truths, and of separating a person from his sins when he has been made to see the faces of the gods."—*Ed.*

[3] The infernal hippopotamus-headed goddess Thoueris, the devourer of the souls. The region of Hades was called *Akar*, as distinct from the other mystical regions in the *kerneter*, viz., the *Aahla*, "Fields of Peace," and the *Auh-naru* or abodes of Osiris. —*Ed.*

genii with monkey's faces,[1] entered into the *pleroma* or state of beatitude ; and having become the companion of Osiris, the chief of all good creatures (Unnefer),[2] he was nourished by him on delicate food. Nevertheless, the just himself did not arrive at the final state of beatitude without having passed through many trials, because as man he was naturally a sinner. The deceased, descending into the Ker-neter, was obliged to pass through fifteen pylons or porticoes guarded by genii armed with swords ;[3] he could only get through by proving his good deeds and his knowledge of divine things, that was his initiation, and he was condemned to the rough work which is the subject of a good part of the sacred Ritual. He had to enter into terrible combats with monsters and fantastic animals raised up by Typhonian power and bent on evil, and he could only triumph by arming himself with sacramental forms and exorcisms which fill eleven chapters of the Ritual.[4] Amongst other means to which the deceased had recourse in order to conjure these diabolical phantoms, was that of assimilation of his members to those of the various gods, and thus deifying in a manner

---

[1] Cap. cxxvi., "The Gods of the Orbit." "Extract ye all the evil out of me, obliterate ye my faults, annihilate my sins, guard ye, and give ye me to pass the pylon, to go from the plains," etc. ; to which the cynocephalus deities reply, "Thou mayest go, we obliterate all thy faults, we annihilate all thy sins, thou hast been severed from the world, we dissipate all thy sins, thou hast severed thyself from earth, thou hast dissipated all the sins which detained thee, come to the Rusta (a dwelling of Osiris). Thou openest the secret doors of the West. Thou comest forth and goest in as thou wishest, like one of the spirits hailed daily within the horizon."—*Ed.*

[2] "The Good Being." A very common funereal title of the deity Osiris.—*Ed.*

[3] Cap. cxlvi., "The Beginning of the Gates of the Aahlu (Fields of Peace) or the abode of Osiris."—*Ed.*

[4] Caps. clii. to clxi., "Mystical Amulets."

his own substance.¹ The wicked in his turn, before being annihilated, was condemned to suffer thousands of tortures, and under the form of a malevolent spirit he returned to this world to disturb men and to bring about misfortune; he entered into the body of unclean animals.²

The sun, personified as Osiris, furnished then the subject of all Egyptian metempsychosis.³ From the god who bestows and nourishes life he became the remunerating and saving god. The myth even went so far as to assert that the sun Osiris accompanied the deceased during his infernal pilgrimage, that he led him to his descent into the Ker-neter, and conducted him to the eternal light. Himself the first to rise from the dead, he raised the righteous in their turn, after having aided them to triumph in all their trials. Indeed the deceased finished by identifying himself completely with Osiris, and by blending himself, so to speak, with his substance, so that he lost all personality; his trials became those of the god he adored, and from the moment of his death every deceased person was called "Osiris himself."⁴

---

¹ Cap. xlii., "The Chapter of Turning Away all Evil, and Turning Back the Blows made in Hades." "There is not a limb of him without a god."—*Ed.*

² Often that of a pig, as on the sarcophagus of Seti I. in the Soane Museum.—*Ed.*

³ The technical name of this metempsychosis was the *Meskem*, and its nature is dwelt upon in some detail in Bunsen's *Egypt's Place in Universal History*, Vol. V. p. 146.—*Ed.*   ⁴ Cap. clxiii.

CHAPTER VII.

The Magic of the Ritual of the Dead.

EGYPTIAN magic was closely connected with eschatological doctrines, and with the development of the Osirian myths which were founded upon them. The soul of the deceased had to assist him during this pilgrimage through the other world, where he was subjected to those trials and exposed to those enemies over which Osiris has already triumphed, on his behalf were sacred rites celebrated near his tomb, and liturgical prayers recited, and it was the operation of these conjoined together with a clear conscience, which finally obtained for him a favourable sentence. The efficacy of these invocatory prayers was considered to be extraordinary. They not only rendered Osiris and the gods of his cycle favourable to the soul of the deceased, but they had also the power of applying to it directly the merits of the labours and sufferings of the god of the dead, and of establishing the complete identity expressed by the phrase " The Osirian." Certain chapters of the

Ritual of the Dead are accompanied by formulæ relating to their spiritual efficacy in the sudden changes of the life beyond the tomb, and by directions regarding their use as talismans, which give them at once the character of magical incantations. Such an one follows the chapter which was engraved on all the scarabei wrought in hard stone which were laid upon the breasts of the mummies:[1]

> Pronounced over the beetle of hard stone which is to be overlaid with gold and to take the place of the individual's heart. Make a phylactery of it anointed with oil, and say magically over this object: "My heart is my mother; my heart is in my transformations."[2]

At the end of another chapter, one of the most obscure and mysterious of the whole book, we read :—

> If this chapter is known, he (the deceased) will be pronounced veracious in the land of the Ker-neter; he will do all that the living do. It was composed by a great god. This chapter was found at Sesennou[3] written in blue upon a cube of blood-stone under the feet of this god;[4] it was found in the days of the king Mycerinus the veracious by the royal son Hartatef, when he was travelling to inspect the accounts of the temples. He repeated a hymn to himself, after which he went into ecstacies; he took it away in the king's chariots as soon as he saw what was written upon it. It is a great mystery. One sees

---

[1] See also caps. c., ci., cxl., and cxxx.—*Ed.*

[2] Cap. xxx., "The Chapter of how a Person avoids that his Heart should be taken from Him in Hades."—*Ed.*   [3] Hermopolis.

[4] "On a brick of burnt clay painted with real lapis lazuli." Birch.

and hears nothing else while reciting this pure and holy chapter. Never again approach a woman; eat neither meat nor fish. Then make a beetle chiselled in stone, and overlaid with gold, put it where the individual's heart was; after having made of it a phylactery steeped in oil, recite over it magically: "My heart is my mother, etc."[1]

We see from these examples, to which we might add many more, that some of the most important chapters of the Ritual of the Dead, when written upon certain objects placed on the mummy, converted them into talismans which protected the deceased with a sovereign efficacy during the perils which awaited him in the other world, before he attained the resurrection of the blest. Others were destined to the consecration of certain symbols made of substances prescribed in the liturgies, and suspended round the neck of the mummy; rubrics were added to them ordering the manufacture of these protecting amulets, and defining the nature of their influence. Lastly, many chapters of the Ritual are in themselves regular magical exorcisms for repulsing the monstrous beings[2] in whom the power of Set was manifested, and who strove to ruin and devour the soul of the deceased.

There is really no essential difference between these chapters of the great hermetical book concerning the destiny of man in the other world, which was supposed to be of divine origin, and certain magical

---

[1] Cap. lxiv., "The Chapter of coming forth as the day."—*Ed.*

[2] More especially caps. xxix. to xli., comprising nearly the whole section of the Ritual of the Dead, which was called "The Preservation of the Body in Hades."—*Ed.*

formulæ written upon leaves of papyrus which are sometimes found attached to the mummies or phylacteries. The texts are of the same kind, but the former only were admitted into the collection of divine writings and the official liturgy for the dead, whilst the latter were probably composed more slowly, and have no place there. We must however remark that the incantations and exorcisms adopted in the Ritual have reference to the protection of the deceased during his subterraneous pilgrimage, whilst the single magical formulæ, which were not so highly regarded, were intended to shelter from malevolent beasts, and all possibility of destruction, the mummy itself while resting in the vault, the preservation of which was so important to the destiny of the soul. These formulæ also kept the body from becoming, during its separation from the soul, the prey of some wicked spirit which would enter, reanimate, and cause it to rise again in the form of a vampire. For, according to the Egyptian belief, the possessing spirits and the spectres which frightened or tormented the living were but the souls of the condemned returning to the earth before undergoing the annihilation of the "second death."

Here is one of these formulæ translated by M. Chabas :—[1]

> O sheep, son of a sheep! lamb son of a sheep, that suckest the milk of thy mother the sheep, do not

---

[1] Chabas, *Bulletin Archeologique*, 1855, p. 44. Other examples are given in Maspero, *Memoires sur quelques Papyrus du Louvre*, sec. iv.; and by Birch, *Magical Papyrus in the British Museum*, in *Records of the Past*, Vol. VI., page 116. —*Ed.*

allow the deceased to be bitten by any serpent male or female, by any scorpion, by any reptile; do not allow their venom to overpower his members. May no deceased male or female penetrate to him! May the shadow of no spirit haunt him! May the mouth of the serpent Am-kahou-ef have no power over him! He, he is the sheep.

Oh thou which enterest, do not enter into any of the members of the deceased! O thou which killest do not kill him with thyself! O thou which entwinest do not entwine thyself round him!

Do not allow the influences of any serpent male or female, of any scorpion, of any reptile, of any deceased male or female to haunt him. O thou that enterest, enter not into him! O thou that breathest, do not blow upon him the things of darkness! Let not thy shadow haunt him when the sun has set and is not yet risen.

I have pronounced the words over the sacred herbs placed in all the corners of the house; then I have sprinkled the whole house with the sacred herbs and the liquor *hak*[1] in the evening and at sunrise. He that is extended will remain extended in his place.

We find as a rule in the chapters of the Egyptian Ritual bearing the character of incantations, and in the other magic formulæ for the protection of the dead, that the words are put into the mouth of the deceased, and his chief means of defence against the attacks of the principle of evil bent on his destruction is to deify, as I mentioned above, his own substance, by assimilating his whole person, or

---

[1] The liquor *hak* was a species of wine, of which there were two qualities, and of which the best was imported from Syria.—*Ed.*

certain of his members, to the celestial gods, proclaiming that he himself is one or other of these gods. There was indeed a formal belief in ancient Egypt, which is attested by numerous passages from the religious texts, that the knowledge of divine things elevated man to the height of the gods, identified him with them, and ended by blending his substance with that of the divine. Certain mysterious words and formulæ, which were hidden from the comprehension of the vulgar, and revealed only to the initiated, brought about this identification or fusion of substance, by an innate or irresistible virtue, the revelation of which was attributed to Thoth, the god of intelligence. It was only necessary to pronounce these formulæ in the name of the deceased over his mummy, and to place a copy of them by his side in the coffin, to ensure for him the benefit of their influence in the dangers which he had to combat in the lower regions.

When so much power came to be attributed to certain formulæ and sacred words in the other world, it followed necessarily that the same power must be recognized in the terrestrial existence. Since the life after death was but a continuation of the earthly life, and was designed to prepare for a subsequent renewal of it, the ideas which were formed of the one condition were extended to that of the other also. If the type of one was the nocturnal course of the sun in the lower hemisphere, the diurnal course of the same luminary was the type of the other. The trials and dangers of the two states were therefore similar; they were connected with the same hostile power, and explained by the same symbolism, which necessarily led to the use of the same magical rites in opposing them. In Set was personified all the evil to be found in nature. He was the god of disorder, disputes, and violence, and all destructive scourges; savage animals and venomous reptiles were considered as subject to him. There was a custom of repelling him and his fatal train of evils by recalling the events of the heroic struggle, in which, after having first succumbed, the principle of order and the preservation of life, symbolised as Osiris, finally triumphed. We see this for instance in an incantation against the bite of venomous serpents, which was written upon a small papyrus now in the Louvre collection,[1] which papyrus was rolled up in a case, and worn as a talisman.

> He is like Set, the asp, the malevolent serpent whose venom burns. He who comes to enjoy the light, may he be hidden! He who dwells in Thebes approaches thee, yield, remain in his home! I am Isis, the widow broken with sorrow. Thou wilt rise against Osiris; he is lying down in the midst of the waters where the fish eat, where the birds drink, where the nets take their prize, while Osiris is lying down in pain.
>
> Tum lord of Heliopolis,[2] thy heart is contented and triumphant, Those in the tombs are full of acclamations, those in the coffins give themselves up to rejoicing, when they see the son of Osiris overthrowing his father's enemies, receiving the white crown from his father Osiris and seizing the wicked.[3] Come! Arise, Osiris, for thine enemies are vanquished.

---

[1] Devería, *Catalogue des Manuscrits Egyptiens du Louvre*, p. 171, et seq.

[2] Tum was the deified personification of the sun in the lower hemisphere.

[3] The white crown, which was more commonly called the *atef* crown, was a grand headdress with disk plumes and pendant uræi. It was symbolical of the kingdom of Egypt and of the divinity of the gods.—*Ed.*

The primary idea of all the magic formulæ which were designed to repel the torments of life and the attacks of malevolent animals (the latter are very numerous) was always assimilation to the gods, an assimilation which sheltered man from danger, and was effected by the power of the words of the enchantment. The virtue of the formulæ lay not in an invocation of the divine power, but in the fact of a man's proclaiming himself such or such a god, and when he, in pronouncing the incantation, called to his aid any one of the various members of the Egyptian Pantheon, it was as one of themselves that he had a right to the assistance of his companions. This is very clearly related in the formulæ of the celebrated Harris papyrus, the object of the studies of M. Chabas,[1] a manuscript of the epoch of the XIXth dynasty, which is perhaps a fragment of the magical collection of tracts which were supposed to be composed by the god Thoth, and were therefore included amongst the hermetical books. Here is one of the incantations of this papyrus which was destined to afford protection from the attacks of crocodiles :—

> Do not be against me! I am Amen.
> I am Anhur,[2] the good guardian.
> I am the great master of the sword.

---

[1] *Le Papyrus Magique Harris*, Chalon sur Saone, 1860.

[2] Anhur, "That which brings to Heaven:" an Egyptian deity, who is always represented as in a marching attitude, and robed with a long dress. He wears a headdress of four plumes, with the usual uræus serpent of celestial deity. He holds a cord in his hands, which is supposed to symbolise one of the forces of the universe. He was a form also of the solar god Shu, and in that character he had for his consort the goddess Tefnut, the Heavenly Cow. He was the Anouris, or Egyptian Mars, of the Greek writers. Anhur was chiefly worshipped in the city and nome of Abot, which was situated in the eastern bank of the Nile, in the Thebaid, and was afterwards called by the Greeks Thinites. (Pierret and Birch).—*Ed.*

Do not erect thyself!¹ I am Month.²
Do not try to surprise me! I am Set.
Do not raise thy two arms against me! I am Sothis.³
Do not seize me! I am Sethu."
Next those that are in the water do not go out;
those that have come out, do not return to the water;
and those that remain floating on the water;⁴
are like corpses on the waves;
and their mouths are closed,
as the seven great secrets are closed,
with an eternal closing.

In another incantation, which was directed against various noxious animals, the man who wished to obtain shelter from their attacks invoked the aid of a god, as being himself a god.

Come to me, O Lord of Gods!
Drive far from me the lions coming from the earth,
the crocodiles issuing from the river,
the mouth of all biting reptiles coming out of their holes!
Stop, crocodile Mako, son of Set!⁵
Do not wave thy tail;
do not work thy two arms;
do not open thy mouth.
May water become as a burning fire before thee!
The spear of the seventy-seven gods is on thine eyes;
the arm of the seventy-seven gods is on thine eye,
thou who wast fastened with metal chains to the bark of Ra,

---

¹ As a cobra serpent raises up himself to inflict his fatal bite.—*Ed.*

² Month or Mentu. The solar deity of Hermonthis. He was the god of war *par excellence*, and the kings of Egypt frequently compared themselves to him in battle. See *Records of the Past*, Vol. II., page 71.—*Ed.*

³ The star Sirius, as consecrated to the goddess Isis.—*Ed.*

⁴ The Egyptians peopled the river of Hades with a multitude of infernal and ghastly deities which are here referred to.—*Ed.*

⁵ See *Ritual of the Dead*, Caps. xxxi. and xxxii.

Stop, crocodile Mako, Son of Set!
For I am Amen, who makes his mother fruitful.[1]

In the third formula the same thing also occurs, for Horus identifies himself with the enchanter, by entreating the support of Isis and Nephthys in all the perils which could possibly menace an Egyptian in a desolate country house.

O thou that bringest back the voice of the guardian,
Horus has pronounced in a low voice the incantation: "Country!"
(At this word the animals which threatened him retired.)[2]
May Isis, my kind mother, pronounce the invocation for me, as well as my sister Nephthys,
May they remain in the act of greeting,
on the south of me,
on the north,
on the west,
on the east!
In order that the jaws of the lions and hyenas may be sealed,
the head of all the animals with long tails,
who eat flesh and drink blood;
that they may fascinate (me);
to lift up their hearing;
to hold me in darkness;
to make me avoid light;
to render me invisible,
instantly in the night!

These magical words did not communicate divine virtue alone to man; animals also could participate in them for the protection of man, as they caused an

---

[1] Amen Khem, or the Ithyphallic Horus, one of whose mystical titles was "The Husband of His Mother."—*Ed.*

[2] Query, Is not this a rubric which has run into the original text, as it has often happened to the rubrics and glosses of the Ritual.

CHALDEAN MAGIC AND SORCERY.

invincible power to dwell in an inanimate object when it had been charmed as a talisman. Thus we have the formula to be pronounced on a watch-dog, to increase his strength by the power of the enchantment.

> Stand up! wicked dog!
> Come! that I may direct thee what to do to day:
> Thou wast fastened up, art thou not untied?
> It is Horus who has ordered thee to do this:
> May thy face be open to heaven!
> May thy jaw be pitiless!
> May thy strength slay like the god Har-sheft![1]
> Massacre them like the goddess Anata![2]
> May thy mane be like bars of iron!
> Be like Horus for this, and like Set for that!
> Go to the south, to the north, to the west, to the east;
> the whole country is given into thy hands;
> nothing shall stop thee.
> Do not turn thy face against me;
> turn it against the savage beasts.
> Do not bring thy face in my way;
> turn it upon that of the stranger.
> I invest thee with a fascinating virtue; raise up thy hearing.
> Be thou a courageous formidable guardian.
> Safety! Word of safety!

In these quotations there appear two facts that have been pointed out by the Greek writers, and which give

---

[1] Harsheft, "terrible face," or "very valiant," a surname of Horus the warrior. He was the local deity of the Heracleopolite nome, and the Arsaphes of Plutarch, *De Iside et Osiride*.—*Ed.*

[2] Anaitis or Anata was a Semitic goddess of a warlike character, somewhat approaching the Bellona of Classic mythology. She was represented as a naked woman standing on a lion, and sometimes on a crocodile, holding a spear or bow, and wearing a peculiar crown formed of tall feathers. Her worship was introduced into Egypt probably about the time of Rameses II. after his Syrian victories, one of his daughters, Bentanath, being named after the goddess.—*Ed.*

quite a distinct character to Egyptian magic. In the first place, there is the absence of demonological development. The Egyptians only admitted into the world of spirits a certain number of genii, who were divided into two antagonistic parties, the one being the followers and servants of Osiris, the other composing the train of Set. On the earth they were merely the natural scourges, the injurious animals that, with the souls of the condemned which returned as vampires, served as instruments to the power of the god of evil. The magic exorcisms did not, properly speaking, combat demons. In the same way the power of the propitiatory incantations was not exercised on the favourable spirits which were inferior to the gods. It was placed at the service of mankind to protect him from the action of the gods themselves.

As to the connection which these formulæ established between man and the gods, that is also expressed in a manner which belongs exclusively to the Egyptian theology. Among other nations the power of magic commanded secondary spirits, and had a coercive action on bad demons alone. The exorcist laid an imperative command on the latter when he told them to retire; but towards the gods, even in the operations of magic, only prayers and supplications were used. In Egypt it was otherwise. Since they admitted that the use of certain sacramental formulæ raised a man to the height of the gods and identified him with each of them, they went on, as an inevitable consequence, to consider these formulæ as containing a force exercisable even upon the most powerful gods, obliging them to obey its commands. The Alexandrian writers also tell us that the Egyptian pretended to constrain the gods by means of evocations and magic formulæ, to obey their wishes, and to manifest themselves to their sight. The god could not resist the effect of the invocation if he were called by his true name.

One of the Harris papyri gives the text of an evocation of this kind which is addressed to no less a personage than Amen, the supreme god of Thebes :—

> Descend! Descend! to the left of heaven, to the left of the earth! Amen makes himself king, life, health, strength ;[1] he has taken the crown of the whole world.
> Close not thine ear.
> The serpents with the oblique walk,
> may they shut their mouths.
> And (may) all reptiles be confounded in the dust
> by thy power, O Amen.

The thoroughly Egyptian opinion which is here indicated continued to be held till the later periods of the Pharaonic religion. It is expressed in the writings of Chæremon, who composed under the Ptolemies a treatise upon the sacred science of the Egyptians. "They not only called the god by name," says M. Maury, "but if he refused to appear they threatened him." These formulæ of compulsion of the gods were named by the Greeks " $\theta\epsilon\omega\nu\ \dot{\alpha}\nu\alpha\gamma\kappa\alpha\iota$." Porphyry in his letter to the philosopher Anebon, expresses his indignation at such a pretension on the part of the Egyptian magicians, and so blind a faith in the power of mere words.

[1] Ankh-uskh-senb. This was the usual phrase which followed the names of divine personages, and especially kings in the official inscriptions. See Birch and Eisenlohr, "The Great Harris Papyrus" in *Records of the Past*, Vol. VI., page 21.

"I am much disturbed," writes the philosopher, "at the idea that those whom we invoke as omnipotent (beings) should receive injunctions like the weakest; and that while exacting from their servants the practice of justice, they should nevertheless appear disposed to do unjust acts if they are so commanded; and that whilst refusing to grant the prayers of those who have not abstained from the pleasures of love, they should act as guides to any immoral man in unlawful and sensual pleasures.'"

This power of magical incantation to compel obedience from the gods themselves became, however, formidable, even to him who exercised it, if he did not show himself worthy to possess it by moral purity and a knowledge of divine things. The romance of Setnau, a curious text of the period of declining Empire, which has been translated by M. Brugsch in the *Revue Archeologique* of 1867, is founded in a great measure,[2] upon the supernatural catastrophes which assail any one who takes possession of the magic book composed by the god Thoth, before he has been sufficiently prepared for initiation into its mysteries.

It is clear, in consequence of this idea which we are considering, that the use of names would naturally have a great importance both in magic and religion. The Egyptian gods were essentially myrionymous, as the Greeks termed Isis. Two whole chapters of

---

[1] Porphyry, *ap.* Euseb. *Præp. Evang.* v. 7.

[2] See *Records of the Past*, Vol. IV., pp. 134-136. "I have undergone these misfortunes on account of this book whereof thou sayest 'Let it be given me.' Speak not to me of it, for because of it we have lost the duration of our life upon earth." And further on, "Beware of taking the book in question. How couldest thou retain it? in consequence of the force of its extraordinary effects."—*Ed.*

the Ritual of the Dead[1] are devoted to the instruction of the deceased in the numerous titles of Osiris, as a help during his travels in the lower world.[2]

The formulæ of the Harris magical papyrus contain constant allusions to the supreme importance which was attached to the names of the gods.

> I, I am the elect of millions of years,
> proceeding from the inferior heaven,
> of which the name is unknown.
> If his name were pronounced on the border of the river,
> yes! he would consume it. If his name were pronounced on the earth,
> yes! he would strike out sparks from it.
> I am Schu under the form of Ra,[3]
> seated in the middle of his father's eye.
> If he who is in the water opens his mouth or snatches with his arms,
> I will cause the earth to fall into the water, putting the south in the place of the north,
> in the whole world.

And this one containing a formal evocation :—

> Come to me, come to me! O thou who endurest for millions and millions of years,
> O Num, only son,[4]

---

[1] Caps. lxli. and lxii, "Festival of the Names of the gods."—*Ed.*

[2] Not only is it recorded on some monuments of the XIIth dynasty that they are dedicated to certain gods in all their names, but the same is said in the tables of the god Ptah the demiurgus, and Ra the solar principle, found on monuments of the time of Rameses II. See Burton, *Excerpta Hieroglyphica*, pl. lvi.-lvii. These "thousand" names, such as Isis is said to have possessed, were part of the mystical nature of the gods, and no doubt traced in some logical order the principal events of the life of Osiris, or recorded his attributes. Birch in Bunsen, *Egypt's Place in Universal History*, Vol. V. p. 151.

[3] One of the names of the rising sun. He was properly a deification of the light of the solar disk, and represented the sun god Ra triumphing over the Typhonic and chaotic powers. He was generally figured as wearing upon his head the hind quarters of a lion, the ideograph of the word "force." Pierret, *Dict. d'Arch. Egypt.*

[4] Or Khnum, the soul of the gods and maker of gods and men. The deity of the vivific force of nature.—*Ed.*

conceived yesterday, born to-day!
He who knows thy name
is he who has seventy-seven eyes and seventy-seven ears,
Come to me! May my voice be heard
as the voice of the great goose Nadak[1] was heard during the night.
I am the great Bah.[2]

I have, I think, already sufficiently proved the importance in Chaldean magic of the doctrine of the efficacy of the supreme and mysterious name of the gods, but this idea assumed a very different character on the banks of the Nile from that which it held on the borders of the Euphrates. In the Chaldean religion, as well in all the religions of ancient Asia, the mysterious Name was considered a real and divine being, who had a personal existence, and therefore exclusive power over the other gods of a less elevated rank, over nature and the world of spirits.[3] In Egypt the traces of an idea attributing such an individual power to the divine name are but rare, and when they occur it is under the influence of the contact with the Semitic religion.

The true and original Egyptian idea was that the mystic name exercised a power upon the god himself to whom it belonged, and that when called by this name he was obliged to obey the incantation. He therefore kept it secret for fear of its being abused, so that only the truly initiated succeeded in learning it.

---

[1] The goose being the mother of the egg out of which the god Seb, the first of the deities, was created.

[2] The deity Hapi or Hapi-moui, the personification of the river Nile.—*Ed.*

[3] Merely as a late Chaldee example of the personification of the theurgic fiat of the Supreme Being, compare the following passages from the Book of Wisdom, vii. 25, and Ecclus. xxiii. 1-7. The connection between these statements and that advanced position of the Jewish Fathers when they endowed the *Memra* with an actual existence and potentiality belongs to the province of the theologian.

In the Egyptian magic of early times, as it is explained by the Neoplatonicians, "they considered it necessary," says M. Maury, "even when the magician did not understand the language from which the name was borrowed, to preserve the primitive form of the name, as another word would not have had the same virtue. The author of the *Treatise on the Egyptian Mysteries*, which is attributed to Jamblicus, maintains that the barbarous names taken from the dialects of Egypt and Assyria have a mysterious and ineffable virtue on account of the great antiquity of these languages, and the divinely revealed origin of the theology of these nations." The use of odd names which were unintelligible to the vulgar, and had been taken, not from their own, but from other dialects, or else composed from imagination, may be traced in Egypt to a much earlier date than might at first sight be supposed. We shall meet with many names of this kind designating Set and Osiris, no one of which is Egyptian, in a magical imprecation of a funereal character which is written upon a papyrus in the Louvre of the date of Rameses II. :—[1]

> O, Ualbpaga! O, Kemmara! O, Kamalo! O, Karkkenmu! O, Aamagoaa! The Uana! The Remu! The Uthun (enemies) of the Sun! This is to command those who are adversaries amongst you.
> He is slain by the violence of the assassin of his brother.[2]
> He has devoted his soul to the crocodile. No one pleads for him. But he takes his soul to the tribunal of double justice[3] before Mamuremukababu[4]

---

[1] Devéria, *Catalogue des Manuscrits Egyptiens du Louvre*, p. 174.   [2] Set.
[3] The Hall of the Two Truths.   [4] This is Osiris.

and the absolute lords who are with him."[1]

The latter replies to his enemy: "O, black-faced lion, with bloody eyes and poison in thy mouth, destroyer of his proper name . . .[2]

. . . of his father, the power of biting shall not again arise in them."

The mystic and magic names, seemingly of a barbarous origin, which are used to designate the gods, hold a very important place in the four last chapters of the Ritual of the Dead, in more perfect copies such as those of the Museum of Turin. Dr. Birch considers these chapters to have been composed about the time of the XXVIth dynasty, and we can clearly discern in them some Semitic roots. We are expressly told that those of the CLXVth chapter are taken from the language of the Anu of Nubia.[3] I have also found in a letter of the late lamented Viscount de Rougé some names of a similar kind mentioned as being derived from the dialect of the Negroes (*nahasi*) in the country of Pount, namely, southern Arabia. This proves that the magic of the African populations must have exercised some influence upon the magic of the Egyptians at a certain time, and within certain limits. The latter in its principle differed greatly doubtless from that of the surrounding nations in doctrine and origin, but in practice it must have borrowed a few rites and names from the customs of the Nubian sorcerers.

---

[1] The forty-two assessors of the tribunal of Osiris.   [2] Lacuna.

[3] "He is Harupuka-ka-sharu-shabau when mentioned by the land of Hes, which is of the land of An, of the land of the Phut. In this way I translate the expression Aabui, which I consider as a word which has been borrowed from the Semitic languages.

CHAPTER VIII.

Contrasts between the Accadian and Egyptian magic.

AFTER having put the reader in the way of comparing for himself the Egyptian and Chaldean magical formulæ, there is no need for me to pursue further the marked difference between the two systems, for this is evident to all students. The fundamental beliefs and ideas of magic superstition in Egypt and Chaldea were as different in their character as were the forms of their incantations.

In the Egyptian documents we perceive no trace of those elementary spirits, some good and some bad, endowed with a distinct personality, which Chaldeans believed to have been spread all over the world, the objects either of propitiatory incantations or the most terrible exorcisms. On the other hand, the Chaldeans in no way entertained the idea of being able to elevate a man into a kind of demigod by means of their formulæ, and of identifying him with the greatest personages of the celestial hierarchy. Neither did they pretend that those formulæ had any power to command the gods or to compel them to obey. Their magic belonged to the intermediate spiritual state, and there its powers were displayed. If they required the help of the supreme gods, that was to be obtained by means of prayers and supplications, and not by compulsion; indeed, and we shall refer to this idea again, even their prayers were not all powerful to accomplish the desires of the suppliant unless they were presented to the gods by a mediator. True indeed there was a supreme name which possessed the power of commanding the gods, and exacting from them a perfect obedience, but that name remained the inviolable secret of Hea. The initiated need never hope to attain to such an awful height of knowledge as he might in the Egyptian system. In exceptionally grave cases he besought Hea, through the mediator Silik-mulu-khi, to pronounce the solemn word in order to re-establish order in the world and restrain the powers of the abyss. But the enchanter did not know that name, and could not in consequence introduce it into his formulæ, even although they were destined to remain for ever concealed in mystery. He could not obtain or make use of it, he only requested the god who knew it to employ it, without endeavouring to penetrate the terrible secret himself.

The primitive simplicity of the incantations of Chaldean magic strikes us forcibly when we compare them with those of the Egyptian magic, and this fact gives to them a stamp of greater antiquity. Every thing is expressed very clearly and simply without any attempt at obscurity, or premeditated complications. The belief in spirits is seen there in its most ancient and perfect form, without any philosophical refinement as to the divine substance, without a single trace of mysticism, and above all without any allusions to the vast number of mythological legends which fill the Egyptian formulæ, and render them perfectly unintelligible without a voluminous commentary.

It is easy on the contrary to understand the magical formulæ in the Accadian language, which were preserved in Chaldea until the breaking up of the sacerdotal schools on the borders of the Euphrates, and which Assurbanipal had copied for the royal library in Nineveh about the VIIth century, B.C. They contain no mysteries, and the sacerdotal secret, if there were one, consisted in the precise knowledge of the exact terms of the incantations, sacred from their antiquity, and no doubt also from the idea that they were of divine origin. The formulæ were the work of a people who possessed as yet no esoteric doctrines and no mystical initiations; amongst whom the science of magic consisted simply in a practical acquaintance by the priests with certain rites and words, by means of which they fancied themselves able to establish a communication with the world of spirits, whilst at the same time their conception of those spirits differed from the popular superstitions only by a little more systematic regularity in their position, hierarchy and privileges.

It is for this reason that the Accadian magic preserved, even during the centuries of the greatest splendour of Babylon and Assyria, the appearance of extreme antiquity and the spirit of the earliest ages, by the side of the learned religion which sprang up later in the same places, and which accepted the existence of this magic by placing in the canon of its sacred books the old Accadian incantations, and giving a place, though indeed an insubordinate one, in its theological system to the genii who were invoked in these incantations. At the bottom, as we shall see, magic was not separated in Chaldea from the religion of the historical centuries; it was a new twig from an entirely different plant which was grafted for good or for evil upon the trunk from the time that its existence was recognized, and tolerated instead of being annihilated. But facts oblige us to see in it also the remains of an earlier religious system, of a still rudimentary and coarse naturalism, which arose from the ideas of a primitive population belonging to a race entirely different from that among which the Chaldaic-Assyrian religion existed. In the civilization which gradually spread over the borders of the Tigris and Euphrates from the fusion of the Sumirians, and the Accadians, the Semito-Kushites and the Turanians, religion and magic were peaceably united, although they originated in the two opposing elements of the people. This I think will be made evident by placing the doctrines of the magic books which were originally written in the Accadian language, and the discovery of which we owe to Sir Henry Rawlinson, in comparison with those of the later official religion and of the public worship, as they appear in many documents.

CHAPTER IX.

The Chaldæo Babylonian religion and its doctrines.

IN order to be able to compare, with a full knowledge of the matter, the information given us by the magic Accadian texts and the Babylonian religious system, let us begin by examining the latter at the time of its most complete development, namely, during the whole of the historical period termed the Assyrian era, when it received an impulse from the sacerdotal schools which were in full activity under Sargon I. and Hammurabi. I shall only need here to resume and complete what I have more minutely explained with quotation and proofs in my *Commentaire des fragments cosmogoniques de Berose*.[1]

The Babylonian religion, adopted by the Assyrians with only one important modification, was, in its essential principles, and in the spirit which guided its ideas, a religion of the same kind as that of Egypt and nearly all other great heathen religions. Underneath the exterior garb of a coarse polytheism with which it had been invested by popular superstition, were the conceptions of a higher order from

[1] Paris, 1872.

which it had originated; and foremost amongst them the fundamental idea of a divine unity, although disfigured by the monstrous illusions of pantheism, which confounded the creature with the Creator, and transformed the Divine Being into a multitude of derivative gods who were manifested in all the phenomena of nature. Below this sole and Supreme God, since he was the All in which every thing becomes absorbed, were ranged in an order of emanation corresponding to their order of importance, a company of secondary gods, which were no other than his attributes and his manifestations personified. In these secondary divine personages and in their reciprocal nature, may be particularly seen the differences between the chief heathen religions, the first principle of which is always the same. The imagination of the Egyptians was, as I said before, especially struck by the successive stages in the daily and yearly course of the sun; they saw in them the most imposing manifestation of the Divinity, revealing most clearly the laws of the order of the world, and they sought in them their divine personifications. The Chaldaic Babylonians on the contrary devoted almost exclusively to astronomy, read in the whole sidereal and planetary system, the revelation of the Divine Being. Like the Syro-Phœnician nations, to whose religions theirs was very closely allied, they considered the stars as the true exterior manifestations of this Divine Being, representing them in their religious system as sentient persons proceeding from the substance of the Absolute Being, whom they identified with the world which was his great work. Only, in its definitive form, their religion classed these emanations in a learned and philosophical scale, which must have been the result of deep thought, and which found no counterpart in the religion of Syria and Phœnicia.

The Supreme God, the first unique principle from which all the other gods took their origin, was Ilu[1] whose name signifies "the god" pre-eminently. He is the One and the Good whom the Neo-platonician philosophers announced as the common source of every thing in Chaldean theology;[2] and indeed the first principle is mentioned as "the god One"[3] in documents of the later epoch, which tell us,[4] the philosophic language having been completely formed in the sacerdotal schools, that in the beginning the Existing Being (Auv Kinuv) was begotten of the Abyss (Apsu), and the primordial sea (Tiamat) and was worshipped under this name by Nebuchadnezzar.[5] But this belongs to a philo-sophical development of quite recent date.[6] In the religion of the classical ages of the basin of the Euphrates, the idea of Ilu was too comprehensive

---

[1] In the Accadian *Dingira*.

[2] Anon., *Compend. de Doctr. Chaldaic.*, see Stanley, *Histor. Philosoph.*, Vol. II., p. 1125.

[3] Or rather the god whose scale in the numerical theological system of the Chaldeans was represented by the sign | a single stroke, which also indicated the sacred cycle 60.   [4] Damasc., *De Princip.*, 125, p. 381, ed. Kopp.

[5] Inscription of Borsippa, col. I., 1, 2, *W. A. I.* 1., 31, 4.

[6] The discovery of the Creation Tablet by Mr. George Smith confirms and illustrates the position of M. Lenormant, and, while tracing the development of the Assyrian religion to a deification of the powers of nature, analogous to the earlier hymns of the Rig Veda, yet at the same time proves that that theoretical explanation was of a subsequent introduction into the faith of Mesopotamia, as the cosmogony is most complex and involved. I shall add this text from Fox Talbot's translation at the end of this chapter, and must refer the reader to the original paper from which it is extracted in the *Transactions of the Society of Biblical Archæology*, Vol. IV., part 1.—*Ed.*

and too vast to receive a very definite exterior form, and consequently the adoration of the people; the Greeks found in him on that account a certain analogy with their Cronos, to whom they likened him. It seems that in Chaldea no important temple was especially dedicated to him, although to him Babylon owed its name of Bab-Ilu[1] or in the Accadian *Ka-Dingira.* The personality of Ilu was not clearly defined for a long time; his office and title as "God One" were at first given to Anu, "the ancient god," and the first person of the supreme trinity, which was afterwards held to emanate from Ilu; the priests did not distinguish the primordial principle from the chief of this trinity. It was only amongst the Assyrians that the worship of a "*deus exsuperantissimus,*" the source and principle whence all the others originate, took almost as important a place as in that of Ahuramazda amongst the Persians, in the person of their national god Assur, from whom the country itself derived its name.

Next to Ilu, the universal and mysterious source of all things came a trinity composed of his three first exterior and visible manifestations, which were placed at the summit of the scale of the gods in the popular worship; Anu, the primordial chaos, the god of Time and the World, (both χρόνος and χόσμος) uncreated matter issuing from the fundamental and unique principle of all things; Hea, the intelligence, or we would willingly say "the Word," which animated matter and rendered it

---

[1] Bab-ilu, "The Gate of (the God) Ilu." The Babylonian name from whence, by an ironical alliteration, the name of Babel, "Gate of Confusion," was derived by the Hebrew historians.—*Ed.*

fertile, which penetrated the universe, directed and inspired it with life; being, at the same time, the king of the element of water, in one word, "the Spirit which moved upon the face of the waters;" and, lastly, Bel the demiurgus and ruler of the organized universe. Damascius[1] describes this great trinity among the Chaldeans, and designates the personages by the Accadian appellations of Anna ('Aνός), Hea ('Aὸς) and Anu ('Iλ-ινος). These three coequal and co-substantial divine persons were not of the same degree of emanation, but they issued on the contrary one from the other: Hea from Anu, and Bel from Nuah.[2]

Corresponding with each of the gods of the supreme trinity was a feminine divinity, his second half, the passive form, or, to use the expression in many inscriptions, "the reflection." Thus, in India, the great Trimurti[3] of the male gods is reproduced in the feminine trinity, or the Sakti-Trimurti. And so in Chaldean mythology Anat or Nana answered to Anu, Belit to Bel, and Davkina to Hea; but the

---

[1] *De Princip.*, 125, p. 384, ed. Kopp.

[2] According to the results of the most recent scholars the following is the pedigree of the gods of Chaldea :—

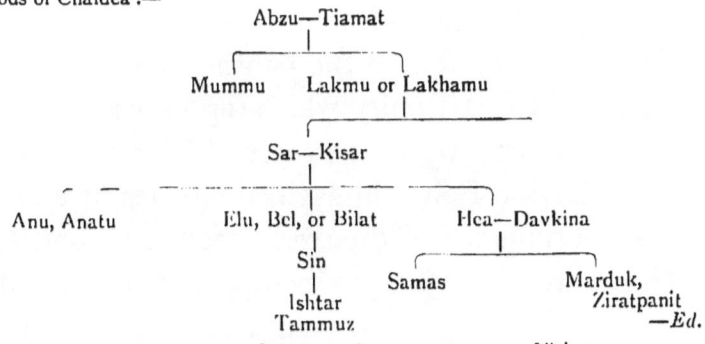

[3] Notably of Elephanta near Salsette: Brahma, creator; Vishnu, preserver; Siva, destroyer.—*Ed.*

distinction between these three female personages was much less clear than that existing between the three male gods. They were often confounded one with the other, and in reality they ultimately become but one, Belit, who was almost always mentioned to the exclusion of the other two in the incantations to the cycle of the great gods. Belit was the principal feminine element of nature, the humid, passive and fertile matter which perpetuates the race of the gods and human beings.

In an Assyrian inscription of Sargon II. Belit is said to grind to powder the elements of the world like paint. Her principal functions are those of "The sovereign goddess," "Lady of the lower abyss," "Mother of the gods," "Queen of the earth," "Queen of fertility." As the primordial humidity from which everything proceeds, she was Tamti, "the sea;" as the chthonian and infernal goddess, Allat or Um-Uruk, "the mother of the town of Erech," the great necropolis of Chaldea. Lastly, in the astronomical world she revealed herself as Istar; but in this last manifestation she took a more distinctly personal character than in the others, and was allotted a special place in the hierarchical system of the pantheon.

After the first Trinity, which represented the genesis of the material world, and issued from the substance of the Divine Being himself, the series of emanation was continued, and thus produced a second trinity. The three personages composing it abandoning henceforth the general and undefined character of those forming the first, and assuming a decidedly sidereal aspect; they represented those celestial bodies in which the Chaldaic-Babylonians saw the most remarkable exterior manifestations of the Divinity, namely, to quote them in their hierarchical order, Sin, the god of the moon, the son of Bel; Samas, the sun, the son of Hea; and lastly, Bin, the god of the atmosphere and its phenomena, of the winds, of the rain and thunder, the son of Anu.

These were the three trinities, "each composed of a father or first principle, a power, and an intelligence," *pater, potentia et mens*, which the philosophers of the Neoplatonician school, who thoroughly understood the Asiatic religions, tell us were regarded by the Chaldeans as emanating from the One and Good "*unum et bonum*," and as constituting the foundation of their religion.[1] And further, since the Chaldaic-Babylonians, like the Syro-Phœnician nations, never recognised a god without dividing his substance into a male and female principle, each of the deities forming the triad of the most important celestial bodies was thus assisted by his spouse. With Sin was united "the supreme lady," whose name we are not yet sure of pronouncing correctly; with Samas the goddess Gula, triform as personating the moon,[2] and who was sometimes replaced by a group of three spouses of equal rank, Malkit, Gula, and Anunit; and, lastly, the companion of Bin was the goddess Sala.

---

[1] Anon., *Compend. de Doctr. Chaldaic.*; see Stanley, *Histor. Philosoph.*, Vol. II., 1125; Damasc. *De Princip.*, 111, p. 345, ed. Kopp.; Lyd., *De Minsib.*, IV., 78, p. 121.

[2] So in Greco-Roman mythology the moon was similarly regarded as a triform goddess under the names of Diana, Luna, and Hecate, a triad often represented in the bronze and marble statuettes.—*Ed.*

In the descending scale of the emanations, and the supreme hierarchy of the pantheon, the gods of the five planets had the next place: viz., Adar (Saturn), Marduk (Jupiter), Nergal (Mars), Istar (Venus), and Nebo (Mercury). As the planets Venus and Mercury each have different aspects in the morning and evening, the Chaldeans admitted later into their astro-mythology a double Istar, and divided the god Nebo into two persons, Nebo and Nusku. The four who were considered as male gods, Istar being a goddess, had each a feminine companion to complete their powers by a conjugal union: Zarpanit being the consort of Marduk; Laz of Nergal; and Tasmit of Nebo; as to Adar, he was represented as both the son and spouse of the great goddess Belit.[1] Istar also possessed a mysterious spouse, Duzi or Dumuzi[2] who was stolen from her in the flower of his youth, and whom she goes to seek in the depths of the infernal regions into which the dead descend; this, however, does not hinder him from indulging in many other passions, of which the mythological legends do not scruple to give some scandalous details.[3]

With these planetary personages ends the series of the twelve great gods who constituted the true Chaldaic-Babylonian Olympus, the superior order of that divine hierarchy, the twelve who were called by

---

[1] In the same manner and by the same idiom as the god Horus-Khem was called "The Husband of his Mother" in Egyptian mythology.—*Ed.*

[2] The Adonis of the Greek writers, "the Tammuz yearly wounded" of Milton and the poets.—*Ed.*

[3] See for these Smith's important translation of the Archaic-Chaldean legends in the *Chaldean Account of Genesis*, 1875, and Sayce in the *Astronomy of the Babylonians*, 1874.—*Ed.*

Diodorus Siculus[1] in a very correct explanation of the astronomical theological Chaldean system, "masters," or "lords of the gods," and who were said by him to preside over the twelve months of the year and the twelve signs of the zodiac.[2] They were generally mentioned alone as objects of a public, official, and universal worship throughout the country, and their titles form part of most proper names; but beneath these great gods, the theology and mythology of Babylon and Assyria recognized legions of *dii minores* which represented inferior orders of emanation, but which do not appear to have been arranged as regularly as were the chiefs of the hierarchy; they formed quite a nation of gods which always remained rather confused, and were worshipped only in certain places. Minor divinities of this kind are mentioned in the cosmogonic story of Berosus in company with Bel; they are said to execute his orders, and to aid him in his work as demiurge. The mythological and astrological tablets give a great number of divine names which must be referred to this class. Those above all should be studied which contain the genealogies of gods, and particularly that precious fragment of a cuneiform text in which the divinities subordinate to the great gods in the principal sanctuaries of Babylon and Assyria are enumerated temple by temple.[3]

Many names which were given in the inscriptions

---

[1] II., 30.

[2] The twelve are arranged in the following order: Anu, Bel, Nuah, Belit, Sin Samas, Bin, Adar, Marduk, Nergal, Istar, Nebo. The best work of reference for English students of these Chaldeo-Greek mythological texts is Cory's *Ancient Fragments*, a most concise and admirable little work edited by an admirable Greek scholar now too rarely referred to.—*Ed.*

[3] *W. A. I.* III., 66.

as belonging to distinct personages were, no doubt, found upon the other mythological tablets as titles of the great gods. Popular worship only gave them a distinct existence, and, in the general and scientific system of religion, they were considered as diverse forms of the same divinity. But some of the *dii minores* have a right to be considered distinct personages, as they perform functions of a certain importance. Such were Serakh, who was also called Nirba, the god of harvests; Manu the great, who presided over fate, as also the goddess Namit; Papsukul, the messenger of the great gods; Bau, the personification of chaos; Martu, the west, the son of Anu; Asmun; Samila; Usu; and many more that it would take too long to mention. Together with them were some local gods of rivers or towns, the adoration of whom never became general in the country, and to whom, in the definite classifications of the pantheon, no higher place was assigned, Subulat, the god of the Euphrates, and Ztak, god of the Tigris, Serrakh of Kis, Kanissura of Cutha; some of the latter being even of foreign origin, and therefore we find certain gods belonging to the Elamite frontier worshipped in the eastern provinces, such as Laguda at Kisik, and in other places Susinka, and Lagamar or Lagamal.[1] The ancient gods of the purely Accadian age were also consigned to the confused crowd of *dii minores*, and their worship consequently abandoned; but they continued to be mentioned in the magical books

---

[1] From whence the name of the early conqueror Kudur Lagamar or Chedorlaomer was derived. Gen. xiv. 1.—*Ed.*

which are preserved, traditionally the remains of another religious phase to be examined shortly.

We must distinguish the long series of stellar personifications, representing " the celestial mansions and the whole army of heaven,"[1] namely, constellations or stars viewed singly; from the gods grouped beneath the supreme cycle as inferior powers and emanations. These corresponded with the astrological and apotelesmatical conceptions, with which the Chaldaic-Babylonian religion had been imbued from the earliest ages in a higher degree than any other religious system of the ancient world. These personifications were distributed into classes and arranged according to their importance and their attributes in a systematic hierarchy, the construction of which is very clearly explained by Diodorus Siculus,[2] and of which we shall hereafter give a detailed account in our book on astrology. They were not all counted amongst the gods properly so called, many stars being regarded only as animated by supernatural beings under the orders of the great gods, thus continuing the chain of emanations in a lower degree; and while they still participated in the divine essence, approaching near to humanity, and consequently interesting themselves pre-eminently in the human race.

In this new sphere were ranged the four principal classes of protecting genii: the Sed, Alap, or Kirub, who was represented as a bull with a human face; the Lamas or Nirgal, as a lion with a man's head; the Ustur, after the human likeness; and the Nattig

---

[1] 2 Kings xxiii. 5.   [2] Lib. ii. 30 and 31.

with the head of an eagle; the emblems of these four classes were adopted by the prophet Ezekiel[1] as those of the four symbolical creatures which supported the throne of Jehovah in his wondrous visions by the river Chebar. Next above them were the angels or spirits, divided into two groups: the Igili or celestial spirits, and the Anunnaki or terrestrial spirits. A tablet from the library of Nineveh gives the names of seven supreme and magnificent gods,[2] fifty great gods of heaven and earth, three hundred spirits of the heavens, and six hundred spirits of the earth.[3] The admission of these choirs of angels and genii beneath the gods, justified the people of that epoch in admitting the demonology of the ancient Accadian books into their religious system, and in placing amongst the sacerdotal sciences the magic of the ancients, who, knowing nothing of the supreme gods of the Assyrian hierarchy, were contented with an earlier religious system, and whose only theology was a system of gods and elementary spirits, of which some were good and others bad.

APPENDIX I.

Tablet I. of the Creation Series.

1 When the upper region was not yet called Heaven,
2 and the lower region was not yet called Earth,
3 and the Abyss of Hades had not yet opened its arm,
4 then the chaos of waters gave birth to all of them.
5 And the waters were gathered into one place.

---

[1] Chap. i. 10; and x. 14.

[2] These are evidently the two superior male triads with Belit, as they are seen in many inscriptions.

[3] G. Smith, *North British Review*, January 1870, p. 309.

6 No men yet dwelt together, no animals yet wandered about,
7 none of the gods had yet been born,
8 their names were not spoken, their attributes were not known.
9 Then the eldest of the gods,
10 Lakhmu and Lakhamu, were born,
11 and grew up . . . .
12 Assur and Kissur were born next,
13 And lived through long periods.
14 Anu . . . .—*H. Fox Talbot.*

APPENDIX II.

Extract from a letter to The Academy, *March* 20, 1875, *by the* Rev. A. H. SAYCE, *on the Creation Tablet.*

"Now the story of the Deluge discovered by Mr. Smith has so fully demonstrated the good faith of Berosus in transcribing the early legends of Chaldea, we may accept without hesitation his account of the Babylonian cosmogony in all its details, even though monumental corroboration of it were still wanting. The cosmogony however belongs to a period of reflection and systematisation.

* * * * *

Sigê, it is stated, was the primitive substance of the universe from whom came *Apason* and his wife *Tavthe*, "the mother of the gods." She bore her firstborn, *Moumis*, "the intelligent world," and afterwards *Dakhe* and *Dakhos*, together with *Kissarê* and *Assôres*, of whom were born the triad Anos, Illinos and Aos, Bel, the demiurge, being the son of Anos and Davke. Now Sigê is the Accadian Zicu or Zigara, "the heaven," "the mother of gods and men," while Apasôn is Ap'su, "the deep," and Tavthe, *Tihamtu*, "the sea." Similarly, *Moumis* is *Mami*, "the waters," *Assôros* being Assur with his wife Scruá. The triad, as well as Davke and Bel are familiar personages in the inscriptions.

* * * * *

Dr. Ewald has shown that the basis of the Phoenician cosmogony (or rather of the various cosmogonies, which a syncretising account fused into one) is the Trinity of *Baau* (or Chaos) Spirit (or Desire) and *Môt*. Môt is interpreted "slime" and is elsewhere termed *Ulâmos*, or Time, and also the "Egg," out of which heaven and earth have been produced. The Trinity corresponds exactly to the old Accadian Trinity of Na or Anu "the sky," Ea or *En-ci*, "the earth," and Mul-ge, "the lord of the under world." Mul-ge is the Bel of Semitic Babylonia, and to him were assigned the functions of a demiurge or creator. Hea was "the lord of life" and "knowledge," as well as "of the deep." He too was "the spirit of wisdom" that brooded over the abysmal waters, and penetrated through the universe, understanding all secrets, and presiding over all theurgic action. His wife, Dav-cina or *Davkê*, "the female earth," was identified with *Bahu ;* and herein we have a curious analogy, not only to the passage of Genesis which states that "the earth had been waste and desolate, and darkness upon the face of the deep; and the spirit of God moved upon the face of the waters," but also to the Phoenician system with its spirit *Môt* and *Baau*. Baau is said to have been the wife of the wind Kolpia, and we thus get a striking resemblance to the Chaldean Triad of the Demiurge, the sky and the earth whose spirit broods over the abyss and is wedded to Baau. Even the language of the Biblical account, in which *Elohim* "carves" the heaven and the earth out of a primeval chaos, his spirit brooding over the deep and wasteness of the earth, shows a similar colouring. The likeness is increased when we recollect that the week of seven days originated among the Accadians, and that each seventh day was one of "rest," on which certain works appear to be done."

CHAPTER X.

Development of the Chaldean Mythology.

THE perusal of such an explanation of this learned and cleverly contrived system as we have just given, following closely the indications of the texts, and giving no play to conjecture or imagination, will suffice to show that it could not have been a very primitive one, and that it must have exacted an immense effort of religious and philosophical thought, which was probably the work of many ages in the sacerdotal schools. And although, through a deficiency of documents, much is still required to complete our knowledge of the ancient history of Chaldea before the development of the Assyrian power, it is sufficient to justify us in affirming that the definitive system of the Chaldaic-Babylonian religion, with its divine hierarchy, and its series of successive emanations, was the result of a great sacerdotal movement. It nearly approached a religious revolution, and corresponded in more than one particular with the transformation which the early

Vedic religion underwent in India under the influence of the Brahmin colleges. Like the latter it was the work of a firmly constituted priesthood, accustomed to the most abstract speculations of thought, and to meditation on the great religious problems, as they presented themselves to minds imbued with pantheistic prejudices; we shall examine later the origin of this priesthood, which was also the source of its religious supremacy. We can even fix the date of 2000 B.C., at the commencement of the dynasty of Agane in Babylon proper, of which Sargon I. was the chief, as about the time when the religious evolution which we are considering, having nearly arrived at perfection, definitely triumphed, and extended its empire over the whole country. The establishment of the same rule in the northern and southern provinces, in Chaldea and in Babylon, first under the dynasty of Agane, and then under the new family which Hammurabi placed on the throne by his conquests, very much facilitated its triumph.

There are many monuments still remaining of the earlier state of the religion. In the numerous inscriptions of the first dynasty of the ancient Chaldean empire which have been handed down to us, we find no trace of the learned system of the Olympus[1] mentioned in the books which are supposed to have been written during the epoch

---

[1] The Olympus of the Accadians has just been illustrated by a translation of "The Hymn to the Mountain of the World." It was a mountain on the summit of which the gods resided, in the interior of which was Hades, the land of "No return," surrounded by seven walls guarded with only one door each. In the midst of Hades issued the river of the water of life, by drinking of which the goddess Ishtar obtained immortality, and was allowed to return to earth after her journey in search of Duzi. See a notice of this discovery by Mr. Boscawen in *The Academy*, No. 187, December 4, 1875.

of Sargon I. The names of the gods are the same as they were later; but these divine personages were not as yet connected with each other by the bonds of the theological system we have just explained, or grouped and arranged according to degrees of importance and emanation from a regular hierarchy. Their attributes were much less definite and distinct than they afterwards became; there was more resemblance amongst themselves, and, above all, they were of an almost exclusively local character.[1] Each of them was worshipped alone with his wife in a town, where he continued to have his principal sanctuary even to the end, and in that town he was looked upon as the first of the gods. Anu[2] reigned thus in Erech with Nana;[3] Bel[4] with Belit[5] in Nipur; Sin with Nana, in Ur; Samas[6] in Larsa of Chaldea, and Sippara of Babylon, where he was united with Anunit; Marduk and Zarpanit were the special deities of Babylon; Nebo of Borsippa, where, as an exception, Nana was his spouse; and Nergal and Laz were worshipped at Cutha. When the dynasty of Ur exercised an actual supremacy over the whole of Chaldea, this supremacy was represented in the religious hierarchy by its giving the pre-eminence to Sin,[7] the patron god of the town; but the same pre-eminence passed to Samas when the power belonged to the king of Larsa. No inscriptions

---

[1] So in Egypt also the eponymous deities and triads of the different nomes became be ultimately regarded as different and even antagonistic deities.—*Ed.*
[2] In the Accadian *Anna*.
[3] In the Accadian *Dingiri*.
[4] In the Accadian *Mul-ge*.
[5] In the Accadian *Nin-ge*.
[6] In the Accadian *Ud*.
[7] After whom many early kings of Babylonia were named, such as Naramsin, the successor of Sargon, Rimsin and Ardusin. See Smith, "Early History of Babylonia" in *Records of the Past*, Vol. III., pp. 15-17.—*Ed.*

of those distant ages (between 3000 and 2000 B.C.) unite the cycle of the great gods in the same worship, as was so often done in later times. The collections of Accadian liturgical hymns, accompanied by an interlinear Assyrian translation, which we have given elsewhere,[1] belongs to the same state of things and the same historical period. The able researches of the Count de Vögué[2] have proved that the religions of the nations of Syria and Palestine always remained in this state, and were never exposed like those of the lower Euphrates to the influence of the work of a sole and powerful sacerdotal corporation.[3] The formula belonging to them, and given by the eminent Academician (now unfortunately for science made an ambassador) could be applied without any modification to the form of the Chaldaic-Babylonian religion previous to its classification, which was really very artificial in many ways. They constituted a group of religions closely connected with each other which may be termed Kuschito-Semitic or Euphratico-Syrian, and they all show the same fundamental data, and have many of the names of their gods in common. This family is one of the most distinctly marked which we can find in the science of the religions.

We see the idea of a sole and universal Divine Being, manifested in the natural world, which is really himself, emanating from his substance and not

---

[1] Un Véda Chaldéen, in Vol. II. of my *Premières Civilisations*.

[2] See De Vögué, *Mélanges d'Archéologie Orientale*, pp. 51 and 57; and also Lenormant, *Manuel de l'Histoire Ancienne de l'Orient*, 3me Éd., Vol. III., pp. 127-303, and 352.

[3] M. Lenormant has shown in his *Lettres Assyriologiques*, Vol. II., that the ancient religion of Arabia bore the same character.

created by him, spread everywhere as the foundation of all religion, and it certainly was the primordial notion of it. But the nature of this god, as in all the ancient pantheisms, was to be at the same time one and many. He was a divine nature working in all the universe, the author of all physical life, destroying his work each year, to renew it afterwards, at the change of the seasons; and following out the pantheistic idea of his nature; he was considered to perform these operations of destruction and renovation not in a world distinct from him, but in his own substance, by a reaction upon himself. A divine name and a distinct person, which became in its exterior form a special personification, corresponded with each phase of these operations. Hence a primitive development of mythology which had taken a local character even upon the borders of the Euphrates and Tigris, until the time of the great work of unification and classification which neither Syria nor Phenicia experienced. Each tribe and town contemplated the Divine Being under one particular aspect, as a certain phenomena of nature or as one of the principles admitted by the coarse philosophy of the time. The result was a corresponding number of gods all different in appearance; but any one who studies them attentively will find that they soon blend one with the other, and return to the primordial unity of the divine substance.

This nature-god had necessarily a double essence, since he was the cause and prototype of the visible world, and united in himself and possessed the two principles of all terrestrial generation, the active and passive, or male and female principles; this conception of duality in unity necessitated the duplication of the symbols, and thus gave rise to the idea of of feminine divinities. In the religions of the Euphratico-Syrian group, the goddess was termed the "manifestation" of the male divinity with which she corresponded. She did not differ from him in any essential point; she was, so to speak, a subjective form of the primitive divinity, a second divine person, distinct enough from the first to be able to form a conjugal union with him, yet at the same time no other than the divinity himself in his exterior manifestation. This general conception of the feminine divinity was subdivided, like the male divinity, into a number of local or attributive personifications. In Chaldea and Babylon, as in Syria and Palestine, every god was necessarily accompanied by a goddess who corresponded to him. The divine personages were not generated separately, but in couples; and each of these couples constituted a complete unity, a reflection of the primitive unity, the two personages which formed it were therefore reciprocally complemental one to the other. When the god had a solar character, the goddess had a lunar nature: if one presided over the day, the other presided over the night: if one personified the active elements, fire and air, the other represented the passive elements, water and earth.'

In this common foundation of the Euphratico-Syrian religions, the divine forms were somewhat vague, undecided and wavering. The gods of Chaldea and Babylon, as they come before us in the most ancient inscriptions, and in the collection of Accadian liturgical hymns, before the great work which defined their respective rank and attributes, resembled those Syrian gods of whom it has been justly said that they had " no firmness of outline, no perceptible determination, nothing to recall the life and personality of the homeric gods; that they were more like those gods of the infant Aryan race, like the feeble divinities of the Vedas, amongst whom Varuna, Indra, and Agni were so often confounded with one another, and the god invoked, be he Indra, Savitri, or Varuna, was always regarded as the highest and most powerful of the gods."[1] By distributing them later into the learned hierarchy of emanations which we have examined; by giving to each a more distinct personality with a clearly defined office; by, so to speak, localising each of them in one of the great heavenly bodies, their primitive nature was sometimes much modified in a way that we can in certain cases thoroughly appreciate. This I think I have proved;[2] and, indeed, it is a generally admitted fact that Adar Samdan, the Chaldaio-Assyrian Hercules, who was considered then as the god of the planet Saturn, was originally a solar personification; he retained even in his new character the features of his first physiognomy, and the mythological tablets still called him "the Sun of the South." In general one may say that in the earliest state of the Chaldaic-Babylonian religion, as also in the

---

[1] J. Soury, in the *Revue des Deux-Mondes* of February 1, 1872.

[2] *Essai de commentaire des fragments cosmogoniques de Bérose*, p. 110, and the following pages.

Syrian, the great majority of the male gods were solar deities, although, in many cases, their physiognomy was much changed in order the better to individualise them, and to make them agree with the newly formed hierarchical system. By way of compensation, the planetary point of view which plays so important a part in the next stage of the religion, hardly appeared during the first epoch, and the influence of the astrological ideas with which it was connected did not begin to predominate in religion until the time of the evolution already mentioned, and then it grew in a great measure out of the new ideas. The only divinity who showed a very decided planetary physiognomy from the earliest times was Istar. In like manner nothing is clearer nor better established than the solar character of her spouse Duzi or Tammuz: he was early recognised in the religion of Phenicia, and had a much more important part there than in the Babylonian mythology. Gods who died and revived periodically belonged to the worship of ancient Asia, and were personifications of the sun in the successive phases of his daily and yearly course. Such was originally Marduk, the tutelary god of Babylon, who was afterwards localized in the planet Jupiter, for he also died to return again to the light, and his tomb was shown in the pyramid of Babylon. His ancient Accadian name of Amar-utuki, changed in the Semitic language to Marduk, signified "the light of the Sun." Bin himself was still termed in some astrological documents the "Sun of the South upon Elam." The principal Epopee of Babylon was composed on a like basis; Izdhubar or Dhubar, its principal hero, was a solar personification, and his twelve great adventures corresponded with the twelve signs of the zodiac.[1]

Some male gods, however, were from the remotest times of the Chaldaic-Babylonian religion exceptions to this common solar character. Sin was the moon, and he bore her name in the Assyrian; he was regarded as both masculine and active, that is to say, in connection with the earth, for the moon was considered to be feminine in connection with the sun, as we saw in the couple Anunit or Gula and Samas. In his great sanctuary of Ur, Nana was his spouse; she was a chthonian goddess personifying the earth, and this connection is clearly expressed by her Accadian name of Hur-ki, peculiar to the worship of the town of Ur, meaning "that which illuminates the earth."[2] On account of the double aspect assumed by the moon according to the point of view from which it is observed, it was represented in many mythological legends, the most important of which has been preserved by Ctesias, as an androgynous god like Men the lunar god of the religions of Asia Minor, whom he very nearly resembles.

In Anu was realised during the earliest period of the religion of the Euphrates, the idea of a cosmic and uranic god, who was at once heaven, earth and time, a deity termed by the Greeks an Æon, in speaking of

---

[1] See Le Déluge et l'Epopée babylonienne, in Vol. II. of my *Premières Civilisations*.

[2] At least it is so translated in the Assyrian, but the original meaning of the name Hur-ki seems still more expressive: "He who extends his action over the earth, he who broods over the earth."

the Asiatic worship, and by the Romans *Sæculum;* he was the same as Ulom or Eschmun of Phenicia, Marna of Gaza, Baal-haldim of the other parts of Palestine, and lastly, the Arabian god Audh or Hobal.[1] He was "the Ancient of days," and of all the divine personifications admitted into the Euphratico-Syrian religions he was the most comprehensive and the most nearly allied to the notion of primordial unity, but at the same time also the most vaguely defined; he was a little like the Vedic Varuna[2] and the Ouranos of the more ancient Greeks. From the time of the oldest Chaldean dynasties, as also at the beginning of that stage which saw the complete classification of religion, he was made the first principle in connection with other gods, and the author of all emanations; indeed he possessed all the qualities which were afterwards given to Ilu, when that deity was distinguished from Anu by a new effort towards the abstract conception of the divine being, and this is the reason why Anu was called pre-eminently "the Ancient," "the Progenitor," and "the Father of the gods."

I could apply these observations also to the personages Bel and Hea, and pass all the gods of the Chaldaic-Babylonian pantheon successively in review, seeking the most ancient idea of each which it is possible to obtain. But to do this would require a regular treatise on the mythology of the basins of the Euphrates and Tigris, which I have not undertaken in this book, and therefore I can only now examine

---

[1] On this conception, see my *Lettres Assyriologiques*, Vol. II., p. 164-178.

[2] For a further analysis of the deities Ouranos and Varuna, see Cox, *Mythology of the Aryan Nations*, Vol. I., pp. 334, 349, 357, and 327, 330; and II., pp. 12, 215. Also Hodges Edition of *Cory's Ancient Fragments*, pp. 10-14.—*Ed.*

such questions incidentally and as they are connected with my subject. The foregoing examples suffice, I think, to show the nature and spirit of the Chaldaio-Babylonian religion in its ancient form, and its identity with the religions which continued to predominate in Syria, Phœnicia, and other countries inhabited by the same race.

CHAPTER XI.

The religious System of the Accadian magic Books.

NOW that we have, by means of numerous documents, thoroughly studied and mastered the system of the religion which was imported into Assyria from Babylon and Chaldea in its two distinct stages, first after the great sacerdotal reform had introduced into it a learned and philosophical hierarchy, and also in its earlier and ruder state; an examination of the ancient Accadian magic books seems to transport us into an entirely new world.

We no longer hear of the same gods, some of the names, which afterwards disappear entirely from the invocations and the mythology,[1] which have not even a settled and generally received equivalent in the Assyrian versions, play an important part in the magic texts. Certain gods, whose titles were to be found in the pantheon of the public and official

---

[1] At least, those names which keep the purely Accadian form and have no Semitic equivalent, only appear in the divine genealogical tables, where a place has still been left them; but it is quite a subordinate place, and does not correspond at all to their ancient importance.

religion, or whom the Assyrian translators had likened indifferently to some of the personages of that religion, appear as a rule, in these texts under an entirely different form, and with entirely different attributes; and further what is particularly remarkable, the sidereal personifications, with the exception of the sun who holds so high a rank in the regular and well organized system of the theology of the great sacedotal schools, and to whom that theology attributes the government of the world and the ordering of events, have no place in the incantations and hymns of the magic collections.[1] At the most we only find a passing mention of the sidereal deities in a very small number of formulæ amongst the invocations at the end after the sacramental words:

> Spirit of the heavens, conjure it! Spirit of the earth conjure it!

While lastly, it is a remarkable fact, which we shall endeavour to explain further on, and which gives a peculiar character to these passages, that not the sidereal gods themselves are invoked, but their spirits,[2] which are imagined to have a distinct existence.

So at the end of an incantation against the plague

---

[1] It is certainly a very remarkable fact that no mention is made of the god of the moon, or even of its Accadian names of Akû and Hur-ki, except in the two invocations which I quote here and the incantation translated farther back, where the account is given in an epic form, of the war of the seven wicked spirits against that planet.

[2] This was essentially the point wherein Gnosticism and Sabaism differed in their conceptions of the heavenly bodies. Taught by, or at least familiar with a certain school of Greek philosophy, the Astro-scientists believed that the planets moved of their own free will in orbits controlled by divine law. The Gnostics taking up this conception, seem to have thought with the doctors of the Cabbala that the spirits of the planets were independent of those celestial spheres, and formed an hierarchy of themselves.—*Ed.*

(*Namtar*),[1] diseases, demons, and witchcraft in general, we read:

> Spirit of the heavens, conjure it! Spirit of the earth, conjure it!
> Spirit of Mul-gelal,[2] lord of the countries, conjure it!
> Spirit of Nin-ge-lal,[3] lady of the countries, conjure it!
> Spirit of Nin-dara,[4] powerful warrior of Mul-gelal, conjure it!
> Spirit of Nusku, sublime messenger of Mul-gelal, conjure it!
> Spirit of Eni-zuna,[5] eldest son of Mul-gelal, conjure it!
> Spirit of Tiskhu,[6] lady of the armies, conjure it!
> Spirit of Mermer,[7] king whose voice[8] is beneficent, conjure it!
> Spirit of Utu,[9] king of justice, conjure it!
> Spirits, Archangels (*Anunna*), great gods, conjure it![10]

In other invocations of the same kind, these spirits of the sidereal gods are associated with those of gods who were no longer known to the public religion of Babylon and Nineveh, and also with other spirits of an elementary character as beings of the same kind and rank; as, for instance, in this enumeration, which is one of the fullest to be found

---

[1] *W. A. I.* IV., 1, col. 3.
[2] In the Assyrian Bel.
[3] In the Assyrian Belit.
[4] In the Assyrian Adar.
[5] In the Assyrian Sin.
[6] In the Assyrian Istar.
[7] In the Assyrian Bin or Ramanu.
[8] In the Assyrian version, "impetuosity."
[9] In the Assyrian Samas.
[10] Compare the litany placed at the end of the incantation immediately preceding this one, on the same tablet:

> Spirit of the heavens, conjure it! Spirit of the earth, conjure them!
> Spirit of Mul-gelal, lord of the countries, conjure them!
> Spirit of Nin-gelal, lady of the countries, conjure them!
> Spirit of Nin-dara, son of the firmament, conjure them!
> Spirit of Tiskhu, lady of the countries, who gives light to the night, conjure them!

CHALDEAN MAGIC AND SORCERY. 139

in the great magic collection copied by Assurbanipal's orders:

> Fever, Spirit of the heavens, conjure it! Spirit of the earth, conjure it!
> Male Spirits, lords of the earth, conjure it!
> Female Spirits, ladies of the earth, conjure it!
> Male Spirits, lords of the stars, conjure it!
> Female Spirits, ladies of the stars, conjure it!
> Male Spirits, lords of hostilities, conjure it!
> Female Spirits, ladies of hostilities, conjure it!
> Spirits Eni-dazarma,[1] conjure it!
> Spirits Nin-dazarma,[2] conjure it!
> Male Spirits, lords of the sublime covering, conjure it![3]
> Female Spirits, ladies of the sublime covering, conjure it!
> Male Spirits, lords of the light of life, conjure it!
> Female Spirits, ladies of the light of life, conjure it!
> Male Spirits, lords of the inferior region, conjure it!
> Female Spirits, ladies of the inferior region, conjure it!
> Spirits, lords of the mother and father[4] of Mul-gelal, conjure it!
> Female Spirits of the mother and father of Mul-gelal, conjure it!
> Spirit of Hur-ki[5] who makes his talismanic[6] ship cross the river, conjure it!
> Spirit of Utu, the king, umpire of the gods, conjure it!
> Spirit of Tiskhu, who directs the Archangels of the earth (*Anunna-ge*), ...[7] conjure it!

---

[1] We have not sufficient information to translate the name of the object of which these spirits are said to be lords, *eni*.

[2] These are the female spirits corresponding to the preceding ones; they are called ladies, *nin*, of the same object.

[3] Or perhaps better "Lord of the heavenly vault."—*Ed.*

[4] In the Assyrian version, "of the father and the mother."

[5] In the Assyrian Sin.

[6] The Assyrian version has only, "his ship." Here we have an allusion to a myth which is as yet unknown.

[7] Lacuna.

Spirit of the goddess Ziku,[1] mother of Hea, conjure it!
Spirit of Ninuah,[2] daughter of Hea, conjure it!
Spirit of Nin-si-ana[3] . . . .[4] conjure it!
Spirit of the god Fire, supreme pontiff on the face of the earth, conjure it!
Spirit of Nin-gis-zida,[5] who upheaves the face of the earth, conjure it!
Spirits of the seven doors of the world, conjure it!
Spirits of the seven locks of the world, conjure it!
Spirit Khusbi-kuru,[6] wife of Namtar, conjure it!
Spirit Khi-tim-kur-ku,[7] daughter of the Ocean, conjure it!

These long litanies are, however, very rare. Up to the present time we possess no criterion which might enable us to judge of the respective antiquity of the different fragments in the great magic collection; but it is clear that, like those of the Vedic collection, they belong to very different epochs, and that the composition of these incantations, formulæ, and hymns might be referred to different centuries far anterior even to the early date at which they were collected and reduced to writing. But it would need careful and deep study, assisted by all the most delicate arts of criticism, to determine the chronology of these fragments, and we are not as yet in a posi-

---

[1] The celestial Ocean. The Nu of Egyptian mythology.—*Ed.*

[2] This rendering is merely provisional and very doubtful; the name is given by the sign which represents the town of Nineveh.

[3] "The lady of the blush of heaven," a name of the planet Venus.

[4] Lacuna.

[5] "The lady of the magic wand," one of the names of the infernal goddess Ninkigal, in the Assyrian Allat.

[6] Or Khusbi-sâ; the meaning is, "his stroke is propitious."

[7] "The spring which surrounds the sublime mountain."

tion to undertake this difficult task. We may however, gather, from the simplicity of the formulæ, which characterises those of a very early date, that the texts containing invocations or litanies, like that we have just quoted, together with two others; the only two of their kind, which have been cited earlier as specimens of long epic stories should be classed amongst the most recent, since they include the idea of punishment of sin by means of disease, and the necessity of repentance, dogmas of a later school. These litanies represent a last phase in the formation of magical documents, a time when the fusion of the Kuschito-Semitic and Turanian elements of the nation had given birth to those religious conceptions which finally predominated exclusively in the exterior and public worship. The old religion of the spirits, upon which Chaldean magic was originally founded, still existed quite independently at this time, and became the peculiar doctrine of the priests of magic, who continued to compose incantations and to add them to the traditional fund which they had received from their predecessors, although this practice seems afterwards to have ceased. But while their doctrine had not changed, and had kept its place side by side with the new religion, the priests perceived plainly the popularity of the gods of this rival religion, and found for them a place accordingly in their infinite world of spirits.

These surmises may seem on a first consideration rather far-fetched, and we shall perhaps be told that the hypotheses we have just advanced rest on no sufficient foundation, but I think anyone who has studied attentively the great collection of magical tablets discovered by Sir Henry Rawlinson must grant that we have in them sufficient and convincing proofs to support our conjectures.

CHAPTER XII.

The Origin of the Myth of the Zi.

WE will now endeavour to give an idea of the religious system explained in the Accadian magic writings, by means of quotations taken principally from the hymns of the third book of the great collection, of which up to this time we have made but little use.

This system was actually that of an adoration of the elementary spirits, as undisputed, as marked, as it ever was amongst the Altaic nations, or in ancient China. Accadian magic was founded upon the belief in innumerable personal spirits distributed in every part throughout nature, sometimes blended with the objects that they animated, and sometimes separate from them. This was certainly one of the rudest conceptions of the supernatural and of the unknown power which governs the world, as it was also one of the most primitive, for it bordered on fetichism and even adopted some of its principles, by confiding blindly in talismans and in their mysterious power.¹ Spirits everywhere dispersed produced all the phenomena of nature, and directed and animated all created beings. They caused evil and good, guided the movements of the celestial bodies, brought back the seasons in their order, made the winds to blow and the rain to fall, and produced by their influence atmospheric phenomena, both beneficial and destructive; they also rendered the earth fertile, and caused plants to germinate and to bear fruit, presided over the birth and preserved the lives of living beings, and yet at the same time sent death and disease. There were spirits of this kind everywhere, in the starry heavens, in the earth, and in the intermediate regions of the atmosphere; each element was full of them, earth, air, fire, and water; and nothing could exist without them.² There were particular ones for each element, each celestial body, each creature, and each object in nature. A very distinct and definite personality was ascribed to them, and we see no trace of the idea of a Supreme God, of a first principle with which they were connected and from which they derived their existence, ruling over this vast number of beings who were superior to man, but inferior to the

---

¹ This was in a sense the theory of even Milton himself when he wrote:
"Millions of spiritual creatures walk the earth,
Unseen both when we wake and when we sleep,"
(*Paradise Lost*, Lib. IV., l. 677-9,)
as it is to this day the belief of the orthodox Turk, who on the conclusion of his prayers, bows to the right and the left as saluting the genii of good and evil respectively, by whom he is attended.—*Ed.*

² This was also known to the Egyptian mythology, the Hieroglyphic inscriptions repeatedly mention the spirits of earth, air, fire, and water, and they were represented as frog-headed and lion-headed respectively. In the long inscription of Darius at El Khargeh these four genii occupy a prominent position, and they also occur in the texts of the myth of Horus in the late Ptolemaic temple of Edfu. See Naville, *Texte de la Mythe d'Horus*, pl. iv.; and *Trans. Soc. Bib. Arch.*, Vol. V., part 1.

notion of the gods cherished by religions of a higher tendency. This feature distinguishes this naturalism, as also that of the Tartar and Mongol nations, from that of the more noble races, such as the ancient Aryas,[1] amongst whom there was always a fundamental idea of a supreme deity, although sometimes very vague and indefinite, besides the adoration of the cosmic phenomena personified in the gods.

As evil is everywhere present in nature side by side with good, plagues with favourable influences, death with life, destruction with fruitfulness; an idea of dualism as decided as in the religion of Zoroaster, pervaded the conceptions of the supernatural world formed by the Accadian magicians, the evil beings of which they feared more than they valued the powers of good. There were essentially good spirits, and others equally bad. Their opposing troops constituted a vast dualism, which embraced the whole universe and kept up a perpetual struggle in all parts of creation. The bad spirits were, like the good, spread everywhere: in heaven, earth, and in the atmosphere, they were in opposition to each other and contended together furiously. Their successive triumphs and defeats caused plagues and benefits to alternate in nature, and they interrupted the regular course of terrestrial things by the intervention of sudden catastrophes. There was a bad as well as a good spirit attached to each celestial body, each element, each phenomena, each object and each being, and

---

[1] See an able article on "The Highest Gods of the Arian Races," by Dr. Roth, in the *Transactions of the German Oriental Society*, Vol. VI., p. 67. Also *Journal of the Asiatic Society*, Vol. I., New Series, p. 51, "Contributions to a Knowledge of the Vedic Theogony by Dr. Muir."—*Ed.*

these were ever trying to supplant each other. Thus discord reigned everywhere in the universe, nothing was free from this continual struggle between evil and good regarded principally from a physical point of view; the moral side of dualism remains quite in the background and hardly appears in the magic writings, or even in the hymns, where it might have been developed more easily. Such writings seem hardly to have recognized any other sin than that of neglecting the propitiatory rites, and entering into communication with the evil spirits by the practices of sorcery, instead of applying to the particular god by means of rites which were considered holy and pious, and through the mediation of the authorized magicians.

Upon this dualistic conception rested the whole edifice of sacred magic, of magic regarded as a holy and legitimate intercourse established by rites of divine origin, between man and the supernatural beings surrounding him on all sides. Placed unhappily in the midst of this perpetual struggle between the good and bad spirits, man felt himself attacked by them at every moment; his fate depended upon them. All his happiness was the work of the former, all the evils to which he was subject were attributable to the latter. He needed then some aid against the attacks of the bad spirits, against the plagues and diseases which they sent upon him. This help he hoped to find in incantations, in mysterious and powerful words the secret of which was known only to the priests of magic, in their prescribed rites and their talismans. By these means the fatal demons were sent away, and the favourable spirits rendered propitious and called to the help of man. The Chaldeans had such a great idea of the power and efficacy of these formulæ, rites, and amulets, that they came to regard them as required to fortify the good spirits themselves in their combat with the demons, and as able to give them help by providing them with invincible weapons which would ensure success. Thus the supernatural power of the magician was not only a protection for man, it also arrested the greatest catastrophes in nature, it influenced the course of the phenomena, and intervened with a decided efficacy in the discords of the world of spirits.

These fundamental data are visible at every point in the great magical collection, and in the formulæ of the same kind which may be discovered elsewhere. They seem to me to stand out so clearly in the quotations which I have already made, as to need no confirmation from other examples.

As the magical doctrines developed and approached nearer to the constitution of a system to which it pretended to give a scientific exactness, it introduced an order and a hierarchy into the crowd of spirits whose existence it admitted. The good spirits were assigned to classes like those we have already noticed amongst the demons. Unhappily the indications of the texts are still less precise as to the distribution and relative rank of the favourable spirits than they are concerning those of the diabolical groups. We can only discern that, in the good as well as in the bad army, were recognized genii, classes called *Alad*, and *Lamma*, and demons termed *Utuq*. The "favourable *Alad*," the "favourable *Lamma*," and the "favourable *Utuq*," are very frequently opposed in the incantatory formulæ to the "evil *Alad*," to "evil *Lamma*," the "evil *Utuq*." Spirits properly so called (*Zi*) are also mentioned, especially elementary spirits, or those attached to beings and definite objects, and angels, more independent, with distinct natural forms, amongst whom we may see the *Anunna*, who are almost always terrestrial spirits, and the *Idede*, who have their dwelling in the heavens.[1]

A certain number of gods even (*ana, dingir,* or *dimmer*) were admitted into the higher regions of the hierarchy. But they did not differ essentially in their nature from the other spirits, and this name (*Zi*) was given to them as well as that of gods. They were beings of the same kind, possessing a distinct title only because their power was thought to be greater and to have a wider scope than that of the other spirits. As far as we can see, the god differed from the simple spirit in that he was less strictly localized, and that he was regarded as animating and directing a great part of the world, many phenomena, and a class of similar beings or objects, each of which individually possessed a spirit. These were then, if they may be so called, the spirits of categories of natural beings or phenomena, considered as distinct from and superior to the individual spirits. Their personality was however as definite as that of the

---

[1] See all this worked out to perfection and adapted to the Judaic system in the *Book of Enoch*, Caps. lxviii. to lxxvii.—*Ed.*

inferior spirits, and we find amongst them no bond of unity of substance, and no common primordial principle. Two of the greatest gods, two holding the first place amongst them, Ana and Hea, had no higher titles than "Spirit of the heavens" (*Zi ana*) and "Spirit of the earth" (*Zi kia*). Therefore the most solemn invocations were addressed to them, and this clearly characterises their original and fundamental nature.

The gods thus conceived appear to have been very numerous. Many such are named in the incantations against demons and diseases and in the magical hymns. But several of these are only mentioned once, and that singly and under such circumstances as to give no precise information about the office and attributes of the god; the more so because the imperfect state of our acquaintance with the Accadian language prevents us from explaining his name, which is sure to have some meaning, and which the Assyrian translator has simply copied without trying to assimilate it to that of a god in his own excessively rich pantheon. What indeed were the gods Nin-akha-quddu, Nin-gur, and many others, whose names are scattered over the magic documents? Fresh texts only can furnish us with the desired information. Some of the names may be nothing but attributes of divine personages better known under other titles. For instance, we know positively that 'Nin-ka-si, "the Lady with the horned countenance," was another name of Nana the wife of Ana; 'Nin-a-su, "the Lord of the numerous waters," and 'Nin-si-ku were titles of Hea, as also Eni-kiga

Mul-kiga, "the Lord of the earth;" whilst Nin-gis-zida, "the Lady of the magic wand," designated the goddess Nin-kigal.

Although we are not yet able to decide precisely on the character and domain of some of the gods, this is only the case with regard to divine personifications of the second rank, who are noticed but rarely. We possess, on the contrary, a great deal of information about the principal gods, owing to the constant mention made of them in the incantations, and particularly by the hymns addressed to them. We can describe them perfectly; and this task we are now about to undertake, but we ought first to notice the peculiar conception of the world with which they were connected.

"The Chaldees," says Diodorus Siculus,[1] "have quite an opinion of their own about the shape of the earth: they imagine it to have the form of a boat turned upside down, and to be hollow underneath." This opinion remained to the last in the Chaldean sacerdotal schools, their astronomers believed in it, and tried, according to Diodorus, to support it by scientific arguments. It is of very ancient origin, a remnant of the ideas of the purely Accadian period; and if we did not clearly understand this conception of the earth, we should find all that the magic texts say about the form and economy of the universe perfectly unintelligible, as also their division of the principal parts of the universe under the dominion of different gods.[2]

[1] Lib. II., sec. 31.
[2] See this idea as a point of the Homeric myth fully worked out in Gladstone's *Homeric Synchronisms*, page 230.

Let us imagine then a boat turned over, not such an one as we are in the habit of seeing, but a round skiff like those which are still used, under the name of *Kufa*, on the shores of the lower Tigris[1] and Euphrates, and of which there are many representations[2] in the historical sculptures of the Assyrian palaces; the sides of this round skiff bend upwards from the point of the greatest width, so that they are shaped like a hollow sphere deprived of two thirds of its height, and showing a circular opening at the point of division. Such was the form of the earth according to the authors of the Accadian magical formulæ and the Chaldean astrologers of after years. We should express the same idea in the present day by comparing it to an orange of which the top had been cut off, leaving the orange upright upon the flat surface thus produced. The upper and convex surface constituted the earth properly so called, the inhabitable earth (*ki*) or terraqueous surface (*ki-a*), to which the collective name of *kalama*, or the countries, is also given. The interior concavity opening from underneath was the terrestrial abyss, *ge*, where the dead found a home (*kur-nu-de, kigal, arali*). The central point in it was the nadir, or, as it was called, "the root" (*uru*), the foundation of the whole structure of the world; this gloomy region witnessed the nocturnal journey of the sun.

Above the earth extended the sky[3] (*ana*) spangled with its fixed stars (*mul*), and revolving round the

---

[1] See Chesney's, *Expedition to the Euphrates and Tigris*, Vol. I., page 57; Vol. II., page 641.
[2] See *The notes to Herodotus*, by G. Rawlinson, lib. I., sec. 194.
[3] *W. A. I.* IV., 20, 2.

mountain of the East (χarsak kurra), the column which joined the heavens and the earth, and served as an axis to the celestial vault. The culminating point of the heavens, the zenith (*nuzku*), was not this axis or pole;[1] on the contrary, it was situated immediately above the country of Accadia, and was regarded as the centre of the inhabited lands, whilst the mountain which acted as a pivot to the starry heavens was to the north-east of this country. Beyond the mountain, and also to the north-east, extended the land of Aralli, which was very rich in gold,[2] and was inhabited by the gods[3] and blessed spirits.

The Chaldean astrologers imagined in later times a spherical heaven completely enveloping the earth; but it seems, from many characteristic expressions, that at the period when the greatest part of the fragments of the magic collection were composed, the firmament was regarded as a hemispherical skull-cap, the lower edges of which, "the foundations of the heavens," rested upon the extremities of the earth, beyond the great reservoir of waters (*abzu*)[4] surrounding the continental surface, and corresponding exactly to the ocean of Homer. We also must give to it the name of ocean in addition to that of reservoir of waters, designating the subterranean

---

[1] *W. A. I.* II., 48, l. 55, 56, c, d, distinguishes between the zenith, *nuzku*, Assyrian *elit same*, and the middle point of the heavens, *ana sâga*, Assyrian *kirib same*.

[2] *W. A. I.* II., 51, l. 11, a, b.

[3] This idea had passed to the Assyrians; see the great inscription of Sargon at Khorsabad, l. 156, published in *Records of the Past*, Vol. VII.

[4] A compound, signifying literally, "abounding in waves." The orthography of this name is derived from a more ancient form, in which the order of the elements was reversed, *zuab*; but the grammars show us that the form *abzu* was substituted for it in the spoken idiom.

cavity or *ge* as the abyss, which word was sometimes used as a translation of the Accadian *abzu* and its Assyrian equivalent *apsu*.¹ The periodical movements of the planets (*lu-bat*), which were assimilated by their Accadian name to animals endowed with life,² took place in a lower zone of the heavens, which was called *ul-gana*, underneath the firmament *e-sara*³ of the fixed stars; astrology afterwards ascribed to them seven concentric and successive spheres, above which the firmament extended, but we can perceive no trace of a similar idea in the magical documents. The firmament supported the ocean of the celestial waters, *ziku*, viewed under the form of a river,⁴ as was frequently the terrestrial ocean, which even assumed the name of "river," *arra* or *aria*.

Between the earth and the heavens was the zone in which the atmospheric phenomena were produced, where the winds (*imi*) blew, and the storms (*imi-dugud*) raged, where the clouds (*imi-dir*) were spread, and at length, rent asunder by the lightning (*nun-gir*) and the hot whirlwind of the thunder-bolt (*amâtu*) from the planets, poured forth rain (*sur*)⁵ through their gutters (*ganul*).

There were then three zones of the universe; the heavens, the terrestrial surface with the atmosphere,

---

¹ This is merely an alteration of the Accadian word.

² *Lu-bat*, translated in the Assyrian *bibbu*, is the goat which leads the flock.

³ The Accadian spelling of this name gives it the sense of "the dwelling of impulse;" it is translated in the Assyrian by *esiru*, from the root אשר. It is evident that one of the two languages has played upon the word which it borrowed from the other, in order to give it a peculiar signification.

⁴ *IV. A. I.* II., 50, l. 27, c, d.

⁵ I have found the decisive proof of this rendering; the usual spelling *A. AN*, does not represent a compound word, it is a complex ideographic expression translated by a simple word.

and the lower abyss. The three greatest gods, Ana, Hea, and Mul-ge or Elim, answered to and presided over those three zones. They corresponded to the gods of the supreme triad of the Chaldaio-Babylonian religion, Anu, Hea, and Bel, the two first of which retained their Accadian names.

But in truth the early conception of these deities with the exception of Hea, as expressed in the magic fragments, is very different from what it afterwards became. Anu certainly preserves some features belonging to the Accadian Ana, but if we compare Bel with the ancient Mul-ge of the magic books we see that a purely artificial assimilation had been made between the Accadian god and a Semitic god of an entirely different character, and, as we have already remarked, probably of a solar origin.

In those parts of the collection which have been handed down to us, there is no special hymn addressed to Ana, but he is' invoked in the sacramental formula of all the incantations under the name of Spirit of the heavens (*Zi-ana*). As his name indicates he was the same as the material-heaven, he was heaven itself, whilst also the soul of it; and he was more completely one with the object to which he was attached than was any other of the supernatural deities.

Ana as described in the most ancient Accadian documents resembled closely the Thian of the early Chinese. But in the oldest religion of China, Thian, "the heavens," was also Chang-ti, "the supreme lord;"[1]

---

[1] See also with relation to the theological use of the names Tian and Shin. Malan's *Who is God in China, Shin or Shang-ti.'* 1855.

he soared above the spirits of nature as sovereign master and first principle, crowning the edifice of the worship of spirits by a thoroughly monotheistic idea. It was perhaps so at the beginning amongst the Accadians; and this supposition is supported by two important arguments, namely, (1) that in their language one of the two words expressing the absolute idea of divinity, *ana*, is the same word which means "heaven;" (2) that the ancient hieroglyph of the sign which, in the cuneiform writing invented by the Accadians renders the idea of "god," is the figure of a star.¹ But although this notion must have existed originally amongst the Accadians, and reappears in the Chaldaio-Babylonian religion, no trace of it is to be found in the fragments composing the magic collection. Ana was in nothing superior to the other two great gods of the two other zones of the universe; he was not even represented as the primordial principle from which they issued.

The name of Hea means "dwelling;"² this name then was manifestly connected with the time when the god was first imagined to be the same as the zone over which he presided, the zone which served as a home for men and animated beings; but he was afterwards regarded as much more separate from the material object than Anna. He was the lord of the earth's surface (*mul-ki*); and this title

---

¹ The use of this sign is not, as appears at first sight, the necessary indication of a primitive sidereal character of the religion. This figure of the star has been appropriated to the expression of the general idea of "the heavens" rather than to that of "god;" it is trebled to represent a "star."

² 'E, *ea*, house.

is applied to him quite as frequently as Hea. In the sacramental formula of the incantations he was invoked as Spirit of the earth, or more exactly still, of the terraqueous surface (*zi-ki-a*). He was also lord of the region of the atmosphere. The spirit of this zone of the universe, he was also the soul which animated everything, penetrated into everything, and made everything which existed in the universe live and move. The Accadians (and they transmitted this idea to the Chaldaio-Babylonians of more recent ages) considered the humid element as the vehicle of all life, and the source of all generation;[1] they saw this element circulating everywhere in the zone which embraces the terrestrial surface and the atmosphere. Hea was the soul and spirit of it, and therefore, according to them, closely connected with the humid element. It was specially his dominion: the waters (*a*), were worshipped in their material reality, and the spirits presiding over them were his children. He had no father assigned to him; but as he was eternally begotten in the bosom of the humid element, he was said[2] to have issued from the celestial ocean personified as a goddess, Ziku.[3] His usual dwelling was in the great reservoir (*abzu* or *arra*), which, as we have already said, surrounded the earth. From this point but one step was necessary to represent him under the ostensible form of a fish-god, and this step was taken; for one of his most usual titles was " the

---

[1] Was not the cosmology of the early Greeks also derived from this source, several of their philosophers holding that all things were produced from water and returned to water again?—*Ed.*

[2] *W. A. I.* Vol. IV., col. 2, l. 36.

[3] As the Egyptian deity Ra from Nut, see Naville, "Litany of Ra," in *Records of the Past*, Vol. VII.

great fish of the ocean" (gal-χana-abzu), or "the sublime fish" (χan maχ).[1]

As the spirit of the inhabited world and the soul directing its phenomena, Hea is the repositary of all science. And here we see the chain of ideas which led to this odd notion, that the learned god should also be an ichthyomorphous god. It passed into the Chaldaio-Babylonian religion with the god Hea himself, and he appeared under this form in the cosmogonic legend, where he was the Oannes of Berosus,[2] revealing religious and social laws to men.[3] According to extracts from the Grecian historian of Chaldea, "he had the body of a fish entire, but underneath his fish's head there was a second human head, while human feet appeared under his tail, and he possessed a human voice. This monster spent the whole day amongst men without taking any food, while he taught them letters, science, and the principles of every art, the rules for the foundation of towns, the building of temples, the measurement and boundaries of lands, seed-time and harvest, in short, all that could advance civilization, so that nothing new has been invented since that period. Then at sunset this great Oannes regained the sea, and passed the night in the vast region of waves, for he was amphibious."[4]

---

[1] For a good illustration of Oannes Dagon, see Bonomi, *Nineveh and its Palaces* pp. 168, 329.—*Ed.*

[2] *Ea χan*, "Hea the fish."

[3] For the identity of Oannès and Hea, see Appendix I, at the end of this part of the volume.

[4] According to Berosus, as quoted by Apollodorus, there were many of these fish avatars of the Supreme Being which were called Annedoti, the first after the lapse of forty *sari*, the second after twenty-six, the third after eighteen (or twenty-eight) *sari*, then a fourth, and finally a fifth named Odacon. See Hodge's *Cory*, pp. 51, 52.—*Ed.*

A representation of the fish-god as a legislator and protector, corresponding exactly with the legend of Berosus, has been found in the sculptures of the Assyrian palaces[1] and on the Babylonian cylinders.[2]

As the soul of that zone of the world inhabited by living beings, of the "dwelling" pre-eminently, Hea was the god who "sees that all is in order," and who defended the frame of nature against the incessant ravages of the wicked spirits. Since he was the god acquainted with science, he knew all their ruses and was able to baffle them; and therefore he alone was possessed of the magic secrets by means of which they could be conquered and repulsed.

Hence the exceptional importance of the position of Hea in the arts of conjurational magic, of which he was the great god. The quotations we have already placed before the reader show clearly his character as supreme protector of men and of nature in the struggle caused by the antagonism between good and evil, as *deus averruncus*, or as the annuller and averter of fatal influences, and as the author of theurgic action. Help was sought from him when neither word, rite, talisman, nor even the intervention of any other of the gods had availed to destroy the demons' power.

The magical texts attributed to Hea the spouse who was afterwards assigned to him in the later mythology, Damkina or Davkina, whilst on the rare occasions when the companion of Ana is mentioned, it was never under the name of Ana, but always as

---
[1] Layard, *Monuments of Nineveh*.
[2] Lajard, *Culte de Mithra*, pl. xvi., no. 7; pl. xvii., nos. 1, 3, 5, 8.

Nin-ka-si. From her name, which can only be exactly translated by the Latin *uxor ex terrâ* (*dam-kina*), she appears to have been originally a personification of the earth's surface, which the god rules and fertilizes. From the union of Hea and Davkina proceeded the material waters which flowed over the earth.[1] Still, as has been before stated, Hea was the only god of the ancient Accadian mythology who was adopted without modification into the Chaldaio-Babylonian religion, whilst he, with his spouse Davkina, never received any Semitic appellation, but kept their Accadian names without any alteration even as far as Nineveh.

In the epic recital of the deluge Hea played the part of protector and saviour of Khasisatra, the Chaldean Noah, the Xisuthrus or Sisithrus of the fragments of Berosus. After having related how the vessel of the just was saved in the flood and rested upon a high mountain, Berosus[2] adds, connecting with this tradition magic and talismanic rites, "A part of this vessel still exists on the Gordyœan heights of Armenia; the pilgrims bring back the asphalt they have scraped from the ruins and use it to avert the influence of sorcery." An extract from Abydenus[3] says also, "The inhabitants of the country make themselves amulets from the wood of the ship and hang them round their necks as a charm against sorcery." The legend has been applied to the ship of Khasisatra, the pretended remains of which were shown to the devotees, the ideas formerly attached

---

[1] *W. A. I.* IV., 14, 2, recto, l. 13, 15.   [2] Fragment 15 of my edition.
[3] Fragment 16.

to the symbolic vessel in which the god Hea was supposed to traverse his humid empire, when he was not represented as a being in part man, in part fish.[1]

One of the hymns of the magic collection,[2] which is extremely difficult to understand because we have only the Accadian text, without the Assyrian version, and that is filled with inexplicable technical terms, treats solely of this vessel of Hea's, "rejoicing the heart at break of day." The planks are ornamented with "seven times seven lions of the desert." The ceiling which covers the inner apartment and the mast are of cedar, the wood which counteracts sorceries. In this vessel are "Hea, who decides destinies, with Damkina, whose word gives life; Silik-mulu-khi, who utters the beneficent name; Munu-abge,[3] who guides the lord of the earth, and Nin-gar,[4] the great pilot of heaven." This hymn enumerates all the parts, points out their magic meaning, and ends by the wish:

> May the ship in front of thee sail upon the canals!
> May the ship behind thee sail upon the face (of the waters)!
> May the joy of the heart be developed in thee in all its fulness!

A fragment of a tablet in the British Museum[5] gives us the remains of a special little collection of prayers, partly of a liturgic, partly of a magical character, and each of them relating to one of the insignia of royalty for which it invokes the protection

---

[1] See also Lenormant, *Le Deluge et l'Epopée Babylonienne*, 1873.
[2] *W. A. I.* IV., 25, col. 1. [3] Beneficent on the waves.
[4] Master of the helm(?). [5] *W. A. I.*, IV., 18, 3.

of the gods. One has reference to the tiara, and has been already mentioned as requesting that the king might be possessed by beneficent spirits; another relates to the precious stones, "which are upon the breast of the king as insignia;" a third to his weapon of war.

> The weapon which causes terror, which wounds, for majesty; the weapon which is raised, which is projectile, beside majesty; the immense force of its blow confuses, none dispute its power, it devastates the rebel country, it crushes its enemies.

This weapon is compared to that of "Hea, king of the ocean," and they invoke in favour of the king who bears it the pilot of the god, called in this case, with a variation of name, Nin-si-gar.

> Come, Nin-si-gar, great pilot of heaven, thrusting forward thy sublime tree, thy lance!

Hea was therefore sometimes represented as an armed warrior; surrounded by other warlike companions, when he was dividing with his ship the waters of the great reservoir (*apsu*), making them a guard round about the earth.

It was probably to Hea,[1] regarded under this warlike aspect, that the ancient poet dedicated another dithyrambus,[2] proud in its style, and peculiarly curious on account of its mythological allusions. A god is celebrating the power of his weapons, particularly his disk with fifty points and

[1] I was more positive about this point in the French edition; now I should remark that this song of triumph may with just as much reason, be placed in the mouth of the son of Hea, Silik-mulu-khi or Marduk, victor in his struggle against the Dragon of the Abyss. But in any case, it was one of these two gods, who specially combated the demons and the powers of darkness.

[2] *W. A. I.* II., 19, 2.

seven concentric rays, like the *tchakra* of the Indian heroes, and the "fiery sword" with which the cherub who kept the gate of the garden of Eden' was armed, as we read in the book of Genesis.[2]

> Who holds his head high before the tremendous terror which my immense strength causes?
> I am master of the steep mountains which tremble whilst their summits reach to the firmament.
> The mountain of alabaster, lapis, and onyx, in my hand I possess it.
> Archangel of the abysses . . . .[3] like a bird of prey which pounces upon the sparrows,
> in the mountain, by my heroic courage, I decide quarrels.
> In my right hand, I hold my fiery disk;[4]
> in my left hand, I hold my murderous disk.
> The sun with fifty faces, the raised weapon of my divinity, I hold it.
> The valiant one who breaks the mountains, the sun from whose influence none can escape, I hold it.
> The weapon which, like a waterspout, stretches in a circle the corpses of the combatants,[5] I hold it.
> That which breaks the mountains, Ana's powerful weapon, I hold it.
> That which bends the mountains, the fish with seven fins, I hold it.
> The flaming blade of battle, which devastates and afflicts the rebel country, I hold it.
> The great sword which overthrows the ranks of the brave, the sword of my divinity, I hold it.

[1] See my *Premieres Civilisations*, Vol. II., p. 193 and the following pages.

[2] See another translation of this hymn by the Rev. Prof. Sayce, in *Records of the Past*, Vol. VII.

[3] Lacuna.

[4] Prof. Sayce has pointed out still further the Aryan analysis of this hymn, especially as regards the *tchakra* or wheel of Buddha, and the mystical disk of Brahma.—*Ed.*

[5] Assyrian version: "which like the waterspout devours everything around it."

The hand of the powerful men of battle, from the attacks
of which the mountain cannot escape, I hold it.

The joy of heroes, the lance which does harm in battle, I
hold it.

The club which crushes the dwellings of the rebel country,
and the shield of battle, I hold them.

The thunder of battle, the weapon with fifty points, I
hold it.

Like the enormous serpent with seven heads, shaking its
heads, the . . . .¹ with seven heads, I hold it.

Like the serpent which scours the waves of the sea,
(attacking) the enemy in front, the destroyer in the
shock of battle, extending its power over heaven and
earth, the weapon with (seven) heads, I hold it.²

The burning god of the East, who makes his glory shine
like that of the day, I hold him.

The creator of heaven and earth, the god whose power
has no rival, I hold him.

The weapon which (spreads) great terror in the country
by its immense power, in my right hand powerfully,
the projectile of gold and onyx . . . .¹ strengthening
by miracles the god, the minister of life, I hold him.

The weapon which like . . . .¹ combats the rebel country,
the weapon with fifty points, I hold it.

While Hea passed into the Chaldaio-Babylonian mythology without changing either his office, his character, or his name, Mul-ge, on the contrary, bore no resemblance in the documents of the magic collection to Bel, the demiurge and god of the organized universe, with whom he was afterwards assimilated, in order to find him an equivalent in

---

¹ Lacunæ.

² Cf. the myth of the *Shesha* serpent of Brahma, which is also seven-headed, and Canopies, the creating deity, who rests upon its folds as the creature floats upon the empyreal waters.—*Ed.*

the religion by which he was adopted. One cause of this assimilation lay no doubt in the fact that the Semitic name Bel had the same meaning as one of Mulge's Accadian titles, Elim, "the Powerful, the Dreaded Being, the Lord." His spouse Nin-ge could better be likened to Belit, regarded as a chthonian deity. Indeed Mul-ge and Nin-ge (or Mul-gelal and Nin-gelal, as they become by adding the second part of a casual suffix, which can be equally well written or omitted)[1] were, as their names indicated, lord and lady of the lower abyss and the bowels of the earth. The Accadian formulæ do not recognize them under any other aspect. We find there the name of Nin-kigal, "the lady of the gloomy pit," used indifferently as a second appellation for Nin-ge, and as the title of a distinct goddess; and she is identified in the bilingual lists with the Semitic goddess Allat.

In some mythological documents the infernal lady Nin-kigal was associated with a god who was called pre-eminently Anunna-ge, "the archangel of the abyss;" he was doubtless another form of Mul-ge; although once in the long incantation which we translated at the beginning of Chapter I, Nin-kigal is called the wife of Nin-a-su, a title of Hea, which would assimilate her therefore with Damkina.

Since Mul-ge and Nin-ge were rulers of the terrestrial mass, the possession of the interior was sometimes considered to entail also the possession of the surface, and they were called "the lord" and "the lady of the countries;" on this account the boundary

---

[1] In the same way one of the appellations of the god of the moon, "the lord of growth," is indifferently *eni-zuna* and *eni-zu*, with or without the casual suffix *na*.

of the empires of Hea and Mul-ge was not very strictly defined. As previously stated the dead were supposed to descend into the lower abyss (*ge*), the undisputed domain of Mul-ge; this place was called "the country whence none return" (*kur-nu-de*), the "tomb" (*arali*), or as a euphemistic expression, the "temple" (*e-kur*), which was sometimes replaced by the plainer name of "temple of the dead" (*ekur-bat*), with which *arali* is synonymous.¹ At the time when the Chaldaio-Babylonian Epopee was composed, the story of Istar's descent into Hades described the country whence none return, designated in the Assyrian by the name *mat-la-tayarti*, in as sombre colours as were used in Hebrew poetry to depict the *schéôl*.

> The daughter of Sin (Istar) has turned her mind towards the place of decomposition, the seat of the god Ir-kalla,
> towards the home which one may enter, but never leave,
> towards the road from which there is no return, towards the dwelling where those entering find blindness (instead of) light,
> where the multitude has nothing but dust to appease its hunger, nothing but mud for food, where they see no light and dwell in darkness, where shades, as birds, press towards the vault, where dust thickens upon the door and its wings.²

In the Accadian magical documents the picture of this land is not less gloomy. A hymn,³ in which

---

¹ Cf. the Egyptian periphrasis Sqeb-hu, "place of freedom," which was also used to designate the tomb.—*Ed.*

² For the remainder of this singular text see *Records of the Past*, Vol. I., page 139, and Schrader, *Hollenfart der Istar*.

³ *W. A. I.* IV., 24, 2.

unfortunately the ends of all the lines are wanting, so that it is impossible to give a connected translation of it, describes this region as "the temple, the place where no feeling exists . . . . the foundation of chaos (*gi umuna*), the place where there is no blessing . . . . the tomb, the place where no one can see . . . ." and announces as its ruler, "Nin-ge upon her raised altars," with her spouse Mul-ge.

In this conception of hell, or Hades, according both to the mythological documents of the Chaldaio-Babylonian epoch and to the magic documents of the purely Accadian period, there is no moral idea of remuneration, no difference of rewards or punishments; the sorrows of the country whence none return, were the same for all, whatever may have been their conduct during life; the only rewards they believed in for piety and virtue were purely terrestrial. However, we read in the epic recital of the descent of Istar, that at the bottom of the country whence none return there was a spring of the waters of life, guarded by the infernal powers with jealous care; which could only be reached by a special permission from the celestial gods, and then he who has drunk the water of the fountain returns alive to the light.[1] The same idea must have existed in the conception of Hades

---

[1] Contrast with this the myth of Euridice, and especially Persephone.
"He said, and sudden from her seat arose
His lovely bride; her heart with transport glows.
Then Pluto feared, lest from the realms above,
And Ceres, object of her filial love,
She'd ne'er return; and, fraudulent, decreed
The fair should taste the rich pomegranate's seed—
A fatal pledge—" etc.—Homer, *Hymn to Ceres*.

The whole of the myths of Persephone and Ishtar will bear, and will repay, the closest analogy.—*Ed.*

which was current at the time when the magical fragments were composed, for we shall see later, that a hymn addressed to the mediator Silik-mulu-khi[1] attributes to him the power "of bringing the dead back to life." But we do not know under what conditions this resurrection was supposed to take place; it was perhaps only admitted in order to justify the pretensions of the priests of magic to work similar wonders by the power of their incantations. We may observe, however, that Diogenes Laertius[2] explicitly attributes to the Chaldean philosophical schools a belief in a final resurrection, after which man was to become immortal. This was the last stage of development reached by the idea of which the first germ appears here.

In the epic narrative of the adventures of Istar, the country whence none return is divided into seven zones, like those of Dante's infernal regions,[3] upon the model of the seven planetary spheres. This resulted from the influence of the astrological doctrines upon religion, and nothing of the same kind can be traced in the more ancient date of the magic books. They mention, however, "seven doors and seven fastenings of the world,"[4] which were probably those leading from the surface of the earth into the lower regions; but they seem to have been considered as scattered around the circumference of the earth.

[1] *W. A. I.* IV., 29, 1. In another bilingual document (*W. A. I.* IV., 19, verse 1) the same power of recalling the dead to life is attributed to the goddess Gula, exceptionally associated in this instance with Silik-mulu-khi, the Maruduk of the Assyrian version.

[2] *De Vit. philosoph.*, proœm.

[3] Dante, *Inferno*, Canto XXXIV. *in loco*.

[4] *W. A. I.* IV., 27, 2.

However that may be, the principal entrance to the infernal regions, the one to which the god Negab was appointed, "the great porter of the world,"[1] was situated in the west, near the great mountain which matched, on that side, "the mountain of the east," or more precisely of the north-east, the cradle of the human race, "father of the countries," the pole of the celestial revolutions, where the Babylonian mythology established the place of the assembly of the gods. The mountain of the west, where the sun set, was a pre-eminently funereal place; from whence arose the god Mul-ge. One fragment of a hymn [2] speaks of it in these terms:

> The great mountain of Mul-gelal, the glory of the mountains, the crest of which reaches unto the heavens, the sublime reservoir of water washes its base; between the mountains (it is) like a powerful buffalo in repose; its summit shines like a ray of the sun, like the prophetic star of heaven [3] perfecting its glory.

The entrance to Hades was then near this mountain of the west, or rather of the south-west, for just as the mountain of the east inclined towards the north in the direction of the blessed country which was occupied by the septentrion, so that part which is directly opposite it must incline to the south, which they imagined a region of death and desolation. This was the result of the Accadian nomenclature for the four cardinal points, which differed fundamentally from that adopted by the Semitic nations. Whilst for the Assyrians the east was *sadû*,

---

[1] His name means porter.   [2] *W. A. I.* IV., 27, 2.
[3] Dilbat, the planet Venus.

"the rising," the west *akharru*, "the point placed behind" the observer, the north *iltanu* (for *istanu*), "the direction of winter," for the Accadians the east was *mer kurra*, "the cardinal point of the mountains," the west *mer mar-tu*, "the point of the road of sunset," the north *mer sidi*, "the point of prosperity, the propitious point," and lastly the south, *mer urulu*, "the funereal point." We shall have to refer later to some of the consequences which seem to flow from attributing this favourable character to the north instead of the south.

The entrance to Hades was also situated beyond the waters of the great reservoir of the ocean. This too was recognized at the time when the poem about the descent of Istar into Hades was composed; for the porter of the gloomy dwellings is there spoken of once as "porter of the waters;" and when he repeats to Allat Istar's request for admittance, he expresses himself thus:—

> These waters thy sister Istar has crossed them.

We also find this in one of the most curious and strangest fragments from the third book of the magic collection.[1] This fragment, which, like so many others, has been handed down to us in a deplorable state of delapidation, for both the beginning and the end are missing, contains a series of invocations which recall those of the Egyptian Ritual of the Dead, and which have reference to all the stages of a descent into the infernal regions. Were they employed as a sort of funereal liturgy

[1] *W. A. I.* IV., 23, 1.

or in rites of evocation?"[1] We do not know; but the information they contain is none the less precious.

One of the first invocations, the greater portion of which is now destroyed, is addressed to the "seven gods, sons of the lord of the infernal region (*Eni-me-sara*), who dwell in the flame,"[2] and to the "twelve gods of bronze placed inside the bronze inclosure, sustaining the bronze inclosure." The invocation which follows is addressed to the ears of the bull placed "on the right of the bronze inclosure," because they imagined the gate of hell to be flanked by human headed bulls like those which guarded the gates of the Assyrian palaces; only these bulls were living genii:—

---

[1] Sir Henry Rawlinson understands the object of these prayers quite differently; he calls the document a "bilingual tablet on the manufacture of a sacred bull in bronze." My readers will no doubt be astonished at this difference of opinion, but the reason of it is that although the sense of the prayers themselves is certain and the translation of them comparatively easy, the executory formulæ which accompany each of them are as yet very obscure, and in some cases incomprehensible. I apprehend that the illustrious founder of Assyriological science translates as the crucible into which the melted metal is poured the word *litis*, which appears both in the Accadian and the Assyrian texts, and which I consider means an enclosure or grating; I shall endeavour later to justify my interpretation philologically from other examples. Sir Henry Rawlinson has also probably been guided by the Assyrian phrase which follows the last prayer quite at the end of the tablet, and where a bull is really mentioned: *enuva alap ana bit mummutu useribu*, "afterwards they lead the bull into the *bit mummutu*." But what is this *bit mummutu?* It seems to me that it is connected with the word *mummu*, "chaos," Hebrew מהמה, "confusion;" it would then be "the abode of confusion, of the state of chaos," which is a very suitable name for the gloomy and infernal region, and so much the more because the Accadian equivalent of *mummu* is *umun*, and because we have just remarked the name *gi-umuna* as applied to Hades.

However if Sir Henry Rawlinson were right in his designation, and had understood better than ourselves the occasion for which these prayers were destined, our translation would still be exact, and the allusions to the disposition of places evident and correct enough to justify our interpretation of these fragments. If the word in question means the crucible in which the bronze is melted, each stage of this process is compared with the entrance to the infernal pit, and consequently in this case also they give us information about the conception of it current at that time.

[2] These seven gods are enumerated in a mythological tablet, *W. A. I.* III., 69, 3.

> O great bull, very great bull, which stampest high,[1]
> which openest an access[2] to the interior, which openest the canals considerably,
> which servest as a foundation to the god Ul-sara,[3] the reaper of the fields,[4]
> my brilliantly pure hands have sacrificed before thee.

The bull on the left of the bronze inclosure[5] is invoked in his turn:—

> Thou art the bull engendered by the god Ungal-turda,[6] the entrance to the tomb is thy act; the lady with the magic wand fashioned thee for eternity!
> The great . . . .[7] the boundaries, the limits, fixing the division between heaven and earth . . . . . may he watch.

The fourth deity is connected with an act which takes place "in the interior of the bronze enclosure." He is invoked as a personal and active god, as the living mountain, in fact, which commands the entrance:—

> O thou who shadest the plain, lord who givest shade by spreading thy shadow on the plain.
> Great mountain, father of Mul-ge, who shadest the plain, pastor who rulest destinies, who shadest the plain.

---

[1] In the Assyrian version, "at the high doors."(?)

[2] In the Assyrian version, "which opens."(?)

[3] The Assyrian version assimilates him to Serakh, the god of harvests.

[4] A metaphorical way of saying he bears the earth with its harvests on his shoulders.—*Ed.*

[5] The tablet only gives the Assyrian version for this one whilst all the others are bilingual.

[6] The text has "the god *zu*," as an allusion to the metamorphosis related above of Ungal-turda into the bird of the same name. This god is called Sarturda by Smith in his *Chaldean Genesis*, who also regards the Zu bird as a species of eagle, but the whole of the myth is at present uncertain. Sarturda appears to have been the personal deity adored by Izdubar.—*Ed.*

[7] Lacunæ.

The two following verses are destroyed, an invocation to Mul-ge and other gods associated with him follows. In consequence of a fracture the ends of all the lines have disappeared, and it is impossible to replace them in full.

> Veritable pastor, (sublime) pastor,
> Mul-gelal, (veritable) pastor,
> Lord of all the countries, (veritable) pastor,
> Lord of all the celestial archangels, (veritable) pastor,
> Lord of all the . . . .[1] (veritable pastor),
> Lord who guards his country, (veritable) pastor,
> Lord who guards his country . . . .
> establishing the riches . . . .
> establishing the possessions . . . .
> . the lofty residence . . . .
> the lofty place . . . .
> the place of lofty repose . . . .
> exalting the town . . . .
> Lord, Master of the earth, (Hea, king . . . .
> Lord Silik-mulu-dug . . . .
> Lord, Father, Mermer . . . .
> Brave Lord, Utu . . . .
> Lord Uras[2] . . . .
> Sublime Lord, Dun-kun-uddu[3] . . . .
> Direct the hand, (strengthen) the hand,

[1] Here is another incomprehensible word in either the Accadian or the Assyrian.

[2] One of the appellations of Nin-dara or Adar, by which he is distinguished in the Assyrian version.

[3] "The hero of the dawn," the god of the planet Mercury under his sidereal name; the conception of this god is necessarily anterior to the time when the same planet was attributed to the Nebo of the Chaldaio-Babylonian religion. The Accadian god Dun-kun-uddu, called in the Assyrian Dapina (as an abbreviation for *yum dapinu*, "accompanying the day") continues, however, to figure in the lists of divine personages, although he is no longer mentioned in the invocations of a later date. *W. A. I.* III., 69, l. 15-20, c, d, gives a list of his Accadian titles, amongst which we notice *eni gusur*, "lord of the light," *ungal gusurra*, "lord of the light," *ungal udda*, "king of the day."

direct the hand, (direct) my steps,
direct this invocation, (make) this invocation (succeed).

Of the last invocation we have only the ends of the lines containing but two or three characters, which allow us to see that most of the verses finish with the word "purify," and that the two last contain a request to open the gate. This is followed by the enigmatical phrase:—

> Then the bull is led into the dwelling of the state of chaos.

Whatever may have been the object of these prayers and the ceremonies with which they were connected, the allusions to the entrance of things are very clear, particularly those addressed to the two bulls. My opinion is, that the numerous mythological allusions which are contained in this piece, thus marking it as so different from the ancient incantations, should decide us to attribute it to a later epoch, as compared with many other parts of the magical collection in which it is contained. But the data with which it furnishes us are nevertheless only a development of ideas that existed in embryo at the most ancient period.

The demons and the spirits of diseases "came forth from hell;"[1] they were "the productions of the *arali*,"[2] "the children which were born of the earth."[3] One of the most formidable of them, Namtar, the plague personified, was described as the "favourite son of Mul-ge, by Nin-ki-gal."[4] Here was a god then not belonging essentially to the bad principle, who was

[1] *W. A. I.* IV., 22, 1, l. 51.   [2] *W. A. I.* IV., 1, col. 1, l. 12.
[3] *W. A. I.* IV., 1, col. 1, l. 22.   [4] *W. A. I.* IV., 1, col. 2, l. 51.

sometimes invoked as favourable; yet he was the father of one of the most wicked demons, to whom the greater number of the others were subject. In the same way, the seven bad spirits which devastated the heavens and made war on the moon, were sons of the god of this zone of the world, of Ana, as well as of the god Fire, who was one of the most powerful adversaries of the powers of darkness.

We may add that the spouse of Namtar was also invoked amongst the good spirits,[1] and that this characteristic is even seen in her name, Khusbi-kuru; "an encounter with her is of good omen, is propitious." This dissipates entirely the idea of any moral symbolism in the dualism of the religion of the Accadian magic books. The good and bad spirits were not connected with different principles; for they could issue from or be united to one another. If some were good and others bad, it was by a sort of blind fatality, and the eternal contest between them more apparent than real, was only the struggle of the elements in their own breast; a condition which was necessary to the life of the universe.

As a logical consequence from this point of view, also it was not only demons who were placed in the gloomy empire of Mul-ge; since amongst the protecting spirits, we find mentioned "the male and female spirits, lords of the infernal regions."[2] The master of the lower abyss had begotten, besides Namtar, one of the warrior gods whose special mission it was to combat demons, monsters, and plagues, like a true Hercules. This was Nin-dara, who is called

[1] *W. A. I.* IV., col. 2, l. 51.   [2] *W. A. I.* IV., col. 2, l. 23, 24.

also Uras, and was afterwards assimilated to the Chaldaio-Babylonian deity Adar, and indeed furnished many characteristic traits of the original physiognomy of this god in the new religion.

Nindara was the nocturnal sun, the sun hidden in the lower world during half his course. Naturally luminous, although plunged in the regions of night, he combated the darkness which surrounded him, and ended by triumphing over it at his rising.[1] He was therefore pre-eminently the warrior god. He regulated the times and hours in his daily course, exercised an influence over life and movement throughout nature, and, like Utu the diurnal sun, he was regarded as an arbitrator, a judge, and a regulator of destiny. There exists a long magical hymn to Nin-dara,[2] which repeats from time to time, as a refrain, this invocation,

> Nin-dara, lord, son of Mul-ge, measure and judge.

Or else,

> Nin-dara, lord, son of Mul-ge, decide the fate.

And in another place,

> The command of the sun is thy command like a judge, rule the lands.
> Everything that exists recognizes thy command.

The hymn, which is very majestic in its style, is in the form of a dialogue between the god and the person by whom he is invoked. It turns upon the exploits of Nin-dara, whose war-like power is forcibly depicted:—

---

[1] Cf. the Egyptian solar myth of the god Ra in his character of Tum, the sun god of Hades, or the underworld. See *Ritual of the Dead*, Cap. III.—*Ed.*
[2] *W. A. I.* IV., 13, 1.

Thou, during thy action, roarest like a bear.

He is represented covered with his armour:—

Thou, thou (coverest) solid copper like a skin.

He is invited to come "from the mountains of the high country," namely from Elam, and from the "mountains of Makan," the country whence they obtain metals for armour, the peninsula of Sinai, so celebrated for its copper mines, which the Egyptians had worked from the time of the fourth dynasty.[1]

This hymn makes frequent mention of certain precious stones which the god possessed, and of which he was the master; their talismanic power was exercised "against the rebel countries." Antiquity always referred to Chaldea the origin of the superstitious belief in the magic power of gems. Pliny[2] points out a book on this subject by a certain Zachalios of Babylon, which was dedicated to the king Mithridates. It was evidently a writing belonging to that Greco-Babylonian literature which was so widely developed during the centuries bordering on the Christian era, and which had the same connection with the real Chaldean doctrines as the Grecian literature of the Hermetical books had with the doctrine of ancient Egypt.

[1] These mines situated in the Wady Magarah at the foot of the Sinaitic mountains, were celebrated also for their production of *mafka* or turquoise, and the goddess Hathor was specially regarded as their local deity. After the period of Shafra of the fifth dynasty the works were abandoned for several centuries, but were again reopened and worked with considerable energy and profit by Thothmes II. and III., and the first three monarchs of the Ramesside line. The neighbourhood abounds with excavations, votive stele, and the debris of neglected workings.—*Ed.*

[2] *Hist. Nat.*, XXXVII., 10.

CHAPTER XIII.

The Mythology of the Underworld.

WE have seen in the preceding chapter that the sun of the lower hemisphere was also the god of the hidden metallic and mineral treasures, which, like him, were only waiting to come out of the earth to shine with a luminous splendour; and this shows an order of ideas of a peculiar nature, and very characteristic of the nations of the Turanian race, namely, the adoration of the spirits which kept in the bosom of the earth the riches concealed there, and who were the gods of metallurgy. As Baron Eckstein has very justly remarked,[1] "There are some nations, like the Pelasgic races, who worship the gods of the abyss, in their connection with the fertility of the soil and agricultural products. There are others, and these are the Finnish, Turkish, Mongolic, and Tungusic races, who worship them from a different point of view, since they do homage to the splendours of a metallic world, connecting this adoration with the magic worship and talismanic superstitions." Traces of these notions are not wanting in the

[1] *Athenæum Francais* of August 19, 1854.

Accadian magical books, and therefore we see invoked[1] in them as protectors, side by side with Silik-mulu-khi;[2] the god of gold, "who purifies gold," the god of silver, of copper, the lord god of the east in his mountain of precious stones, with the god of the cedar, to which tree was ascribed a peculiar power to avert fatal influences and sorcery.

The demons issuing from the lower abyss had, like the sorcerers who held intercourse with them, a particular preference for the darkness in which they originated. They liked to profit by the gloom, and so to slip into the world and to work evil there. Darkness was itself a visible manifestation of the evil principle, as light was a manifestation of the good. The primitive Accadians appear to have had the same terror of the night as the Aryas of the Vedic ages; in this idea they were very different from the Chaldaio-Babylonians of earlier times, who delighted in the sight of the starry firmament, and knew no higher, no more splendid expression of the divinity than those starry hosts to which their worship was addressed.

According to the magical hymns, the diurnal sun, shining in the highest regions of the heavens and dissipating the darkness, was one of the most active protecting gods, a great enemy of demons and sorcerers. One hymn[3] addressed to him begins thus:—

> O thou, who causest lies to disappear, thou who dissipatest the bad influence of wonders, of auguries, of evil prog-

---

[1] *W. A. I.* II., 58, 6.

[2] While these sheets were passing through the press, M. Lenormant has seen fresh reason for restoring the last syllable of this name as it stood originally.—*Ed.*

[3] *W. A. I.* IV., 17 verso.

nostications, of dreams, of wicked apparitions, thou who defeatest wicked plots, thou who leadest men and countries to perdition who abandon themselves to sorcery and witchcraft, I have shut up before thee their images (of the bad spirits)[1] in the raised heaps of corn .... Do not allow those who cast spells and are hardened, to rise.

* * * * * *

May the great gods, who have created me, take my hand! Thou who curest my face, direct my hand, direct it, lord, light of the universe, Sun.

The sun was not one of the highest gods of the religious system which had served as a foundation for Accadian magic, his power did not approach that of the three great spirits of the zones of the universe. But it was just his lower rank that made him more accessible to the prayers of man; and the fact that his influence upon man and the phenomena of life was so sensibly felt, made them assign to him the office of arbiter of events and of fate; while lastly, as he dissipated darkness, and consequently was engaged in a struggle with the bad spirits, he became one of the supernatural personages to whom the magical invocations were most frequently addressed. The collection contained many hymns addressed to him. These have often a touch of real poetry, like the following, the opening portion of which has unfortunately disappeared:—[2]

Sun, thou shinest in the deepest heavens;[3] thou openest the bolts which close the high heavens; thou openest the gate of heaven.

---

[1] Here we have a fresh indication of the talismanic use of images of demons in order to repulse their attacks.

[2] *W. A. I.* IV., 20, 2.   [3] In the horizon.

> Sun, thou raisest thy head above the countries.
> Sun, thou stretchest the vast heavens above the countries,[1] like a covering.

Cite we also the beginning of another hymn, the mythology of which was very fully developed:—[2]

> Great lord, from the centre of the high heavens thou (comest) into our sight.
> Sun, valiant hero, from the centre of the high heavens thou (comest) into our sight.
> At the opening of the high heavens, at the door, thou appearest.
> The bolts of the high heavens . . . . . .[3]
> In the great door of the high heavens, in the opening, which belongs to thee, in the highest summits of the high heavens, high in thy rapid course (the celestial spirits) respectfully and joyfully approach thee, ...[3] they exalt thy crown, they raise thee up rejoicing.
> In . . . .[3] in the repose of thy heart the days fly.
> The (spirits) of all countries greatly surround thee. The (spirits) of heaven and earth turn towards thee.

This hymn was composed for the cure of some malady, as the text shows from the place where it recommences, on the original tablet, after a gap of about a dozen lines. The priest addresses the god, speaking of the invalid in the third person; and he pretends that his power is of divine origin, which gives him the right to command the sun.

> As for me, the lord has sent me, the great lord, Hea, has sent me.
>
> .   .   .   .   .[4]
>
> Thou, at thy coming, cure the race of man, cause a ray of health to shine upon him, cure his disease.

---

[1] The terrestrial surface.   [2] *IV. A. I.* IV., 17 recto.   [3] Lacunæ.
[4] Here occurs a verse which I am not yet competent to translate.

> The man, son of his god, is burdened with the load of his omissions and transgressions.
> His feet and his hands suffer cruelly, he is painfully exhausted by the disease.
> Sun, at the raising of my hands, come at the call, eat his food, absorb his victim, turn his weakness into strength.
> By thy orders may his omissions be forgiven! may his transgressions be blotted out!
> Break his chains, ... may he recover from his illness!
> May the king live!
> May thy majesty protect him during the remainder of his days!
> Confirm thy sentence upon the king!

The invalid for whose sake they uttered the invocation was then the king. I have already spoken of the peculiar idea of penitence which it expresses, and which does not bear a very primitive stamp.

In this hymn we come upon a new and important idea which we have not encountered before, but of which the hymns already cited have suggested indications. The idea is this, that diseases were oftentimes sent as chastisements for sin, and by the permission of the celestial and benevolent deities, one of the chief of whom was the pre-eminently propitious deity Hea. But Hea could not cause evil by himself, and therefore, if he chastised, it could only be by suspending for the time his protecting influence, and by abandoning the doomed man to the action of evil spirits, and to the demons of disease. Man could also obtain a cure for the evils which Hea had allowed to come upon him, through the help of a god less high in rank than Hea, such as the sun, which would not be possible if this evil were the direct personal work of Hea.

The beneficent office of protector attributed to the sun, the facility with which men could hold intercourse with him, so much more easily than with the three superior gods, was also the peculiar property of the deities of the pure elements of the atmospheric zone, intermediate between heaven and earth. They were worshipped either in their material reality, or in the persons of the spirits which animated them.

As amongst the Vedas the winds present themselves sometimes as a single god Vayu, and sometimes as an assemblage of gods, the Maruts, so the fragments of the Accadian magical collection recognized, besides the special spirits for each wind, some of which were good and some bad,[1] one god or spirit of the winds in general, Imi or Mermer,[2] who is often mentioned, but always in an incidental manner, in the fragments which have been handed down to us; and they represent him chiefly as producing the fertilizing rains. He was afterwards identified with the Chaldaio-Babylonian deity Bin or Ramanu,[3] whose attributes were of a wider scope since they embraced all the atmospheric phenomena, and who indeed appears to have originally personified one of the aspects of the solar system.

One of these hymns is addressed to the waters which flow over the earth:—[4]

---

[1] The reader will consult what has been said farther back of the demon of the west wind, and the mention of the evil winds in the long incantation, a translation of which opens the first chapter of this work.

[2] The augmentative and factitive form of sea, "the cardinal point, from whence the wind blows."

[3] The Rimmon of the Old Testament.   [4] *W. A. I.* IV., 14, 2 recto.

> Sublime waters (waters of the Tigris), waters of the Euphrates, which flow in their place, abundant waters which dwell together permanently in the great reservoir, children of the ocean which are seven, the waters are sublime, the waters are brilliantly pure, the waters glisten,
>
> In the presence of your father Hea, in the presence of your mother, the spouse of the great fish,[1] may he be sublime! may he be holy and pure! may he shine! may the malevolent and destructive mouth have no effect! Amen.

Another tablet invokes the river as a special and personal god:—[2]

> River god, who pushes forward like the beak of a ship,[3] drives before him the evil fate like a formidable deer.
>
> . . . .
>
> May the sun rising dissipate the darkness! they will never again prevail in the house.
> May the evil destiny depart into the desert and high places.
> The evil fate, Spirit of the heavens, conjure it! Spirit of the earth, conjure it!
> Amen. The evil fate, which stretches over the earth. River god, break it.

This river god (Aria) re-appears later in the lists of gods of the second rank,[4] with various Accadian names, amongst others, that of *Aria-mulu-rutik*, "River which rushes forward like a spike, a spur;" and the same lists mention his spouse, Ki-kuru-nir, his son Sazi, and his messenger; they occur side by side

---

[1] The Assyrian version substitutes for this title the name of Davkina.
[2] IV. A. I. IV., 14, 2 recto and verso.
[3] The Assyrian version omits this comparison.
[4] II. A. I. II., 56, l. 26-32, c, d.

with Hea's six sons. The same lists[1] notice several other divinities of the humid element which have purely Accadian names and belong to the ancient Accadian elementary mythology: Ungal-a-abba, "the king of the sea;" Ungal-ariada, "the king of the river;" and Ungal-aba, "the king of the wave."

Amongst the magic fragments we have one more hymn[2] to the wave of the ocean, personified as a protecting divinity, whose waters are celebrated as "the waters shining with purity," the "sublime waters, holy waters, vivifying waters," collected in "the holy and pure ocean."

Amongst the personifications of the waters we must place "Khi-tim-kur-ku, daughter of the ocean,"[3] since her name appears to mean, "the spring which surrounds the sublime mountain;" and it was therefore the paradisiacal spring celebrated in the traditions of so many different nations.

The theological importance of fire was very different to these deities. He was worshipped in his material reality as a god superior even to the sun, under the very same name which is used to designate the element of fire in the ordinary language, *iz-bar*, or rather *bar*, for the first sign seems to be simply a silent determinative which is the equivalent of the ideographic character "god." He, or rather it, is still more frequently called Bil-gi (indeed that seems to have been the first title assigned to it), which must be translated as "the fire of the rushes," the fire issuing from an instrument analagous to the

---

[1] *W. A. I.* II., 59, l. 38-40, d, e.   [2] *W. A. I.* II., 58, 6 recto.
[3] *W. A. I.* IV., col. 2, l. 53.

arani[1] of the primitive Aryas, which was made out of a ligneous reed. This conception of him and the attributes assigned to him connect him evidently with the Agni of the Vedas.

A hymn[2] says:—

> Fire, supreme chief rising high in the country!
> Hero, son of the Ocean, rising high in the country;
> Fire, with thy pure and brilliant flame,
> thou bringest light into the dwellings of darkness,
> thou decidest the fate of everything which has a name.
> Thou mixest copper and tin,
> thou purifiest gold and silver.
> Thou art the offspring of the goddess Nin-ka-si.[3]
> May the works of the man, son of his god, shine with purity!
> May he be high as heaven!
> May he be holy and pure as the earth!
> May he shine as the midst of heavens!

In the formula quoted above enumerating the different kinds of sorceries, we have already seen fire invoked as the great agent in dissipating spells, the hero who puts the demons to flight. So also he is represented in this fragment of a hymn.[4]

> (Thou) who chasest the wicked *Maskim*,
> who (developest)[5] the blessing of life,
> who strikest terror into the heart of the wicked,
> guardian of the oracle of Mul-gelal.
> Fire, destroyer of enemies,
> terrible weapon which chasest the plague,
> fertile, brilliant.

---

[1] The *pramantha* or fire wheel.—*Ed.*
[2] *W. A. I.* IV., 14, 2 verso.
[3] Davkina.
[4] *W. A. I.* IV., 21, 1st verse.
[5] Not understanding the exact meaning of the word here, I have replaced it by a conjecture based on the general sense of the passage.

Universal peace and shelter from the attacks of the malevolent were due to the protection of this god:—

> Repose of the god Fire, the hero,
> may countries and rivers rest with thee!
> May the Tigris and (the Euphrates) rest with thee!
> May the sea . . . .¹ rest with thee!
> May the road of the daughter of the gods rest with thee![2]
> May the interior of the productions (of nature) rest with thee!
> May the hearts of my god and goddess, spirits . . . .¹ rest with thee!
> May the hearts of the god and goddess of my town, spirits . . . .¹ rest with thee!
> In this day . . . .¹ may the interior of the hearts of my god and goddess open,
> and may the evil destiny be expelled from my body.[3]

The last verses, which are very much mutilated, call upon the god Fire to act as a judge and saviour.

Hymns to the deity Fire abound in the magic collection. He was worshipped principally in the flame of the sacrifice, and therefore he was called "the supreme pontiff upon the face of the earth."[4] But this god was also recognized in the flame which burnt on the domestic hearth, and protected the house against evil influences and demons; hence arose the titles he sometimes received of "god of the house" (*dimmer êa*), "protector of the house" (*uru êa*), "protector of the family" (*uru sûχar*).

This god, who resided in the flame of the sacrifice

---

[1] Lacunæ. [2] There seems to be an allusion here to the milky way.
[3] *W. A. I.* IV., 8, col. 4. [4] *W. A. I.* IV., 1, col. 2, l. 42.

and in that of the hearth, was also the cosmic fire, distributed throughout nature, which was necessary to her existence, and which shone in the stars. Regarded in this light, he was adored as the son of Ana, the heavens personified, and addressed as "the god who rises high, the great chief who commands by the supreme power of Ana," and this was the reason why we have seen him struggling vainly to prevent the ravages made by the terrible *Maskim* throughout the economy of nature.[1] Another hymn,[2] addressed to him in his highest and widest office, begins thus:—

> Lord with the exalted heart, owner of the wealth of the great gods,
> . . . .[3] of Mul-ge, who exaltest the heart upon the earth, owner of the wealth of the great gods.
> Lord of the immense space, who exaltest the heart in the heavens, owner of the wealth of the great gods,
> hero, Fire, heroic male, who risest,[4]
> who risest like a garment, who clothest space.
> Powerful Fire, who raisest[5] the high mountains,[6]
> who deliverest from maledictions, who illuminest the darkness.

I think these quotations show clearly enough how great was the importance of the god Fire in the religious system of the Accadian magic books. He belonged exclusively to them; in the documents of the Assyrian period he is only mentioned once amongst the *dii minores*, and then as a symbolical

---

[1] *W. A. I.* IV., 15.   [2] *W. A. I.* IV., 26, 3.   [3] Lacuna.
[4] In the Assyrian version, "hero, Fire, who risest, male warrior."
[5] Literally, "who pushes forward."
[6] In the Assyrian version, "the steep mountains."

personification rather than a god, when Sargon calls the month of Ab[1] "the month of the descent of the Fire chasing humid clouds."[2] The Assyrian translators of the magic hymns generally simply transferred his name in their versions. But at other times they tried to assimilate him to the gods of the Chaldaio-Babylonian religion, likening him sometimes to Nebo, and sometimes to Bin. His character changed with his rank; from the beneficent and protecting god that he was at first, he became a terrible and formidable king. For in my opinion he is to be recognized, under the name of Isuv (and not Itak), in the personage mentioned in a tablet lately discovered by Mr. George Smith,[3] as walking before Nitara or Lubara the god of epidemics, to herald his destructive approach.

But although the old Accadian god Fire lost his place in the Pantheon, he was frequently mentioned in epic poetry. Assuming a solar character, he became, under the name of Izdhubar, or rather Dhubar (*dhu-bar*, mass of fire),[4] the hero of one of the principal epic histories, the one containing the narrative of the deluge. No one who is endowed with a critical mind can doubt that Izdhubar or Dhubar is a god transformed in epic poetry into a terrestrial hero, and not an historical king, as Mr. Smith would have him considered. His solar

[1] July-August.

[2] Oppert, *Inscriptions de Dour-Sarkayan*, p. 18; and *Records of the Past*, Vol. VII.

[3] *Chaldæan Account of Genesis*, p. 131.

[4] The insertion of the element *dhu* between the sign *iz* and *bar* proves that *iz* is in this case simply a mute determinative, since if *izbar* or *gisbar* had been conjoined the compound would necessarily read *duizbar* or *dugisbar*.

nature comes out clearly in his exploits in epic poetry, in twelve great enterprises corresponding to the signs of the zodiac, as also in his position as son of Samas. At the same time his primæval character of an elementary god, his identity with the Fire, Bar or Bilgi of the Accadian magic books, seems to me strongly marked in an invocation in the Assyrian tongue against the spells of sorcerers,[1] which is addressed to him in conjunction with the earth.

> Earth! Earth! Earth and Dhubar! O ye masters of talismans!

A fragment of a tablet brought back by Mr. Smith from his first journey into Assyria contains the beginning of a prayer to this god,[2] who is described there by the Assyrian titles of *gitmalu*, "generous," *gitmalu emuqi*, "generous in his power."

Fire was naturally the greatest and most active of the gods with whom man could hold direct communication by means of sacred rites and magic incantations; an intercourse of the most intimate nature might be established with him, since man himself produced him, or at least placed him at will upon his altar, by lighting on it the sacrificial flame. As to Hea, the chief *averruncus*, the soul of the super-terrestrial zone, the supreme protector, the god to whom they had recourse when all else failed, he was too high and too far from humanity, in spite of all the power attributed to sacramental words and magic operations, for the prayers of man to go straight to him and influence his will. They imagined therefore a

---

[1] *IV. A. I.* IV., 56, col. 1, l. 37.
[2] See *Transactions of the Society of Biblical Archæology*, Vol. III., p. 460.

god specially charged with the office of mediator between man and Hea, who does not appear to correspond with any phenomena of nature, and who had no other office but that of mediator. This was Silik-mulu-khi, whose name means "he who distributes good amongst men."[1] He says, according to one hymn,[2]

> I am he who walks before Hea,
> I am the warrior, the eldest son of Hea, his messenger.

The insignia of his office was a reed, which took the place both of the royal sceptre and of the magical wand, and which was transmitted later to Marduk of Babylon, as a consequence of the assimilation by which he obtained the attributes of Silik-mulu-khi. A magical formula[3] describes the divine sceptre itself, and assigns the following words to it:—

> Golden reed, great reed, tall reeds of the marshes, sacred bed of the gods,
>
> .   .   .   .   .   .
>
> I am the messenger of Silik-mulu-khi,
> who cause all to grow young again.

This formula seems, however, to identify it with the reed of the utensil resembling the *arani*, the reed which serves to kindle the sacred fire, because after the words supposed to be spoken by the divine attribute, the invocator says in his own name:

> May the god of the house be installed in the house!
> May the favourable demon, the favourable god enter the house!

---

[1] His name sometimes has variations, of which we cannot understand the sense, such as Silik-ri-mulu. We may notice that of Silik-kuru, meaning "he who arranges the good omen."

[2] *W. A. I.* IV., 30, 3.   [3] *W. A. I.* IV., 6, col. 5.   [4] Lacuna.

The wicked demon, the wicked (*Alad*), the wicked *Gigim*,
the wicked *Telal*, (the wicked god,) the wicked *Maskim*,
the phantom, the spectre, the vampire,
Spirit of the heavens, conjure them! Spirit of the earth, conjure it![1]

The title of "god of the house" was as we have seen peculiar to the deified Fire. We may suppose, therefore, that this formula in question was to be pronounced during the act of kindling, by means of Silik-mulu-khi's reed, the flame of the domestic hearth, the protecting god who banished demons and evil influences from the house.

Silik-mulu-khi revealed to man Hea's will and knowledge. We have seen him a prominent figure in all the incantations of a dramatic character; he was there represented as carrying to Hea the appeals of men who were tormented by malignant spirits and diseases, he explained their sufferings to him and asked his help; it was to this divine personage that Hea unfolded the secret which had power to ensure the defeat of the demons, imposing upon him the duty of carrying out the rites of liberation. Further, when gods such as the Sun or the Fire desired to implore the aid and supreme intervention of Hea, they also first had recourse to the mediation of Silik-mulu-dug.[2] After the quotations in the first chapter, however, we do not need to develop this conception more fully or to add any new proofs of its truth.

It was to Silik-mulu-khi that this beautiful fragment is addressed, in which the language bears a strong

---

[1] Or "Spirit of the house, expel them."—*Ed.*   [2] *W. A. I.* IV., 15.

resemblance to that of the 147th Psalm,[1] and which expresses in forcible terms the power of the command imposed upon the whole of nature in the name of the god:

> Who can escape thy hail?[2]
> Thy will is the sublime scimitar with which thou rulest heaven and earth.
> I commanded the sea, and the sea became calm.
> I commanded the flower, and the flower ripened its grain;[3]
> I commanded the girdle of the[4] 'river of Sippara,'[5] and by the will of Silik-mulu-khi I overturned its course.
> Lord, thou art sublime, what transitory being is equal to thee?[6]
> Silik-mulu-khi, amongst all the gods who are named, thou art the remunerator.
> Hero, amongst the gods who . . . .[7] the enemy . . . .[7]
> Silik-mulu-khi, the enemy . . . .[7]
> Lord of battles . . . .[7]

A hymn composed posterior to the assimilation which was afterwards made between Silik-mulu-khi and the Babylonian Marduk, explains his benevolent office in terms worthy of attention:[8]

> (Great lord) of the country, king of the countries, eldest (son) of Hea who bringest back (into their periodical movements) heaven and earth,
> Silik-mulu-khi (great lord of the country, king of the countries, God amongst the gods,

---

[1] See my *Premières Civilisations*, Vol. II., page 169 and the following. The translation of the text that is given here is considerably amended.

[2] *W. A. I.* IV., 29, 1.   [3] In the Assyrian version, "the flower is withered."

[4] In the Assyrian version, "of the Euphrates."

[5] The Assyrian version omits this word.

[6] *W. A. I.* IV., 26, 4.

[7] Lacunæ.   [8] *W. A. I.* IV., 29, 1.

Director) of Ana and Mul-ge,[1]
Merciful one amongst the gods,
Generator[2] who bringest back the dead to life,
Silik-mulu-khi, king of heaven and earth,
King of Tin-Tir,[3] king of E-saggadhu,[4]
King of the E-zida,[5] king of the E-makh-tila,[6]
to thee are heaven and earth!
To thee are heaven and earth round about!
To thee is the lip of life!
To thee are death and life!
To thee is the sublime bank of the pit of the ocean!
All men belonging to the human race,[7] all who breathe,[8] all who bearing a name exist on the surface of the earth,
the whole of the four regions of the world, the archangels of the legions of heaven and earth, how many soever they are,

. . . .[9]

Thou art the (propitious god;)
thou art the (favourable giant;)
thou art he who gives life;
thou art he who saves,
the merciful one amongst the gods,

---

[1] Here taken in the sense of heaven and earth.

[2] In the Assyrian version, "merciful one."

[3] Babylon, as the Assyrian version has it.

[4] "The house that attires its head," the name of the Pyramid of Babylon, the principal seat of the worship of Marduk in Babylon.

[5] "The house of the right hand," or "the house of equity," the name of the stepped tower at Borsippa.

[6] "The supreme house of life," the name of another temple at Borsippa.

[7] In the Accadian *sak miga* or *sak gigga*, in the Assyrian *zalmat qaqqadi*, literally "those with black heads," a not unfrequent designation of mankind, which appears to relate to the traditions of the primitive existence of two races of men, one of a dark complexion the other of a fair, not unlike the children of men and the children of God, mentioned in the first chapters of Genesis.

[8] In the Assyrian version, "the development of life."

[9] Here occurs a gap of several lines.

the regenerator[1] who bringest back the dead to life.
Silik-mulu-khi, king of heaven and earth,
I have invoked thy name, I have invoked thy sublimity.
May the gods (celebrate) the glories of thy name!
May they (bless) his submission unto thee!
May the invalid be delivered from his disease!
Cure the plague, the fever, the ulcer!
The wicked *Utuq*, the wicked *Alal*, the—
wicked *Gigim*, the wicked *Telal*,
the wicked god, the wicked *Maskim*
the phantom, the spectre, the vampire,
incubus, succubus, nightmare,
the bad (plague), painful fever, the bad malady,
he who causes (evil), he who produces evil,

. . . .[2]

the wicked sorcery, the philter . . . .[2]
(Spirit of the heavens, conjure it! Spirit of the earth, conjure it!)

Silik-mulu-khi is thus very clearly identified in this hymn with the Marduk of the Chaldaio-Babylonian religion, and the Assyrian translators of the magic texts have always rendered his name as such. But this assimilation does not correspond precisely with the primitive conception of him, for we see yet nothing which attributes to Silik-mulu-khi the planetary character which was assumed by Marduk in the definitive organization of the Chaldaio-Babylonian system, nor the solar character which he had originally. This assimilation was probably made when Marduk had become decidedly the god of the planet Jupiter, "the Great Fortune" of the astrologers, which justified them in connecting with his other attributes the

---

[1] In the Assyrian version, "the merciful one." [2] Lacunæ.

favourable and protecting office of Silik-mulu-khi. Or perhaps it is still more likely to have taken place before this, and to have had its foundation in the cosmogonic legend, which represented Marduk as the champion of the celestial gods, fighting and conquering "the scaly Tiamat." In fact this exploit agreed perfectly with the usual *rôle* of Silik-mulu-khi, and on the other hand, the struggle with the powers of darkness was also very naturally attributed to a solar god, which character Marduk originally possessed. Here then, according to all appearances, lies the analogy between the myths, which produced the assimilation. But we must also remark that the old Accadian orthography of the name of this god was never used in the documents of the Chaldaio-Babylonian or Assyrian religion as an ideographic or allophonic notation for the name of Marduk. The identification is only to be found in the lists of gods, like the Assyrian versions of the magic formulæ; while other fragments of those mythological tablets seem to admit a distinction between Silik-mulu-khi and Marduk.

No one can fail to be struck by the close connection between the earliest conception of Silik-mulu-khi, in the Accadian magic books, and that of the archangel Çraoscha, "the holy and strong," in the most ancient texts of the religion of Zoroaster; and particularly with the office of mediator attributed to Mithra,[1] probably under the ever increasing influence of the Median Magism, which tended at that

---

[1] See G. Rawlinson, *The Five Great Monarchies of the Ancient Eastern World*, Vol. II., p. 328; Vol. III., p. 348.

time to deeply corrupt the ancient purity of Mazdeism.¹ Any one well versed in the science of comparative theology will at once perceive the striking points of resemblance which exist between the doctrine of ancient magic and that of the religion of Zoroaster, principally in its latest books, namely, a fundamental dualism, fire-worship, and the existence of a god who acted as a special mediator between man and the pure and supreme spirit Ahuramazda.² These are very striking analogies, which need to be examined by the light of a deep study of the Accadian documents, and which, from henceforth, open new fields for research. Already several learned men, who have devoted their vigils to the study of the sacred books of the Iranian religion, like M. Spiegel, have sought at Babylon the source of some of the data found in the writings attributed to Zoroaster, but which do not belong to the older traditions. This opinion should without doubt be somewhat modified, because the influence, thus introduced into the ancient fund of pure Aryan traditions, was rather that of the true Accadian system than of the Chaldaio-Babylonian religion, the sister of the religions of Syria and Phœnicia. We must also keep in mind an important point in this question, Mithra, and particularly his office as mediator (since the name itself was already applied amongst the Vedas to a solar personification), is nowhere mentioned in the most ancient portions of the collection of the Avesta, that is, in the hymns called *Gathas*. The

---

¹ See my *Lettres Assyriologiques*, Vol. I., p. 103.
² See Bleek's edition of *Haug's Translation of the Avesta*.

analogies we have just pointed out appear most prominently in those parts of the collection which bear reference to a development posterior to Mazdeism, and scholars are now unanimous in admitting that these portions of the Avesta belong to a new phase of the Persian religion, when its original spirit had been already much modified by the influence of Median Magism. This Magism itself, which long remained at variance with the orthodox Mazdeism resulted from a mixture of the old Iranian doctrines expressed in the *Gathas*, with extraneous doctrines, as, for instance, those of the religion belonging to the ancient Turanian people of Media, who were nearly allied to the Accadians of Chaldea, and thus ultimately foreign ideas predominated in Magism over its Iranian notions. All that can be gathered of the fundamental data of Magism from the classical writers, its worship of the elements and their spirits, added to the importance it attributed to the magic rites, recalls very forcibly to our minds the religion of the Accadian tablets. It is possible then that these analogies indicate an original community of doctrine and race between the Accadians and the Turanian foundation of the Medic nation, rather than a direct influence of the beliefs of the most ancient Chaldean inhabitants upon Mazdeism. Sir Henry Rawlinson[1] has clearly demonstrated the fact that fire-worship, the permanent and principal rite of Mazdeism, was borrowed by Magism from the ancient Turanian religion, which was a thing un-

---

[1] "Memoir on the Atropatenian Ecbatana," in *Journal of the Royal Geographical Society*, Vol. X., and *Journal of the Royal Asiatic Society*, London, Vol. XV., p. 254.

known to the primitive system of Zoroaster, and that it originated in Atropatine. At first I myself opposed this idea, by dwelling principally upon the importance of the worship of Agni amongst the Vedas, but I must confess that now I am less positive, considering the part played by the god Fire and his worship in the primitive Accadian religion, whilst the *Gathas* contain nothing similar to the worship of Agni in the Vedic hymns. It seems to me indeed that the subject must be considered again, and the explanation of it will henceforth partly depend upon the results of further study of the Accadian books. Henceforth we ought to place amongst the allowable hypotheses that one which supposes that fire-worship was at first common to both the Turanians and the Aryans, and therefore of an extremely ancient origin, and that it may have been repudiated by the Zoroastrian reform, and then afterwards restored in Mazdeism, itself already somewhat changed by the influence of the Medic magic.

How many new and important questions in religious history arise from these Accadian magic books, which we have as yet only begun to examine, and which still necessitate long and patient study! Many are the questionable points which rise up before the mind of the scientist, definite answers to which cannot be expected for many years to come. But much has been gained when a problem is clearly stated, since that is the first step towards its solution; and among the most striking analogies existing between the beliefs of our magic documents and certain points in the secondary development of the Mazdean religion, we have not yet mentioned the most important of all, the doctrine of the Mazdean Fravishis, or the Fervers of the modern Parsees.

The Fravishis of the religion of Zoroaster were the simple essences of all things, the celestial creatures corresponding with the terrestrial, of which they were the immortal types. Stars, animals, men, angels themselves, in one word every created being, had his Fravishi, who was invoked in prayers and sacrifices, and was the invisible protector who watched untiringly over the being to whom he was attached. These were obviously the Chaldean personal spirits of each being and each object of nature thus introduced into the Mazdean theology, and taking a place in the inferior rank of the celestial hierarchy of the Good Principle.[1] The prototype of the human Fravishi was as clearly established as those of the Fravishis of other beings in the system which served as a foundation for Chaldean magic. In the same way that every man had his Fravishi according to the most recent books of the Avesta, so also, according to the Accadian magical tablets, and this doctrine was continually brought out in them, had every man from the hour of his birth a special god attached to him, who lived in him as his protector and his spiritual type; or, as they also expressed the same idea, a divine couple, "a god and a goddess, pure spirits," for they liked to divide every supernatural being into a conjugal duality. Hence the

---

[1] The Good Being, the Pure One, the Brilliant, all titles of Ahuramazda, and all analogous to those ascribed to the Chaldean deities.—*Ed.*

expressions so frequently repeated, "the man, son of his god, the king, son of his god," meaning, the pious man, the pious king; as also in the incantations, when the one speaking says to the god Fire, for instance, "May he be given back to the favourable hands of his god." The god attached to each man, whether he were regarded as single or divided into a divine couple, was a god of a peculiar character, partaking of human nature, its imperfections and its foibles. He was not indeed as entirely good, powerful, and protecting as we might imagine from the formula which have just been quoted. Like the man to whom he was united, he could be conquered by demons or by spells, and thus become their servant; and therefore he himself, being bound by the power of the imprecation, worked in the man's body the evil commanded him.[1] When Namtar, the plague personified as a goddess, seized upon an individual, his god and goddess, as well as his body, were at the mercy of the spirit of the disease;[2] and we have already referred to the texts which prove this idea. We may say, in conclusion, that the god and goddess belonging to each man were a part of his soul, as also were the Fravishis, according to the Mazdean books, only in these latter the conception arose to a higher degree, detaching itself from the materiality and imperfections of the terrestrial man.

The purely spiritual beings, like the Amshaspands, the Yazatas, and even the supreme god, Ahuramazda, had their Fravishis, which may be distinguished from themselves, and is not that exactly

---

[1] *W. A. I.* IV., 7.   [2] British Museum, K 1284.

the strange and subtle distinction made in the magical texts of the Chaldeans, in the quotations at the beginning of this chapter, between such and such a god, and his spirit who was regarded as a separate entity? The idea itself was a complicated one, and presupposed a great nicety of speculation upon the nature of spiritual beings, but it was nevertheless explicitly expressed, and it allowed, at one time, the admission into the incantatory litanies of the spirits of the planet gods belonging to the Chaldaio-Babylonian religion, which yet were not accepted as national gods.

This system of beliefs, as we have just shown it, without affirming anything that was not supported by a passage from the texts, has left its mark in the great Accadian collection discovered by Sir Henry Rawlinson, and it is clear that it must necessarily have given birth to an entirely magical worship. It merits a place by itself in the history of religions, where it will remain the type of the richest and most perfect development to which the exclusive worship of the spirits of nature and the elements, which was characteristic of the Turanian race, has ever attained.

APPENDIX I.

The Relationship between Hea and Oannes.

I CANNOT possibly continue to maintain the assimilation which I, in common with many others, established many years ago between the Oannes of

Berosus and the Ana of the Accadians, or as he is in the Assyrian Anuv. The form described as that of this personage in the fragments of the Chaldean historian is found resembling that of a god, both in the sculptures[1] and upon the cylinders.[2] But there is positively nothing in the cuneiform texts to indicate that Anu possessed the double character of a fish-god and a god of science and government which is ascribed to Oannes in the narrative of Berosus. It is on the contrary an exact representation of the physiognomy and office which these same texts assigned to Hea.

Now there is a very precious story preserved by Helladius,[3] which corresponds exactly with that of Berosus except in the name of the god referred to. He relates the fable of a man named Oes, who came forth from the Erythrean Sea, with the body of a fish, and the head, feet, and arms of a man, and who taught astronomy and letters. "Some say that he issued from the primordial egg, whence his name of Oes, and that he was wholly human while he seemed to be a fish, having "clothed himself in a cetaceous skin." The name here is 'Ωῆς, which is not more different from Hea than the 'Αὸs of Damascius, who must also be identified with him.

But if Hea is the subject of the narrative of Berosus, how are we to explain the origin of the form 'Ωάννης,

---

[1] Layard, *Monuments of Nineveh*, New Series, pl. vi.
[2] Lajard, *Culte de Mithra*, pl. xvi., No. 7; pl. xvii., Nos. 1, 3, 5, 8.
[3] *Ap. Phot. Biblioth.*, cad. 279, p. 1593. But the Babylonians, like the rest of the barbarians, pass over in silence the *one* principle of the universe, and they constitute two, Tauthe and Apason, making Apason the mother of Tauthe, and denominating her "the mother of the gods" ... From these proceeds an only-begotten son Moymis, from them also is derived another progeny, Dache and Dachus, and again a third, Kissare and Assaros, from which last three others proceed, Anus and Illinus and Aus (Oes). Damascius in Hodge's *Cory*, p. 92.

which his name has assumed? I think the answer is to be found in this passage from Hyginus,[1] "Euahanes, qui in Chaldea de mari exiisse dicitur, astrologian interpretatus est." Euahanes is a more correct and fuller form than Oannes, and explains its origin, for it is clearly the Accadian *Ea χan*, "Hea the fish."

Another fragment of Berosus[2] terms this divine personage τον Μυσαρὸν 'Ωάννην, τον 'Αννήδοτον. I proposed to substitute μυστικὸν for μυσαρὸν, which appeared to be impossible; C. Muller wrote δεύτερον. All these conjectures are now known to be needless, a capital μ only was needed, for Μυσαρὸς is one of the god's surnames simply copied from the Assyrian. It is really *musiru* (participle of the Aphel of אשר) or *musaru*, "he who ordains justice, law." As to 'Αννήδοτος, I also recognize in that a surname of Accadian origin, with the meaning of which we are not yet acquainted, but which is written in the lists of those belonging to this god,[3] and which, like many others, preserved its ancient pronunciation, *Nin-dutur*, in the Assyrian tongue.

A third fragment[4] enumerates the five successive theophanies or avatars of Oannes posterior to Annedotus, between the creation and the deluge. In almost all the titles which he gives them we can easily recognize the Accadian surnames of Hea with a slight alteration:

Εὐέδωκος, Εὔδωκος = *Dunga*,[5] *U-Dunga*;[6] correct Εὐδωγκος.

---

[1] *Hab.* 264.
[2] No. 10 in my edition.
[3] *IV. A. I.* ll., 58, l. 63, a, b.
[4] No. 11 in my edition.
[5] *IV. A. I.* ll., 58, l. 60, a.
[6] Documents which are as yet unpublished.

Ἐνεύγαμος = Nukimmut,[1] Nakimmut;[2] corr. Νεύγαμος.
Ἐνεύβουλος = Eni-bubu,[3] a variation of Nin-bubu;[4] corr. Ἐνεύβουβος.
Ἀνήμεντος = Ana-Amman.[5]
Ἀνώδαφος .... the rest is yet to be discovered.

I think these various coincidences will not allow any one to doubt that the Oannes of Berosus is the same as Hea, and not as Anu.

We must notice, however, that all the mythical names of the narratives translated into Greek by the Chaldean priest which have been found as yet in the fragments of the epic cycle, are purely Accadian, and therefore contradict the idea of a Semitic etymology, as at first proposed, both for themselves and for those of which the original form is still wanting.

These names, besides those already mentioned, are:—

Ἄλωρος = Adiuru; corr. Ἄδωρος.
Ἀμεγάλαρος, Μεγάλαρος = Mulu-urugal; corr. Μελάργαλος.
Ὀτιάρτης = Ubaratutu; corr. Ὀπάρτης.
Ξίσουθρος, Σίσιθρος = Xasisatra.
Τιτάν = Eta-ana.

APPENDIX II.

The War of the Seven Wicked Spirits against the Moon.[6]

In the beginning, they were the wicked gods,[7] the rebellious genii who were formed in the interior of the heavens.

[1] W. A. I. I, 55, 2, l. 2; 11, 58, l. 54, a, b.   [2] W. A. I. II., 58, l. 55, a, b.
[3] Documents which are as yet unpublished.
[4] W. A. I. II., 58, l. 62, a, b.   [5] W. A. I. II., 58, l. 52, a, b.
[6] Translations of this have already been published by Mr. Smith, *Assyrian Discoveries*, p. 398 and the following, and Mr. Fox Talbot, *Records of the Past*, Vol. V., p. 161.
[7] "Days of storm, powers of evil." Fox Talbot.

They, they were the agents of violence.

. . . .[1]

They were seven: the first . . . .[2]
the second, the hurricane . . . .[2]
the third, a leopard . . . .[2]
the fourth, a serpent . . . .[2]
the fifth, a watch-dog which . . . .[2]
the sixth, a rebellious giant who submits neither to god nor king;
the seventh, the messenger of the fatal wind who . . . .[2]
They were seven, messengers of Ana, their king;
from town to town they directed their steps.
They were the tempest which rages violently in the heavens;
they were the floating clouds in the sky, the rainy clouds which are driven onward,
the gale of wind which blows violently and causes darkness on a brilliant day.
With the violent winds, in violent winds they rose;
the tempest of Mermer[3] was the result of their war-like power,
to the right of Mermer, they advanced;
from the foundations of the heavens like lightning they (shoot forth),
flowing like rivers they march forward.
In the vast heavens, dwelling of Ana, their king,
they had established evil (they had no rival).
Behold Mul-ge heard this news,
and he meditated a resolve in his heart.
He took counsel with Hea, the supremely wise amongst the gods,
and they placed Uru-ki,[4] Utu,[5] and Tiskhu[6] in the lower part of the heavens to govern there,

---

[1] I here omit two partly defaced verses which are particularly difficult to translate.
[2] Lacunæ.   [3] In the Assyrian Bin or Ramanu (Rimmon). Im. Fox Talbot.
[4] In the Assyrian version Sin.   [5] In the Assyrian Samas.
[6] In the Assyrian Istar.

they established them with Ana in the government of the legions of heaven.
These three gods, his children,
them, he commanded them
to watch day and night without fail.
Behold the seven wicked gods who rose from the lower part of the heavens
effectually obscured the light of Aku.[1]
The noble Utu and Mermer the warrior, passed by them;
Tiskhu with Ana[2] rose from the higher seats
and installed himself in the kingdom of the heavens.[3]

. . . .

Behold these seven . . . .[4]
at the head . . . .[4]
the evil . . . .[4]
for the drink of his sublime mouth . . . .[4]
Aku, the pastor of mankind . . . .[4] of the earth . . . .[4]
was overturned and stopped in the midst (of his course),[5]
fearing night and day, and sitting no more on the throne of his power.
The wicked gods, messengers of Ana their king

. . . .[6]

plotted mischief
from the midst of the heavens like the wind they came down upon the earth
Mul-ge saw the anguish of the noble Aku in the heavens
Master, he spoke to his servant Aku:
"My servant, Nusku, carry this message for me to the Ocean,

---

[1] In the Assyrian Sin. Paku. Fox Talbot.
[2] In the Assyrian version, "with Ana the King."
[3] Four verses are missing here, they having been destroyed by a fracture of the tablet.
[4] Lacunæ.
[5] This verse is translated according to the Assyrian version, which in this place does not keep strictly to the Accadian text. The latter is mutilated and consequently very obscure.
[6] Here follows a verse which is still untranslatable.

the news that my son Aku is in great trouble in the heavens,
tell it to Hea in the Ocean."
Nusku obeyed the command of his king,
to Hea as a quick messenger he went.
To the lord, the supremely wise, the unchangeable master,[1]
Nusku gave the message of his king.
Hea, in the Ocean, listened to this message;
he opened his lips and his mouth was filled with wisdom,
Hea called his son Silik-mulu-khi[2] and said these words to him:
"Go, my son Silik-mulu-khi,
(here is) news of my son[3] Aku who is in great trouble in the heavens,
his anguish in the heavens is evident.
These seven wicked and murderous gods, who know no fear,
these seven wicked gods (destroy) like lightning (devastate) the life of the earth;
they came down upon the earth like an angry whirlwind,
they effectually obscured the light of Aku;
the noble Utu and Mermer (passed) by them."[4]

. . . .

A fracture of the tablet has unfortunately deprived us of the rest of the narrative, and we have nothing left of the verses which related the defeat of the seven malevolent spirits as well as the deliverance of Aku

---

[1] Nu-kimmut, an Accadian title of Hea, which has passed into the Assyrian language and occurs frequently in the texts.

[2] In the Assyrian version Marduk.

[3] These words are translated according to the Assyrian version; the meaning of the Accadian seems to be different, but it has partly disappeared. It seems, however, that the Assyrian translator must have made a mistake, for Akû, some verses farther back, is called the son of Mul-ge, and not of Hea.

[4] *W. A. I.* IV., 5.

the god of the moon. This struggle about the origin of things was supposed to break out afresh each time that the star was eclipsed; so we read in an astrological document,[1] that when certain phenomena are produced "the gods of heaven and earth reduce men to dust and ruin them; there will be an eclipse, a deluge, diseases, death; the seven great and wicked spirits will exercise their powers of oppression before the moon."[2]

The incantation containing the narrative of this war of the seven demons of heaven against the moon was destined to cure the king of a disease caused by the wicked spirits. The god Aku, in the Assyrian Sin, was considered as the type of royalty, the first divine monarch who had reigned upon the earth; the sufferings of the king were then assimilated to his, the remembrance of his deliverance became an augury for that of the prince; the formulæ which had chased away from him the demons eager to extinguish his glory were repeated to procure the safety of the sovereign. This intention of the deprecatory formulæ is plainly shown in the fragments which remain to us of the conclusion of this text:

> In the dwelling of government and justice . . . .
> at the gate of the palace the cry . . . .
> A dyed wool of various colours, the skin of a . . . .
> which has never known the male, the skin of a . . . .[3]
> which has never known the male, fashion them;

---

[1] *W. A. I.* III., 62, col. 2, l. 11, 12.

[2] Cf. the dragon and sun myth of Chinese mythology, and the practice adopted by the priests of beating gongs to drive away the demon which was swallowing the sun, whom he by ultimately vomiting forth restores to his place in the heavens.—*Ed.*

[3] These two names of animals are still doubtful.

cover the feet and hands of the king, son of his god.

The king, son of his god, like the light of Aku, will cause the country to live again; like the brilliancy of the flame he raises his head.

Then after a new gap of ten verses:

. . . . make on his head
present . . . .
exhibit . . . .
. . . .
. . . . may he be pure and holy; may he shine!
The wicked demon, the wicked (*Alal*), the wicked *Gigim*, the wicked *Telal*,
the wicked (god), the wicked *Maskim*,
they shall never enter (the palace);
they shall never approach (the gate) of the palace,
they shall never attack the king;
. . . . they shall never follow;
. . . . they shall never enter.

CHAPTER XIV.

The Religions and the Magic of the Turanian Nations.

I HAVE already spoken of the coarse naturalism manifested in the worship of the spirits of nature, which is professed up to the present time by the Ugro-Finnic tribes of the regions about the Ural and Altai mountains, and which exists amongst the Mongols, as a popular superstition under the Buddhism which they have now for some centuries adopted. This variety of religious beliefs appears in its most rudimentary form with a confused demonology, in which the good are not clearly distinguished from the evil, and no one of the spirits is sufficiently elevated above the rest to become a god. Things remained in this primitive state, without making any progress in the development of belief, without any effort towards a more philosophical, a more reasonable classification, amongst those tribes who preserved from the earliest times their nomadic and barbaric character, and who dwelt apart in unfertile and uncivilized countries.

The nations under consideration know no other worship than the magical rites, no priests but their sorcerers. The Ugric and Altaic tribes have their Shamans;[1] the Mongols, with the Buddhist Lamas, keep the priests of magic from their ancient worship, which they call abysses.[2] As I said before, these magicians, who take the place of the priests, are at once diviners, exorcists, and physicians, thaumaturges, and fabricators of amulets. They do not perform the functions of a minister of worship as a permanent and settled thing. "They are only called upon in cases of necessity," says M. Maury,[3] "but they exercise, none the less, a considerable power over the nations whom they govern as sacred ministers. Their power, particularly their resentment, is much feared, while their knowledge is as blindly trusted. These enchanters have, as a rule, something in their look and attitude that inspires fear and acts upon the imagination. This results no doubt from the care which they take to give to their physiognomy an imposing or savage look, but this particular expression is perhaps still more often the effect of the over-excited state in which they are kept by the rites to which they have recourse; they make use of various stimulants to excite their faculties and produce an artifical muscular force, and to cause hallucinations, convulsions, and dreams, which they consider to be a divine enthusiasm, for they are

---

[1] See De Wrangell on the shamans in *Le Nord de la Silérie*, translated by the Prince E. Galitzin, Vol. I., p. 268; also P. Hyacinthe, *Du chamanisme en Chine*, in the *Nouvelles Annales des Voyages*, 5th series, June 1851, p. 287, and foll.

[2] P. De Tchihatchef, *Voyage scientifique dans l'Altai oriental*, p. 45.

[3] *La Magie et l'Astrologie*, p. 13.

the dupes of their own delirium; but even if they perceive the worthlessness of their predictions, they still all the same claim to be believed."

Amongst all nations, of whatever race, disease is always regarded as a possession, and as the work of a demon.[1]

"The Baschkirs," says M. Maury again,[2] "have their Shaitan-kuriazi, who expel devils and undertake to treat the invalids regarded as possessed[3] by means of the administration of certain remedies. This Shaitan, whose name has been borrowed from the Satan of the Christians, since the Baschkirs have come into contact with the Russians, is held by the Kalmuks to be the chief author of all our bodily sufferings. If they wish to expel him they must resort not only to conjurations, but also to cunning. The abyss places his offerings before the sick man, as if they were intended for the wicked spirit; it being supposed that the demon, attracted by their number or their value, will leave the body which he is tormenting, in order to sieze upon this new spoil.[4] According to the Tcheremisses, the souls of the dead come to trouble the living, and in order to prevent them from doing so, they pierce the soles of the feet and also the heart of the deceased, thinking that being thus nailed into their tomb, the dead could not possibly leave it.[5] . . . . The Kirghis tribes apply to their sorcerers, or *Baksy*,

---

[1] Castrèn, *Vorlesungen über die Finnische Mythologie*, p. 173.

[2] *La Magie et l'Astrologie*, p. 283 and foll.

[3] C. d'Ohsson, *Histoire des Mongols*, Vol. I., p. 17.

[4] P. de Tchihatchef, *Voyage scientifique*, p. 45.

[5] Haxthausen, *Etudes sur la situation intérieure de la Russie*, Vol. I., p. 419.

to chase away demons, and thus to cure the diseases they are supposed to produce. To this end they whip the invalid until the blood comes, and then spit in his face. In their eyes every disease is a personal being.[1] This idea is so generally received amongst the Tchuvaches also, that they firmly believe the least omission of duty is punished by some disease sent to them by Tchemen, a demon whose name is only an altered form of Shaitan.[2] An opinion strongly resembling this is found again amongst the Tchuktchis; these savages have recourse to the strangest conjurations to free them from disease; their Shamans are also subject to nervous states, which they bring on by an artificial excitement."[3]

There is therefore it will be seen a close connection between this sorcery, which takes the place of all other worship in the beliefs in which it originated, and that which is enunciated in the Accadian magical books.

Among the Turanian nations the system is still rudimentary, coarse and confused, as must necessarily be the case amongst tribes which have never got beyond a state of barbarity. Nevertheless we see plainly the germ which was developed, under more favourable circumstances, upon the banks of the Euphrates and Tigris, before the ethnic element from another stock became incorporated with the Accadian

---

[1] Levchine, *Description des hordes et des steppes des Kirghiz-Kazaks*, French translation, p. 356, 358.

[2] *Nouvelles Annales des Voyages*, 5th series, Vol. IV., p. 191.

[3] Wrangell's, *Le Nord de la Sibérie*, translated by Galitzin, Vol. I., p. 265 and foll.

nation. But if the comparison could only be established with the beliefs and rites of these half savage tribes, who have no literature, and who are only known to us from the imperfect stories of travellers, and who dwell moreover in the distant regions of Siberia, the demonstration would be very poor and of no great weight, the analogies too vague and far-fetched to be accepted by the critic. Some almost as striking might be pointed out with the creeds and magic of the Red Skins of America and the Blacks of Africa, for as M. Maury judiciously remarks, " it is not only in the general features, but even in the details, that we see such a strong resemblance between the magic of all barbaric nations."

This comparison may lead us to really decisive results, if we apply it to facts which can be established in the two countries where the people of the Turanian race, in the definite and narrow sense in which we understand this word, were able, by rising to a higher degree of civilization, to establish a true system of religion from the fund of their primitive beliefs, still keeping the train of magic superstitions, while developing them and adopting more reasonable conceptions: namely, amongst the Medes and the Finns.

Median Magism is the result of the combination of an ancient Turanian religion with Mazdeism, upon which it afterwards exercised a very great influence; Finnish mythology on the contrary is a spontaneous creation from the Turanian fund, but it developed itself in the north, where nature assumed an entirely different aspect from what it did amongst the

Accadians, and we see the marks of it in their mythology. In spite of the differences which necessarily resulted from such various stages of development, I think that, after glancing at Median Magism and the beliefs of the ancient Finns, as they are expressed in the great Epopee of the Kalewala, the affinities with the system we have just explained from the remains of the Accadian magic collection, will seem so numerous and striking, that the reader will feel bound to allow with us the existence of a very strongly marked family of religions. And this family, which has been too much lost sight of up to this time, corresponds exactly with a great ethnic and linguistic division, for which henceforth a place must be found in the universal history of mankind.

CHAPTER XV.

The Early Median Mythology compared with that of the Chaldeans.

THE facts relating to Media have a particular importance for us. A very few of the most distinguished scholars hesitate to admit the fact, an unexpected one I must grant, of the existence in Chaldea of a primitive population from the same stock as the Ugro-Finnish and Tartarian nations, which had a large share in the Chaldaio-Babylonian civilization. I shall endeavour later, for I think it very necessary, to answer the objections of these learned men, whose judgment is of too great importance not to be disputed seriously and respectfully, as I have great confidence that the new facts brought out in this book may perhaps help to overrule their scruples. They require, indeed, formal proofs of the fact which seems to them *a priori* very unlikely, and, if I am not mistaken, our researches furnish data which are not without value. However, one of the most important elements of the question rests in facts showing that if the Accadians belonged, by their language and religion, to the real Turanian race, they did not constitute a sporadical phenomena difficult of explanation, but belonged to a chain of nations of the same race which spread in the earliest ages from the plain of central Asia to the Persian Gulf. I shall also need to revert to the admirable efforts by which MM. Westergaard, De Saulcy, Norris, Oppert, and Mordtmann have proved that Media was originally inhabited by a people whose language was closely allied to the Turco-Tartaric and Mongolian philological branches on the one hand, and on the other to the Accadian of Chaldea.

This people, who for want of a better designation must be called Proto-Medic, preserved exclusively the sovereignty of the country until the establishment of the Medes proper, belonging to the Iranian race, of which event, since it is one of great importance in the history of Asia, I have endeavoured to fix the date at the eighth century B.C., in accordance with the data furnished by the Assyrian inscriptions.[1] Even after the invasion, the Iranians only constituted a caste, powerful, but small in number. From the time of the Achaemenian dynasty, the mass of the people still spoke the old language, to which was granted the honour of being counted amongst the official dialects of the chancery of the Persian kings. Turanian Media kept not only its

---

[1] In the first of my *Lettres Assyriologiques*, Vol. I. See the articles written by M. Maury in the *Journal des Savants* of February, March, April and May 1872.

language, but also its own religion, and only after a long time did it cease to struggle, with so many vicissitudes, against the religion of Zoroaster; its peculiar beliefs penetrated even to those of the Iranian conquerors, and produced, by their amalgamation with the religious ideas of these conquerors, the system of *Magism*, so called after the tribe of the Magi, who were at that time in possession of the sacerdotal privileges.[1]

This name of Magism has long been applied to the religion of Zoroaster, causing a confusion which must be ascribed to the Greek authors, beginning with Herodotus, who had travelled in Media and not in Persia proper: but this use of the name is a decided error, and the discoveries of contemporaneous scholars have helped to show the two systems as not only distinct from, but even at enmity with each other.[2]

Darius, the son of Hystaspes, who ought to know even better than Herodotus, relates in the annals of his reign, engraved upon the rock of Behistun, that the Magi, being for the time masters of the empire, with Gaumata the false Smerdis, had undertaken to substitute their religion for that of the Iranian nation, and that he, Darius, at his accession, overthrew their impious altars.[3]

---

[1] Herodotus, lib. I., 132.

[2] See Westergaard, in the preface of his edition of the *Zend-Avesta*, p. 17. And above all Sir Henry Rawlinson, *Journal of the Royal Asiatic Society*, Vol. XV., p. 247 and foll.; Canon Rawlinson's translation of *Herodotus*, Vol. I., p. 426-431; and *The Five Great Monarchies of Ancient Eastern World*, 2nd edition, Vol. III., p. 322-355.

[3] See Rawlinson, "Inscription of Darius at Behistun," Persian text, in *Records of the Past*, Vol. I., p. 107.

While Cambyses was in Egypt, the people fell into impiety, and false beliefs (*dranga*, the lie) flourished in the country, in Persia, in Media, and in the other provinces[1] . . . .

The kingdom which had been taken away from our race I regained; I re-established it. The temples which Gaumata the Magi had destroyed, I built again. I gave them back to the people; I restored the sacred songs and rites to the families from which Gaumata the Magi had taken them; I re-established the state upon its original basis, Persia, Media, and the other provinces.[2]

In the inscription on his tomb at Nakch-i-Rustam, he says again, "When Ahuramazda saw that this world was given up to superstition, he confided it to me."[3] The word used in the Persian text at this place is *yatum*, the religion of the Yatus, a name given to the enemies of Zoroaster in the Zend-Avesta; in the Babylonian text the expression is paraphrased thus: "When he saw that these countries worshipped according to the doctrines of perdition."[4] We understand from the expressions of these texts, the massacre of the Magi by the Persians directly after the false Smerdis had been killed, and the institution, otherwise inexplicable, of the festival of the Magophonia, by which for a long time the anniversary of this massacre was celebrated.[5] In no truly Zoroastrian document of

---

[1] *Inscription of Behistun*, Table I., § 10.
[2] Table I., § 14.
[3] See *Records of the Past*, Vol. V., p. 149.
[4] See Oppert, *Expédition en Mésopotamie*, Vol. II., p. 178.
[5] Herodotus, III., 79; Ctes., *Persic*, p. 68, editor Baehr; Agath., II., 47, edition of Paris.

ancient date, and of Persian or Bactrian origin, do we find the Magi mentioned as ministers of religion. However, the corruption of the national and primitive doctrines of the Iranian race, that is, of the pure Mazdeism of the *Gathas* and the first *Fargards* of the Vendidad-Sadé, took place early amongst the Medes, from their contact with the Turanian nations, even before they had conquered the whole region to which they gave the name of Media, for the Vendidad[1] names Ragha and Tchakra as the places of their residence; that is to say, it considers their residence in Ragæ and Khorasan to have been the origin of serious religious heresies, one of which was characterized by the practice of burning the body after death. The same fact is proved by a curious text which M. Haug quotes.[2] At the time of the foundation of the Achaemenian empire, and under the first kings of this dynasty, when the Persian religion still existed in all its purity, there was a deep-rooted antagonism, both in doctrine and position, between the Medic priesthood known as *Magus*, and the Persian, termed *Athrava*.[3] This antagonism afterwards diminished, as the Persian religion lost its purity. Foiled in their attempt to exalt their system above Mazdeism, which had only succeeded for a short time under the false Smerdis, the Magi tried another plan, more prudent and more complicated, endeavouring to enter by cunning the fortress which they could not overthrow by strength. From the time of Xerxes,

---

[1] I., 59-66.

[2] In Bunsen, *Aegyptens Stelle*, Vol. V., p. 116.

[3] See Spiegel, *Avesta*, Vol. II., p. 6 and foll.

they began to be in favour at court,[1] and this favour continued to increase. To their influence are to be ascribed nearly all the changes which, towards the end of the Achaemenian dynasty, corrupted deeply the Zoroastrian faith, so that it passed into idolatry; these changes have been very ably examined by Canon Rawlinson.[2] In this way pure Mazdeism was substituted for a syncretic religion, in which the elements of Mazdeism predominated, and which recognized both the *magus* and *athrava*. The portions of the Zend-Avesta belonging to the second period of the composition, bear very evident marks of this introduction of strange ideas, although they are not so far developed there as they were in the public worship through the decrees of some of the Achaemenian kings. Many centuries later, when the Sassanian princes undertook to restore Mazdeism in a state of greater purity, yet without taking it back to its primitive condition, they preserved the sacerdotal title of Magi, the heterodox meaning of which had passed away with time.

All the Greek and Latin writers acquainted with the Persian religion at this period give to its ministers the title of Magi.[3]

In the great Pehlevi inscription of Nakch-i-Rajab, the Roman title *Pontifex maximus* is rendered *magūpat û aiharpat Rûm*.[4] These two words, derived from the the Zend *magupaiti* and *aêthrapaiti*, "chief of the Magi," and "chief of the Athravas," are used again

---

[1] Herodotus, VII., 19, 113, 191.
[2] *The Five Great Monarchies*, 2nd edition, Vol. III., p. 357-362.
[3] Ammian. Marcell., XXIII.; Agath., II., 36.
[4] Haug, *Essay on the Pehlavi Language*, p. 37.

indifferently in other Sassanian inscriptions to express the idea of "supreme pontiff," and they have given rise to the two titles of the religious ministers of the more recent Parsism, *Mobed* and *Herbed*. The fundamental distinction existing from the beginning and during the first periods of the Achaemenian dynasty between Magism and Mazdeism explains the contradiction between the spirit and doctrine of the religion of Zoroaster, on the one hand, as it is expressed in the ancient parts of the Zend-Avesta, and as we find it in the inscriptions of Darius and Xerxes, or in the admirable refutation of Persian dualism addressed to Cyrus which forms the forty-fifth[1] chapter of the book of Isaiah, and on the other hand the information respecting the religion of the Medes and Persians furnished by Herodotus and Dinon.

The Mazdean doctrine, so clearly and repeatedly expressed by Darius, was essentially spiritualistic. It rested upon an idea of dualism, in which the superiority of the Good Principle, Ahuramazda, shone forth in the most brilliant manner. Ahuramazda was in reality the only god, "the Lord God of the heavens," "he who has given (created) heaven and earth;" all the official decrees of the kings begin by a proclamation of the greatness of the god Ahuramazda; and they mention no other god. The princes were called sovereigns by favour of Ahuramazda; from him came victory, conquest, safety, prosperity, and all wealth. The "law of Ahuramazda" was the rule of life; his protection was

[1] Isa. xlv. 5-7.

a blessing which they invoked continually in fervent prayers.[1] There is nothing astonishing, consequently, in the sympathy which was manifested by the first Persian kings for the Jewish religion, and in the manner in which Cyrus identified Jehovah with his own god.[2] The Persians certainly spoke of other gods, but without specially naming them, and this must have been the opening by which strange influences entered into the religion and corrupted it. Thus Ahuramazda, instead of being called exactly "the Great God," was sometimes designated as "the greatest of the gods," and after him we find that "the other gods," or "the gods who guard the house," are invoked several times. But these gods were certainly personages of an inferior order, powerful spirits created by Ahuramazda, and dependent upon him, yet having a right to the worship of men; they corresponded to the Amshaspands and the Yazatas of the Zend-Avesta. As to the adversary of Ahuramazda, the representative of the bad principle, the Angromainyus or Ahriman of the books attributed to

---

[1] Cf. the following extracts from the *Avesta*:—
  1 I desire by my prayer with uplifted hands this joy.
    First the entirely pure works of the holy spirit, Mazda.
    (Then) the understanding of Vohumano (goodmindedness), and that which rejoices the soul of the Bull.
  2 I draw near to you, O Ahura Mazda with goodmindedness,
    Give me for both these worlds the corporeal as well as the spiritual,
    Gifts arising out of purity, which make joyful in brightness.—*Gatha* i.

Also—
  12 We praise thee, we acknowledge ourselves as thy debtors, Mazda Ahura.
  13 With all good thoughts, with all good words, with all good works, we draw nigh unto thee.
  14 This thy body, the fairest of all bodies, we invite Mazda Ahura.
  15 The greatest among the great lights,
  16 That which they call the sun.—*Yacna* xxxvi.

[2] Ezra i. 2, 3.

Zoroaster, he was "the enemy" who was regarded with horror and loaded with curses; the kings were usually represented as fighting with him or his genii, symbolized as horrible monsters.[1] He is only mentioned once in the inscriptions at Behistun,[2] where Darius calls him Dranga, "the lie" personified, and ascribes to him all the revolts which he had to subdue.

Herodotus and the other classical writers describe the true spirit of Mazdeism, when they represent the Persians as having a horror of idolatry and strange religions, or when they show them in their expeditions as hostile to everything bordering on paganism, burning temples,[3] destroying the images of the gods or raising them as trophies,[4] outraging or killing the priests,[5] hindering the celebration of festivals,[6] thrusting the sacred animals through with the sword,[7] and even carrying their hatred of the rites of strange worship so far as to desecrate the sepulchres.[8] But when the same Herodotus pretends to give exact details about the true Persian religion, he does not even know the name of Ahuramazda. He speaks of homage being rendered to the

---

[1] Lajard, *Culte de Mithra*, pl. ii., xxv.; see G. Rawlinson, *The Five Great Monarchies*, 2nd edition, Vol. III., p. 355. Especially on the monuments at Persepolis, and the Pehlevi seals in the British Museum.—*Ed.*

[2] Table 4, § 4.

[3] Herodotus, lib. III., 25; VI., 19, 96, 101; VIII., 33, 53; Cic., *De Leg.*, II., 10; Strab., XIV., p. 634; Pausan., X., 35, 2.

[4] Herodotus, lib. I., 183; III., 37.

[5] Herodotus, lib. I., 183; III., 27, 29.

[6] Herodotus, lib. III., 29.

[7] Herodotus, lib. III., 29.

[8] Herodotus, lib. I., 187; III., 16, 37; Diod. Sic., lib. X., 13.

sun, the fire, the earth, the water, and the winds,[1] a worship which has nothing in common with the precepts and spirit of the Zend-Avesta, but an entirely naturalistic religion quite distinct from the Mazdean spiritualism, resembling rather the Vedic Aryas, and still more that of our Accadian magic books. It is true he says explicitly that the Magi were the necessary ministers of this worship, and this shows us that under the name of the Persian religion he is speaking of Magism, the rites of which he had seen performed in Media. Dinon[2] and Diogenes Laertius[3] also bear witness that the Magi worshipped the elements; but the former remarks that they honoured fire and water principally with their worship. These were exactly the same elements which were directly worshipped by the Accadian magicians in their material reality, hence we gather that their spirits were not clearly distinct from each other. If we consider attentively the terms of the passages which we point out as the chief of those relating to the elementary worship of the Median magic, the impression they leave upon us will be that of a worship of the spirits of nature, in which the personality of these spirits was confused in many cases

---

[1] Herodotus, lib. I., 131; cf. III., 16. "The Persians, according to my own knowledge, observe the following customs. It is not their practice to erect statues, or temples, or altars, but they charge those with folly who do so, because, as I conjecture, they do not think the gods have human forms as the Greeks do. They are accustomed to ascend to the highest parts of the mountains and offer sacrifice to Jupiter. And they call the whole circle of the heavens by the name of Jupiter. They sacrifice to the sun and moon, to the earth, fire, water, and the winds; to these alone they have sacrificed from the earliest times, but they have since learnt from the Arabians and Assyrians to sacrifice to Venus Urania, whom the Assyrians call Venus Mylitta, the Arabians Mylitta, and the Persians Mithra." Herod., Clio, 131.

[2] *Ap.* Clem. Alex., *Protrept.*, I., 5.

[3] *De Vit. philos., proœm.*, 6.

with the objects and elements which they were supposed to animate and govern.

I have previously mentioned the difficulty raised by the rite of a worship of the fire kept burning upon the altars. But whatever may be the solution of it, if it is proved, which is quite possible, that this rite formed an integral part of the system of Mazdeism in its primitive purity, it certainly existed also, and had a very important place in the religion of Magism, and even in the cultus of the Turanian Medes, before any Persian invasion. Sir Henry Rawlinson[1] and his brother historian[2] appear to me to have demonstrated this position in a most convincing manner, and also, this fact is conformable with what we have noticed amongst the Accadians. The Magi pretended to have the power of making fire descend on to their altars by means of magical ceremonies.[3]

The worship of the stars was very fully developed in the system of Median magic. This worship appears very seldom in the Zendic books,[4] and that only in one of the most recent portions; clever modern critics have no hesitation in pronouncing it, as it appears there, to be the result of a later introduction, and due to some foreign influence.[5] Towards the end of the Persian empire, on the contrary, it assumed a great importance, as it did in the Zoroastrian writings of a very early epoch.[6]

[1] *Journal of the Royal Asiatic Society*, Vol. XV., p. 254.
[2] *The Five Great Monarchies*, 2nd edition, Vol. II., p. 345 and foll.
[3] Dio. Chrysost., *Orat.*, XXXVI., p. 149, editor Reiske; Clem., *Recognit.*, IV., 29; cf. Ammian. Marcell., XXIII., 6.
[4] Only in the 21st fargard of the *Vendidad-Sadé*.
[5] See Spiegel, *Avesta*, Vol. I., p. 258, 271 and foll.; Vol. II., p. 119, 120.
[6] See Spiegel, *Avesta*, Vol. I., p. 273 and foll.

Evidently it came from the Magi. The principal office of this worship amongst the Medes is made known to us by the description which Herodotus gives[1] of the seven walls of Ecbatana, each with the sacred colour of one of the seven planets. The same sacramental arrangement was observed in the town of Ganzakh, the Gazaca of the classical writers, and in Atropatene, since Moses Chorenensis[2] calls it "the second Ecbatana, the town with seven walls." Later, at the period of the Sassanian dynasty, the Persian poet Nizami, author of the Heft-Peiher, describes this style as prevailing in the palace of the seven planets built by Bahram-Gour or Varahran V.[3] It was borrowed direct from the customs of civilization, from the Babylonian religion, for the famous tower of Borsippa had seven storeys with the colours of the seven planetary bodies,[4] after its restoration by Nebuchadnezzar, and the same arrangement was observed in the *ziggurrat* or sacred tower of the palace of Khorsabad.[5] But the worship of the stars and planets must have come originally, M. Spiegel thinks, from the introduction of the religious doctrines of Babylon, in which it held such a prominent position, and the Kushito-Semitic doctrines, for we have seen that it was quite foreign to the old Accadian beliefs. Most probably, however, the Turanians of Media received it from the

---

[1] I., 98.

[2] Quoted by Sir Henry Rawlinson, *Journal of the Royal Asiatic Society*, Vol. X., 127.

[3] Vahran V. ascended the Persian throne A.D. 420.

[4] Sir H. Rawlinson, *Journal of the Royal Asiatic Society*, Vol. XVIII., p. 1-34.

[5] Victor Place, *Ninive et l'Assyrie*, pl. 36, 37. See my *Essai de Commentaire des Fragments cosmogoniques de Bérose*, p. 369 and foll.

Assyrians, just as they got the worship of Anat, changed into Anahita,[1] from their constant contact with the civilization of the countries round the Euphrates and Tigris, and they, in their turn, transmitted it to the Magi, by whom it was afterwards introduced amongst the Persians and the rest of the Iranian races.

This spirit of a peculiar naturalistic pantheism analogous to that of the Accadian magical books, which is revealed by this worship of the elements and the stars, is the very antipodes of the spiritualism of the pure Mazdean religion in its earliest documents. The Magi adopted it into the sphere of the most elevated personages of their religious system, in which they had completely altered the fundamental conception of Mazdeism, although they still preserved the dualistic form which the old Proto-Medic religion must have admitted even before any contact with the Iranians, since we found it amongst the Accadians. There is no doubt that they placed at the top of the scale the antagonistic worship of Ahuramazda and of Angromainyus. For certainly Ahuramazda is the same as the Zeus whom Herodotus[2] mentions as being worshipped by the Magi, and the same Herodotus[3] represents these later, armed with the *khraf-*

---

[1] See my *Essai de Commentaire des Fragments cosmogoniques de Bérose*, p. 157 and foll. This goddess was also introduced into the Egyptian Mythology in the time of the Ramessides probably from Asiatic sources also.—*Ed.*

[2] I., 97.

[3] I., 140. "But what follows relating to the dead is only secretly mentioned and not openly, viz., that the dead body of a Persian is never buried until it has been torn by some bird or dog, but I know for a certainty that the Magi do this, for they do it openly. The Persians then having covered the body with wax conceal it in the ground. The Magi differ very much from all other men, and particularly from the

çthraghna,' pursuing and killing the wicked animals of creation, reptiles and insects, with as much zeal as the more orthodox Mazdeans. But the Magi considered the antagonism to be only superficial, for they regarded the representatives of the two opposing principles as consubstantial, equal in power, and emanating both from one and the same pre-existent principle. I do not hesitate indeed to refer to Median Magism the origin of the personage Zarvana-akarana, "Time without limit," the common source of Ahuramazda and Angromainyus; which conception substitutes the most complete Pantheism and the greatest indifference as to morals for the dualism of Zoroaster, of which it still maintains the outward semblance. This personage, who was of great importance in the books which were composed before the time of Alexander, and the conception of whom became in the middle ages the fundamental dogma of a heresy from Mazdeism, the heresy of the Zarvanians, did not belong to the ancient fund of the Zoroastrian religion. He was not mentioned in its earliest books, and all the scholars who are best versed in these matters agree that his presence later points to a corruption of the original doctrine, attributable to foreign influences.² Endeme, the favourite

Egyptian priests, for the latter hold it matter of religion not to kill anything that has ife, except such things as they offer in sacrifice: whereas the Magi kill everything with their own hands, except a dog or a man, and they think they do a meritorious thing when they kill ants, serpents, and other reptiles and birds." Herod., *Clio*, 140.

¹ *Yaçna*, lvii., 6.

² D'Eckstein, *Questions sur le Antiquites Sémitiques*, § xv.; Oppert, *Annales de Philosophie Chrétienne*, January 1862, p. 61; Spiegel, *Avesta*, Vol. I., p. 271; Vol. II., p. 119, 216 and foll. See also what I have said in my *Manuel d'Histoire ancienne de l'Orient*, 3rd edition, Vol II., p. 316.

disciple of Aristotle, describing very precisely this personage and the dualistic couple from which he proceeded, writes of this being as a conception of the Magi.¹ It is interesting to remark here that, in a passage the first date of which may be ascribed to Berosus,² this same name of Zarvana is applied to the legendary personification of the ancient Turanian race, under the form which had been assumed by the Chaldaic-Babylonian legend in Armenia about the origin of the different races.³ We discovered in the fragments of the great Accadian magic collection ideas analogous to those resulting from the conception of Zarvana-akarana; we saw odious demons, like Namtar, and propitious gods opposed to the demons, like Nin-dar, both emanating from Mul-ge. We suppose, also, that in a religion which resembled nearly that of ancient Accad, and represented the same ideas of the spirits and gods under a rather different form, the dark side of Mul-ge's character had been brought out in strong contrast to the favourable attributes of Hea; and that at the same time they attributed to Ana something of the idea of a first principle which he originally possessed, slightly modified, as was the conception of all the other gods; it will be thus seen that the three gods connected by the Accadians with the three zones of the universe were grouped in such a manner that they would naturally be represented in Iranianism by the couple of Ahuramazda and Angromainyus with Zarvana-akarana above them.

---

¹ *Ap.* Damasc., *De Princip.*, 125. ² Mos. Choren., I., 5.
³ See my *Essai de Commentaire des Fragments cosmogoniques de Bérose*, p. 422 and foll.

Magic Magism however goes even further than the conception of a common principle, from which both Ahuramazda and Angromainyus were supposed to have emanated. Whilst in the true Mazdeism of of the Persians, Ahuramazda alone was worshipped and Angromainyus loaded with curses, in Magism the two principles of good and evil, Ahuramazda and Angromainyus, received equally alike the homage of the altars.

Plutarch[1] relates that the Magi offered sacrifices to Angromainyus, Ἄιδης, Ἀρειμάνιος, and describes the rites used, which consisted of an offering of grass and sedge, called ὄμωμι, evidently the *haoma*, sprinkled with the blood of a wolf, and placed in an obscure spot. Herodotus[2] tells us that Amestris, the spouse of Xerxes, who was entirely under the influence of the Magi, sacrificed seven children " to the god of darkness and the infernal regions." He also mentions a like sacrifice as having been offered to the same god in the passage of the Strymon, when the Persians were marching into Greece. This shocking practice of human sacrifices was entirely opposed to the fundamental principles of the Zoroastrian doctrine, as was also the worship of Angromainyus, and it never appears again in Persian history. We recognize in it, in concert with Canon Rawlinson,[3] a trace of the influence of Magism.

In this worship of the bad principle placed upon a footing of perfect equality with the good, Median

---

[1] *De Is. et Osir.*, p. 369, editor Reiske.   [2] VII., 114.
[3] *The Five Great Monarchies*, 2nd edition, Vol. III., p. 359.

Magism reveals itself as inferior, from a moral point of view, to the doctrine of Accadian magic. But we must remember the peculiar circumstances in which the people of Media had been placed by the Iranian conquest. There are very strong indications which would lead us to believe that before the conquest the form of a serpent was attributed to one of the gods.[1] This worship of serpent-gods is found amongst many of the primitive Turanian tribes.[2] The Accadians made the serpent one of the principal attributes, and one of the forms of Hea,[3] and we have a very important allusion to a mythological serpent in these words from an Accadian dithyrambus uttered by a god,[4] perhaps by Hea, as I mentioned before in quoting the whole piece:

> Like the enormous serpent with seven heads, the weapon with seven heads, I hold it.
> Like the serpent which beats the waves of the sea (attacking) the enemy in front,
> devastator in the shock of battle, extending his power over heaven and earth, the weapon with (seven) heads, (I hold it).[5]

When once the Iranian traditions were fused with the ancient beliefs of the Proto-Medic religion, the serpent-god naturally became identified with the representative of the dark and bad principle, for, according to the Mazdean myths, the serpent was the

[1] See my *Lettres Assyriologiques*, Vol. I., p. 99.
[2] See Fergusson, *Tree and Serpent Worship*, London 1861, in 4to.
[3] George Rawlinson, *The Five Great Monarchies*, 2nd edition, Vol. I., p. 122.
[4] *W. A. I.* II., 19.
[5] I have compared elsewhere (in my *Premières Civilisations*, Vol., II., p. 136) this allusion with the Brahmanic legend of Manthanam. See *Records of the Past*, Vol. III., p. 127.

form assumed by Angromainyus, in order to penetrate into the heaven of Ahuramazda.[1] In the heroic cycle, also, the serpent Dahaka,[2] or Azhi-Dakaha,[3] conquered by Thraetona,[4] an Iranian form of the Vedic myth Trita, son of Aptya,[5] was a personification of the bad principle. Moses Chorenensis[6] attributes to the dynasty of the Aryan Medes and to the descendants of their subjects, who were transported into Armenia, the preservation of the ancient Turanian worship of the serpent, connecting with it the name of Astyages.[7] So also the descendants of Thraetona, becoming one with those they conquered, ended by worshipping Azhi-Dahaka. And as the people of Turanian origin were inclined to honour their ancient national god rather than that of the Iranian conquerers, Angromainyus or Azhi-Dahaka certainly out-shone Ahuramazda. From this point of view, I think M. Oppert[8] was right in recognizing a trace of the Magism of the ancient Medes in the odd religion of the Yezidis or "worshippers of the devil," who dwell at the present time in Irak-Adjemy and the north of Mesopotamia; for this religion professes in its doctrines the Mazdean dualism, but in its worship it only renders homage to the wicked principle.[9]

[1] Lajard, *Memoire sur les bas-reliefs decouverts en Transylvanie*, Section ii., iii. at the end.
[2] *Yaçna*, IX., 25.   [3] *Vendidad-Sadé*, I., 69.
[4] Burnouf, *Journal Asiatique*, 3rd series, Vol. XLV., p. 497 and foll.
[5] See Roth, "Die Werke von Feridun in Indien und Iran," in the *Zeitschr. der Deutsch. Morgenl. Gesellsch.*, Vol. II., p. 216 and foll.; Spiegel, *Avesta*, Vol. I., p. 7.
[6] I., 29.
[7] See my *Lettres Assyriologiques*, Vol. I., p. 97-101.
[8] *Rapport au ministre de l'instruction publique*, Paris 1856.
[9] Layard, *Nineveh and Babylon*, p. 41 and foll., 81-94.

Herodotus tells us [1] that the Magi borrowed from the Assyrians the worship of their celestial Aphrodite, that is, of the Anahita introduced afterwards into the Persian religion by a decree of Artaxerxes Mnemon; [2] and I may here be permitted to repeat my own words upon the place of this goddess in the Magism of Media. [3]

The Father of History, in pointing out that the Magi adopted the Chaldaio-Assyrian goddess, adds that they called her Mithra. This information from Herodotus has occasioned many conjectures and many theories of an entirely mythological character, which have disappeared before a more intimate acquaintance with the Asiatic religions. At present, the most generally received opinion amongst scholars naturally results from the study of the original Iranian sources; it decides that the view taken by Herodotus is inadmissible, that the historian of Helicarnassus has committed an error and occasioned a confusion, as he has also done in other places.[4] But what was the cause of it? This question although it has not been asked as yet, still I think finds an answer in the close alliance between the worship of Anahita and Mithra in the system of Median Magism. The conception of the personage of Mithra as a form of the sun dates back to the primitive Aryan fund of religious ideas; we find in it one of the Adityas of Vedic mythology, and it is impossible that the authors of the first Mazdean

---

[1] I., 131. [2] Berosus, *Ap.* Clem. Alex., *Protrept*, I., 5.
[3] *Essai de Commentaire des Fragments cosmogoniques de Bérose*, p. 157 and foll.
[4] See Bréal, *De Persicis nominibus apud Scriptores Graecos*, p. 5 and foll.

reforms should not have known this analogy. But this view of Mithra evidently did not assume in their system the importance which was afterwards attributed to it in the latest Zoroastrian books; he was a secondary personage, inferior, perhaps, even to the Amshaspands, not a deity of the same or nearly the same rank as Ahuramazda; for Mazdeism, in its primitive purity, recognized only in the latter the supreme and perfect divine nature. And Canon Rawlinson[1] has very judiciously remarked that the introduction of Mithra into the public worship took place at the same time as that of Anahita, and that the two facts point to a historical connection which must not be overlooked. Indeed, the inscription of Artaxerxes Mnemon at Susa is the first official document of the Achaemenian dynasty which mentions other gods with Ahuramazda, and these gods were Anahita and Mithra, united together and forming an indivisible group. The legal establishment of their worship in this supreme rank must therefore have been simultaneous, and must have arisen from the same source. And it was in the time of Artaxerxes that Xenophon[2] began to speak of Mithra as one of the principal national gods of the Persians.

After this it is very difficult not to think that Artaxerxes Mnemon, among the innovations which during his reign modified the Zoroastrian religion so much, introduced not only a new personage, but a divine couple, that of Mithra and Anahita, which the

---

[1] *The Five Great Monarchies*, 2nd edition, Vol. III., p. 360 and foll.
[2] *Cyrop.*, VII., 5, 53; *Econom.*, IV., 24.

presence of Mithra justified them in grafting as an alien branch upon the ancient stock of Mazdeism, and which had already been grafted upon it in the system of Median Magism. In this latter system, as far as we can understand the economy of it, the worship of the sun and moon, spoken of by Herodotus, was established under the influence of the Chaldaio-Assyrian religion, with the form of the worship of the couple of a solar god and lunar goddess, Mithra and Anahita,[1] placed immediately beneath Ahuramazda. Hence the mistake made by Herodotus, who confounded the two personages of this couple. Perhaps it was not after all an error, and the divine couple of which we are speaking may have been sometimes designated as a double Mithra. So also might we explain, as the remains of this state of things, the expression in a passage from the Yaçna,[2] which has much puzzled the commentators, *Ahuraêibya Mithraêibya* "the two divine Mithras."[3]

I do not think we need to qualify this opinion; since our study of the Accadian magic texts allows us to confirm it. We have noticed the close resemblance between the office of mediator, attributed to Mithra in the Persian religion from the time of Artaxerxes Mnemon, with that filled by Silik-mulu-khi between man and Hea in the Accadian system. The name of Mithra, signifying "the friend," might be taken as an Iranian equivalent or as a sort of

---

[1] Whilst the Aryan-Medes borrowed the person of Anat from the Chaldaio-Assyrian religion the latter received from them the name of Mithra, as an appellation of the sun. *W. A. I.* III., 69, 5.

[2] I., 29.

[3] See Burnouf, *Commentaire sur le Yaçna,* p. 351.

translation of Silik-mulu-khi, "he who sheds abroad good for men." It seems that in Magism Mithra must originally have taken the place and the attributes of some mediator-god of the Proto-Medic religion, analogous to the Silik-mulu-khi of the Accadians, who bore, no doubt, the same kind of name. He was later divided into an original couple, like the god attached to each person in the Accadian system, and with him was associated the goddess Anahita, who was borrowed from the Chaldaio-Assyrian religion.

Lastly, to complete the picture of Median Magism, and to finish the comparison of points of resemblance with the system we studied amongst the Accadians, we must mention that the practices of incantation and sorcery were greatly developed in it. These practices are formally forbidden and severely condemned by all the books of Mazdeism, which attributed the invention of them "to the Yatus, the enemies of Zoroaster."[1] The name *yâtus*, used by Darius in the inscription of Naksh-i-Rustam[2] to designate the religion of the Magi, would alone strongly favour the notion that these rites were considered very important. Dinon[3] also describes the incantations to which the Magi devoted themselves with their divining wand in their hand. They foretold the future by throwing little sticks of tamarisk wood;[4] this custom is said by the classical writers to have been of Scythian or Turanian origin. The *Bareçma*,[5] having become after a certain period an

---

[1] *Vendidad-Sade*, I., 52-56.   [2] See *Records of the Past*, Vol. V., p. 149.
[3] *Ap.* Schol. *ad* Nicandr. *Theriac.*, V., 613.   [4] Ibid.   [5] *Yaçna*, LVII., 6.

essential part of the insignia of the ministers of the Mazdean worship, was originally nothing else than a bundle of these wands, the use of which was introduced into Persia under the influence of the Magi.¹ Following the enquiries which we are going to make into astrology and divination in Chaldea and Babylon, we shall prove that the throwing of these wands was known and practised there,² and that this was even the most ancient mode of divination used in the time of the Accadians.³

We said that the Magi pretended to have the power of drawing fire down from heaven upon their altars by means of certain woods and rites.

Herodotus⁴ and Diogenes Laertius⁵ speak of the supernatural power the Magi thought they possessed. The last of these writers had particularly consulted the special treatise upon the Magi by Hermippus, where they were represented as jugglers and enchanters.⁶ About the time of the Median wars a book attributed to the Magus Osthanes was circulated in Greece; this book was the origin of the magic substituted by the Greeks from that time forth for the coarse and ancient rites of *Goetia*.⁷ From what we know of this book, it seems to have taught, as the

---

¹ See G. Rawlinson, *The Five Great Monarchies*, 2nd edition, Vol. III., p. 351.

² Ezekiel xxi. 26. The wands or arrows of fate are marked on many Babylonian cylinders as held in the hand of Marduk (Lajard, *Culte de Mithra*, pl. xxxii., No. 2; liv., A, No. 5), or of Istar (Lajard, pl. xxxvii., No. 1), the divinities of the planets Jupiter and Venus, the most favourable deities according to the ideas of astrologers.

³ There is certainly a resemblance between this divination and the magic throwing of dice that we see mentioned in the tablet K 142 of the British Museum.

⁴ I., 103, 120; VII., 12.   ⁵ *De Vit. philosoph. præm.*, 6.

⁶ Plin., *Hist. Nat.*, XXX, 2.

⁷ Plin., XXX., 1; Euseb., *Chronic.*, I., 48; *Præpar. Evangel.*, I., 10; V., 14; Suid., V.; Apul., *Apolog.*, 27.

supreme secrets of the caste of the Magi, all sorts of spells and divinations, even to the invocation of the dead and the infernal spirits.[1] Further, these priests who had spread from Media over the whole of Persia were regarded in the west as types of enchanters and magicians,[2] hence the meaning attached by us to the word magic. Their magic was known, however, to have resembled very nearly that of Chaldea,[3] which ended by causing in the minds of the Greeks an inextricable confusion between the Magi and the Chaldeans.[4]

It has been necessary to explain these things very fully in order to give a complete idea of our knowledge of the Median Magism, which is still after all a very obscure subject. But I think that from these explanations the reader will be able to distinguish fairly well between the three elements composing this mixed system: the Iranian and Mazdean element, which may be compared to a garment cast over the ancient conceptions of a very different origin as a result of the conquest by the Medes proper; the doctrines borrowed from the Chaldaio-Assyrian religion, consisting chiefly of the worship of the stars and Anahita; and lastly, the ancient fund of the popular Turanian beliefs before the invasion of

---

[1] Plin., XXX., 5.

[2] Strab., I., p. 24; XVI., p. 762; Lucian, *De Necromant.*, p. 11, edit. Lehmann; Ammian. Marcell., XXIII., 6; Origen, *Adv. Cels.*, VI., 80; Minut. Fil., Octavian, 26; Clem. Alex., *Protrept.*, I., p. 17, edit. Potter; S. Cyprian, *De Idol.* in Opp., Vol., I., p. 408.

[3] Ammian. Marcell., XXIII., 6.

[4] Plat., I., *Alcibiad.*, 37; Justin, I., 1; Diogen. Laert., I., 8; Plin., *Hist. Nat.*, XXX., 2; XXXVII., 49; Apul., *Florid.*, II., 5; Tatian, *Orat ad Graec.*, I.; Suid., Μαγική and Ζωροαστρης; *Constitut. Apostolic.*, IV., 26, Clem. Alex., *Stromat.*, V., p. 598, edit. Potter; Arnot., *Adv. gent.*, I., 52.

the Iranians. Finally, these beliefs have therefore a close resemblance with the doctrines of the old Accadian magic books, a resemblance analogous to that existing between the dialects of anti-Aryan Media and Accadian Chaldea.

CHAPTER XVI.

Finno-Tartarian Magical Mythology.

THE connection with the Finnish mythology and magic is still more striking. We have a fertile mine of information about the rites and religion of this nation in the great Epopee of the *Kalevala*, which M. Léouzon-Leduc has undertaken to lay before the French public, and of which, although it is translated into many European languages,[1] our scholars and literary men are almost entirely ignorant; this is much to be regretted, for the poem should be placed next to the Epopees of Greece, India, and Persia, on account of its beauty and importance. The subject of it has been clearly explained in the works of Ganander,[2] Castrèn,[3] and other Finnish scholars.[4]

---

[1] The best of these translations is the German, published by M. Schiefner at Helsingfors in 1852.

[2] *Mythologia Fennica, eller forklarung ofver afgudar*, 1789.

[3] *Vorlesungen ueber die Finnische Mythologie*, 2nd edition, St. Petersburg, 1856. See also the two dissertations, *Ueber die Zauberkunst der Finnen*, and *Allgemeine Uebersicht der Goetlesen und der Magie der Finnen waehrend des Heidenthuns*, in his *Kleinere Schriften*, published by M. Schiefner.

[4] We cannot enumerate here all the works of Toppelius, Parthan, Téngström, Gottlund, Lönnrot, and Koskinen.

The ancient Finnish paganism had as a foundation the worship of the spirits of nature, which we have already seen existing in such a primitive and coarse state amongst the Siberian tribes. The fact that the two are closely connected, and that the Finnish worship of spirits was derived from the Siberian, needs no further demonstration, for it has been clearly proved by all who have written upon the subject. But on this foundation the imagination of the Finns built up a fine mythological structure with a numerous hierarchy of gods and genii differing in rank, while each preserved the mark of his origin and became the subject of various legends. Amongst the people of Suomi, first in their ancient eastern domain, where they lived under brighter skies and of which they preserved some vague remembrance, and then in the new homes in northern Europe to which they gradually receded, the same thing took place as with the Accadian nations upon the banks of the Euphrates and Tigris. The old demonological and magical superstitions of the Turanian race gave birth to a perfect religious system and a fertile mythology. Although the difference of countries and climates gave a different colouring to many personifications belonging to both mythologies, the religions of these two nations were manifestly inspired by the same genius, derived from the common fund of ideas of one and the same race. We may well be astonished at finding so great a resemblance, so many gods and spirits retaining the same character under different names, and such a perfect similarity between certain formulæ of incantations in spite of the wide distance both in time and space which separates heathen Finland, which did not embrace Christianity until the middle ages, from purely Accadian Chaldea, which was utterly annihilated fifteen centuries before the Christian era.

The Finns never had any other priests than their magicians, their worship consisted only in domestic offerings on certain fixed days, with the parents of the family as ministers, and in mysterious ceremonies to which was attributed a supernatural power, while those entrusted with the science which prescribed how these were to be performed, were called prodigies. Amongst these latter there were on the one hand the *Tietajat*, "the learned," *Asaajat*, "the intelligent," or *Laulajat*, "the incantators," magicians of a benevolent character who had recourse only to an artificial excitement in order to learn the future and enter into direct communication with the spirits, and to the sacred songs and rituals which act upon the latter and induce them to protect man; M. Rein, in treating on this subject at Helsingfors in 1844, attributes to them a sacerdotal character, to which the *Noijat* or sorcerers properly so called had no claim. These *Noijat* pretended to be in connection with both bad and good spirits, they used their knowledge and power for evil as well as for good, according as they were well or evilly disposed towards any person. To these incantations they added the use of philters and other strange practices; their chief rite was that which was called by the Scandinavians *Seidr*, which consisted in pronouncing certain words over the flame, together with ceremonies of which only the initiated possessed the secret; by means of the *Scidr* a person could assume any form he wished, or become invisible, or be transported instantaneously from one place to another.¹

The *Tietajat* and *Noijat* alike claimed the power to cure or rather expel diseases, which they considered as personal beings, by means of their formulæ, their songs, and enchanted drinks which were really pharmaceutical ingredients; they were the only physicians of the nation.² There existed between these two classes of persons the distinction which we have observed in the Accadian books between the priest of magic and the malevolent sorcerer, considered as an impious being. In the Kalevala, spells held a very important place; they were considered as a divine work, and the gods themselves had recourse to them continually during the course of their heroic life; but the sorcerers were depicted as perverse men, who abused these supreme secrets, and put them to a wrong use. The Finns attributed to the incantations and magic rites, whether used for a good or bad end, an absolute power over the whole of nature, and also the elements and spirits. The earth and the air, the visible and invisible regions, water and fire, were subject to the power of spells; they brought the dead back to torment the living; they even acted upon the most powerful gods, neutralized their influence, or exer-

---

¹ For further interesting details respecting the Greenlanders, Finns, and the Asyekoks of the Esquimaux, see Dr. Rink's *Legends and Tales of the Esquimaux, and Letters from Greenland.—Ed.*

² See Lönnrot, *Abhandlung über die magische Medicin der Finnen.*

cised a sort of constraint over them. Finnish poetry describes the effects of these sorceries under the most hyperbolical forms. Of this we will give an example:

> Lemminkäinen entered the house; it was full of men talking freely; men clothed in long garments upon the benches, singers upon the pavement, *runoias* under the wide opened doors, instruments ranged around the walls, and upon the principal seat, near the hearth, sorcerers.
>
> And Lemminkäinen began his spells.
>
> He sang, and the most accomplished singers only brought forth ridiculous sounds.
>
> Their hands became covered with stone gloves, masses of stone bent their backs, a stone hat crushed their heads, stone collars squeezed their necks.
>
> So they mocked the most famous singers, the most clever *runoias*.
>
> Lemminkäinen sang again: and the men were thrown into a sledge drawn by a discoloured cat; and the cat, in its rapid course, bore them off to the extreme limits of Pohjola,[1] as far as the vast deserts of Lapland, where the horse's footstep no longer resounds, and the mare's foal finds no pasture.
>
> Lemminkäinen sang again: and the men cast themselves into the great gulf of Lapland, into the strait which swallows up heroes, into those waves of which the sorcerers drink in order to quench their burning thirst.
>
> Lemminkäinen sang again: and the men rolled into the impetuous torrent of Rutja, into the fatal gulf which swallows up trees as a prey, into which the pines fall with their roots, in which the crested firs are engulfed.

[1] The world of darkness, the abode of wicked spirits.

> Thus Lemminkäinen mocked at young men, old men and men in the prime of life, by means of his incantations.[1]

But whatever the power of these spells may have been, which governed nature and supernatural beings, spirits and gods, there was a talisman more powerful even than they, for it controlled their power and protected its possessor; this was the "celestial wand," resembling the wand of the Median Magi. The gods themselves found their only protection from certain enchantments in this wand. Wäinämöinen, threatened by the great sorceress of Lapland, answers her:

> The Laplander cannot hurt me with his spells, for I hold in my hands the celestial wand, and he who hates me, and would bring evil upon me, does not possess it.[2]

We will now proceed to enquire into the mythology and the hierarchy of the Finnish gods and spirits.

At the head of all, we find three gods who divided the sovereignty of the universe, Ukko, Wäinämöinen, and Ilmarinen. Ukko, whose name signified "the ancient, the venerable," was "the celestial old man," *Vanha taivahinen*, "the god of heaven," *Taivahan jumala;* in his connection with the two others he had a marked superiority and appeared sometimes even as a first principle, whence his surname of *ylijumala*, "the supreme god." Wäinämöinen, "the friend of the waves," was the ruler of

---

[1] *Kalevala*, part i., 12th runa. Cf. the Aryan Mediæval legend of the Pied Piper of Hamelin in its various forms.—*Ed.*

[2] *Kalevala*, 24th runa of the first edition; the text of the second, published in 1849, seems to be inferior in this place. Cf. the Greek myth of the golden bough which alone secured the living in their visit to Hades.

the humid element and the atmosphere; Ilmarinen, "the eternal forger," the master of the terrestrial globe and of the treasures which it contains, which he alone had succeeded in working. The three highest gods of Finnish mythology, who together "fixed the gates of the air, established the celestial vault, and sown the stars in space,"[1] Ukko, Wäinämöinen, and Ilmarinen, corresponded then almost exactly to the three superior gods who presided over the three zones of the universe in the system of the Accadian magic collection, Ana, Hea, and Mul-ge. The resemblance is particularly striking between Hea and Wäinämöinen, whose adventures form the subject of the Kalevala. Like the Accadian deity, the Finnish god was not only king of the waters and the atmosphere, he was also the spirit whence all life proceeded, the master of favourable spells, the adversary and the conqueror of all personifications of evil, and the sovereign possessor of all science. He sent the celestial fire to man, and invented music and incantations. Every one needed to invoke his protection, warriors, fishermen, magicians, all felt the effects of his protection. The sweat which dropped from his body was a balm for all diseases.[2] He alone furnished efficacious assistance against the charms of the sorcerers, and an appeal to him was a last resource against the encroachments of the demons. He is also the depositary "of the Runes of science," of the

---

[1] *Kalevala*, part ii., 14th runa.

[2] Cf. the Egyptian myth of the salutary virtues of the sweat of the god Ra, as related in the Magical Papyrus in the British Museum, *Records of the Past*, Vol. VI., p. 116.—*Ed.*

"supreme words," of the "creative words," which he discovered in the ancient Wipunen,[1] words which gave life to everything that existed and which had power to bind the gods as well as the inferior beings. These words, like the mysterious name of the Accadian books were the last point in supernatural science, the spell above all spells; they had in themselves an unparalleled virtue quite independent of the agent who uttered them. When Wäinämöinen, who is continually represented in the epopee as a hero in spite of his divine nature had been wounded by the axe of Pohja, the personification of the infernal region, he sought the old man of Suomi, that he might staunch the torrent of blood flowing from the wound; and the old man replied to him:

> We have staunched greater wounds, we have bound up more terrible ones, we have triumphed over greater difficulties, we have broken through sterner obstacles by the three words of the creation, by the holy and original words. The mouths of rivers, the currents of lakes, and rushing cataracts have been conquered. We have joined isthmuses to isthmuses.[2]

Below the three superior gods, the Finns included in their worship all the objects and beings of nature, which they peopled everywhere with personal spirits, sometimes distinct from their object, sometimes blended with it. They rendered homage to mountains, stones, trees, seas, rivers, and fountains. Fire was to them a divine being, being worshipped in the

---

[1] *Kalevala*, part i., 9th and 10th runas.
[2] *Kalevala*, part i., 3rd runa.

flame on the domestic hearth; to which, at the festival of the *joulu*, the mother of the family offered a libation with this invocation:

> Rise ever higher O my flame,
> But do not become greater nor shine brighter!¹

This festival of the *joulu* took place immediately after the winter solstice, when the days began to lengthen; the rite of the worship of the flame seems then to indicate that the Finns identified the fire, honoured by them in its elementary reality, with the sun, just as we have seen the Accadian god Fire become a solar personage in the Babylonian epopee, under the form of the hero Izdubar, or Dhubar. However this may be, the Finns invoked the sun under the name of Paiwa,² to protect them from the demons of the night, and to cure certain diseases, especially any infirmity of the brain, as the Accadians invoked the god Utu, who personified the same planet. They worshipped in addition Kuu, the male god of the moon, who corresponded exactly with the Aku, Enizuna or Itu of the Accadians; and they had also many stellary divinities, like Otava the great bear, and Tahti, or the stars in the abstract.

According to the Finnish mythology, each place had its Haltia, spirit or genius, each house its familiar gnome or Tonttu, each element and natural phenomenon a spirit belonging to that class called by the Scandinavians Dvergues, every action of man, every circumstance of life, its genius or special god.

---

[1] H. J. Wille, *Beskrivelse over Siliejords Præstegield i over Tellemarken i Norge*, p. 243.

[2] We must compare it with one of the Accadian names of the god Sun, *Biselva*. Beiwa was also the solar god of the Laps.

Some particular spirits called Egres made the plants grow which the labourer cultivated, and watched over their development. Others, the Keijuiset, winged spirits, some black, and others white, some wicked, and others again beneficent, indicated their presence particularly by entering houses where a corpse was lying.

From this vast crowd of spirits scattered over the whole of creation arose the gods who were also very numerous, presiding over a class of beings, a collection of phenomena, some phase in the development of man, animals or plants, stand out characterized by a more general nature and a higher power.

Here Finnish mythology differed entirely from that of the Accadians; it assumed a peculiar idiosyncrasy, and attested the influence of the soil and climate where it attained perfection. Under the burning sun of the borders of the Euphrates and Tigris, and in the midst of the gloomy forests and icy marshes of Finland, the same principle of the personification of natural phenomena, objects, and classes of beings belonging to the animated world, necessarily produced gods of a different aspect. We need not therefore be surprised to find that all this part of Accadian mythology was represented among the Finns by mythological creations differing entirely from the popular superstition. Widely separated, both in time and space, these two nations have added, each in their own way, to the common foundation of the same conception of the supernatural world and its relation to nature, which we see plainly manifesting itself through the diverse colours and forms of the embellishments. Two trees of the same kind, planted in different soils and climates, do not grow in the same way; but the botanist can recognise, nevertheless, their specific identity and their common origin. After all, there is not more difference, nay, indeed there is even less, between the Finnish mythology and that of the Accadian magic books, than there is between the mythologies of the Greek and Indian nations, which are but different branches arising from the same root, the primitive beliefs of the Aryan race.

I have not undertaken to give in this place a treatise on Finnish mythology; I desire only to show the community of spirit and the points of resemblance it has with the ancient Accadian mythology, as already pointed out by Prof. Sayce. I shall decline to enumerate the Finnish gods created by the aspects of nature in the north, who could have no counterpart in those countries where the Accadians dwelt, divinities, for instance, presiding over the great birch and fir woods, like Hiltaainen, Tapio, the shepherd of the wild beasts of these forests, "the bearded old man of the joyous forest," to whom a very poetical invocation is addressed in the Kalevala,[1] together with all the minor divinities in their train, whose duty it was to propagate and distribute the different species of forest trees and the wild beasts which dwelt under their shadow. Popular imagination multiplied these indefinitely, and epic poetry ascribed to them, genealogies and histories resembling those of mankind. Not less

[1] 7th runa of the first edition, 14th of the second.

numerous were the gods who watched over the flocks, like Käitös, Käkri, Suvetar, and those who protected the fishermen of the Baltic, increasing the fishes and sending them into his nets, like Juolitar and his spouse Hillewo, the goddess of the otters, and so many other divinities of the second rank, presided over by Ahto, the king of the ocean and the waters.

CHAPTER XVII.

Further Analysis of Finnish Demonology.

ALL these considerations take us back to the conceptions we observed in the Accadian books, which were indeed the fundamental conceptions of all the Turanian nations and a prevailing characteristic of their religion; and this was the importance of the gods and spirits presiding over the treasures buried in the bosom of the earth, and the works of metallurgy.[1] Here was the empire of the great Ihuarinen, the divine smith, who forged upon his anvil the celestial vault; and it is in this connection that we meet with the genii of the rocks and mines, the Wuorin Väki, who worked under the guidance of Kämuläinen. However, here again, while we notice a certain analogy, there was also an important difference, which resulted from the diverse conditions of the two nations of Accad and Suomi. In the Accadian books, the most important place amongst the gods of metallurgy was given to the god of copper. In Finnish poetry, not copper but iron held the first rank, of which the special god

[1] See on this subject my *Premières Civilisations*, Vol. I., p. 114-126.

Rauta-Rekhi was surrounded by a retinue of relations corresponding with the principal operations used in working that metal: and the legend of the birth of iron is one of the most remarkable and original in the Kalevala.¹ But this application of all the metallurgic myths to iron was certainly not always to be found amongst the Finns; it resulted from the peculiar conditions of their sojourn in the country from which they were finally expelled, where iron abounded, and the lack of copper and bronze rendered it less likely that they would remember the ancient traditions which their Livonian brethren kept so jealously. The Accadians, on the contrary, although they had already worked iron, were much more abundantly supplied with bronze; it was the common metal which they used for their instruments and utensils.² At this point philology draws our attention to a fact, the exact parallel of that shown in the mythology. The word (*windu*) which designates copper in the Accadian, is identical with that signifying iron amongst the Finns (*rauta*), and the Laps (*rude*), and which passed thence to the Sclavonians and Lithuanians as the name of the same metal (*ruda*). Thus in the Aryan languages a word that originally meant "metal" in a general sense, became in Sanscrit the name of iron especially (*ayas*), and in Latin that of bronze (*æs*).

According to the Finnish creed, each man bore within him from his birth a divine spirit who was his inseparable companion for life. This spirit became

---

[1] Part i., 4th runa.
[2] G. Rawlinson, *The Five Great Monarchies*, 2nd edition, Vol. I., p. 96-99.

more closely united to its subject, in proportion as the latter tore himself away from earthly things to retire into the sanctuary of his soul. This was an important source of the magician's supernatural power; he aspired "to a transcendental ecstasy, *tulla intoon*, to a great state of excitement of the soul, *tulla haltiorhin*, in which he became like the spirit dwelling in him, and entirely identified with it. He used artificial means, intoxicating drugs for instance, in order to attain to this state of excitement, for it was only then that he succeeded, so to speak, in deifying himself, and received the homage of the genii and spirits of nature.[1] This doctrine, which M. Rein has explained very clearly, and which held a chief place in the Finnish religious ideas, as also in their magic, is just that of the special god attached to each man and dwelling in his body, which prevailed also in the Accadian magic books. This furnishes an affinity of conceptions and beliefs which is of great importance, since it is not one of those natural ideas which arise independently amongst widely differing nations. To find elsewhere a similar notion, we must go to Persia for the doctrine of the Fravaschis, which we have already decided that the Iranians obtained through the Medes, from Accadian sources. Every demonological religion, as soon as it becomes elevated and purified, leads to dualism: it lays down the doctrine that spirits are spread over all parts of nature, and to explain the spectacle of good by the side of evil, decay and destruction with regeneration

---

[1] Cf. the cultus of the Pythian Apollo, in the intoxication of the priestess at Delphos.—*Ed.*

and life, which nature constantly affords, it assumes the existence of two opposing armies of good and evil spirits. This, as we have seen, was the case with the Accadians, and it was the same also among the Finns. They likewise recognized two worlds at enmity with each other; that of the gods together with the propitious spirits, and that of the demons, respectively the kingdom of light and that of darkness, the region of good and that of evil. But they placed these two worlds upon the earth, instead of adopting the Accadian view, by which the demons were supposed to issue from a subterraneous abyss; one was the blessed region of the Kalevala, situated under the direct and beneficent influence of the sun's rays, the other the Pohjolo, "which devours men and swallows up heroes," where the demons dwelt, and where the dead found their home, Tuonela, governed by the severe Tuoni. The Finns imagined the region of Pohjola to be situated amongst the uninhabitable solitudes of the poles, Lapland on one side serving it as a boundary. There the most wicked sorcerers loved to dwell, and there the demons laid in ambush to watch men. The icy plains of Lapland were to the Finns what the burning sands of Arabia were to the Accadians, an accursed country and a resort of foul spirits.

The demons who were born in the darkness of Pohjola were quite as numerous as the good spirits; they were scattered over the whole universe, and brought trouble and destruction everywhere. They misled hunters, caused diseases, disturbed the silence of the night, increased the number of wolves and foxes; and in short, all the sufferings of the sad and desolate northern winter were attributable to their influence.

Finnish mythology invented unlimited classes of wicked spirits and demons for all kinds of misfortunes and trouble. In epic poetry we find that a more human form is given to the influences dispersed throughout the world, where they opposed and strove to destroy the work of the gods and propitious genii. In this case, the wicked principle was personified by the giant Hiisi, who had a wife and children, horses, dogs, cats, and servants, all hideous and wicked like himself; in one word, the complete household of the chief of a tribe. The bad influence of Hiisi extended everywhere: Hiisi-Hejmoläinen, his servant, reigned over the mountains; Wesi-Hiisi, another of his servants, over the waters; Hiiden-Lintu, his bird, carried evil into the air; Hiidën-Ruuna, his horse, traversed the plains and deserts; Hiidën-Kissa, his cat, spread terror around her, and forced thieves to avow their misdeeds, thus occasionally turning her wicked action to a good purpose; the Hiidën Väiki, analogous to the Furies, were his messengers. Hiisi, scouring the plains on his horse, while his bird preceded him in the air, seems to have been originally a personification of the icy and fatal north wind. The Finns considered him as one of the most terrible demons, just as the Accadians feared the personification of the west wind, which produced by its excessive heat in their country quite as fatal effects.

As we have already stated, the sorcerers held communication with these demons as frequently as, or even more frequently than, they did with the good spirits; and to this diabolical intercourse they owed a great deal of their power. The priests of magic brought about this communication entirely by means of a spiritual frenzy and sacred words. As to the demons, they exorcised them by the power of their formulæ and by the help of the spiritual beings of the good principle; many of their incantations were destined thus to repulse the wicked demons, to break diabolical spells, and to invoke in this work the aid of the pure spirits. But Finnish magic was chiefly medical, being used to cure diseases and wounds: this view of its development has been admirably explained by Lönnrot in a special treatise.[1]

Here we meet again the fundamental notion, which is so characteristic of certain races of mankind, that every disease was itself a personal being, or a demon, and that its invasion constituted an actual possession of the diseased person.

According to the Finns diseases were the daughters of Louhiatar, the old lady of Pohjola, just as the Accadians considered them to have issued from Ninkigal, the lady of the gloomy abyss and of the dead. They regarded pleurisy, gout, colic, consumption, leprosy, and the plague, as so many distinct personages. These had their residence at Kipümäki, the hill of pains, situated on an island in the river of Tuonela, the river of the country of the dead, the analogue of the river Dahilla of the Accadian tablets.

---

[1] *Abhandlung uber die magische Medicin der Finnen.* See also for an illustration of the Egyptian demono-medical system which had a like basis, "Le Grand Papyrus Ebers" in *L'Egyptologie*, par M. F. Chabas, and also the original text itself, *Papyrus Ebers*, Leipzig, fol., 1876.—*Ed.*

The hill of Kipümäki recalls also by its conception the "mountain of the West," of the Accadian books, whence the principal demons issued to spread over the surface of the earth. This hill of Kipümäki was high: on its summit was a great flat stone, surrounded by many other large stones. In the middle one were nine holes, in which the diseases were buried with the help of conjurations. We read in one of our Accadian incantations:[1]

> May the disease be swallowed up into the earth like passing waters.

Kivutar, or Kipu-tytö, daughter of Tuoni, went to collect the diseases in a brazen vessel, and had them cooked upon a magic hearth.

The sorcerer or priest of magic recognized the disease from which a man was suffering by the special diagnostic faculty that the state of divine ecstasy, whether natural or artificial developed. When he had once decided what the disease was, he set about exorcising the demon, using enchanted drinks, talismans, magic knots, incantations, and occasionally, as the highest means to which he could have recourse, if he had succeeded in discovering the secret, the all-powerful words with which Wäinämöinen was entrusted.

The Finnish incantations for exorcising the demons of diseases were composed in exactly the same spirit, and founded upon the same data, as the Accadian incantations destined for the like purpose. They were formulæ belonging to the same family, and they often showed a remarkable similarity of language;

[1] *W. A. I.* IV., 3, col. 2.

the Egyptian incantations, on the contrary, having been composed by people with very different ideas about the supernatural world, assumed quite another form.

This is an incantation from one of the songs of the *Kalevala:*

> O malady, disappear into the heavens; pain, rise up to the clouds;[1] inflamed vapour, fly into the air, in order that the wind may take thee away, that the tempest may chase thee to distant regions, where neither sun nor moon give their light, where the warm wind does not inflame the flesh.
>
> O pain, mount upon the winged steed of stone, and fly to the mountains covered with iron. For he is too robust to be devoured by disease, to be consumed by pains.
>
> Go, O diseases, to where the virgin of pains has her hearth, where the daughter of Wäinämöinen cooks pains, go to the hill of pains.
>
> There are the white dogs, who formerly howled in torments, who groaned in their sufferings.

This other incantation against the plague was discovered by Ganander:

> O scourge, depart; plague, take thy flight, far from the bare flesh.
>
> I will give thee a horse, with which to escape, whose shoes shall not slide on ice, nor whose feet slip on the rocks.
>
> Go where I send thee. Take for thy journey the infernal steed, the stallion of the mountain. Flee to the mountains of Turja, to the rock of iron. Go across the sandy plains of the infernal regions, and precipitate thyself into the eternal abyss, whence thou wilt

---

[1] "May the disease of his head be carried away into the heavens like a violent wind," says an Accadian incantation (*W. A. I.* IV., 3, col. 2.) And another, "May the diseases of the head, the infirmities fly away into the sky like grasshoppers, may they dart into vast space like birds."

never return. Go where I send thee, into the thick forest of Lapland, into the dark regions of Pohja.

The Accadian formulæ banished the demons which they had expelled from a man's body to the sandy desert; the Finnish *runa* sends the plague away to Lapland.[1] Such is the different form we should expect the same idea to take with two nations placed in such opposite geographical conditions, although originally from the same stock.

When wounds alone were to be cured, there were no demons to exorcise. They used special incantations, words of conjuration (*manous*), which they pronounced over the place to stop the flow of blood. The ninth *runa* of the Kalevala furnishes us with a good example in the recital of the cure of Wäinämöinen's wound:

> Listen, O blood, instead of flowing, instead of pouring forth thy warm stream. Stop, O blood, like a wall; stop like a hedge; stop like a reef in the sea; like a stiff *carex*[2] in the moss, like a boulder in the field, like the pine in the wood.

When the flow of blood was staunched, the incantation called upon certain divinities, who could repair the damage which the weapon had done to the body; thus Helka closed up the wound:

> Come here, come, Helka, beautiful woman, close with turf, stop the gaping wound with moss; hide it with little stones, in order that the lake may not overflow, that the red blood may not inundate the earth.

---

[1] Cf. the Jewish ceremony of expelling the goat of Azazel into the desert.—*Ed.*

[2] The common sedge, *Carex palustris* (?) of which there are about thirty English species.

The goddess Suonetar healed and renewed the flesh:

> She is beautiful, the goddess of veins, Suonetar, the beneficent goddess! She knits the veins wonderfully with her beautiful spindle, her metal distaff, her iron wheel.
>
> Come to me, I invoke thy help; come to me, I call thee. Bring in thy bosom a bundle of flesh, a ball of veins to tie the extremity of the veins.[1]

These are called the *runas* of the *synty*, or of regeneration or recovery.[2] But in order to complete and consolidate the work of the secondary divinities, the intervention of the ancient Ukko was needed, he being the highest personification of the divine power:

> O glorious god, prepare thy chariot, put the horses to, mount to thy splendid seat, and march across bones, members, wounded flesh, severed veins. Cause silver to flow into the empty space of the bones, cause gold to flow into the wounds in the veins.
>
> Where the flesh has been torn, may new flesh be produced; where bones have been broken, may new bones be formed; may the severed veins be united; everywhere that a wound has been made, may health return complete and beautiful.

The cure of a wound needing the formation of new flesh was considered a regular act of creation, and therefore the help of the creative power himself was necessary.

---

[1] *Kalevala*, 15th runa.

[2] They extended also the name *synty* to the supernatural faculty by which the curer recognized the disease and discerned the remedy.

CHAPTER XVIII.

The Accadian People and their Language.

THE comparisons which we drew in the foregoing chapter have obliged us to recognize a close connection between Chaldean magic and that of the Altaic or Turanian nations, and particularly of the Finns. The religious ideas from which it sprang constituted a perfect and united system of mythology, which was only a natural and logical development of that form of naturalism peculiar to all those nations, and of the worship of the spirits of nature and the elements. It presented striking analogies with the ancient ante-Iranian element on the one hand, which became united with the Mazdean data in Median Magism, and on the other with Finnish mythology, despite the peculiar colour assumed by the latter as the result of its development in the most northern latitudes of Europe.

Having arrived at this point, we cannot fail to attach great importance to the fact that in Chaldea and the countries which come under its rule, like

Assyria, there was a special magic language, and that that is the language which is now named by both French and English scholars the Accadian tongue.[1] The sacred books of the magicians, which Assurbanipal had copied again in the seventh century, for the instruction of his priests, were written in the Accadian, only a Semitic Assyrian version had been added to them at a very early epoch, in order to render the incantations intelligible to those who had to recite them, but the Accadian was clearly the only properly liturgical text. We have a proof of it in the fact that some lines which are repeated or are very easy to understand, have no translation attached to them. Thus at the present day the Coptic priests always have an Arabic version accompanying their missals, so that they may understand the words of the ritual while they recite them in the Coptic tongue. The magic formulæ engraved upon the amulets of hard stone, even upon the amulets found in Assyria, evidently of Assyrian work, and belonging to the last epoch of the empire of Nineveh, are at least most of them in the Accadian language; and while more than a hundred have their legends in Accadian, I have as yet only met with three bearing Assyrian inscriptions in all the various European collections. So also in the fragments of the great magic collection copied by the scribes of Assurbanipal, there are many incantations and hymns of which the primitive Accadian text was, no doubt, lost at an early period, since only an Assyrian version exists at the present time, bearing marks

---

[1] There is positive proof that the Assyrians themselves entitled the ante-Semitic idiom of Chaldea "the Accadian language," and we have no real reason for differing from them.

however of great antiquity. Still there are not more than ten in this condition amongst many hundred formulæ in the Accadian.

Chaldea possessed, then, a special magic language which preserved this character for the Assyrian people also, and that language is the Accadian. It was regarded as having a particular power over the world of spirits, both good and evil. It seems that the idea of supernatural virtue inherent in the words of this language, increased in proportion as it ceased to be used as a spoken idiom, becoming for the priests a dead language exclusively applied to religious uses, while to the people it was an unintelligible gibberish. It was the result of the natural tendency in man to attribute a mysterious power to mysterious words, the same tendency which led the Egyptians to use names which were incomprehensible to the vulgar in their magic formulæ, and even add names and words belonging to no language at all, and composed at will for theurgic operations.

Now this bond of union between the magic rites and a definitive language is an important point in determining the origin of Chaldean magic; for since we have established the relationship of the latter with the sacred sorcery of the Turanian nations, the Accadian, its language is thus a dialect of the great Ural-Altaic family. Everything concurs, therefore, to refer us to the same race of mankind, for the origin, truly at a very remote period, of the demonological and magic superstitions adopted on the banks of the Euphrates and Tigris.

It does not, however, suffice to affirm that the Accadian language had a Turanian character; we must give the reader proofs of it. The question of the origin of Chaldean magic leads us to a series of ethnographical linguistic problems, which are henceforth of the greatest importance in the history of early antiquity. They concern the elements which contributed to civilize Babylon, the existence of a primitive Turanian civilization, extending over the greater part of interior Asia, before the dispersion of the Semites and Aryas. If we would not limit ourselves to assertions which are not sufficiently proved, we must examine into these problems somewhat, and indicate at least the principal facts which afford us the means of their solution.

Then, after having established that a close and constant connection existed in Chaldea between magic and the Accadian language, I must say a few words about this language and the ground we have for attributing it to the Turanian class. Like Dr. Hincks, Sir Henry Rawlinson, Dr. Oppert, M. Grivel, and Prof. Sayce, I have made a special study of the Accadian dialect, and have brought out also an elementary grammar of the language;[1] it is a purely

---

[1] In my *Etudes Accadiennes*, Vol. I., parts 1-3. I have treated further of this subject with numerous additions and references, in another volume *La langue primitive de la Chaldée et les idiomes Touraniens* (Paris 1875), which has been received in a most flattering manner by the philological public of England and Germany. I may be excused for passing over the polemics which were the origin of this last work. I have only to do here with what partakes of a really scientific character, and do not therefore need to speak of the fantastical notions of M. Joseph Halevy, which will ever remain a strange monument of ignorance and false assertions. This scholar has presumed to speak of the Accadian tongue, without a full knowledge of it, and all that he says is inexact. He has been contradicted by the master hand of M. Eberhard Schrader in *Zeitschrift der Deutsch. Morgenl. Gesellschaft*, Vol. XXIX.

philological work of a difficult nature, which is only addressed to a few special readers. With great pleasure, therefore, I seize the opportunity here afforded me of summing up, for the benefit of my readers in general, the conclusions which I arrived at by means of this special study, which was necessarily very incomplete; but I think some of the data are already firmly established, and can stand the proof of being examined by the light of a direct examination and a philological analysis of the texts. The reader must excuse my devoting this chapter exclusively to the language. Although such a theme may seem rather dry to those who do not go into it deeply, the question is important enough to make one forget that it is uninteresting for a few pages. The fact of the presence of a Turanian nation in early Chaldea once proved, it becomes quite a large branch of the human race, to which a place must be henceforth assigned in the history of civilization, although no notice has been taken of it up to the present time.

CHAPTER XIX.

The Accadian Language.

THERE are four fundamental principles, which are now universally acknowledged by all Assyriologists to be incontestable and clearly proved.

1st. The Accadian, or Sumerian language as some would call it, exists, and no one can deny it without ignoring altogether the teaching of science.

2nd. It is the dialect of the inventors of the Cuneiform Anarian writing, a people who predominated about the lower basins of the Euphrates and Tigris, before this tract was inhabited by a nation speaking the Semitic language.

3rd. It is an agglutinative language, the genius and grammar of which are totally different from the Semitic dialects.

4th. It is closely related to the agglutinative languages of anti-Aryan Media, and Susiana, which have also become intelligible to us by means of inscriptions.

There is a fifth point, upon which the verdict of scholars is not universally agreed, and the proofs of which are not quite so perfect, namely the relation of this dialect to the Turanian or Altaic languages.

Although all the Assyriologists of the English school, headed by their illustrious chief, Sir Henry Rawlinson, MM. Oppert, and Karl Eneberg agree with me in thinking this connection firmly established, yet there are others, such as M. Schrader, Friedrich Delitzsch, and Gelzer, who, while they do not deny it in theory, show themselves more reserved, and even rather undecided in expressing their opinion.

We cannot be surprised at meeting with a certain degree of hesitation upon this subject. On the one hand, our acquaintance with the Accadian is as yet very imperfect; we have still much to do before completely mastering the language and especially its vocabulary. On the other hand, the Altaic dialects have not until now entered into the category of languages ordinarily studied by philologists, so they are only known to a special few; the works of the great linguistic school, founded by Castren and Schott, and brilliantly represented at the present day by such men as Schiefner, Ahlqvist, O. Donner, Yryö Koskinen, Paul Hunfalvy, and Budenz, remain for the most part unread and unstudied. Lastly, it seems rather singular, nay even imprudent and unscientific, to attempt a comparison of a language which has ceased to be spoken some three thousand years at least, with dialects in use at the present day, the most of which do not possess one single written record of an ancient date, while those which can produce a few of less recent origin, as Finnish, Magyar,

Turkish, and Mongolic, cannot trace them back further than the Middle Ages. In order to understand the feasibility of such an effort, we must remember that the object of comparative philology is to deal with a family of languages, the most striking feature of which is a singular relative immobility as compared with others, and this peculiarity preserves intact even to our days the remains of a state of language much more primitive than that which is revealed by the ancient monuments of the Aryan or Semitic languages. From those few documents of the Middle Ages which this family of languages offers for our perusal, we gather that they have undergone no visible change during the last five or six centuries.

There is consequently no ground to justify an assertion that our supposition is inadmissible, and no fundamental and valid objection to be opposed *à priori* to an enquiry after a relationship which may also be proved between the Accadian and Altaic languages of the present day. Although this is a very delicate question still it is one from which we hope for favourable results. Having established this, I shall indicate briefly the principal facts which can be proved with relation to the affinities and grammatical differences between the Accadian and the Altaic or Turanian languages, and I think the conviction of this correspondence will justify the theory in which I become daily more and more confirmed by my own studies.

To begin with the subject of the evident affinities.

1st. *The almost universal thematic harmony of the vowels, to which there are but few exceptions.*

The vocal harmony in the Accadian is exclusively thematic. It is threefold; that is to say, it admits of three classes of vowels.

Strong: *â, a, û.*
Neuter: *î, i, u.*
Weak: *e.*

The same root may contain both strong and neuter vowels, or neuter and weak vowels, but not strong vowels with the weak; the great majority of the disyllabic or trisyllabic roots show, however, a repetition of the same vowel in all the syllables. The diphthongs *au, ia,* and *ua* harmonize with the strong vowels, the diphthong *ie* would seem to have been regarded as neuter, and so to be used indifferently with both strong and weak. There are fewer exceptions to these laws of harmony in the Accadian than in most of the Altaic languages.

On the other hand, in the Accadian, as in Ostiac, the vowels of the suffixes of derivation are not made to agree with those of the root. It would seem, too, that there is not necessarily an agreement between the vowels of the two parts of a compound word, although we sometimes see this harmony established; it is so at the present time in the Magyar dialect. This point, however, is one of the most difficult to explain clearly, on account of the great number of Accadian roots that are expressed in writing by ideographic signs. In that case, indeed, the ideograph remains constant, whatever phonic modifications the root may have undergone in the spoken idiom; the writing does not allow of these modifications, where they otherwise exist.

Lastly, although the Accadian possesses incontestably a thematic harmony, we find no trace of a terminational concordance, and this is also the case with some of the Altaic dialects.

2nd. *The formation of the greater number of derivatives by means of suffixes.*

The principal and best known of these suffixes are: -*Ga*, which indicates dependence. It is used to form certain substantives like *guga*, "title, name," from *gu*, "to speak, to say;" *kubabbarga*, "a fine," from *kubabbar*, "silver." It is chiefly employed in the formation of adjectives, as *kalaga*, "powerful," from *kala*, "to be powerful;" *ziga*, "living," from *zi*, "to live;" *sega*, "happy," from *se*, "happiness."

-*Ik*, which is employed in forming the names of agents and adjectives with an active signification, as χ*ulik*, "malevolent," from χ*ul*, "wicked;" *nirik*, "prince," from *nir*, "to govern;" *uddaik*, "preeminent," from *uddu*, "to go out, to rise."

-*Da*, which serves to individualise and specialise: for instance, in *muda*, "renowned," from *mu*, "name;" *tarda*, "judge," from *tar*, "to judge;" *ada*, "watercourse, river," from *a*, "water;" χ*irda*, inclosure," from χ*ir*, "to bind."

-*Ma*, which expresses an idea of locality, and being joined to the name of a town characterises the surrounding district of which it is the capital.

-*A*, which forms ethnical words, as *Mulgekia*, "man of Mulgeki," the town called in the Assyrian *Nipur*, *Urunua*, "man of Ur."

3rd. *The same system of declension by means of casual suffixes which are joined to the root without effecting any change in it, and the identity of the more important of these suffixes.*

We must distinguish three series of declensions amongst the fourteen which have been proved to exist in the Accadian, and of which thirteen are marked by the addition of suffixes, the nominative showing the word in its original purity. The first series consists of the primitive suffixes which belong to the most ancient type of declension in the Altaic languages, and are found in other languages of the various branches of this family; in the Accadian itself they are mere attributive roots. These suffixes are:—*na*, which designates the genitive and expresses the idea of instrumentality; the formation of the genitive by means of the suffix *-na, -niu- -in, -ni*, is common to all the Turanian or Altaic languages without exception, in the Ugro-Finnic, the Samoyedic, the Turco-Tartaric, the Mongolic, the Tungusic, and the Corea-Japanese groups. *-ta*, which expresses the idea of an internal or external locative, that is to say, both the inessive "into" and the elative or ablative "from, from within;" the locative is indicated by *-tt* in Magyar, *-dann, -tann* in some of the Samoyedic dialects, *-da* in Turkish, *-da* in Buriatic, and *-dur* in Mongolic, *-de* in Mantchoo; the abessive by *-ta* and *-tta* in the various Ugro-Finnic dialects; the ablative by *-dan* in Turkish, *-tan* in Yakut; lastly, we must point out the connection between the sign of the dative in the Samoyedic dialects, *-d* and *-t*, and the same sign which marks the locative and the dative in the Mongolic and Tungusic languages. *-ku*, is the sign of the illative; our minds naturally turn to the Turkish datives in -*ke*, -*ga*, and -*ge*, and possibly to the Samoyedic locatives in -*kan*, -*gan*.

-*as*, -*es* indicates the adverbial case, by means of which adverbs are formed from substantives; the same case is shown in Tcheremissian by -*s*, and in the language of the Lapps by -*s*; then, too, some verbal adverbs are formed in Votiac by -*sa*, and in Mordvinian by -*z*. Lastly, we may mention, in connection with it, the inessive in -*ssa* and -*s* in the Ugro-Finnic dialects.

-*la* is the suffix of the adessive, and this case is formed by -*lla* and -*l* in all the Ugro-Finnic languages.

-*li* which shows an action done by a person and seems sometimes to have a comitative signification; in Yakut we find a comitative in -*lin* and an adverbial case in -*li*; in Turkish the idea of the comitative is expressed by the postposition *ilé*, which is sometimes contracted into *le* and used as a suffix.

-*bi*, -*b*, is the sign of the absolute case where the use of the article is omitted; it is really a pronoun in the third person affixed to the word. We must place with it the accusatives in -*b*, -*v* of the dialect spoken in Lapland, in -*m* in Tcheremissian and the Samoyedic dialects (which also have it sometimes in -*p*), in -*ben* in Mongolic, in -*be* in Mantchoo. Castren recognized in these latter, "*ein Ueberrest eines Pronomens der dritten Person;*" this is his own expression. The Altaistic philologists agree in admitting that the Turanian languages had originally but one accusative of construction and position, as we find in the Accadian, and that when this case was omitted, its place was supplied by a form possessing in its primitive use a determinative character.[1]

Besides these casual suffixes of the first formation, there is in the Accadian a second series formed by taking attributive roots from the vocabulary of the language. Thus:

The sign of the dative, *-ra, -r*, is the root *ra*, "to bear towards."

The sign of the suppressive, *-ge*, "that which is below;" to express the superior position of the subject with relation to the object, the inferior position of the object is expressed: "upon the mountain" is χarsak-ge, "the mountain beneath."

The sign of the possessive, *-lal*, is the root *lal*, "to take."

The sign of the equative, *-tum*, is the root *tum*, "to produce, to reproduce.

The sign of the oppositive, *-gab*, is the root *gab*, "before, that which is in front."

This grammatical process is essentially Turanian, and is entirely foreign to the other families of languages. We find numerous instances of it in the Magyar. The word *bel*, "interior," is used as the illative suffix (formerly *-bele*, now *-ba, -be*); the verbal root *raj*, "it is above," as that of the superessive (at present *-ra, -re*); *vel*, "companion," becomes the sign of the comitative (*-val, -vel*); *kep*, "image," that of the equative (*-kép*); and *kor*, "age, time," that of the temporal (*-kor*).

Lastly, some of the casual suffixes of the Accadian are formed by the combination of two roots, which

[1] See Lucien Adam, *Revue de Linguistique*, Vol. IV., p. 259.

are both transformed into signs of cases; such are those of the sublative, *-gelal,* and the delative, *-lalge,* consisting of the same elements *ge* and *lal,* placed in a different order. Combinations of this kind, for forming secondary suffixes, are also a Turanian peculiarity; each group of the family furnishes examples of it, which have been long noticed by grammarians.

4th. *The analogous formation of the plural and the dual.*

The Accadian, like Mantchoo and Japanese, possesses some rare specimens of the most ancient mode of forming the plural in the Turanian languages, by doubling the root; for instance, *ana ana,* "the gods," *kur kur,* "the countries, as in Mantchoo, *jalan jalan,* "the countries," and the Japanese *fito-bito,* "men," in the singular *fito.* But its most common plurals are obtained by means of the suffixes *-mes* and *-ene.* The first becomes *-es* in the formation of verbal plurals; we must therefore compare with it suffixes of the same number in Zyriainian *-jas,* and in Votiac *-jos,* the ancient Turkish plural in *-z,* which is only to be seen in *biz,* "we," and *siz,* "you;" lastly, the Buriatic plurals in *-s.* Max Müller thinks the primitive form of the Ugro-Finnic plural was *-äs*; but this is still a point of discussion amongst Altaic philologists, we will not therefore pursue this subject, as we wish to deal only with incontestable facts.

It is still more important to notice that the two Accadian suffixes of the plural are attributive roots meaning "much, union," and that the primitive formation of Altaic plurals by roots of this kind transformed into suffixes really takes place in Mantchoo. In the Accadian, *mes* and *ene* may be employed both as suffixes and as distinct words, following the inflected noun of which they denote the plurality; just as in Mantchoo we find some plurals formed by a suffix *-sa*, and other cases in which the same sign under the form of *sei* is a separate word, which preserves a distinct existence.

The dual number is only found in a few of the Altaic languages; in the language of the Lapps it is indicated by the sign *-g*, in Ostiac by *-kan, -gan*, in the Samoyedic dialects by *-ha, -g, -k*. Boller recognizes in these suffixes a remains of the word *kat*, meaning "two;" the Accadian confirms this opinion, for it forms its dual (which is only used for things which are naturally in pairs, like the duplicate members of the body) by affixing to the substantive *kas*, "two:" *si-kas*, "the two eyes," *pi-kas*, "the two ears."

5th. *The absence of any distinction between the masculine and feminine genders.*

This is one of the principal facts of the grammar; constituting one of the most striking features of the Altaic as compared with the Aryan and Semitic languages. It is very marked in the Accadian.

6th. *In a good many words the root is only to be found in a perfect state in the oblique cases, or in the verbal moods which cause it to be followed by a suffix; this suffix has the effect of preserving the root by keeping the final part of it, which either becomes contracted or is lost in the absolute and isolated form, in the nominative of the nouns for instance.*

Thus χ*a*, "fish," becomes in the illative χ*anaku*,

whence we conclude that the real root is χ*ana*, shortened in the absolute form. The verb "to give" takes in the third person singular of the preterite the form *insî*, and in the third person plural *insimus*; "to do good," in the third person singular *in*χ*i*, and in the third person plural *in*χ*iges*; "to commemorate, pronounce, conjure," in the third person singular *inpâ*, and in the third person plural *inpânes*. The roots are not therefore *sî*, χ*i*, *pâ*, but *sîmu*, *tîla*, *pâni*; without the suffix there is an ellipsis of the last syllable. This is very often the case with the words in which the second syllable of the root contains a guttural, a liquid, an *n* or an *m*. This characteristic is also decidedly Turanian, and is peculiar to this linguistic family; the Altaistic philologists pointed it out long ago in the Ugro-Finnic dialects.

7th. *The identity of the pronouns.*

First person: Accadian, *mu*; Proto-Medic, *mi* (genitive); Finnic, *mä*; Esthonian, *ma*; the language of the Lapps, *mon*; Tcheremissian, *min*; Mordvinian, *mon*; Zyriainian, *me*; Ostiac, *ma*; Magyar, *n*; Samoyedic, *man*; Yakut, *min*; Turkish, *ben*; Mongolic, *bi* (gen. *mini*); Mantchoo, *bi* (gen. *mini*); Ancient Japanese, *wa*.

Second person: Accadian, *zu*; Finnic, *sä*; Esthonian, *sa*; the language of the Lapps, *ton*; Tcheremissian, *tin*; Mordvinian, *ton*; Zyriainian, *te*; Magyar, *te*; Samoyedic, *tan*; Turkish, *sen*; Mongolic, *si*; Mantchoo, *si*.

Third person: Accadian, *na*, *ni*; Finnic, *ne* (plural); Esthonian, *need* (plural); Zyriainian, *nja* (plural); Magyar, *ön* ("soi"); Yakut, *kini* (accus.

onu); Turkish, *ol* (gen. *onun*); Buriatic, *ene;* Tungusic, *nun;* Mantchoo, *i,* (genitive *ini*).

The plural pronoun of the first person is *me* in the Accadian. The same change of vowel in the singular pronoun marks the Ugro-Finnic, Samoyedic, and Tungusic dialects.

Finnic, *me;* Esthonian, *meie;* language of the Lapps, *mi;* Tcheremissian, *mä;* Mordvinian, *min;* Zyriainian, *mi;* Ostiac, *men;* Magyar, *mi;* Samoyedic, *mé, mi;* Mantchoo, *be.*

The two other persons of the plural pronoun in the Accadian are formed by a particular process: the third person, *nene,* by the reduplication of the singular *ni;* the second, *zunene,* by the addition of this pronoun *nene* to the singular *zu, zu* + *nene,* "thou + they, you." They cannot, therefore, be subject to the same comparisons. However, it is curious to notice that the Tcheremissian dialect, which has not kept the pronoun in *n* for the third person singular, has in the plural a pronoun *nina,* like that of the Accadian *nene,* which must have been formed in the same way by a reduplication of the typical pronoun in *n.*

The Accadian has one more parallel series of singular pronouns.

First person, *du;* it appears again in a corrupted form in the possessive suffix -*ta* of the Proto-Medic.

Second person, *mun;* compare the Proto-Medic *ni,* the Ostiac *nen,* the Yakut *än,* and the verbal terminations in -*n,* of the second person in the Samoyedic dialects.

Third person, *bi;* which is also used as an enclitic

demonstrative; this is the verbal pronoun -*pi* in Finnic, -*b* in Esthonian, -*be* in Tcheremissian, the demonstrative *by* in Yakut, and *bu* in Turkish; lastly, the possessive suffix -*ba* in the Samoyedic dialect of the Yenessee.

8th. *The same principle for the construction of one of the conjugations of the verb, the postpositive.*

The Accadian possesses three systems of conjugation: prepositive, postpositive, and periphrastic. The last takes the place of the passive with the verb *men*, "to be," as its auxiliary; it is like the periphrastic conjugation of the Altaic languages; but this point of grammar is not peculiar enough to furnish a precise element of classification. I shall speak later of the prepositive conjugation, which is the most common in the texts, and constitutes perhaps one of the most striking characteristics of the Accadian language. As to the postpositive conjugation, there we get such forms as *enimu*, "I am master," literally, "to be master + I," from *eni; garranin*, "he has had made," literally, "to have made + he," from *gar;* it may be described, therefore, as the root + the termination of tense, and if necessary + the personal suffix; and in the derived forms the root + the formative of voice + the termination of tense, and if necessary + the personal suffix. This is precisely the mechanism of the Ugro-Finnic and Turco-Tartaric verb. Only in the Accadian, being an ancient language, the pronominal suffixes are not used as they are in the modern languages; they remain intact, and are not reduced to mere grammatical terminations.

9th. *The use of the same particle in forming the causative of verbs.*

This particle, added before or after the root according to the conjugation, is *tan* or *dan* in the Accadian, and corresponds exactly with the suffixes of derivation to which the same meaning is attached in the Ugro-Finnic verbal formations *ta*, and the Turco-Tartaric *tar* or *dar*.

10th. *The existence of a negative conjugation unknown to any other family of languages.*

This is one of the most important and decisive points in the classification of the Accadian. The negative verb may be formed by means of one or other of the two particles *nu* and *me*, which are prefixed also to substantives or adjectives in *-ga*, in order to make compounds of a negative or caritive signification. The first is certainly identical with the two negations *ani* or *inne* of the Proto-Medic, the *nem* of Magyar, the *ent* in Ostiac, *it* (a contraction of *int*) of certain moods in the Tcheremissian conjugation of the negative verb. The second is none other than the incorporated verbal negation *me* of the languages of the Turco-Tartaric group.

11th. *The use of verbal forms instead of conjunctions.*

The Accadian verb possesses a conjunctive mood, which it uses instead of placing the copulative after a verb; it also substitutes one of its indicatives for a conjunction, to express the idea of " in order that."

12th. *The use of postpositions where the Aryan and Semitic languages employ prepositions.*

There is no need to enter into a detailed explanation of this point, the simple statement of the fact suffices; but it is to be remembered as another important feature.

13th. *The same process in the formation of adverbs taken from substantives and verbs; the existence of an adverbial or essive case in the declension.*

CHAPTER XX.

Differentiation of the Accadian and its allied Languages.

I SHALL now proceed to consider the differences, more or less striking and decisive, which are observable between the grammar of the Accadian language and the customary mechanism of the Altaic dialects.

1st. *The existence of a small number of prefixes of derivation.*

We have sufficient proofs of two of these prefixes which were both originally attributive roots; *id*, giving an idea of locality, and *ki*, used to form the name of the agent. This process of derivation is unknown in the Altaic languages. But the Proto-Medic, belonging to a linguistic family of which the origin has never been questioned, has also prefixes of derivation: the augmentative *far*, and the localizative *it*. The latter is manifestly identical with the Accadian prefix *id-*, which has the same meaning. This strange fact, this derogation from the ordinary rules, is therefore common to the two contemporary languages spoken by the neighbouring lands of Chaldea and ante-Aryan Media. There are also some prefixes in modern Magyar, one of which is used to form the superlatives of adjectives, the others in the formation of derived verbs. Their introduction is explained to be due to foreign influence. For my part, I should have no objection to make, if any one suggested the same explanation of the origin of the rare prefixes of the Accadian and Proto-Medic.

We can, however, compare with this fact one other, which may be sometimes found in the Accadian, touching the presence of a kind of vocalic augment, which is prefixed to the root in derivatives. They form thus *usar*, "shore," from a root *sar*; *enim*, "act of raising," from a root *nim*; *ugude*, "act of proclaiming," from *gude*, "to proclaim," which was itself a compound. This peculiarity seems at first sight quite anti-Turanian; but there are evident traces of it to be found in the Ugric dialects. From a root *tar*, *ter*, Vogul has *ätär*, "clear, brilliant," and Ostiac *eder*, *eter* with the same meaning, whilst in Magyar we find *därü*; in another case Magyar has *élég*, "enough," (*lég-* being the superlative prefix); the form in Finnic is *lika*; in Esthonian, *lég*; in the dialect of the Lapps, *like*, "too much: again, the word "dog" is in Finnic, *penu*; in Zyriainian, *pon*; in Votiac, *punu*; in Mordvinian, *pinä*: but in Vogul it becomes *emp*; in Ostiac, *amp*; in Magyar, *eb*: these facts prove that there is in these dialects a true vocal augment analogous to that of the Accadian.

2nd. *The position of the adjective or genitive generally after the word which it qualifies.*

This rule is almost invariable, but there are exceptional cases of an inverse position to be found occasionally in the texts. Besides, we may be sure that the custom of placing the adjective or the genitive before the word which it qualifies, according to the customary rule of the Altaic languages, was much more common at the early period when the Cuneiform writing was first invented, than it afterwards became; at the same time, it may even have been the regular rule. Indeed, the syllabaries and commentaries of the lexicographical tablets display a good many complete ideographic groups formed out of compounds of genitive and subject, or adjective and substantive, which at the time when these documents were written used to be rendered by compounds containing the same elements placed in an inverse order: subject and genitive, or substantive + adjective. A change had therefore taken place in the language with regard to this subject; this rule, which was at variance with the general rule of the Altaic languages, triumphed finally after a period of uncertainty, perhaps owing to the influence of the Semitic language flourishing side by side with the Accadian.

We must remark, however, that the rule for the qualificative to precede the verb which it qualifies in the respective positions of the attributive genitive or adjective and the word qualified, is by no means inflexibly observed in some of the Altaic languages; to keep to the Ugro-Finnic group, we find that the rule in Tcheremissian is that the syntactical genitive (without any suffix) should precede the subject, and the grammatical genitive (formed by means of a suffix) follow it; in ancient times there was this same rule in the Proto-Medic, thus: "son of Cyrus" was expressed as *kuras sakri*, or else *tar kurasna*. In Zyriainian, the purely syntactical genitive can follow the word which it qualifies in certain fixed cases. In Votiac, the position of the genitive, either syntactical or grammatical, and of the adjective is indifferently before or after the word described.

I have just mentioned the rule for the position of the genitive in Proto-Medic, with regard to the adjective, that it always follows the noun to which it refers. In Susian even the syntactical genitive always follows the word which it qualifies, while the adjective precedes it.

3rd. *The verbal conjugation most frequently in use is prepositive, and not postpositive.*

The order of conjugation is as follows: pronominal subject prefixed + root + termination of tense, etc., if necessary, + termination of number if necessary; and in the derived voices:[1] pronominal subject prefixed + formative of the voice + root, and termination of tense if necessary + termination of number if necessary. The postpositive conjugation is the most original characteristic of the Accadian; it is exactly the opposite of the mechanism of the Ugro-Finnic and Turco-Tartaric verbs.

I do not however think that this last mechanism can be considered as an essential and fundamental feature of the Altaic languages.

[1] By this term, which seems to me best suited to the facts observable in the Accadian, I understand what is spoken of commonly in the Ugro-Finnic or Turkish grammar as "derived verbs."

Two of the principal groups of the Altaic family, the whole of the Mongolic group, and Mantchoo in the Tungusic group, have an entirely different verb, which allows of no personal suffixes, and which prefixes to the root the personal pronoun intact in its absolute form, in order to express explicitly the person indicated, which it cannot otherwise do. It is certainly always written separately, whilst in the Accadian it seems more entirely incorporated with the word; but that is simply a question of custom and orthography, which has nothing to do with the essential process of grammatical construction, and the order established by the mind in the elements of the postposition.

Philologists of Castren and Max Muller's standing have no hesitation in affirming that the word in Mongolic and Mantchoo represents the most ancient type of the Altaic verb, which remained intact in these two groups, whilst in others it was so modified that it assumed an entirely different aspect. Some languages have remained in the purely radical stage which always precedes agglutination, like the ancient Chinese; they have the pronoun before, and not after the verb. This is the order which presents itself most naturally to the human mind. The correctness of such an opinion is further proved in a most decisive manner by the fact that, even in our own day, Mantchoo has passed from the first stage to the agglutinative, placing the sign of the person at the end in some dialects of the Tungusic group. Castren has proved that the use of pronominal suffixes for the different persons of the verb has only lately become general amongst the tribes round Njertchinsk, as was the case rather earlier with the tribe of the Buriates belonging to the Mongolic group; but the other Tungusic dialects, and particularly Mantchoo, remain strangers to this innovation.[1]

It is interesting to compare the verb in Mantchoo with that of the Accadian. In the indicative mood it is conjugated like either of the personal indicatives of the simple voice in the Accadian: pronoun + root + termination of tense. Thus, in the present: *bi ara-mbi*, "I write," *si ara-mbi*, "thou writest," *ere ara-mbi*, "he writes," are exactly like the Accadian, *mu-śar-ri*, *iz-śar-ri*, with the same meaning. More often the personal pronoun is omitted in Mantchoo, so that the verb seems at first to be of no person.[2] That is precisely similar to the impersonal indicative of the Accadian, one of the moods most frequently used in the texts, in which there are no pronominal prefixes.

There is another construction in Mantchoo exactly like the Accadian: I refer to the practice of placing between the pronoun and the root, that is to say before the latter, a formative which has itself the meaning of a root existing independently in the vocabulary; the first concessive is an instance of this: present, *bi baha-fi ara-mbi*, "I can write;" perfect, *bi baha-fi ara ha-bi*," "I have been able to

[1] Castrén, and a still better authority, Schiefner, have shown that the introduction of this new principle in Buriatic was due to the influence of Yakut, a language of the Turco-Tartaric group, and in Tungusic, which belongs to the circle of Njertchinsk, to the influence of Buriate.

[2] Lucien Adam, *Grammaire de la Langue Mandchou*, p. 51.

write." Sometimes, instead of the termination of tense, a termination of the mood is placed after the root, like the gerund and supine are conjugated in the Accadian; it is so with the first optative: *bi ara tchi*, "that I may write," and the first subjunctive is made by the addition of a formative which is originally a conjunction: *bi-aika-ara-tchi*. I repeat that the division into several words is only a form of orthography; in Mantchoo we even find the casual suffixes of declension written separately. Nevertheless, the principle of construction is the same as in the Accadian, although the verbs of the two languages have taken different paths, as might be expected, considering the immense distance and length of time which separates them.

Therefore, although the prepositive conjugation of the Accadian may differ completely from the verbal mechanism of the Ugro-Finnic and Turco-Tartaric dialects, which really agrees with the Accadian postpositive, it presents striking analogies with the fundamental principles upon which the mechanism of the verb is built up in Mantchoo, a language which belongs itself to the great family of Altaic languages. And, in spite of the vast distance of time and space which extends between the Accadian and Mantchoo dialects, these analogies are worthy our serious attention, more especially since the first to notice them was no less remarkable a scholar than Prof. Sayce.

For myself I have even ventured to go farther; I suggested a connection between the construction of the Accadian verb and that of the Ugro-Finnic negative verb, at the same time propounding a new theory about the formation of the latter. This theory has been supported by O. Donner, the learned professor of Helsingfors; but elsewhere it has met with a cool reception. The present is no fit occasion to examine its merits and defend it. I prefer adhering to the rule which I made at the beginning of this chapter, that I would only set forth certain linguistic similarities which are acknowledged to be incontestable; and therefore I must leave this conjecture, as being up to this time insufficiently proved, though I would wish to add that my own opinion has in no way changed respecting it.

4th. *The other verbal voices, with the exception of the causative, are formed by means of particles peculiar to the Accadian.*

It is difficult to attach any great importance to this point, because we should find great differences between the dialects belonging to the different groups of the Altaic family, and often an individual originality, quite as marked as in the Accadian, with respect to the particles used in the formation of the verbal voices or derived verbs, according to whichever designation best suits the reader's taste. We may remark, however, that although most of the formatives of the Accadian verbal voices are without analogy, so far as we can see in the modern Altaic languages, one of them presents a striking similarity with the proto-Medic. This is the incorporation of a particle, *ra*, for the reciprocal and co-operative forms of the Accadian verb, and in the second edition of the trilingual inscriptions of the Achemenides, we find an enclitic reciprocal pronoun *ir*, *irra*. This fact seems to point forcibly to a regular relationship.

5th. *The use of certain periphrastic constructions which at a cursory and superficial glance have deceived people into thinking them prepositions.*

I only mention this last point on account of the discussion there has been about the so-called Accadian prepositions, and the conclusions which some would derive from them. Their presence has been regarded as a decisive disproof of any relationship between the Turanian or Altaic languages and the Accadian dialect. There need now be no more discussion about the matter. The Accadian has no prepositions, but only periphrastic constructions which may contain any words which express an idea of situation or relation. And in reality these periphrastic constructions, instead of constituting an essential and organic feature of the language, are but a fact of syntax of secondary importance, and much less remarkable than it at first appeared. They are a syntactical peculiarity, which furnishes no decisive information to guide us in the classification of the language.

CHAPTER XXI.

Altaic affinities of the Accadian Language.

THE conclusions to be drawn from the foregoing remarks are obvious to any one who is serious in his researches, and has resolutely laid aside all prejudices. The grammatical affinities between the Accadian and Turanian or Altaic languages far outweigh the differences which might be discovered, even supposing the least of these to be reckoned. Besides, the affinities are certainly of a much more essential and organic character than the differences. The latter are by no means incompatibilities, whatever people who know nothing at all about the Accadian may affirm. They must need some degree of audacious frivolity and ignorance, who would venture upon such an assertion. Now, in each instance in which the Accadian departs from the ordinary rules of the Altaic dialects, we find a parallel peculiarity appearing sporadically in some or other of the languages of this family. Such exceptions cannot therefore be regarded as entirely foreign, and certainly not as contrary to the fundamental genius of the great linguistic family. We had some difficulty, I own, in finding an analogous case to the prepositive conjunction, which constitutes one of the most striking peculiarities of the Accadian, and we found it at last at the opposite extremity of the geographical tract over which the Altaic dialects extend. But our comparison with Mantchoo was justified by the opinion certain illustrious philologists had previously expressed, that this language was a monument of the most ancient type of the Turanian verbal conjugation. A knowledge of the Accadian is therefore of great use in the general philology of the Altaic languages, by confirming decisively M. Castren's opinion. We can now discern that the languages belonging to this family must have passed through three successive stages, with regard to the pronominal subject of the verb.

1st. Prepositive juxtaposition, in which the incorporation has taken place to a greater or less degree.

2nd. Simple positive juxtaposition.

3rd. Transformation of the subjoined pronoun into an affixed termination, distinct from the perfect form of the pronoun.

The Tungusic group, with the exception of the dialects spoken around Njertchinsk, became crystallized at the first stage, and even at the very beginning of that period, when the pronoun was entirely distinct from the verb which it preceded, and which was itself impersonal. The Ugro-Finnic and Turco-Tartaric dialects have all reached the third stage. As to the Accadian, it had formed its grammar at the time of its transition from the first to the second stage, when the pronoun could be indifferently prefixed or suffixed to the root; it possesses, therefore, a very rich prepositive conjugation, which is the most generally used, and a postpositive conjugation of less frequent occurrence, which seems to have the same number of voices and moods, but no objective or negative forms. Altaistic scholars, such as the Professors Paul Hunfalvy of Pest, and O. Donner of Helsingfors, concur with the author of the present work, and the greater number of Assyriologists, in assigning the Accadian to the family of languages that they have made their special study. In their opinion, its philological classification is indisputable.

But although the Accadian should be ranged amongst the Turanian and Altaic dialects, and its affinities seem generally very close with the Ugro-Finnic and Turco-Tartaric groups, yet, since some of its characteristics are decidedly original, it is better to consider it as the type of a separate group of this family. At a later date, a closer examination than any that has as yet been instituted may enable us to recognize in it the most ancient form, the primitive type of one of the groups existing at the present time; but any attempts to establish such a connection now would be premature, in spite of the striking analogies with the Ugric dialects, which appear to M. Donner so remarkable.

The grammar of the Accadian language exhibits a very primitive character in its processes of agglutination. Possessive or verbal pronouns, suffixes of derivation, casual suffixes or those of number, particles forming the verbal voices, in short, all the elements out of which the grammatical mechanism is formed, are joined together or remain separate without losing their identity by reciprocal contact, and without becoming corrupted for the purposes of incorporation. We see nothing analogous to the state of semiflexion at which some of the modern Ugro-Finnic languages have arrived; and at which it is now proved that the ancient dialects of Media and Susiana became crystallized: the latter had, therefore, attained to a further degree of development than the Accadian.

A no less important proof of grammatical antiquity is furnished by the fact that Mantchoo alone amongst the Altaic languages possesses, in the same degree, the power of dispensing with the casual suffixes of the declensions, and of expressing cases by words which indicate position, the substantive remaining uninflected. This occurs most frequently in the epigraphic style, in monumental inscriptions, for instance. Lastly, we must observe a peculiarity of the same kind, pointing to the primitive phase of the language, when it was still at the rhematical stage, in the number of words formed from simple roots without any suffixes of derivation, and used indifferently as verbs and substantives. There is not one of the Altaic languages that has not preserved a few of these forms, which remain invariable, whether used as verbs or substantives; but in the Accadian they constitute a large part of the vocabulary.

Besides these facts, which only show the Accadian grammar to be in a more ancient state than any other of the known Altaic dialects, this language exhibits, at the same time, peculiarities of syntax, which are in reality very striking, but which are by no means contrary to the Turanian or Altaic genius, although they may appear rather exaggerated. The agglutinative tendency holds such sway there that it almost approaches polysynthetism, or a holophrastic construction. Two important and well defined instances will prove the truth of what I say.

1st. The casual suffixes and the possessive pronouns used as suffixes of a substantive that governs a genitive, or is accompanied by an adjective, are not placed after the substantive itself, but after the genitive or adjective. Thus, *kar kâdingirata*, "upon the quay of Babylon," reads literally, "the quay of Babylon—upon;" and *sam tillabiku*, "for its whole price," is also literally, " price—whole—its—for."

2nd. When there is an enumeration of things in the same case, no matter how long, and even if each word of the enumeration be accompanied by an adjective or genitive which it governs, the whole series is regarded as a single polysynthetic group, and treated as a regular compound word; instead of giving to each term of the enumeration its casual suffix, one only is used for the whole, and is placed at the end of the series. For instance: χ*arsak taq sirgal taq guk taq zakurna*, "the mountain of alabaster, lapis, and marble," is literally, "mountain—stone—of the great light—stone—blue—stone—shining—in."

This is not polysynthetism properly so called, such as we find in the American languages; but it is a tendency towards such a principle, resulting from agglutination. In the American languages, and it is needless to say we are merely drawing a comparison, not pointing out a relationship, all the elements of a complete proposition become one single word, and the incorporation is so perfect as to allow the different words incorporated to interpenetrate each other and otherwise assume corrupted forms. In the Accadian, on the contrary, all the elements of polysynthetic agglutination remain intact, without any alteration or corruption of form, each preserving its identity; the group of words united by a common suffix does not become one single word, it remains a proposition, a member of a sentence composed of distinct words, which become agglutinated into a new kind of unity intermediate between the separate word and the complete phrase.

This remains a fact of syntax, without reference to morphology or grammar.

There are other constructions which I have termed incapsulations, which resemble somewhat a characteristic feature in the American languages. They not only unite into one group all the elements of the most complex idea, but the words become mixed up one with the other. F. Lieber has named this peculiarity incapsulation, thus comparing the way in which the words are placed in the phrase to a box which contains another, itself containing a third, the third a fourth, and so on. There is the same tendency visible in the Accadian, though not carried to so great an extent. Just as synthetic agglutination has no power to form a single word of the elements which are thus brought together, but merely constitute a homogeneous group of a peculiar kind, in which the words, far from being corrupted by constant contact, remain entire, and preserve their own identity to a certain extent, yet at the same time coalescing sufficiently for the whole group to be declined as one word: so incapsulation introduces into this long series, as you might insert a small box into a large one, a member of a sentence perfect in itself, or a less complicated synthetic group. Properly speaking, there is no fusion of one holophrastic word into another, but simply of a sentence complete in itself, and in the elements of which synthetical union has sometimes already begun, between a word and its casual suffix, or else in the midst of a conglomeration of words which are declined as a whole, and are joined by a common suffix. Furthermore, this fusion is not as complicated as in the American languages; I have never met with it double, triple, or quadruple, as occurs in those cases, but it is always simple.

We have in Accadian thus one example of this phenomena, which may very easily be analyzed, in the expression, *egir sam nutillabiku*, "after his instalment," literally, "the remainder—of the price—not complete—his—to," in which *sam nutillabi* is inserted between *egir*, "remainder," and its casual suffix, *ku*, forming together *egirku*, "after."

CHAPTER XXII.

Accadian and Altaïc affinities.

OUR knowledge of the Accadian is as yet far from perfect. The subject of the grammatical forms has received the most attention up to the present time, and is therefore the most clearly understood. On this point, the most essential facts are already fully established; we possess a sure method of comparing languages, and it is consequently easy to weigh the affinities existing between the Accadian and the Altaic languages, as we have just done. On the other hand, questions of pronunciations and the vocabulary have hardly been examined at all in a scientific manner. So we ought to be much more careful in speaking of the connection between the lexicon of the Accadian dialect and that of the modern languages of the Turanian or Altaic family.

However, some very remarkable analogies have already been discovered between a large number of Accadian words and the corresponding words of the Ugro-Finnic or Turco-Tartaric idioms.

Such for instance, as the names of the numbers up to seven:

	ONE.	TWO.	THREE.	FIVE.	SIX.	SEVEN.
Accad.	*id*[1]	*kas*[2]	*is*	*bara*	*as*	*siesna*
Fin.	*yksi (yhden)*	*kaksi*	*kol-me*	*viisi*	*kuusi*	*seicemän*
Esth.	*üks*	*kaks*	*kol-m*	*viis*	*kuus*	*seice*
Lap.	*akt*	*kvekte*	*kol-m*	*vit*	*kot*	*ćeć*
Tcher.	*ik*	*kok*	*ku-m*	*vis*	*kut*	*sim*
Mord.	*väike*	*kavto*	*kol-mo*	*väte*	*koto*	*sisem*
Zyr.	*ötik*	*kyk*	*kuj-im*	*vit*	*kvait*	*sizim*
Vog.	*äkvä*	*kit*	*kor-om*	*ät*	*kot*	*siu*
Ost.	*it*	*kat*	*ćud-em*	*vet*	*ćut*	*tabet*
Mag.	*egy*	*kettö*	*har-om*[3]	*öt*[4]	*hat*[5]	*het*[6]

I shall give some instances of analogies which present themselves at the first glance.

1st. In the terms used to designate the parental and filial relationships.

	FATHER.	FATHER.	FATHER.	MOTHER.	MOTHER.	SON.
Accad.	*ad, adda*	*ai*	*abba*	*umu, umma*	*nene*	*tar*
Fin.	*isä*	*äijä*[7]		*emä*		*tär*[8]
Esth.	*issa*			*ömma*		
Lap.	*attje*	*aija*				
Tcher.	*ätjä*			*ävä*		
Mord.						*tsóra*
Zyr.		*aj*				
Vog.		*jaj*			*an*	

[1] A contraction of *ikd*, according to the phonetic laws of the language.

[2] A contraction of *kaks*.

[3] In Yakut, *üs;* Ujgur, *üć;* Tchouvache, *visse;* Osmanli, *uć*.

[4] In Yakut, *biäs;* Ujgur, *biś;* Tchouvache, *pil-ik;* Osmanli, *leś*.

[5] In Yakut, *al-ta;* Ujgur, *al-tj;* Tchouvache, *ol-ta;* Osmanli, *al-ti*.

[6] I do not give the name of the number "four" in this table, because in the Accadian it seems to be quite distinct, *sana, san*.

[7] "Old man, grandfather."

[8] This is only used in the duplicate form *tytär*, "girl;" but the simple *tär* has a share in the formation of a great many mythological names.

	FATHER.	FATHER.	FATHER.	MOTHER.	MOTHER.	SON.
Ost.	ata				ana, ane	
Mag.	atja				anja	dér[1]
As. Turk.	ata		baba		ana	tura[2]
Osm.	ata		baba		ana	

2nd. In the names of limbs and parts of the bodies of men and animals.

	HAND.	HAND.	FOOT.	MOUTH.	EYE.	BLOOD.	BONE.
Accad.	qat	id	arik	du	si, silim	us[3]	lum
Fin.	käte		jalk-a	sū	silmä	ver-i	luu
Esth.	käsi		jalg	sū	silm	verr-i	
Lap.	kät, kiet		juolk-e	čo-d[4]	čalme	var	
Tcher.	ket, kid		jal, jol	sü[5]	sinzä	ver	lu
Mord.	ked, käd				selme	ver	
Zyr.	ki				sin	vir	ly
Vog.	kåt			tu-s	sem	vujr	lu
Ost.	kêt			tu-t	siem	ver	ly
Mag.	kéz		gjalog[6]	sa-j	szem	vér	
As. Turk.		il	ajoq				
Osm.		él[7]	ajaq				

	SKIN.	WOOL, HAIR.	TAIL.	URINE.	GERM, SEED OF ANIMALS.
Accad.	śu	sik	kun	kas, kisi	kul
Fin.				kusi	kull-i[8]
Esth.				kusi	kol-i[9]
Lap.				koj	kuol[9]
Tcher.				kuź-vüt[10]	
Mord.					
Zyr.					
Vog.					kus'

[1] "Girl;" this ancient word is only preserved in certain mythological appellations.
[2] "Royal race, chief." The Accadian *tur* has also the secondary meaning of "chief."
[3] A contraction of *vus*.   [4] "Throat."   [5] "Aperture."
[6] "One who goes on foot."   [7] Ostiaco-Samoyedic, *ude*; lurak, *uda*.
[8] "Male member."   [9] "Testicle."   [10] Literally, "urine-water."

	SKIN.	WOOL, HAIR.	TAIL.	URINE.	GERM, SEED OF ANIMALS.
Ost.				χos-em[1]	kila
Mag.				hud	
As. Turk.	soi-maq[2]	sać	kin[3]		
Osm.	soi-maq	sać			

3rd. In the names of living beings.

	MAN.	MAN.	OX.	FISH.
Accad.	gum, kū	mulu	χar	χana, χa
Fin.			här-kä	kala
Esth.			här-g	kala
Lap.			här-gge[4]	kuele, guolle
Tcher.		maar-a		kol
Mord.		mord-va		kal
Zyr.	kom-i	mor-t	kör	
Vog.	kum, χum			kul, χul
Ost.	χu-i		kār, χār	χut
Mag.	hīm[5]		ö-kör	hal[6]
As. Turk.			ö-küz	
Osm.			ö-küz	

4th. In the designation of parts of plants.

	STALK, BRANCH.	ROOT.	LEAF.[7]	FRUIT, SEED.
Accad.	gis	ur	dub	kalumma (kaluvva)
Fin.	oks-a	jur-i	leht-i	külvii
Esth.	oks	jūr	lehhed	külv-a-n[9]
Lap.	äks-e			gilv[10]
Tcher.	ukś			
Mord.		jor	lop-a	
Zyr.				
Vog.			lop-t	

---

[1] "To make water."
[2] "To flay, gall, skin."
[3] "Hinder part, that which comes after."
[4] "Reindeer."   [5] "Male."   [6] Mongolic, *kal.*
[7] And also "leaf, table of writing."
[8] *kulv-ün,* "to sow."   [9] "To sow."   [10] *Gilvv-it,* "to sow."

	STALK, BRANCH.	ROOT.	LEAF.[1]	FRUIT, SEED.
Ost.		jor	lip-et	kir-em[2]
Mag.	ág[3]		lev-él[4]	
As. Turk.				
Osm.				

5th. In the names of the heavenly bodies, the elements, and the great phenomena of the terrestrial surface.

	HEAVEN, GOD.	SKY, TEMPEST.[5]	SUN.	DAYBREAK.	DAY.	LIGHT.
Accad.	ana	imi	utu[6]	kun	tam	sir[7]
Fin.		jymj[8]				sar-a stan[9]
Esth.						sor-a-n[10]
Lap.						sarra[11]
Tcher.		juma				sar[12]
Mord.		jom[13]				
Zyr.	jen[14]	iym[15]				
Vog.						sar-ni[16]
Ost.						
Mag.						sār[12]
As. Turk.			udun[17]	gun[18]	tan	sari[12]
Osm.				gun		sari[19]

[1] And also "leaf, table of writing."
[2] "To sow."
[3] There is here a metathesis of the radical vowel which is medial in the Accadian and initial in the Ugro-Finnic languages.
[4] In the language of the Lapps "leaf, page."
[5] Generally all kinds of meteorological phenomena.
[6] Cf. ud, "day."
[7] Cf. ser-zi, "ray;" ser-ka, "brilliancy, splendour."
[8] "Thunder."
[9] "To become light;" sir-khu, "light."
[10] "To shine;" sor-a, "ray."
[11] "Light."
[12] "Yellow."
[13] "Sky."
[14] "God." In the Votiac, in, "sky."
[15] "Thunder." It is the well-known root of the word juma-la, juma-l, which becomes, in most languages of the Ugro-Finnic group, the title of the divinity.
[16] "White."
[17] "Day." Mongol, ud, "sun;" ed-ür, "day."
[18] "Day." Mongol, kün.
[19] For the root sar, ser, sir, "to shine, to be clear, white," in all the groups of the Altaic family, see Schott's Ueber der Altaische Sprachengeschlecht, Vol. I., p. 136; O. Donner's, Vergl Woerterb. der Finnisch-Ugrischen Sprachen, p. 109 et seq.

	MOON.	MOON.	NIGHT.	EARTH, COUNTRY.
Accad.	idu[1]	ai	gig, gie	ma, mada
Fin.	kuta-ma[2]			maa, mu-ta
Esth.	kû			mei-sa[3]
Lap.				
Tcher.				
Mord.	kuu			mj-landa
Zyr.				mo-da
Vog.	kölitä[4]			mu
Ost.	χoda-j[4]			ma, ma-g
Mag.	hold			me-g
As. Turk.		ai	gije	me-zö[3]
Osm.		ai	gije	

	MOUNTAIN.	FIELD.	STONE.	WATER.
Accad.	kur	sa	taq	a
Fin.	kor-k-o[5]	sia[6]		
Esth.	kör-g-e[7]	sia[8]		
Lap.	kar-as[9]			
Tcher.	kor-ok			
Mord.				
Zyr.				ju[10]
Vog.				ja, je[10]
Ost.	ker-eś			
Mag.				já[11]
As. Turk.			taś	
Osm.			taś	

[1] Cf. Hesych v. αἰδής.

[2] The form *kû*, contracted from *kuta* is more frequently used.

[3] "Field."   [4] "Morning."

[5] "Elevation;" all philologists are agreed in considering the root *kork*, in the Ugro-Finnic languages, as a secondary root, derived from a primary root *kor*.

[6] "Situation, place."   [7] "High."   [8] "Here."

[9] "Great;" cf. in the Accadian *gur-us*, "exalted, powerful." In the Votaic, the word for "mountain" is formed with the same suffix of derivation, *gur-ez*.

[10] "Water-course."

[11] Only preserved in certain names of places.

6th. In a few essential verbs.

	TO BE.	TO BE FINISHED, TO COMPLETE.	TO PLACE, TO PUT.
Accad.	men (ven)	til	ku
Fin.	ol-en[1]	täj-si[2]	
Esth.	olle-ma	täi-s[2]	
Lap.		täva-s[2]	
Tcher.	yl-em		
Mord.	al-ems		
Zyr.	völ-nj[3]	tjr[2]	
Vog.			
Ost.	ūd-ém	tet[2]	
Mag.	(val, van)	tele[2]	
As. Turk.	ol-maq	tol-maq[4]	qo-maq
Osm.	ol-maq	tol-maq[4]	qo-maq

	TO COMPLETE, TO FINISH.[5]	TO ADJUST, TO PLACE, TO ADD.	TO CUT.
Accad.	kak	tab	χas
Fin.	kok-o[6]	tap-ā-n[7]	([8])
Esth.	kokk[9]	tab-an[7]	
Lap.	cok-e[10]	tap-a-tet[7]	
Tcher.	kog-o[11]		kiz-e[12]
Mord.			
Zyr.			
Vog.			käs-äi[12]
Ost.			kej[12]
Mag.		tap-ni[13]	kes[12]
As. Turk.		tab-maq[14]	qaz-maq[15]
Osm.			qaz-maq[15]

---

[1] Of course the comparison only refers here to the radical subject, leaving the terminations, which vary according to the languages, out of the question.

[2] "Full."   [3] Votiac, van.   [4] "To be full."   [5] Substantively "all."

[6] "Piece, all;" kokö-n, "to assemble, to collect."

[7] "To reach, arrive at, seize."

[8] It is perhaps necessary here to write veic-i, "knife," which some philologists identify with the words placed below.

[9] "Heap;" kokk-u-ma, "to assemble, to collect."

[10] "Heap."   [11] "Complete."   [12] "Knife."   [13] "To touch."

[14] "To find, attain;" tab-la-maq, "to beat, to smooth."

[15] "To hollow, to engrave."

	TO PUT IN A LINE.	TO BIND.	TO CRY.	TO EAT.
Accad.	śar[1]	χir	χir	ku
Fin.	sar-ja[2]		kir-ju-n	sjö-n
Esth.	ser-an[3]		kir-u-n	sö-n
Lap.		kar-et		
Tcher.	sur[4]			
Mord.				sev-en
Zyr.	zor[4]	kör-to		sjuj-a
Vog.	sir[5]			te-m
Ost.				tev-em
Mag.	śor,[6] sär[7]	kö-t-ni	hir[8]	en-ni (ev-ni)
As. Turk.				je-mék[9]
Osm.				je-mék

	TO VOMIT.	TO GO TO BED, REST.	TO PUT AN END TO, DIE
Accad.	aχtu	gud	bat
Fin.	okse-nn-an		
Esth.			
Lap.			
Tcher.			
Mord.			
Zyr.		kuil-a	
Vog.		kol-em[10]	
Ost.	aχt-em	kud-em, χod-em[10]	
Mag.		hál-ni[11]	
As. Turk.			bat-maq,[12] bit-mek[13]
Osm.			bat-maq,[12] bit-mek[13]

These are only a few examples which it would be easy to multiply, but they suffice to give the reader an idea of the striking resemblance existing between

---

[1] Substantively, "line."
[2] "Lengthening, length, extent;" sor-e-a, "straight, extended."
[3] "To put in order, regulate;" sor-a, "upright, just."
[4] "Perch." [5] "Time, turn." [6] "Series, line."
[7] "Rank, order, time." [8] "Cry."
[9] Yakut, si ; Tchouvache, śe. [10] "To spend the night."
[11] "To sleep." [12] "To descend, to give way."
[13] "To be done, completed, to finish."

the words of the Accadian lexicon, so far as we can understand them, and those of the Altaic lexicons, particularly the Ugro-Finnic and the Turco-Tartaric groups. It is true that we ought to beware of a simple analogy between words of different languages, for it is often deceitful; I am also quite willing to admit that all the similitudes in the vocabulary which can be discovered at present between the Accadian and the modern Altaic languages should be revised as our studies progress, when some of them will very likely prove of no value. But at the same time I must observe that many of those I have just quoted are based on facts that would defy the most minute scientific examination, facts which refer to the roots and not to the word as it stands, the examples being the result of a critical analysis or dissection of the word.

From this point of view there is another circumstance of great importance referring to the grammatical peculiarity mentioned above, namely, that there are in the Accadian many propositions or roots which retain the same form without any development or modification whether they are used as substantives or verbs. This dialect exhibits, in an absolute and living state, a number of verbal or substantive roots in daily use formed from primitive roots, which it needs close examination to discover in the derivatives of the Ugro-Finnic languages. Here are a few examples:

UGRO-FINNIC ROOTS.	ACCADIAN.
kal, kil, "bruise, break:"	*qut,* "cut, cut in pieces."
kar, kor, kur, kir, "echo, murmur, speak:"	*kir,* "word, murmur."

UGRO-FINNIC ROOTS.	ACCADIAN.
kor, ker, "ask, seek, collect:"	*kur,* "to obtain, to conquer."
kan, kan, kun, ken, kin, "to be stiff, straight, strong, solid:"	*gan,* "to stand up, to exist, to be."
	gin, gen, "to stand up, to be firm, exist."
kam, kam, kum, kim, "to be bent, round:"	*gam,* "to be bent."
tar, tor, ter, tir, "break, share, cut:"	*tar,* "cut, separate, decide."
kar, kor, ker, kir, "to be bent, round, in a circle:"	*χar,* "circle, collar, viscera."
sak, sok, suk, sik, "to taper, to be first, to push forward:"	*śak,* "head, summit, point, chief."
sar, sor, sur, sir, "to increase, to enlarge, push forward, to be long, to expand:"	*sar,* "push forward, grow."
	sur, "push, expel."

CHAPTER XXIII.

Phonology of the Accadian Language.

NOW the comparisons which we have just drawn between the different vocabularies, and how illustrated by examples, reveal the unexpected fact that the Accadian roots resemble the Ugric much more than they do the Finnic. They are less full, less developed than those of the latter language, while they resembled those of the former in the frequent omission of the vocalic termination and the modification of two rival consonants into one.[1]

Some philologists have stumbled at this fact, as they considered it necessary to the proof of the Altaic character of the language that the Accadian forms should resemble more closely those of the Finnic dialect. But in this, to my mind, they are only yielding to a preconceived idea; they should give the character of recent alterations to the differences of form which distinguish the Ugric from the Finnic roots. But really nothing justifies this

---

[1] But not however the internal contraction which suppresses a syllable in the middle of a word. No example of this is found in the Accadian, though it is often to be met with in the ancient dialects of Susiana.

opinion, which is pretty generally adopted by Altaistic philologists. The points in question are not necessarily of any fixed date; they may have belonged to a much earlier period than is generally supposed, and constituted, perhaps long ago, the individual originality of the Ugric idioms as well as of the Accadian in comparison with the regular Finnish dialects. This is the conclusion to which I have been led by the study of the Accadian language.

But we must now examine the phonetic phenomena which are allowed to exist in the Accadian itself; and for this purpose we must study it apart from any exterior comparison. This language reveals, indeed, a very curious contrast, which is also highly important. On one hand, it is a language which was formed and crystallized at a very early epoch in the original phase of agglutination, and its grammar possesses, consequently, some forms of a most ancient stamp, to which, from this point of view, none but those of the Mantchoo can be compared. On the other hand, in the monuments we possess, it seems to be a language of long standing, spoken for centuries, the words of which are as though worn out by long use. We discover in it the effects of very powerful agents of phonetic change.

These influences, as we gather from the transformations which the roots undergo in the heart of the language, may be distributed into two classes, a tendency to omit the final vowels, and an attempt to soften the pronunciation.

The Accadian is peculiarly prone to the omission

of final vowel. For a certain number of words we find equally both forms, with or without the final vowel: for instance, *dara* and *dar*, " race ;" *utu* and *ut*, " sun;" *eni* and *en*, " lord." The influence of a tendency to omit the final vowel strikes us even in words of which we discover the formation by means of suffixes ending in a vowel. Thus, *ma*, " country," produces *mada*, by means of the individualizing suffix *da*, and *mada* becomes contracted into *mad*; *turi*, " to pass, leap over, enter," is certainly derived by the addition of the suffix *ri*, and the more simple root *tu*, " to assail, attack, enter," and it becomes *tur*. All the casual suffixes which do not end in a heavy vowel are susceptible of this contraction ; we find *ungalmur*, " to my king," for *ungalmura*; *ennunak*, " for the guard," instead of *ennuneku*; χ*ilib*, " the splendid and magnificent," for χ*ilibi*.

This endeavour to modify the pronunciation gives rise to three principal facts, which we shall illustrate by several examples.

1st. The alteration in the root by the omission of the final vowel is not the only one made, for that often leaves a consonant at the end of the word; when the consonant is *m*, *n*, or a guttural, it is often suppressed, in order to render the sound more agreeable; the parallel forms *erin* and *eri*, " servant," *gig* and *gie*, " night," etc., etc., furnish us with a proof of this modification. Hence a fact, traces of which which are now beginning to be discovered in the Accadian, and which have long been proved to exist in Finnic, Magyar, and all the Ugro-Finnic languages; we do not possess the full and perfect form of the root in many words, except as joined to a suffix of declension or conjugation, because in the absolute form the root is contracted through the influence I have just mentioned.

Take therefore as an example the verbs "to give" and "to accomplish;" in the infinitive and singular of the preterite they are *sî* and *śî;* but directly it becomes necessary to add a suffix of number or time, in the plural of the present, they assume the forms *simus* and *simue*, *śigies* and *śigi* (for *sigi-e*), because in reality the root is *simu* and *sigi*, and the addition of the suffix (acting here as an element of preservation, quite contrary to its usual functions in inflected languages) keeps it perfect, and arrests the contraction of the final letter, which takes place when there is no suffix to protect it.[1]

2nd. In its effort after euphony, the Accadian pronunciation rarely allows of two adjacent consonants. We should not be able to find more than twenty such instances among the polysyllabic roots expressed by ideograms, and explained by the syllabaries, or those written phonetically in the Accadian texts. But we can easily fathom the reason of this peculiarity. The harsh sound resulting from the juxtaposition of two consonants is avoided by con-

---

[1] Great attention should be paid to facts of this kind, for they often exercise a modifying influence on the ideas which we connect with certain words. Here is an example of it. We have two forms (expressed by two different ideograms) for the Accadian word "fish," χ*a* and χ*an*. I compared it to the Finnic *kala* and the Hungarian *hal*, to which χ*an*, from a phonetic point of view, really corresponds. But I believed so far in the anteriority of the form χ*a*, which was my reason for not agreeing with M. Donner's opinion connecting *kala-kal* with a root *kal*. Well! I was wrong, for it is only a contraction of χ*an* and even χ*ana*; the proof of it rests in the statement that I made about the illative χ*anaku* (and not χ*aku*) in which the root assumes its original form to support the suffix.

tracting them into one. Here is the proof. Although we seldom find two consonants in roots which allow of no further analysis, yet we often see them in the numerous compound words of the Accadian. Now, in this case, the peculiar character of the cuneiform Anarian writing, while it places the two ideograms side by side, gives no indication of the phonic modification undergone by the two roots thus brought together; but we are helped out of this difficulty by the commentaries on the pronunciation, which the Assyrian scribes so often added on the lexicographical tablets.[1]

From them we learn that the first consonant was almost always assimilated to the second. Thus, suppose we had the two roots *ut* and *sû* represented by the ideograms χ and *y;* when they were united into a compound, they were written as χ-*y;* only the commentaries inform us that the compound became *ussu* by assimilation, not *utsu*. This modification went still further. The same commentaries inform us, by various examples, which all point to the same fact, that double letters had no effect upon the pronunciation, they were sounded like simple letters. Thus, in the compound *ut-sû*, literally, "sun—to set," we follow the change operated by a modification of the pronunciation through the successive forms *utsû, ussu, usû;* in the word "while," and the substantive "break of day," we have the same series, *barbar, babbar, babar*. Finally, I will only remind my readers of the forms mentioned above, which are written phonetically in the texts; such as *gagarra*

[1] See my *Langue primitive de la Chaldée*, p. 47, et seq.

for *gargarra*, *nanam* for *namnam*, *ganamga* for *garnamga*, etc., etc.; their origin is now easily accounted for.

3rd. We have just seen that there is a tendency to omit the final guttural of a root; but the initial guttural is often aspirated under the influence of different circumstances, becoming χ from *k* or *g;* then this aspirate is modified, and finally almost disappears, or loses itself in the *h* which is always inherent in the initial vowel. The particle which is prefixed to form the precative of verbs, exhibits the following scale of degeneration: *gan*, *ga*, χ*a*, *a (ha)*, in a root signifying "light, day" (compare the Finnic *koi*), we can follow the same progression: *ku*, χ*u*, *u (hu)*.

Such are the principal processes of phonetic decay, which may easily be verified in the Accadian itself, as we have already pointed out. But these processes are the result of certain tendencies, which have brought the Accadian roots to forms so closely resembling those of the Ugric roots, whilst the Finnic have preserved fuller, and therefore more ancient forms; at least, as a rule, for there are some exceptions as in every case: for instance, although the Accadian *hidu*, "moon," has the initial guttural aspirated, it is less contracted than the Finnic *kuu*, which rather resembles the Vepse *kudai*, and the form that most nearly approaches the original here seems to be the Vogul *kolita* (cf. Mag. *hold*), the fundamental root being *kal*, *kul*, *kil*, as M. Donner has proved.

No one can deny that an exact linguistic method

imposes upon us the duty of testing the comparisons established between the Accadian vocabulary and that of the Ugro-Finnic languages by the laws of phonetic change, which we find in this language, operating upon the roots themselves. To act otherwise would be to deviate from the paths of science. In examining the lexicon, therefore, we acknowledge these laws, and their application may be observed in those comparisons we gave above as examples. Some have seen in them also specimens of certain laws of correspondence in articulation between the Accadian and those Ugro-Finnic dialects which we can thoroughly understand, independently of the processes of phonetic change which I have just mentioned; for we are already advanced to such a point in this study, that, instead of contenting ourselves with simple approximative analogies, we begin to trace firm and unalterable laws of permutation.

1st. The Accadian soft checks, *b, g, d*, correspond to the Finnic hard checks, *p, k, t;* as a rule, they are only found when some of the languages belonging to the Ugro-Finnic group (exclusive of the dialect of the Lapps) allow also the soft check in the same word.

2nd. Whenever the Ugric languages substitute χ or *h* for a Finnic *k*, the Accadian also has χ, and sometimes even as the initial letter the simple vowel in which the aspirate *h* is inherent; there are very few exceptions to this rule.

3rd. If an *f* in Magyar is found to correspond with a Finnic *p*, we may be sure that the Accadian will also have *p*, and not the soft check, *b*.

4th. In the diverse forms under which the same root presents itself, some of the Ugro-Finnic roots have a dental, others a sibilant; in such a case, the Accadian usually gives the preference to the dental, which is generally *d*, and not *t*.

5th. Although in the Accadian *l* is not so systematically changed into a dental, as is the case in Ostiac, still it is frequently done, and *d* is then the dental chosen.

6th. The Accadian sometimes substitutes *n* for *l*, like the Ugro-Finnic languages; but this change is only made at the end of the root.

7th. *Vice versâ*, it allows *l* to be used for *n* before a guttural.

8th. Whenever the proto-Medic has *r*, and the Ugro-Finnic languages *l*, the Accadian has also *l*.

9th. If the Ugro-Finnic languages have a final sibilant, the Accadian may substitute *r*, and reciprocally.

10th. An Accadian *k* or *g* corresponds in certain cases to a liquid sibilant or a sonant in the Ugro-Finnic and Turco-Tartaric languages.

11th. The words beginning with *ja, jo, ju, je, ji*, in the Ugro-Finnic languages, have *a, u, e, i* in the Accadian; for the latter has no initial *j*, or at least it coalesces with the *h* inherent in the vowel.

Any one who is acquainted with the Altaic languages will see at once that these phonetic laws agree in their essential data with those of the Ugro-Finnic dialects, and especially with Ostiac, as has been already observed by M. Donner. Again, then, we find ourselves face to face with new and weighty arguments, which unite with the tendency to omit the final letter, the rare occurrence of two adjacent consonants, several grammatical peculiarities, and the separate existence of the suffixes and the root in compounds, to prove the same fact, namely, that the Accadian bore a closer resemblance with the Ugric languages, and particularly Ostiac, than with the real Finnic languages. It exhibited in its vocabulary, at a period some thirty centuries before the Christian era, most of the changes and phonetic tendencies which characterize the Ugric tongues. It therefore bore witness to the fact that these points are not of recent date, although Finnic has remained untouched up to the present time by some of these phonetic changes, and is an example of preservation only equalled in Lithuanian amongst all the Aryan languages. So striking is the analogy, that some day, perhaps, in the progress of our study of the Accadian, it may come to be regarded as the primitive type of the Ugric languages, belonging really to this special subdivision of the great Turanian or Altaic family.

However this last conjecture may turn out, for of course it is as yet but a conjecture, we may yet confidently affirm, in spite of our imperfect acquaintance with the Accadian vocabulary, that, as regards the lexicology and grammatical morphology, the affinity of the Accadian with the Altaic languages is clearly established. New inquiries can only strengthen our opinion, and confirm this principal fact, by enabling us to judge better of the degree of relationship between the ancient Turanian language of Chaldea and certain groups which are still represented by the same linguistic family.

CHAPTER XXIV.

The origin of the Kushito-Semitic religion.

THE triumph of the Kushito-Semitic religion is still more ancient than the triumph of the Assyrian over the Accadian language. Only in the formulæ and hymns of the magic collection which must have been gathered from oral traditions, do we find the old religious system peculiar to the Accadians which was so thoroughly conformable to the characteristics of their race, and so connected with the beliefs of the Finns and other Turanians as to suggest that it was derived from them. Although the affinity of the Chaldaio-Babylonian official religion with that of the Syrian, Canaanitish and Arab populations, proves that this religion must have been originally promulgated by the Kushites of Babylon, yet it was the same religion as the old kings of Ur professed in spite of their purely Accadian names. The Accadian inscriptions of the Likbabi (or Likbagas, the reading of this name is still doubtful) and the Dungi[1] are dedicated to the gods who remain to the last day of Babylon the

---

[1] See Inscriptions of Dungi, king of Ur, in "Early History of Babylonia," in *Records of the Past*, Vol. III., p. 1.

objects of public adoration, and whom the great sacerdotal system of classification places in the highest ranks of the celestial hierarchy. Even at this point the gods peculiar to the magical books are no longer mentioned.

At the same time, the most ancient liturgical documents we possess about the Chaldaio-Babylonian religion, that collection of hymns which I called, in a first and very imperfect attempt at a translation of its principal parts, the *Chaldean Veda*,[1] are in the Accadian tongue, although the songs are not generally addressed to the primitive gods of Accad, but to those whom I regard as having been worshipped at first by the Kushites. It seems that the priesthood of Babylon and Chaldea in the seventh century, regarded these hymns as the most ancient trophies of their own religion which had been preserved in a settled form. So the Accadian became for them the sacred language of prayer to the gods, as well as the tongue which commanded the spirits, owing to the co-existence of the liturgical collection and the magical collection forming a sort of double Veda, only with this difference from the Indian, that in Chaldea the collection corresponding to the Atharva Veda consisted of older pieces, which were more suited to the primitive doctrine of the people in whose language they were composed, than those of the collection analogous to the Rig. There was another thing that tended still more to give to the Accadian the character of a sacred language, even in a religion

[1] See the part under this title in Vol. II. of my *Premières Civilisations*.

which was not primarily adopted by the Accadians. As the cuneiform graphic system had been invented by the Turanian portion of the population, and according to the genius and requirements of that language, the Chaldean people wrote in Accadian long before they wrote in Assyrian; consequently the significant names which were applied in Accadian to the Kushito-Semitic divinities had a written form prior to their Assyrian names. When writing was first applied to the Semitic language, these forms were adopted in preference to the phonetic orthography of the corresponding Assyrian names as ideographic groups consecrated by custom. This point once established, the Accadian became later, in the eyes of the Chaldean priests, the language in which they wrote the names of the gods, even when they read them in their Semitic form, and therefore, Accadian pre-eminently the language of religious symbolism.

All these facts show how ancient was the diffusion of the Kushito-Semitic religion, the sister to those of Syria and Phenicia, amongst the Accadian nation, while it still preserved its own characteristics and language. This event must have been nearly contemporary with the juxtaposition of the two races on the soil of Chaldea and Babylonia, and the Nimroditish conquest, which the book of Genesis points out to us as temporarily subjugating Erech and Accad together with Babel to the power of Kush, had no doubt some connection with it.

We must however make the best use of such knowledge as we possess, and go back further than authentic history and the original records which have been handed down to us, in order to reach the epoch when the people of Sumir and Accad, at that time the sole inhabitants of the southern basin of the Euphrates and Tigris, whilst another division of the same race dwelt in the mountains of the east, and professed that religion of demonological naturalism, to which the other Turanian nations continued to cling, together with a hierarchy composed of the priests of magic and a worship consisting of their rites and incantations.

But there is no need to go back as far as might at first sight seem necessary for the era of the establishment of the Chaldaio-Babylonian religion, and its final triumph over the Accadian faith, in a country specially noted as the "country of Accad," the southern provinces where the Turanian language was last spoken and where the proportion of Kushites was small as compared with the Turanians. The most ancient epigraphic monuments that we possess of this reign, the empire of the old kings of Ur, may perhaps mark the establishment of the new religion. It is indeed a very striking fact which has been already pointed out by several scholars,[1] that at the base of all the pyramidical temples of Chaldea proper, at Ur, Erech, Nippur, and Larsa, the name of the same king, which I have temporarily rendered Likbabi, is to be seen upon the bricks. "Although the whole of Chaldea has been thoroughly explored," says Canon

---

[1] See G. Rawlinson's *The Five Great Monarchies*, 2nd edition, Vol. I., p. 156 et seq., 176.

Rawlinson, "no trace is to be found of any sacred monument that could be attributed with any degree of probability to a date prior to this prince." He is the first of whom we possess any inscriptions, as yet, but he belongs to the regular historical period and does not open an era in it like a Menes in Egypt. Temples in the form of pyramids at certain distances one from the other must therefore be considered quite a recent institution in Chaldea as compared with what they were in the country of Shinar or Sumir, where national tradition, like that of the Bible, placed the construction of the first of these temples side by side with the confusion of tongues, and no one dared to attribute the foundation of the original pyramids of Babylon and Borsippa to any historical king; for they were said to be the work of a "very ancient" king, or perhaps even more correctly " of the most ancient king, the first king."[1] In the land of Accad, instead of being an ancient and indigenous growth, the construction of this kind of edifice was really only an imitation of Babylonian customs, undertaken and carried out in all the cities at once by the same king, who is not lost to sight in the gloom of the times, but appears on the contrary in the full light of history. Now the pyramidical temple is the tangible expression, the material and architectural manifestation of the

---

[1] See my *Commentaire des Fragments cosmogoniques de Bérose*, p. 55. Mr. Boscawen in *Trans. Soc. Bib Arch.*, Vol. IV., p. 167-170, has published the fragments of a bilingual text of an ancient king whose name is unfortunately lost, relating to some works carried on at the Pyramid of Babylon, from a copy made in the time of Assurbanipal; but the expressions of this text seem to me to imply the notion of a restoration and improvement on the original, considered as the completion rather than the foundation of the edifice.

Chaldaio-Babylonian religion. Serving both as a sanctuary and as an observatory for the stars, it agreed admirably with the genius of the essentially sidereal religion to which it was united by an indissoluble bond. The king Likbabi, who erected pyramidical temples in all the Chaldean towns, for up to that time they were unknown in the country, appears consequently as a sort of crowned apostle of the Chaldaio-Babylonian religion; he was particularly devoted to the god Sin, who became henceforth the god of the town of Ur, yet honouring equally Anu and Nana in Urukh, Samas' in Larsa, Bel in Nipur, or rather in each town the god who was regarded from that time forward as its special protector. His works of religious architecture show the activity of his followers in favour of the religion which he embraced, and which he endeavoured, as it would seem with a certain amount of success, to substitute for the ancient Accadian magical religion which possessed no temples and no fixed public worship.

On first beginning to study these details, the mind is struck by the unity of language and civilization in Babylon and Assyria. "The only variation, it was said at the time, in the long list of the Chaldaio-Assyrian kings is the fluctuation between the centres of gravity of their power. Sometimes transplanted from the south, where it had taken root, to the north, sometimes from the north to the south, the Semitic empire of Mesopotamia was termed conformably to these changes, either the Chaldean empire or the Assyrian empire. The worship, manners, language and extent of these two kingdoms remain exactly the same."[1] But in proportion as our knowledge of the monuments and cuneiform texts has increased, the period has come, as it does in all sciences, when we detect distinctions in what appeared at first to be quite uniform; and underneath a general unity many diversities are now found to exist. It is universally agreed, and this point has been maintained chiefly by English scholars, that in spite of the adoption of Chaldaio-Babylonian cultus by the people of Assur, the Assyrians and Babylonians were two distinct nations, possessing in many things a peculiar physiognomy, special customs and opposite characteristics, almost as different the one from the other as were those of the Greeks and Romans. The spectacle of their common interests and the difference between them, the initiative part played by Babylon and the originality which Assyria managed to keep in spite of it, has an exact parallel in the reciprocal relation still existing between China and Japan. Besides we know from the most reliable documents, and from the testimony of the Assyrians themselves, that Babylon remained almost entirely independent of Assyria until the eighth century B.C. and always had its own special history.[2] We must now go back still farther into the most remote antiquity and distinguish Babylonia, inhabited principally by the Kushites, from Chaldea, which retained its Chaldean or Turanian character much later. There

[1] Oppert's, *Histoire des Empires de Chaldée et d'Assyrie*, p. 6.

[2] See particularly Smith's "Early History of Babylonia," *Trans. Soc. Bib. Arch* Vol. I.

was originally, no doubt, a non-Semitic or ante-Kushite Babylon, using this name in anticipation, for to be quite correct we should say a town of Tin-tir, in the same way that there was an Agane and a Sippara to which we ought probably to give the title Sumirian. But the whole of this northern division of the land lost its Turanian character much more quickly than the towns of the south. Babylon and Chaldea were united for a short period, but at the time of the Kushite invasion under the legendary empire of Nimrod they quickly separated again, and their progress through many centuries was quite independent of each other, corresponding with the characteristics of the races, which predominated respectively in the two countries. During this state of things the authentic history of these two countries begins, supported by contemporary documents. From that time, even under the powerful monarchs of Ur, who united the two countries under their sway, and whose dominion seems to have extended over a part at least of the territory which was afterwards called Assyria, the difference between the races predominating in Babylon and Chaldea is plainly shown by a difference in the language most generally used in each of the countries. We have a positive proof of this fact in the official inscriptions of the vice-regents of the monarchs of Ur in the principal cities.' In the southern towns, as Sirgilla, Is-baggi-Hea, Eridhu, these governors

---

' These vice-regents have two different titles, like the towns, between which we still find it impossible to distinguish:

    1st. Accadian *patesi*; Assyrian *nuab*.
    2nd. Accadian *nir-nitu*; Assyrian *sakkanakku*.

generally had Accadian names, and even when they themselves bore Semitic names (as Idadu at Eridhu) their inscriptions were always in the Accadian, like those of their sovereigns in all the region of the south, from Nipur to the Persian Gulf. But at Diru in the neighbourhood of Babylon (the ancient name of this town was *Bat-ana*), as also at Assur, the vice-regents had Semitic names, and their inscriptions were written in Assyrian;[1] in the north also the kings of Ur, Dungi for instance, used the Assyrian for their official documents. In the same way, the independent kings of Agane show by the form of their names that they were of Kushito-Semitic origin, and there were some princes, Sabuv amongst the number, who were referred back to a period of extreme antiquity by certain indications connected with the monarchs who succeeded them. From this time the predominance of the Semitic language and the ethnic element that spoke it in Babylonia is so certain, that there was no need to fear the effects of the Elamite conquest of the Kassians, which took place a little later, and their dominion during many centuries. In the inscriptions of some kings of this dynasty there is an attempt made to substitute a duality, *Kassi u Ak-kadi* for the ancient formula *Sumeri u Akkadi;* but these Kassi did not however succeed in making their own language predominate, although it continued to furnish their regal names; their inscriptions as kings of Babylon were written in

---

[1] See in my *Choix des Textes cunéiformes*, No. 5, the inscription of *Ilu-mutabil*, vice-regent of Diru, whom I have erroneously represented as a prince of Babylon itself, by a false assimilation of the Archaic form of the initial letter in the ideographic group representing the name of his town.

the Accadian or Assyrian, and it was under their supremacy that the Assyrian tongue finally supplanted the Accadian everywhere, a circumstance evidently owing to the predominating influence of their capital Babylon.

The annals of the northern and southern provinces of Babylonia and Chaldea, the countries of Sumir and Accad, became intermingled a little before the invasion of the Kassi or Cissians, about the twentieth century B.C., when for the first time a king of Agane in the north, Sargon I.,[1] united the two countries under his sceptre and formed them into a single empire.

That was the time when the great work of classification and reform of the religion took place, when the text of the sacred magical and astrological books was definitely settled, in one word when the priesthood determined to unite into a complete whole, subordinate to its own religious ideas, the various institutions which the different elements of the population had founded in Babylonia and Chaldea, and which were independent of and even perhaps antagonistic to each other.

The Chaldaio-Babylonian civilization was thus fairly established; it was essentially of a very mixed character, but the contributions of the two races, the Turanian and Kushito-Semitic, were so thoroughly combined that it is now extremely difficult in many cases to distinguish them. This civilization became from that time common to the whole territory between Assyria and the sea. The

---

[1] See "Inscription of the Birth of Sargina," in *Records of the Past*, Vol. V., p. 1.

bilingual lexicographical tablets with their methodically classified enumerations of animals, plants, and minerals, natural and artificial objects, the anatomy of their different parts, weapons, utensils, all kinds of agricultural and industrial implements, food, drinks, means of transport by land and sea, diseases, professions, and classes of persons, furnish us with a complete picture of the state of civilization at the epoch when they were written, and the social state and knowledge upon which part of this civilization rested. It is the same that we see afterwards with a few changes existing at Babylon until the end of the great city's independence, and spreading all over Assyria. It was quite different from the Chaldean civilization under the ancient kings of Ur, of which Mr. George Rawlinson has given such an interesting picture in his *Five Ancient Monarchies*,[1] from the ruins of Mugheir and Warka; great progress has taken place since those early times.

The improved civilization which is brought before us in the lexicographical tablets possesses this striking peculiarity that it is a civilization in two languages. If all the civilization were the work of one of the two ethnic and linguistic elements of the population, while the other only borrowed such improvements, we ought to find amongst the people who instituted these reforms a complete indigenous nomenclature for everything connected with the different branches of civilization; the others on the contrary would have copied from them by translating the necessary terms into their own

[1] Vol. I.

language; in the same way the latter element would have had recourse to the vocabulary of the other to designate objects with which it had become familiar since intercourse had been established between the two. Now we find that this is not the case; the borrowing of designations for the most necessary objects and inventions which are essential to a perfect civilization is reciprocal, almost as many names are imported from the Accadian into the Assyrian as from the Assyrian into the Accadian. There are several utensils, instruments and institutions which must have been introduced by the population speaking a Semitic language, and have formed part of its contribution to the common fund, for they were designated by a simple word in the language; while they are expressed in the Accadian by round about phrases, compounds of an artificial nature, where the Assyrian word itself has not been boldly adopted into the vocabulary. A thorough and attentive analysis of the lexicographical tablets, with a view to ascertaining what words one language borrowed from the other, would be a most interesting and useful study. These tablets would then serve as a faithful mirror, reflecting in part the work of the formation of the Chaldaio-Babylonian civilization; my own studies have led me to the discovery that in some branches of culture the Kushito-Semitic element took the initiative, as the Turanian did in others.

I must add that as regards political matters at the time when the great work of religious, scientific, and social organization took place in connection with the Chaldaio-Babylonian civilization, such as it was to remain, the northern provinces, speaking even then hardly anything but a Semitic language, took the principal management, as they really possessed the supremacy under Sargon and his son. The northern sacerdotal schools, those of Sippara, Babylon, and Borsippa, played a more important part in the politics of the country than the southern schools, those of Urukh and Ur. Or at least the great sacerdotal schools both in the south and north are an institution connected primarily with the Kushito-Semitic religion, although in the latter days, about the time of Nabukuduruzur and the Achæmenides, the caste which they represented called themselves specially Chaldeans; this title would have been perhaps more correctly applied to some division amongst them, the priests of magic for instance.

CHAPTER XXV.

The two Ethnic elements in the Babylonian nation.

THE diversity of races of men and languages is a fact which struck all the ancients. In the interior of Babylon itself at the time of the first Chaldean empire different languages were spoken, which were hardly intelligible in any other part but the one where they were spoken.[1] Æschylus[2] also calls the inhabitants of this town πάμμικτος ὄχλος, "a mixed crowd of every origin." And all the edicts of the kings of Babylon mentioned in the book of Daniel[3] begin with these words, "Be it known to you, O people, nations, and languages, . . ." The vast commerce of Babylon and Chaldea both by sea and land, as also the great influx of captives who were brought into the country by the conquering kings, such as Nebuchadnezzar, was an

---

[1] Quatremère, *Mémoire géographique sur la Babylone*, p. 21.
[2] *Pers.* 51.   [3] Dan. iii. 4; v. 19; vi. 26; vii. 14.

important influence in the production of this variety in race and language.

Foreign peoples, forming as the Jews did regular colonies with their own religion, civil laws and language, had come, in consequence of successful wars, and established themselves in the lower provinces of the Tigris and Euphrates, side by side with the ancient population and the Armenian tribes which the cuneiform texts teach us were so numerous even in the eighth century before the Christian era, and the native population itself had always been of a very mixed character from the earliest times.

That two ethnically different races existed in the population of Babylonia and Chaldea at the commencement of the historical era, is an established fact which the labours of every Assyriologist have tended to confirm, although some ignorant and superficial devotees of the Semitic language have ventured to doubt this as well as the existence of the Accadian tongue. A dualism of language corresponded to this dualism of race. Around the lower basin of the Euphrates and Tigris two languages were spoken, belonging to quite different families; the Accadian, which we claim as a branch of the Turanian or Altaic family, and the language of the so-called Semitic group, to which the name of *Assyrian* has been given because it was used in Assyria as well as in Babylon and Chaldea. As this title of *Assyrian* has been universally adopted, we must fall in with the general custom inconvenient as it is in this case, though the name is by no means suitable; it is too limited and has the misfortune to resemble that of the people by whom it was most recently spoken. We could not however venture to change it for a more correct designation, as that would render an already complicated question still more complicated by creating confusion in the terms used. I therefore continue to call the language by this name, but I would remind my readers that in Babylon and part of Chaldea, Assyrian was spoken long before the existence of the Assyrian nation, in other words, the people of Assur adopted in later times the Semitic language of Babylonia.

The most ancient of the Babylonian kings, some of whose epigraphic writings we possess, kings who can vie in antiquity with the builders of the Egyptian pyramids, Dungi for instance, had their official inscriptions engraved in the Semitic Assyrian as well as in the Accadian, although their proper names bear witness to their Accadian origin. Long after, about the date 2000 B.C., when Sargon I. had his great astrological work compiled which we shall elsewhere examine, there was no idea as yet of the Assyrians as a nation. The composers of the astrological collection knew only in that direction some mixed tribes *gutium*,[1] the *goim* of the book of Genesis,[2] from the midst of which rose the town

---

[1] The Assyrian tribes continued up to a late period in their nomadic mode of life. We have a curious proof of this in the fact that the word which in Assyrian means "town," and which is in every case peculiar to Assyria proper, was *alu*, a word radically and ethnologically identical with the Hebrews אהל, "tent." In Babylon it seems that they used the word *ir*, which also had a place in the Hebrew language with the same meaning; Prof. Sayce ascribes its origin to the Accadian *uru*, "town," but this last point is still doubtful.

[2] Gen. xix. 1.

of Assur (now Kalah-Shergat), the first seat of civilization, which was by degrees to conquer these tribes and unite them into a compact whole. The god of this city was then called Ausar,[1] a name which was afterwards changed to Assur, and the place itself partook of the nature of a Babylonian colony.[2] We may remark by the way, what important grounds these facts furnish for translating Genesis x. 11, "Out of that land he, Nimrod, went forth towards Assyria."

In every case the existence of the two languages has been fully proved, and this leads us to believe in a dualism of race. But owing to a rather curious circumstance, we are unable to find any exact time when the domains of the two races, as well as of the two languages, were clearly defined. From the earliest era of which we possess any written records, we see the two races mingled and intermixed, although each kept its own language and distinguishing characteristics, spreading over the whole surface of the country which extends from the Assyrian frontiers to the sea. We can only make out that in the north more people spoke the Semitic language than the Turanian; in the country of

---

[1] *W. A. I.* I., l. 1; IV., 18, 2. The town itself seems to have been called *Ausar* before the god, whose name appears to have taken this form and then that of *Assur* only in order to join artificially to a Semitic root (Assyrian אשר Hebrew ישר), the name of the ancient *Sar* of the Accadians, the ideographic expression of which became the usual orthography of the god Assur. The choice of the characters generally employed in writing Ausar as the name of a town are of such a nature as to lead us to conclude with Prof. Sayce that the name of the place, *a-usar*, "the border of the water," is of Accadian etymology, an etymology which agrees perfectly with the situation of the town.

[2] See Smith's "Notes on the Early History of Assyria and Babylon," in *Records of the Past*, Vol. III., p. 1.

Shinar properly so called in the south, the latter language was the more general, so also in the country called Accad, and later (from the ninth century) Kaldi. But that is a question of minor importance; the two elements existed alike in the two countries.

CHAPTER XXVI.

The Origin of the Chaldaio-Babylonian Cosmogonies.

THE Chaldaio-Babylonian cosmogonic traditions seem to have recognized the creation of two races of men, one with a brown, the other with a white skin.[1] But our data with reference to this point are still too imperfect to be of much use to us here, or to aid us in discovering a connection between this belief and the two different races existing together from the earliest times in the country where this belief arose, or to allow us to compare them with that enigmatical account given in the sixth chapter of Genesis about "the sons of God" (ver. 2), "the daughters of men" (ver. 4). Our study of these things must be reserved until we are better acquainted with traditions of this kind.

A good deal of light is thrown upon this subject by the celebrated passage of Hellanicus,[2] which

---

[1] See Smith's *Chaldean Account of Genesis*, p. 86. This very solution of many apparent geological and ethnographical difficulties has been already anticipated by Domenick M'Causland in his singular and plausible work, *Adam and the Adamite*.—*Ed.*

[2] Steph. Byz.

informs us that the primitive dualism of the Chaldean and Babylonian nations was known to the Greeks, and was expressed by their use of the names of Chaldeans and Cephenes. A whole cycle of traditions is connected with these names by the writer and other Greek authors, some of which seem really to possess an historical character, while others, in which Perseus plays the principal part,[1] are mythical; but the latter have acquired a great value since the discovery of the fragments of the Babylonian Epopee of Izdhubar or rather Dhubar, because one of the principal episodes of the legend of Perseus, the delivery of Andromeda, resembles in every detail an episode in the Epopee of the shores of the Euphrates.[2]

To the Greeks the name Cephenes was synonymous with Ethiopians. The opinion which has been preserved by Hellanicus counts them as one of the two elements of the race inhabiting the countries watered by the lower course of the Euphrates and Tigris, the famous Ethiopians or Kushites of Babylon, whose existence is proved by so many passages of classical antiquity and the sacred writings.[3] The Bible connects with these Kushites the name of Nimrod,[4] which is used both as the name of a hero

---

[1] Arrian., *Ap. Eustath. ad Dionys., Perieg.*, 1005; Apollodor., II., 4, 5; *Chronic.*, posch. l., p. 74, ed. Dindorf; cf. Herodot., VI., 54, and VII., 61; Lucan, *Phars.*, VI., 449. The name of Perseus must be here the Hellenic form of a Babylonian name with which we are not yet acquainted, probably the same that had given rise to the Parsoudos of Ctesias.

[2] See my *Premières Civilisations*, Vol. II., p. 23, et seq.

[3] Ch. Lenormant's *Introduction à l'Histoire de l'Asie occidentale*, p. 240, et seq.; Movers', *Die Phœnizier*, Vol. II., part 1, p. 269, 276, 224, et seq.; part 2, p. 104, 105, 388; Knobel's *Die Völkertafel der Genesis*, p. 251, 339, et seq.; D'Eckstein in the *Athenæum Français*, April 22nd, May 22nd, and August 19th, 1854.

[4] Gen. x., 8-12.

and as the name of a place, like all those contained in the same chapter of Genesis.¹ The more recent Semitic language gave to the name of Nimrod the meaning of "rebel," (from the root מרד,) in consideration of the character assumed by the heroic form of this personage; but that is certainly a forced etymology of later origin. After the labours of M. Grivel² and Prof. Sayce,³ there is no room to doubt that Nimrod was properly the Babylonian god Marduk reduced to the position of a hero, and we are ready to admit that Namarud was derived from an Accadian variation of the name of this god *ana amar-utu*.⁴ At any rate the god became here the personification of the people of his town.

The other element of the nation in the dualism of the Chaldees and Cephenes consisted of the Chaldees, who are described by Diodorus Siculus⁵ in a very correct passage about their discipline and their ideas as "the most ancient of the Babylonians." Hellanicus said in the same way, following the example of Stephen of Byzantium that " before the king Cepheus," that is to say, before the Cephenes, "there were some Chaldees who extended beyond Babylon as far as Choche," as far as the place where Seleucia afterwards stood. In the opinion of Berosus, the kings who reigned immediately after the flood are Chaldees. Without

---

¹ Oppert's *Comptes-rendus de la Sociélé française de Numismatique et d'Archeologie*, Vol. I.

² *Comptes-rendus de l'Acadèmie des Inscriptions*, 1874, p. 37-46; *Trans. Soc. Bib. Arch.*, Vol. III., p. 136, et seq.

³ *Trans. Soc. Bib. Arch.*, Vol. II., p. 243, et seq.

⁴ See my *Langue primitive de la Chaldée*, p. 369.   ⁵ II. 29.

speaking in such exact terms of the existence of this nation anterior to the Kushites, the Bible clearly admits the fact by mentioning, as the origin of the empire of Nimrod son of Kush, four towns which where already in being long before his time.[1] It also refers to the Chaldees at a very early epoch under the name of the *Chasdim.* Thus in the time of Abraham the great city of Ur, now Mugheir, was called "Ur of the Chaldees,"[2] and before that a chief of the Semitic tribe from which the Hebrews sprang is mentioned as Arphaxad, or Arpachashd, "neighbour of the Chaldees."[3] This notice of Ur in the most ancient records of the Terachites as that of the principal town of the Chaldees, whilst the same records establish no connection between them and Babel, becomes a very important point in determining the true ethnographical character of this nation. In fact Ur appears in all the numerous epigraphic monuments as the city most exclusively Turanian of them all; it is only much later that we can trace any vestige of the use of the Semitic-Assyrian language, all is in Accadian at the period of which we are speaking, and even under the Semitic kings of the dynasties of Karrak and Larsam.

In the cuneiform documents the term Kaldu or Kaldi occurs as the name of a tribe of the great Accadian nation[4] which was at first very obscure, but which began to be renowned about the ninth

---

[1] Gen. x. 11.   [2] Gen. xi. 22, 31; xv. 7.
[3] Gen. x. 22, 24; xi. 10-13.
[4] Stèle de Samsi-Vul, col. 4, l. 38 (*IV. A. I. I.*, 34).

century before our era.¹ Already under Assur-nazirhabel, Salmanassar III. and Samsi-Bin,² it had become mistress of the whole region bordering on the sea coast, which was then called Kaldu, and was divided into a great many small principalities governed by the chiefs of this tribe. From the eighth century the tribe of the Kaldi became important enough to furnish kings of Babylon,³ and after that period the Chaldees (using the word in a special sense) inhabited the southern part of the basins of the Euphrates and Tigris, and may be counted as the great adversaries of the Assyrian power, until by overthrowing Nineveh itself they founded the last Chaldaio-Babylonian empire under the dynasty of Nabopolassar. The tradition preserved by Hellanicus and other Greek writers substitutes, therefore, the name of Chaldees for that of Accadians, and even perhaps, as we shall see later, the indigenous traditions themselves used the double appellation of Sumir and Accad.⁴

But this discloses a question of great importance. We have proved the identity of the languages spoken by the Assyrians and the non-Turanian portion of the inhabitants of Babylon, but the Bible affirms that the inhabitants of the two countries were of a different race, by placing Assur amongst the descendents of Shem, while the people of Babylon are referred back to Ham for their origin. This would be no great stumbling-block

---

[1] See my *Premières Civilisations*, Vol. II., p. 218. [2] Or Samsi-Vul I.
[3] The same work, Vol. II., p. 221.
[4] We shall touch upon the question of Sumir and Accad, again in the Appendix.

after the facts revealed to us by the civilization imparted to the Assyrian tribes by the Babylonian colony of Assur; it is quite natural that they should have adopted at the same time the language of their teachers which must have resembled somewhat the dialect they spoke before. The difficulty of our problem lies in the fact that the Assyrian, or more correctly the Babylonian tongue belonged to the family commonly called the Semitic, and neither the Scriptures nor any other tradition mention the establishment of a Semitic colony in Babylon or the neigbouring provinces. These were really the Ethiopians, Cephenes or children of Kush, which three names were given to them indifferently, who existed side by side with the Chaldeans proper; these Kushites founded the first great political power in Chaldea, the empire of Nimrod or the king Cepheus; and there is no question of a Semitic invasion having supplanted them, though we have certainly notices of a few Semitic tribes, wandering between the Kushite towns in the uncultivated tracts of land like the Terachites, who finally emigrated, doubtless before the great increase in the settled population and the Aramean tribes of later origin.[1] But these may always be distinguished from the two really indigenous

---

[1] I agree entirely with M. Schrader's theory, that the various Semitic nations of the north and west, who originated in Arabia, the common cradle of their race, had, previous to the final migration which placed them in their settled habitations, one and all been subject to the contact and influence of Accadian Babylon, and that this affected them forcibly, and modified to a certain degree their peculiar characteristics. But there is no need to suppose on this account that they had ever settled in Babylon itself. The contact must have taken place in a neighbouring country, in the plains on the right bank of the Euphrates, where the ancient tribes of these nations, if they came from the centre of Arabia, naturally encamped before they began their march to the north.

elements, and as regards dualism of language, which corresponds to the dualism of race found in the ancient inhabitants of the country, we are obliged to come to the conclusion that the so-called Assyrian dialect was the one spoken by the Cephenian or Kushite portion of the population, although it belonged to the family of the Semitic languages. The Cephenian legends confirm this opinion by referring the origin of the Terachites themselves to the Ethiopian element in the nation: "Aethiopum proles quos rege Cepheo metus atque odium mutare sedes perpulerit." [1]

This is no isolated case either. Scholars of note whose opinion is of great weight have already remarked that the term Semitic is not suitable of application here. A large part, if not the majority, of the nations mentioned in the Bible as the descendants of Ham, particularly those of the branch of Kush, spoke languages of this class.[2] Hebrew was originally none other than the dialect of the Canaanites; a nation itself profoundly Hamitic; and Isaiah even calls that tongue "the language of Canaan." The family of Abraham heard and adopted it during their long residence among the Canaanites, in place of the language they spoke previously which probably resembled the Arabian as the tribes of Heber and Joctan were descended from the same stock.

Ghez is spoken by a people of Kushite origin in whom the Semitic elements made themselves strongly

---

[1] Tacit., *Hist.*, V., 11.

[2] See Oppert's *Athénæum français*, October 21st, 1854; De Rougé's *Revue ethnographique*, 1859, p. 109-111; and my *Manuel d'Histoire ancienne de l'Orient*, 3rd edition, Vol. I., p. 122, et seq.

felt, yet the latter can hardly have furnished the language of the country, for in that case we should have expected it to be Yemen, just as we know that this people imported the writing of Southern Arabia. The Himyaritic or Sabæan language itself is the dialect of a country where the Kushite nations had established themselves before the tribes descended from Joctan, and where they always continued to form an important part of the population. Therefore if the Joctanides of Southern Arabia spoke at the time of their civilization a different language from the tribes of the same stock inhabiting other parts of the peninsula, are we not justified in attributing it to the influence of the primitive settlers in the country with whom they mingled? Thus we arrive at the same conclusion as we did in speaking of the Assyrian; and this is also the case with Hebrew. It is a so-called Semitic language which was originally spoken by a people classed by the book of Genesis among the descendants of Ham, and which that people afterwards introduced and established by means of their superior civilization amongst the purely Semitic tribes who were still leading a nomadic and pastoral life.

These facts form a powerful argument, from a linguistic, and, to a certain extent, historical point of view, in favour of the theory of those writers who see in the Kushite and Canaanite nations "the most ancient branch of the Semitic family of the human race spreading over the entire interior of ancient Asia, from the sources of the Euphrates and Tigris into the heart of Arabia, from the shores of the Persian

Gulf to those of the Mediterranean, and on both coasts of the Gulf of Arabia, in Africa and in Asia." Some scholars hold an opinion that this ancient branch of the Semitic family was the first to leave the common home, and having established itself in Chaldea, Ethiopia, Egypt, and Palestine, became civilized, and was thus both an object of execration and envy to its pastoral brethren. Hence they say arose the wide separation between the descendants of Shem and Ham, the latter in the south and west, the former in the east and north, although both belonged originally to the same family, speaking one language though cut up into many dialects, and professing the same religion under different symbols, which may be called as a whole the Syro-Arabic or Syro-Ethiopian family in opposition to the Indo-Persian or Indo-Germanic family, the other great section of the white races.[1] This view would coincide very well with the way in which the Kushites frequently coalesced with the pure Semitic races, so that they could no longer be distinguished from them, whenever the two elements have followed each other, as in Southern Arabia and possibly in Assyria.

But, on the other hand, it would seem anthropologically evident from the figures on monuments and the skulls which have been examined so far, that there was a distinction between the descendants of Shem and Ham which is not found in the language, and which corresponded to that established by the biblical narrative; the people of Ham had also to a certain

[1] Guigniaut's *Religions de l'Antiquité*, Vol. II., part 3, p. 822.

degree peculiar characteristics, more materialistic and more industrial than those of the purely Semitic races, though they had likewise many common instincts; lastly, although a good many of the descendants of Ham spoke languages which were decidedly Semitic, others, like the Egyptians, possessed dialects which were doubtless closely connected with the Semitic family, but which possessed so far their own originality that they ought to be placed in a family apart. It is perhaps possible to explain and reconcile these contradictory data by modifying the formula thus obtained by a regard to the facts which have been ascertained by anthropology. In that case, we should have to suppose that the first branch detached from the parent stem was represented by the people of Ham, who coalesced with a Melanian race (black with smooth hair, like the Ghonds of India) which they found settled previously in the country into which they first spread, whilst the Semitic races were more behindhand and preserved the blood of the white race in all its purity. Thus their intermixture with another people would have sufficed after a certain time to make the descendants of Ham quite a different race from those of Shem, without, however, effacing their original affinities, especially those of language. At the same time, the mixture of blood which would in this way become the distinctive characteristic of the descendants of Ham, would not be found everywhere in equal proportions; the Melanian blood would predominate more in one instance than in another. Thus the nations referred by the biblical narrative to the family of Ham, would really exhibit a gradation of admixture with others, more or less decided, from the people who so strongly resembled the Semitic races as to be with difficulty distinguished from them, like the Kushites of Babylon or the Canaanites of Phenicia; to the people of decidedly ethnical characteristics, like the Egyptians. And we shall discover, if we study the history of the descendants of Ham, that there was a greater or less degree of affinity between the dialects spoken by the different nations, corresponding to the degree of resemblance of the people themselves to the anthropological type of the pure Semitic races; and this is itself a most important fact in determining the question how far a stranger element entered the pure blood of the white race.

It is extremely probable that there was some mixture of a tolerably pure Melanian race with the population of Chaldea and Babylonia, and that this circumstance would have caused that portion of the people who spoke a Semitic dialect to be classed amongst the Kushites. In fact part of the region of the great marshes round the Persian Gulf appears always to have been inhabited by almost black tribes,[1] who lived in a very savage state, and over whom the culture of the great cities in the neighbourhood never had much influence. These appear to have been the ancestors of the Lemluns of the present day, of whom we have heard a good deal from the French traveller Texier; they are closely allied as an anthropological type to the Bissharris of the neighbouring land of

---

[1] The bas-reliefs of Susiana prove to us the existence of tribes with a stronger Melanian element in them, and of an almost pure Negroid type; see G. Rawlinson's *The Five Great Monarchies*, 2nd edition, Vol. II., p. 500.

Egypt. We meet with them again in the same marshes, where the Assyrian bas-reliefs of Sennacherib and Assurbanipal exhibit them as coalescing with other tribes of a more or less Mongolian type.[1] They probably spoke "the language of the fishermen," which is mentioned in some Assyrian documents as being a different dialect from those of Assur and Accad. In my opinion these tribes were really of Ethiopian origin, and represented the first *substratum* of the historical Kushites of Babylon; there are even now the remains of that most ancient population of the country who dwelt there even earlier than the Turanians, and were conquered by the latter before the dawn of the historic ages. These first Kushites only remained select in the shelter of the inaccessible marshes where they had retreated; in other parts of the land they mixed with a few tribes speaking the Semitic language, who established themselves there before the Semitic race properly so-called, and thus arose the second Kushite nation of the era of Nimrod and Cepheus, the only people who belong to history and who spoke the language called Assyrian; the purely Semitic races, like the Hebrews, treated these in the same way as the Canaanites, and refused to consider them of the same race as themselves in spite of the affinity of language.

However I will not insist too strongly upon these latter conclusions, as they are at present conjectures which could not be fully examined and proved without necessitating explanations of a far too complicated

---

[1] Mr. George Rawlinson (*The Five Great Monarchies*, 2nd edition, Vol, II., p. 497) had made a similar remark about the figures on the bas-reliefs relating to the Babylonian war of Assurbanipal.

character to be introduced here. Of one fact we may be sure, namely, the existence of the Kushito-Semitic and Turanian or Altaic races following each other, and coalescing over the whole of Babylon and Chaldea, as long as we can discover from the monuments in our possession, one predominating in the north, the other in the south. An eminent anthropologist Dr. Hamy has discovered amongst the figures of kings and other inhabitants of the country represented in the ancient Babylonian sculptures, the existence of two entirely distinct ethnological types of race. One has a slender figure, the other is short and dumpy; the first was a remarkably long shaped, the second a round skull; and finally, one shows very remarkably the arched profile of the Syro-Arabic or Semitic races with its aquiline nose; whilst the other is distinguished by prominent cheek-bones and a nose with highly curved nostrils. In the words of M. Hamy, the second Babylonian and Assyrian type "differs radically from the Syro-Arabic type, in the same degree that the peasants of our central table-land do from the Jews and the Arabs;" and this second type resembles rather than any other known to us that of the Ugro-Finnic and Siberian races, to whom several anthropologists have assigned the name of Mongoloides.[1]

In our previous researches we have thus seen that there was a dualism of language corresponding to the dualism of race, and that one of the languages, the Assyrian, belonged to the Semitic family, while the other, the Accadian, formed a separate group of

[1] See my *Langue primitive de la Chaldée*, p. 382-386.

the Altaic family, closely allied to the Ugro-Finnic dialects. It is not improbable that this ancient fusion of two entirely different dialects spoken in the same land, had much to do with the origin of the tradition which placed at a very early epoch the origin of the confusion of languages at Babylon. Lastly, the special researches we have prosecuted in the present work lead us to point out another parallel dualism; that of the religions. Side by side with the Semitic and Turanian languages in Chaldea, we have seen on the one hand a religion closely related to those of Syria and Phenicia, belonging to the same group and founded on the same conceptions; and on the other, a system of magic resulting from very different views, with its own gods and spirits, resembling forcibly the magic of the Finns and all the Altaic nations, and connected with a perfect religious system which is explained in the magic books, and which was only a normal development of that demonological naturalism which is peculiar to the Turanian nations.

All these facts combine in a most striking manner; and the fundamental difference, the first opposition of the two elements constituting the population of Chaldea and Babylonia in the most remote ages, appears in the religion as in the language. There were doubtless two races of men whose history can be traced back to the time of their divergence from each other, each having its own characteristics and possessing its own language.

CHAPTER XXVII.

The Priority of the Accadian Population of Chaldea.

THE fragments of the narrative of Berosus which we possess begin thus: "There were (originally) in Babylon many men of a *foreign race* (ἀλλοεθνεῖς), who inhabited Chaldea, living in a savage state after the manner of animals." There is no other way of translating this phrase; the word ἀλλοεθνὴς has only one meaning in Greek, it is synonymous with ἀλλόφυλος. It has a stronger signification than ξένος, since it gives not only the idea of foreigner, but also that of "man of a very different nation, of another race."[1] So in the eyes of Berosus the first inhabitants of Babylonia, whom the god Oannes (Hea) came to civilize in person, and whose first place of abode was Chaldea, were foreigners of another race.

But with relation to whom were they foreigners and of another race? Plain common sense tells us that it was as compared with the Babylonians of the time of Berosus, namely, the people speaking the

[1] See my *Langue primitive de la Chaldée*, p. 327.

Semitic language to whom the writer belonged. We cannot even imagine him to have had any other intention. In the same way we often find the name of the Philistines changed in the Septuagint into ἀλλόφυλοι used absolutely, meaning there a people of a different race from the Israelites.

From these observations we are led to conclude that the Chaldean priest who translated the annals of his native land into Greek under the first Seleucidæ, regarded the non-Semitic, the Accadian or Turanian people, as the first occupier of the soil. This was the national tradition. The question is, was it correct? We have at present no means of ascertaining this; and there are reasons for thinking, as we said just now, that this element which possessed a certain amount of civilization had superseded a primitive savage population, itself almost Melanian, which is to this day represented by the Lemluns. But one thing however seems certain; all the Assyriologists who have studied the subject admit unanimously that an Accadian or Turanian element furnished the first civilized inhabitants of the vast plains, of the lower part of the basin of the Euphrates and Tigris, and that from this point of view they had decidedly the priority over the Semitic or Kushito-Semitic element. The Turanian remained during long centuries, and particularly in the southern provinces, the predominating element with regard to politics and language in the dualism of the population, even after that dualism had become too decided for anyone to deny that the civilization common to the tribes speaking the two languages was the work of one race alone.

That the Accadians or Turanians had the priority over the Semitic or Kushito-Semitic races is proved by the geographical names of Chaldea and Babylonia which the Semitic portion of the population adopted; for these do not certainly belong to their language, nor have they any precise etymology in it; they were beyond doubt borrowed from the Accadian. Examples of this are furnished by the two great rivers the Tigris and Euphrates, and some of the most important towns of the land, as Ur (*uru*, "the town" above all others), Uruk, the Erech of the Bible (*uru-uku*, "the eternal city"), Larsam, Agane, Surippak, Eridhu, Nipur, Borsippa, not to mention the names of many towns of which the non-Semitic character is clearly manifest. These instances of geographical nomenclature are quite decisive, although their number is limited, for in most cases the towns of Babylonia and Chaldea had a double name, as is the case at the present day in Hungary and other countries where two races speaking different languages exist together, neither having absorbed the other. Thus one of the most important towns of Babylonia was called in the Assyrian *Kuti* and in the Accadian *Tiggaba*. In the Bible it is called Cutha, a modification of the Assyrian form, but the classical geographers copied from the other name; Pliny writes it Digba; Ptolemy, Digua; the Peutingerian table has Digubis, all coming from the Accadian Tiggaba, the tradition of which was evidently preserved down to the Roman epoch. In these cases of double appellation, when we know the meaning of the Accadian name we generally find that the Assyrian appellation was an exact translation of it. For instance, the Accadian name of Babylon *Kâ-Dingira* and the Semitic name Bab-il both alike meant "the gate of the god;" but these two synonymous appellations were themselves preceded by a more ancient Accadian name *Tin-tir*, of which there seems to have been no Semitic translation. There is positively not a single town south of the Assyrian frontier sufficiently ancient to have had only a Semitic name. Appellations of this kind taken from the Assyrian, as Dur-Sarkin, Dur-Ummu-banit, Kar-ramani, which are some of the most ancient, first begin to appear much later, in the full light of the historic ages, under dynasties of kings posterior to the great monarchs of Ur (the first princes of whom we have any record), and dynasties whose surnames attest the Semitic origin of the family. Such towns owed their foundation to those kings.

In a former chapter we touched upon the subject of the names of divinities borrowed from the Accadian language and mythology, which the Semitic portion of the population received into its pantheon, and which remained there up to the last days of Babylon and Assyria; for they were also common to those disciples both in religion and literature of the Chaldaio-Babylonian civilization. The few fragments that we possess of the cosmogonic epic legend, describing the events of the earliest ages up to a few years after the Deluge and the destruction of the tower of Babel, suffice to show us that the names used in it are entirely Accadian; and when we say that they remain almost unaltered in the extracts of Berosus, we may be sure that under the Seleucidæ the ancient Accadian form was preserved intact in the traditions of the sacerdotal schools, and that no Semitic substitutes were adopted.'

As regards the anteriority of the Turanian or Accadian element to the Semitic or Kushito-Semitic element, we have a proof that the former was in possession of a remarkable state of civilization, a sedentary and agricultural life, a steady industry, and above all an organized government, in the fact that the Assyrian vocabulary has borrowed many words from the Accadian with reference to these things, particularly names of offices which it would be impossible to explain supposing them to be of Semitic origin, while that is readily done in the Accadian.² We may give as examples *tur-tanu* "Generalissimo of the armies" (Accadian *tur-dan*, "powerful chief"); *sak* "officer" (which is used in the composition of the hybrid form *rab-sak*); *dubsar* "scribe" (in the Bible טפסר); *patesi* "viceregent vicar;" *aba* "magistrate of the judicial order;" *emga* a sacerdotal title which was applied to the Chaldean Magi, and which meant originally "glorious, august." I have long thought, in common with all other Assyriologists following in the wake of M. Oppert, that the ethnic dualism of the population of Chaldea and Babylonia was expressed by the nomenclature so often used in speaking of the inhabitants of those countries, *Sumeriu u Akkadiv*, "the Sumirians and the Accadians," I saw in these two names the designation

---

¹ Those names of which we already possess the original forms are, if we compare the forms given in the extract of Berosus with the original forms: = Adi-Uru = Mulu-urugal = U-bara-tutu = Khasis-adra or Adra-khasis (the two forms are equally used) = Etana. All these personages are specially classed as Chaldeans by Berosus.

² See my *Langue primitive de Chaldée*, p. 363. et seq.

of the two races, applying that of Accad to the Turanians and that of Sumir to the Semitic or Kushito-Semitic tribes. I set forth this opinion in the first French edition of this present work, but I must confess that my convictions have been shaken since then by the objections that M. Schrader has raised against seeing any distinction of race expressed in these two names. Although we may be certain that the Assyrians themselves used the term "the Accadian language" to designate the non-Semitic tongue, and although consequently we may be justified by their example in using the term Accadian as a general designation of the ethnic element which we hold to be connected with the Altaic nations, yet there is nothing to prove that the name Sumirians described another race. It is possible and even probable that M. Ménant and M. Schrader are right in thinking that the two names of Sumirians and Accadians were anterior to the introduction of the Semitic element, and originally designated rather two geographical divisions of the same people and the same race, the inhabitants of the northern and southern provinces of Chaldea and Babylonia proper.[1] If it is so, the duality of Sumir and Accad would have no connection with the ethnic duality, which is to be seen just as much in the land of Sumir as in the country of Accad, taking these two words in the geographical sense. The Sumirians and the Accadians would both therefore have belonged to the non-Semitic race.

[1] I shall recur, however, in an Appendix to the difficult question of Sumir and Accad, and I shall then make use of the new documents on this subject with which science has lately been enriched.

CHAPTER XXVIII.

The Sumirian Influence in Chaldean and Babylonian Civilization.

FROM the fusion of the characteristics and institutions of the two races who, though of different origin, inhabited the lower valley of the Euphrates and Tigris, arose that great civilization of Chaldea and Babylon, which made its influence felt over the whole of ancient Asia, and moulded the latter after its own pattern. The Chaldaio-Babylonian civilization was essentially of a mixed nature, resulting from the combinations of different elements, and in this lay its greatness, richness, and power; the capabilities and the instincts of two different races were united to construct it.

We cannot as yet, and perhaps we may never be able to determine precisely and minutely what is Turanian and what Kushite in a mixed creation which we have no means of studying except as a whole. However we can trace a good many things back to their original source, even in the present state of our knowledge.

Thus we know for certain that the Turanian portion of the population introduced the peculiar system of cuneiform writing into Babylon and Chaldea. The careful researches of M. Oppert have settled that point beyond dispute.[1] The characters that compose the writing have either an ideographic or syllabic value, but more frequently they may be used both ways, according to the position in which they occur. They consisted originally[2] of a rough drawing or symbolical image, which has since undergone but little alteration, of the concrete object or abstract idea expressed or brought to mind by the syllable composing their phonetic value, not in the Assyrian tongue but in the Accadian, that is, in the language of the Turanians of Chaldea.[3] The idea of "god" is rendered in the Assyrian by the word *ilu*, but the character which represents ideographically this word, which character was originally in the form of a star, is pronounced *an* where it is employed as a syllabic sign, because in that language "god" was spoken of as *ana*. The sign meaning "father," in the Assyrian *abu*, is phonetically *at* or *ad*, because the word "father" was *ad* (lengthened form *adda*) in the Accadian; another has the double form of the verb "to go" (in the Assyrian *alak*), and the syllable *du* "to go," pronounced *du* in the same language. The value of the compound syllables is of the same origin. One sign represents the syllable *tur* and the idea of "son," the Accadian word for "son" (in the Assyrian *ablu* or *maru*) being *tur*; another the syllable *gal* and the idea of "great"

---

[1] *Rapport au ministre de l'Instruction publique*, Paris, 1858; *Expédition en Mésopotamie*, Vol. II., p. 77-86; Schrader's "Ist das Akkadischer der keilinschriften eine Sprache oder eine Schrift," in Vol. XXIX. of the *Journal of the German Asiatic Society*.

[2] Oppert's *Expédition en Mésopotamie*, Vol. II., p. 63-68.

[3] See Sayce, *Lectures on Assyrian Philology*, lecture iii.

(in the Assyrian *rabu*), the Accadian for "great" being *gal*; a third has the meaning of "chief, prince," and gives the compound syllable *nir* after the form of the Accadian word *nir* "prince." Even the phenomena of polyphony itself, or the existence of many phonetic expressions for the same sign, independently of the Assyrian reading corresponding to its ideographic signification, finds its explanation in the different words which note the various shades of the ideographic meaning in the Accadian. For instance, one and the same sign gives the idea of "sun" (Assyrian *samsu*) and "day" (Assyrian *yumu*); but it is used phonetically to represent the simple syllable *ut*, *ud*, and the compound syllable *par*, and it also became in the Accadian *utu* "sun" and *par* (in its lengthened form *parra*) "day." Another has the double signification of "sheep" (Assyrian *sinu*) and of the verb "to take" (Assyrian *sabatu*); the first of these ideas was rendered in the Accadian by the word *lu*, the second by the word *dib*, so the character has the double phonetic value of *lu* and *dib*.

At the same time, facts of the most convincing nature bearing upon the pronunciation would deter any serious mind from the opinion that the cuneiform syllabary could have been invented by a Semitic people. These facts show beyond a doubt that it was the work of a race speaking quite a different language, who were not capable of rendering a language of the family of Shem otherwise than very imperfectly. The principal of these facts is the absence of any particular sign for the articulations ט, ע, ה, א, characteristic of the Semitic organ; the confusion of *m* with *v*; the want of distinction between the sibilants, ז, ס, צ, *za* and *ṣa* having only one sign, as *az*, *aṣ*, *aṣ*, or *iz*, *is*, *iš*, or else again *zib*, *ṣib*, and *sib*, etc.; the want of a different notation for ב and פ, or כ and ק as a final, the same character being *ap* and *ab*, or else *ag*, *ak*, *aq;* lastly, the absence of a different written expression for כ and ק before the vowel *i*, ב and פ before the vowel *u*, for neither *qi* nor *pu* can be written, and we must substitute for them *ki* and *bu*.[1]

We obtain some very important information concerning the progress of the syllabary by studying the primitive and elementary characters of the cuneiform writing, 180. in number, the combination of which gave rise to a great number of new signs.[2] If we examine them with a view to discovering what the internal objects were which they originally represented, we find that the nature of the objects thus formed into graphic signs seems to indicate as the original seat of this writing a land other than Chaldea, a more northern region with a very different fauna and flora;[3] where, for instance, the lion and the other great carnivora of the feline race were unknown, whilst the bear and the wolf were common animals; where neither the palm nor even the vine[4] flourished, their place being supplied

[1] The attempt at a distinction between *ki* and *qi*, *bu* and *pu*, did not appear until quite a late period, towards the end of the eighth century B.C., and its use never became general.

[2] Smith's *The Phonetic Values of the Cuneiform Characters*, p. 4; and my *Études accadiennes*, Vol. I., fasc. 1, p. 45, et seq.

[3] Oppert's *Comptes-rendus de la Société française de Numismatique et d'Archéologie*, Vol. I., p. 74.

[4] The character which is used to designate the vine, and afterwards wine, is a compound sign, and of the secondary formation, the combination of which has been traced to the compound *ges-tin*, "tree of life," which is its Accadian rendering.

to a great extent by conifers. It would be worth while to pursue these observations in a special treatise, and some day it will certainly be done. One of the most significant facts that could be brought forward is that the Accadians designate every kind of camel, that of Arabia amongst the rest, by a name that can only be etymologically explained as a description of the peculiar characteristic of the camel with two humps of Upper Asia. The important and suggestive remark of M. Oppert which we have just quoted, with illustrations of our own, would lead us to decide that even if the cuneiform writing received its final development and organization in Chaldea itself, after the Accadians had settled in the plain and round the junction of the Euphrates and Tigris, yet they must have brought the first elements of it with them from another region to which their migration was first directed.

In fact the Accadians had no ground for affirming themselves to be the first occupants of the land of Chaldea, they could not call themselves the aboriginal inhabitants; they remembered that their ancestors had come from another region of a very different character physically, and therefore, after having dwelt for centuries and centuries in the great plains, they continued to use the name of *Akkadi*, which meant "mountaineers" in their own language. The original force of Sumirians and Accadians in the Accadian was, "the people of the plain and the people of the mountain;" so the ancient title of supreme royalty which we should translate "king of the Sumirians and Accadians," *unga kiengi ki akkad*, really means "king of the plain and mountain." Therefore, although the names of Sumirians and Accadians became at the historical epoch the designation of the north and south of Babylonia, this was only after an alteration in the respective positions of the races to whom these names applied originally in order to show what part of the country they inhabited.[1] The names remained like monuments of an anterior epoch, when the two divisions of the Turanian people, instead of inhabiting the north of Babylonia and the south of Chaldea, were spread over the plain watered by the two great rivers, while the Sumirians and Accadians still dwelt in the mountains of the east and north-east, the common cradle of the race, or rather the last stage of their migration before they reached the Euphrates and Tigris.

I have pointed out elsewhere[2] the curious coincidence existing between this fact and the witness of classical literature, which ascribes to the nations dwelling in a part of Armenia the names of Χαλδαῖοι, Κάρδακες, Καρδοῦχοι, Κορδυαῖοι, Γορδυηνοὶ, Κύρτιοι, *Gordiani, Kardu;*[3] and I by no means agree with those

---

[1] See my *Etudes accadiennes*, Vol. I., fasc. 3, p. 72, et seq.; and farther on the Appendix II.

[2] *Commentaire des Fragments cosmogoniques de Bérose*, p. 51, et seq.; *Etudes accadiennes*, Vol. I., fasc. 3, p. 71-75.

[3] Lassen's *Die altpersische keilinschriften von Persepolis*, p. 81-86, and in the *Zeitschrift für die Kunde des Morgenlandes*, Vol. VI., p. 49, 50; Wester's *Zeitschrift für die Kunde des Morgenlandes*, Vol. VI., p. 370, et seq.; Jacquot's *Journal Asiatique*, June 1838, p. 593, et seq.; Ritter's *Erdkunde Asien*, Vol. II., p. 788-796; Vol. VIII., p. 90, et seq.; Vol. IX., p. 631; Gesenius', *Thesaur.* v. כשדים; Rödiger and Pott's *Zeitschrift für die Kunde des Morgenlandes*, Vol. III., p. 6, et seq.; Ewald's *Geschichte des Volkes Israel*, Vol. I., p. 333; Kunick's *Mélanges asiatiques de l'académie de Saint Petersburg*, Vol. I., p. 53, et seq.; Hitzig's *Ugeschichte der Philistäer*, p. 46, Pott, in the Encyclopædia of Ersch and Guber, art. *Indogerm. Sprachstam*, p. 59, Lengerke's *Kenaan*, p. 220; Renan's *Histoire des Langues semitiques*, 1st edition, p. 60.

scholars who look upon this as a chance coincidence to which no further value is to be attached. In fact, Berosus mentions the Gordyan mountains as the resting-place of the ship of Xisisthrus after the Deluge; and these mountains correspond exactly (judging from the narrative of Assurnazirpal's campaigns)[1] to the mountain Nizir, which a national tradition in the cuneiform writing preserves as the scene of the same occurrence. Therefore, the mountains which were still inhabited at the classical epoch by a people whose name resembled very closely that of the Chaldeans, proved to be the very ones from which the people of Babylon and Chaldea imagined the post-diluvian founders of humanity to have descended, and which the Accadians remembered as the home of their ancestors. The inhabitants of these same mountainous regions, who have kept the name of Kurds up to the present time, became Aryanized many centuries ago by means of successive migrations of other nations, and it would seem that this had already taken place in the time of Xenophon; but before that, and until the period of the last conquests of the Assyrian kings, the cuneiform monuments exhibit their country as occupied exclusively by Turanian tribes closely allied to the most ancient population of Media, and therefore also to the Turanians of Chaldea.[2] I might go further still, and trace the route of the Accadians' first migration according to their own traditions, and it would then prove to be the same as that ascribed in

---

[1] *W. A. I.* I., 20, l. 33, et seq.
[2] See my *Lettres Assyriologiques*, 1st series, Vol. I., p. 19, et seq.

the book of Genesis to the builders of the tower of Babel, who went "from the east into the land of Shinar." By these means I should reach at length that mountain of the north-east, which played so large a part in the Chaldean traditions under the double title of "Cradle of the human race," and "Place of the assembly of the god."[1] But in so doing I should be introducing matter quite foreign to the subject of this chapter, and losing myself in digressions which could not but weary the reader. It suffices for me to have pointed out these peculiarities in such a manner as to prove that the Turanian part of the population who introduced the cuneiform writing into Chaldea, already possessed the first rudiments of this writing before they reached the last stage of their migration on the banks of the Euphrates and Tigris. Abel Remusat has shewn in a special treatise,[2] that the same was the case in Eastern Asia with the ancestors of the Hundred Families, who invented the fundamental elements of Chinese writing when living still in a state of singular barbarity.

The earliest characters of the cuneiform writing would not lead us to conclude that the Accadians were much more advanced than the Chinese, when they began to use them as a means of expressing their thoughts. But the Accadians were already at that time in possession of a complete metallurgy, whilst the ancestors of the Chinese still used weapons

---

[1] See my *Commentaire des Fragments cosmogoniques de Bérose*, p. 317, 393; and my *Etudes accadiennes*, Vol. I., fasc. 3, p. 73, et seq.

[2] "Recherches sur l'origine et la formation de l'écriture Chinoise," in the *Mémoires de l'Académie des Inscriptions*, 2nd series, Vol. VIII.

of stone; for amongst the fundamental elements of the primitive hieroglyphism of the Accadians there is a sign for copper and another for the precious metals, as gold and silver.

In consequence of the information gathered from the latest discoveries, we may, I think, place amongst the Turanian contributions to the Chaldaio-Babylonian civilization not only writing, but also magic with its attendant train of beliefs and practices. I have endeavoured elsewhere to prove that to this element was due the credit of introducing the working of metals, which was such a flourishing branch of industry in Chaldea and Babylonia from the earliest times.[1] Lastly, I hold that there are many powerful arguments to be drawn from the vocabulary and writing in support of the opinion, that the first Turanian strata of the Accadian population introduced, with its system of canals and irrigation, the agriculture which was peculiar to this country, and I hope some day to arrange these arguments in a special work on this subject.

On the other hand, we are now in a position to prove that astrology and astronomy were the work of the Kushito-Semitic element of the population. It has long been observed, that the whole world owes its first information about astronomy, mathematics, and certain branches of industry,[2] to the nations of this family, who were essentially materialistic and constructive. Whilst the Accadian always remained the magical language, even in Assyria, all the

---

[1] See my *Premières Civilisations*, Vol. l., p. 118, et seq.

[2] Boeckh's *Metrologische Untersuchungen*, Berlin, 1838; Bertheau's *Zur Geschichte der Israeliten*, p. 99, et seq.

astrological and astronomical documents were in Assyrian. Sir Henry Rawlinson and Mr. Norris brought out a most interesting series of these latter documents, Vol. III. of the *Cuneiform Inscriptions of Western Asia*, but a great number of them are still unpublished. The most ancient even, like the great work in seventy tablets,[1] in which Sargon I. and his son Naram-sin collected the traditions and rules for augury belonging to the astrological schools that existed before their era, were written in this language, as we plainly see, in spite of the multiplicity of ideograms and allophonic words in their archaic orthography. So the language devoted to astrology is that of the Kushito-Semitic people,[2] just as the Accadian is the magical language. This fact is a very important guide to the origin of the science,

---

[1] The *Namarbili*, or "Book of the Illumination of Bel."—*Ed.*

[2] I have adhered to the original form of this paragraph as it appears in the French edition, because I fully believe in its fundamental data which ascribe the origin of astrology and astronomy to the Kushito-Semetic element. But I now think that some of these assertions are too positive, and require explanation in a note.

For instance, it was going rather too far to conclude from the fact that all the fragments of astrological and astronomical books in our possession at present are in Assyrian, that none were ever written in any other language, and so not in the Accadian. And *W. A. I.* III, 55, 2, ought perhaps to be considered as an astronomical table drawn up after the documents in "the language of Assur" compared with those in "the language of Sumir and Accad." The Accadian language possesses a complete scientific nomenclature for astronomy and astrology, and some of the expressions are often independent as their formation of the corresponding Assyrian expressions. Again in the great work compiled by order of Sargon I. and Naram-Sin, we find in place of Assyrian terms written phonetically, ideographic expressions, which might just as well have been invented by people speaking the Semitic languages as by those speaking the Accadian. We are also ready to grant that even with regard to such fundamental terms as "conjunction" (in the Accadian *ribana*, in the Assyrian *qasritu*), that are regular allophonic words, that is to say Accadian words written phonetically, and taken afterwards improperly as indivisible ideographic groups rendered by the corresponding Assyrian words. This proves, at least, that the element speaking the Accadian language cultivated early and attentively the science of the stars, and did not leave the monopoly of it to the doctors of the Assyrain element. But I fail to see in it with Prof. Sayce an absolute proof that this science was invented by the Accadians. As I have already

and it will be seen to be still more important in connection with the other proofs I am about to adduce, on account of the close relation existing between astrology, and the sidereal religion which we have termed Chaldaio-Babylonian.

remarked above, considering the long co-existence of the two populations, each keeping its own language, although they were consolidated into one and the same political state, I cannot think it necessary that everything written or expressed in the Accadian should necessarily be of Accadian origin.

On the other hand, it seems to me impossible not to attribute to the Accadians the sexagesimal computation, which was the basis of the whole Chaldean system of mathematics. The double cycle of 60 and 600 years, exactly like the *sosses* and *neres* of Chaldea, exists amongst the Uigurs, the Mongols, and the Mantchoos; like the cycle of Hoang-ti in China from the earliest historic epochs, a cycle of 60 years mixed with others of 61 days and 60 months, which was brought into this country from the countries of the Kuen-lun like all the primitive civilization of the Hundred Families. Cycles which are born one of another, and proceed from the sexagesimal numeration, have been also introduced into India, where a Babylonian computation hardly accounts satisfactorily for their appearance; such are the cycle of 60 years attributed to Parâsara, and the figures of 3600 years assigned to the period of Vâkpaii, of 216,000 to that of Pradjâpati, and of 432,000 to Kali-yuga. We have nothing analogous on the part of the Semitic races or the Canaanites like the Egyptians. Fréret, Ideler, Bunsen, and Lepsius, were struck, as no one can fail to be, by the connection between all the chronological computations which I have just mentioned, and their relation to the Chaldean system. But no one could explain this connection; now, however, we begin to see more clearly since we have proved the Turanian or Altaic character of the Accadians who introduced the sexagesimal numeration into Chaldea.

CHAPTER XXIX.

The Influence of the Kushite Mythology in Chaldean Faith.

THE Kushito-Semitic element appears to have predominated in both the religion and language of the people of Chaldea, particularly during the last period of the Chaldaic and Babylonian civilization.

The religion of the Kushites was allied to those of Syria and Phenicia, and after having adopted some Accadian characteristics, it became the official religion of Babylon and Chaldea; the ancient Accadian magic was cast out, and obliged to occupy an inferior position as we explained above; and the Assyrian language entirely supplanted the Accadian. It is as yet impossible to determine precisely at what moment this change took place, or was finally settled, for it must have been gradual. But twelve centuries before the Christian era, the title of Accadians, which was still used to designate the inhabitants, had become little else but a name. The ancient Turanian population, which was established there before the Kushites, coalesced with them entirely, even adopting their language, and the mixed civilization which had resulted from the amalgamation of its own customs and institutions with those of the new comers.

A little later the tribe of Kaldi appears upon the scene, they were the Chaldeans, properly so-called[1] who boasted that they, more than any other tribe, had preserved in all its purity the blood "of the most ancient amongst the Babylonians," which was considered on account of its antiquity even more noble than that of the Kushites or Cephenes. The chiefs of this tribe of Kaldi, such as Yakin and Merodach-Baladan, bore thoroughly Assyrian names, as also the monarchs of the last Babylonian empire, the dynasty of which claimed to be of thoroughly Chaldean origin in the strictest sense of the word.[2] The Accadian language had fallen into disuse long before; we cannot even be sure that it was still spoken under the last kings of the Cissian dynasty of Babylon, who were reigning some thirteen or fourteen centuries before the Christian era, although they had some inscriptions engraved in it, such as

[1] It is not difficult now to understand the origin of the apparent contradiction with regard to the Chaldeans, concerning the information collected by Diodorus of Sicily, and the accounts of the prophets of Israel. As a fraction of the people of Accad, the Chaldeans had the right, as Diodorus tells us, of calling themselves the most ancient of the Babylonians; while as the peculiar tribe of Kaldi ruling over all the countries as far as Babylon, Isaiah was not mistaken in terming them a new nation. On the contrary, these two assertions are both alike equally true, according to the point of view from which we regard them.

[2] Many years before, the king of Babylon, who belonged to the type acknowledged as Mongolic, and whose image may be seen on one of the black stones in the British Museum (see pl. i. of my *Langue primitive de la Chaldée*), bore a Semitic-Assyrian name, Maruduk-idin-akhe.

Burna-buryas and Durri-galzu.[1] We may assert with truth that the Accadian became from that time what Latin was in the middle ages, a classical and sacred language. It kept this sacred character on account of the old collections of liturgical hymns and magical formulæ in the Accadian, which served as a foundation for sacerdotal teaching, and which were still sung at certain ceremonies, or recited during theurgical operations in the seventh century B.C., when Assurbanipal had the Accadian books copied for his library at Nineveh.[2] But there are indications that these books were only intelligible by means of the ancient Assyrian translations which accompanied them, and that even in Babylon, the priests could not write Accadian inscriptions as they had done five or six years before Assurbanipal tried to restore the study of the sacred language, which, he said, none of his predecessors had done. Therefore he had not only the Accadian books copied, but also all the documents concerning grammar and the vocabulary, which were to be found at Erech and other places. His project succeeded well enough to produce some scribes who composed a few Accadian documents[3] in

[1] I have shown elsewhere (*Etudes accadiennes*, Vol. I., fasc. 3, p. 79) that the use of the Accadian began to decline from the time that Sargon I., king of Agané, by subjecting the whole of the country, as far as the Gulf of Persia, to a new dynasty, proceeding from the northern provinces, secured the political preponderance of the Kushito-Semitic element. From that moment the custom was established, that private contracts were written in Assyrian, whenever one of the contracting parties bore a Semitic name, and consequently belonged to the same race as the reigning dynasty. This decline went on rapidly under the Cissian kings, of whom Hammurabi was the first, when the capital was definitely fixed at Babylon. It must have been under these kings, who occupied the throne for many centuries, that the Accadian ceased to be a living and spoken language.

[2] *History of Assurbanipal*, p. 325.

[3] Now that one of these documents has been published (*W. A. I.* IV., 18, 2) and can be minutely studied, I find it difficult to allow that it was really composed under

his honour, Mr. Smith pointed out this fact which never occured again, either before or after him, from the twelfth to the sixth century B.C.

Assurbanipal. It seems much more like an ancient hymn. I imagine that the copyist inserted the name of this monarch (under the Accadianized form of *Ausar-ban-ibila*) in the final prayer for the king, where there must originally have been a blank, filled up according to convenience by the name of the king reigning when the hymn was to be used. I should attach more importance to the fact that an Accadian name reappears for the last king of Babylon. The title of this monarch means, "Nebo is majestic, glorious;" we have two forms of it, one purely Assyrian, *Nabu-nadu*, the other Accadian, *Nabu-nîtuq*. Now the second is not an allophonism for *Nabu-nadu*, for although in the Canon of Ptolemy Alexander Polyhister this king is called according to Berosus Ναβονάδιος or Ναβοννήδος = *Nabu-nadu*. Abydene called him Ναβούνιδοχος, *Nabu-nîtuq*; therefore this king elected by the Chaldeans from their very midst (Bérose, fragment 14, ed. C. Muller; Abyden, fragment 8, ed. C. Muller), who calls himself in his own inscriptions "chief magus," *rubu emga* (*W. A. I.* 1., 68, 2, 3, 4), the רב־מג of the Bible (Jer. xxxix., 3) bore simultaneously two synonymous names; the one Assyrian *Nabu-nddu*, the other Accadian *Nabu-nîtuq*, and used them indifferently in his official inscriptions; some of the Greek historians of Babylon adopted the first form in writing of him, others the second. This indicated a kind of renaissance of the Accadian as the sacred and classical languages of the time of the last Babylonish empire. It also proves that the Accadian is indeed the "language of the Chaldees" in the sacerdotal sense of the name, which the book of Daniel describes as one of the principal paths of study marked out for young people destined to a learned career.

CHAPTER XXX.

The Turanians in Chaldea and ancient Asia.

I HAVE briefly but completely explained the light that a study of the original texts, and particularly the fragments of the Accadian books, has thrown upon the difficult problem of the true origin of the Chaldaic-Babylonian nation. Regarded in this way, which, with clearly defined limits, seems to me the correct one, the position of the Turanian nation of the Accadians may perhaps be more easily understood by scholars in whose minds the fact still awakens a sort of defiance.

"No one in the present day," said M. Renan quite lately in one of his remarkable annual reports to the Asiatic Society of Paris,[1] "can doubt that this (Turanian) civilization possessed and most probably created the writing called cuneiform. If we take the word Turanian as a synonym of what is neither Semitic nor Aryan, then the expression is exact, but we see no great advantage in it. A classification of animals as fishes, mammals, and what is neither fish nor

[1] *Journal Asiatique*, 7th series, Vol. II., p. 42.

mammal would not be of much use to science. But we acknowledge that it does astonish us to find the word Turanian taken in its strict sense, and to see that ancient substruction of the learned civilization of Babylon assigned to the Turkish, Finnish, and Hungarian races; in one word, to races which have never done anything but pull down, and have never created a civilization of their own.

"The truth may not always seem very probable, and if any one can prove to us that the Turks, Finns, and Hungarians founded the most powerful and intelligent of the ante-Semitic and ante-Aryan civilizations, we will believe it; every consideration *a priori* ought to be made subordinate to proofs *a posteriori*. But the force of the proofs must be in proportion to the improbability of the result."

M. Renan will allow us to endeavour to dissipate his doubts with all the deference due to his vast store of knowledge and his great renown; I am the more eager about this because I think the facts mentioned in the preceding pages partly answer his principal objections.

In the first place, I think he is rather severe upon the Turanian race; he seems to associate it only with the savage devastations of the Ghingis Khan and of Timur, and his judgment concerning the office of this vast family of nations ought to be challenged. The race which has furnished Christian Europe with one of its greatest, most intelligent, most chivalrous, and most eloquent nations, the Hungarians, which has produced, moreover, amongst the Finns at the northern extremity of the European continent an epic monument of such great worth as the *Kalevala*, which possessed a real civilization before the arrival of the Scandinavians amongst these same Finns, whose aptitude for appropriating all the resources of modern culture to a much greater degree than the Russians themselves has been only lately pointed out by a traveller interested in political economy; such a race cannot certainly be described with justice as "only able to pull down." And although the Turks are less supple, less sharp, more solid and heavier than the Hungarians or the Finns, their part in the history of Islamism is by no means exclusively that of the destroyer; they have their great men and their glorious pages, and above all, they display remarkable qualifications for government, which have always been wanting to the Arabs.[1]

It is quite true that the Turanian nations which hold the most important place in history, the Hungarians and the Turks, first appear at the time when they were just becoming subject to a civilization foreign to their race, having adopted, with the new religion of which they made themselves the champions, at first of Christianity, then secondly of Mohammedanism, the whole inheritance of the culture which grew up elsewhere under the auspices of this religion. It is true they do not appear in history possessing a civilization of their own, but do they stand alone in this point? The facility with which the Hungarians adopted the Christian culture of the West,

[1] Cf. the various papers on the "Westerly drifting of Nomads," by H. Howorth, in the *Transactions of the Anthropological Institute of Great Britain*, Vol. I., Part 7, p. 2, 226, and of the *Ethnological Society of London*, and his *History of the Mongols* lately published.— *Ed.*

and the Turks an Arab civilization with the Mussulman faith, would lead us to think that they were not amongst the most enlightened of the Turanian nations, or at least that their ancient national culture was very inferior to that for which they exchanged it. But this is no decisive proof that there was not amongst other nations of the same stock a very ancient Turanian civilization also with its own physiognomy and exclusive characteristics, resulting from the development of certain peculiar instincts which are found, at least in a low degree, amongst the most unenlightened Ugro-Finnic tribes of Siberia.

At this point, however, I must define the exact limits of the facts relating to the Accadians, for I think that scholars of the English school, and Prof. Sayce amongst others,[1] have gone rather too far in considering them as the originators of all Semitic civilization, and I myself in former treatises, without going as far as that, have rather transgressed the bounds of probability in espousing this belief. I think there are decisive proofs that the first civilized occupants of the soil of Babylonia and Chaldea, before the Kushites of Nimrod, were a people of Turanian race, more closely connected with the Ugro-Finns than with the Tartars. Even before this people had reached the banks of the Tigris and Euphrates, in the first stage of their migration, they had invented the first rough rudiments of a hieroglyphic system, which as it became further developed produced the cuneiform writing; they were then acquainted with the working of

[1] "The Origin of Semitic Civilization," *Trans. Soc. Bib. Arch.*, Vol. I.

metals, and the processes of certain necessary branches of industry. In the fertile plains where they settled, they engaged in sedentary and agricultural pursuits; they built towns, cultivated the soil, planned irrigation, and practised all the trades demanded by such a mode of life. Thus they had a regular civilization, peculiar to themselves, which had grown up spontaneously in their midst before any Kushite, Semitic, or Aryan influence had made itself felt among them. But of course this civilization was very imperfect, so far at least as we can judge by the poverty of its fundamental vocabulary, and the number of fictitious compounds which the Accadians were obliged to adopt in order to adapt the language which they were still speaking to the requirements of a more advanced culture. There is nothing to prove that the civilization of the Accadians of Chaldea was more learned and perfect except in the possession of their writing (and the example of the Chinese shows that this art may sometimes be cultivated by races who are still plunged in complete barbarity), than that of the Pagan Finns, as pictured to us in the Kalevala, and who are in that epic shown to bear so close a resemblance to the Accadians from a religious point of view. As a rule I think that the primitive Turanian civilization, vestiges of which might still be found in other countries, was essentially incomplete, developed only in certain directions, while in others it remained quite in a rudimentary state, and that if it was one of the first to exist, it was settled and arranged early, just as the Turanian languages became crystallized at the earliest stage in the formation of a language. It was civilization, and civilization in quite an advanced stage as compared with the state of barbarity in which most of the other races were still plunged when it arose; but it became in its turn a comparative barbarism by the side of the more perfect civilization which sprang up afterwards amongst other races, the Kushites for instance, who superseded the Turanians in Babylonia and Chaldea, and whose influence had already penetrated as far as to affect that portion of the Accadians who still kept up a national life, and continued to use their old language, in the time of the builder kings of Ur, the Likbabi, and the Dungi.[1]

[1] This opinion of mine is not so different as may appear at first sight from that expressed by M. Schrader in his works which are so justly renowned throughout scientific Europe, and particularly in his excellent paper in the *jahrbücher für Theologie* for the year 1875, entitled "Semitismus und Babylonismus." I agree with him cordially in his view that Babylonism, as he calls it, differs radically from a pure and original Semitism as represented by the Arabs; further, that the influence of the most ancient Babylonish civilization which held sway over the Semitic tribes of the north, was the result of constant communication before the establishment of their nations in their definite regions, and which introduced amongst them all the ideas, institutions, religious, social and scientific traditions foreign to Arabia, which they had in common with Babylon.

The point on which we differ is that he considers the old Babylonish civilization as a homogeneous whole, referring it entirely to the first element of the population who spoke the non-Semitic language, whilst I have made a bolder attempt to penetrate the darkness of the prehistoric past connected with the countries watered by the Euphrates and the Tigris.

Instead of attributing this civilization to a single race, I see in it a mixed product of the contributions of two nations of different origin, and I am trying, with a certain degree of success, to analyse it and discover what belongs to its two factors. M. Schrader seems to me rather too absorbed in the presence of the Semitic race in Babylonia, and consequently considers everything which does not belong to pure Semitism to be quite unconnected with it. I think, on the contrary, that the population who spoke the Semitic language in Babylonia and Chaldea was not composed of the Semitic race properly so-called, but of Kushites or people belonging to a neighbouring ethnic family endowed with peculiar characteristics, somewhat resembling those of the Egyptians. So I think the comparison with original and pure Semitism is not enough for the solution of the problem of the origin of the Chaldaio-Babylonian nation. We must also compare it with the ethnology of Egypt under the primitive dynasties, and with as much as we can discover of the genius and institutions of the Kushites in other countries, in Yemen for instance, before attributing to the Accadian Turanians everything which was not thoroughly Semitic in the civilization of Babylon.

It must be evident that I by no means attribute to the primitive Turanians of Chaldea all the foundation of the learned civilization of Babylon. I only see in them one of its factors, and that not even the principal one. The first to establish themselves round the lower course of the Tigris and Euphrates, they bequeathed to posterior times some of the stones which served to erect the Chaldaio-Babylonian civilization, their agricultural and industrial processes, the rites and formulæ of their magic, and above all, their writing, falsely assigned to the Semitic-Assyrian nation, yet really preserved through many centuries by force of tradition and custom. But in this great and learned civilization the most noble part came from the Kushito-Semitic element, which spoke the Assyrian tongue; for that element furnished some of the science and the religion of the country, and finally established its language entirely, substituting it for the Accadian even amongst the Chaldeans properly so called, the descendants of those Accadians whose blood remained the purest. Babylon in particular became very early an almost entirely Kushite town. This was the reason why she was able to exercise so great and decisive an influence over the Canaanitish and Semitic nations; and their connection in race and language favoured this influence, so that the Babylonian civilization was partly, with a little help from other sources, a more complete, more learned, and more highly wrought development of characteristic instincts peculiar to the nations over whom it ruled both by precept and by example.

CHAPTER XXXI.

The Archaic Legislation of the Accadians.

THE existence of a Turanian nation in the strictest sense of the word, or if any one prefers it, an Altaic nation in Babylonia and Chaldea, is as we have seen an established fact; this nation preceded the Kushito-Semitic tribes, and was possessed of quite a remarkable degree of civilization analogous to the culture of the populations who are incontestably Turanian. Though M. Renan demands a number of forcible proofs before he will believe this fact, still I consider that such a collection of proofs henceforth exists, and in the present work I have been trying to add to their number. The learned Academician whom I have thus been endeavouring to convince, said himself, and rightly, "From the point of view of the historical sciences five things are essential to a race, to give us a right to speak of it as an individuality amongst the human species: a Language of its own, a Literature imprinted with a peculiar physiognomy, a Religion, a History, and a Legislation."[1]

[1] *Revue des Deux-Mondes*, 1er Septembre, 1873, p. 140.

A good many of these conditions we now know to be fulfilled amongst the Accadians, thus connecting them with the Turanian stock, and the Ugro-Finnic nations in particular.

First there is a Language to which we have just devoted a special chapter, an epitome of more extensive philological studies. We have already pointed out the organic and indisputable characters, which ought, in our opinion, to determine its linguistic classification.

As to a Literature, we can certainly find one amongst the Accadians, a literature of a very original stamp, and inspired by a breath of true poetry, in the existing fragments of the liturgical collection, the incantations and hymns of the great magical collection. At the other extremity of the Accadian nations' domain, the Finns likewise possess a brilliant and poetical literature. A literary comparison of the genius which inspired the Kalevala and that which dictated the religious and magical Accadian lyrics would be an interesting study; we should see that the common instincts of race may exist in the poetry of two nations so widely separated both by time and space, to say nothing of the difference of colour which was the necessary result of two such opposite aspects of nature as are furnished by the shores of the Persian Gulf and the northern forests of Finland.[1]

As concerning a Religion, that is the subject to

[1] It is very probable, as M. Schrader's judicious and suggestive remark would imply, that the example and influence of the Accadians was the means of introducing amongst some of the Semitic tribes, the *parallelismus membrorum*, which became the foundation of Hebrew poetry, though it was quite unknown to the Arabs.

which we have applied ourselves in this volume by the help of documents now for the first time brought to light, the study of which has led us as a corollary to the examination of the ethnographic question of the Accadian nation. By revealing to us a primitive religious system, which was really indigenous to the Accadian nation before they adopted and propagated the worship of the gods common to all the religions of the Euphratico-Syrian group, the magical books have opened up a new and unexpected perspective on one of the most important points. We have compared the data of the system of these books to the ante-Iranian part of Median Magism and the Finnish mythology, and so have been able to prove the existence of an independent family of religions which must be called Turanian, religions having no other worship but magic, and proceeding from the old fund of demonological naturalism which has remained in so coarse and rudimentary a state amongst the tribes of Siberia, those Turanian hordes who still exist under the primordial conditions of the race, for the circumstances which have clogged their progress from the beginning have never allowed them to attain to a true state of civilization. Here then are three of the conditions essential to the existence and individuality of a race, fulfilled in such a manner as clearly to connect the Accadians with the typical Turanian nations, the Finns for instance, in spite of the immense hiatus of time and space which occurs between them. The primitive history of the different Turanian groups, their dispersion and first attempts at civilization, can certainly never be fully discovered; we must be content with proving satisfactorily the linguistic, ethnographic, and religious affinities which show their common origin.

The most we can do for the Accadians especially is to trace by induction, in the absence of contemporary records, by the help of their own traditions, the principal and most important features of their early history, from the time when they established themselves in Chaldea up to the period when they began those inscriptions which have been handed down to us; we must then proceed to unravel the course of their pre-historic migration as far as to that mountain of the north-east which was their point of departure.

It remains for us then now to consider the question of legislation or the social constitution. Here again the requisite documents are wanting or at least insufficient; but we may hope that future discoveries may fill up this gap. At present we possess only a very small fragment of the ancient Accadian laws, which, it appears, had been reduced to writing and translated into Assyrian at the same time as the religious books. This fragment[1] treats of the relations and duties of domestic life. It concludes with a curious note, "Placed opposite to the Assyrian, written and engraved like the ancient originals." Here is the translation:

---

[1] *W. A. I.* II., 10. It is more complete in my *Choix de Textes cunéiformes*, No. 15; some corrections in Friedriech Delitzsch's *Assyrische Lesestücke*, p. 37 et seq. Translations, differing a little from mine, in the minor details, but agreeing with it in the really important facts, have been brought out by M. Oppert (*Journal Asiatique*, 7th series, Vol. I., p. 37, et seq.), and by Prof. Sayce (*Records of the Past*, Vol. III., p. 23, et seq.). I now correct on a few points the version which I made in the first French edition of this work.

In future, in any case :[1]
1st sentence.
A son to his father;
Thou art not my father,
(if) he has said to him,
and (if) he has made a mark with his nail to confirm it,[2]
he will make honourable amends to him[3]
and he will pay a fine.
2nd sentence.
A son to his mother:
(if) he has said to her, Thou art not my mother
his hair and his nails[4] shall be cut off,
in the town he shall be banished from land and water,[5]
and he shall be driven from the house.
3rd sentence.
A father to his son:
Thou art not my son,
(if) he has said to him,
from his house and home
he shall be banished.[6]
4th sentence.
A mother to her son:
Thou art not my son,
(if) she has said to him,
she shall be chased from the house and the place.
5th sentence.
A wife to her husband
(if) she has wronged him
Thou art no (longer) my husband,

[1] Assyrian version: "In any case, in future."
[2] That is to say if he has agreed to it in proper form by a deed, in which case the mark of his nail serves as a signature.
[3] Assyrian: "he will acknowledge his paternity."
[4] Assyrian: "his hair" only.
[5] Assyrian: "in the town they banish him" (literally, they confine him).
[6] It is most likely that here, as well as in the following sentence, the disowned child is the one driven from the house.

(if) she has said to him,
she shall be thrown into the river.
6th sentence.
A husband to his wife :
Thou art no (longer) my wife,
(if) he has said to her
he shall be made to pay half a mina of silver.
7th sentence.
The ruler [1]
(if) the slave
he kills, mutilates,
ruins him by wounding him,
(if) the latter flees from the property
or falls ill [2]
his hand every day
half a measure of corn
shall weigh out (as compensation).[3]

The document which we have just translated forms a short but complete whole. On the same tablet, which was one of the last of a collection of bilingual documents of various kinds collated with a view to philological analysis, there was formerly another series of legal sentences, but owing to their mutilated state and the obscurity of the expression some of them cannot be translated. Two extracts will suffice to show the patriarchal constitution of society and a state of things in which property could be acquired by occupation, as a great part of it was uninhabited and consequently *res nullius*.

---

[1] Literally, "the chief;" but we cannot take it in the sense of proprietor as Prof. Sayce does. It refers on the contrary to the fact that the country manager is answerable to him for any harm done to the slaves committed to his care.

[2] By his own fault.

[3] Cf. the Mosaic law, Ex. xx. 7-10; xxi. 20, 21.—*Ed.*

> 2 A married man may always settle an estate on his child, without making him live there.
> 10 Of all that she has had enclosed,
>   the married woman shall be the owner.

Other sentences treat of the erection and ownership of places of worship.

> 2 In future a sanctuary on a private estate may be very lofty.
> 3 Of the sanctuary situated in his own high place the individual shall have possession.
> 6 The distinct property of the sanctuary the son shall inherit.

Another expresses in a few words the precept of filial respect, to which a penal sanction was given as we saw just now.

> 7 Thou shalt not disown thy father or thy mother.

Finally there is one which determines the validity of marriage by its consummation.

> 8 (An individual) has taken a wife [1]
>   and has not come near her [2]
>   he may change. [3]

All these legal arrangements bear the mark of their extreme antiquity and of the incomplete social state to which they were adapted. But while they exhibit a respect for woman not often found in a like condition of semi-barbarity, yet she was certainly not regarded as the equal of her husband; he could easily get rid of her by giving her pecuniary

---

[1] Literally, "elected her, declared her."
[2] Literally, *subigendo eam non compressit*.
[3] The right of rejection after the completion of the marriage is not the thing here referred to. The terms employed seem to imply that a legal union could be contracted only with one woman.

compensation, whilst the woman could not claim a divorce under pain of death. In the same way several passages of the magic books show that the master had the right to take advantage of all his female slaves, and they seem to consider it the greatest misfortune for a slave not to have attracted the attention of her master, just as much so as for a free woman of rank to have found no husband. But the free Accadian woman was not the creature of her spouse; she had her own rights and her own fortune. Even under the control of a husband she could possess personal property and take the necessary steps to acquire it. If she disowned the child attributed to her, she was only in the same position as the husband by the disavowal of his paternity. But the most striking point was the importance attached to the mother in her relations with her children, which was superior even to that of the father.

In the fragments of the Accadian law, the son who denied his father was sentenced to a simple fine; but he who denied his mother was to be banished both from land and sea. Amongst the ancient Finns, before their conversion to Christianity, the mother of a family took precedence of the father in the rites of domestic worship. This is a remarkable point of contact in such a short fragment, and that with reference to a subject itself characteristic enough to be regarded as an individual peculiarity of race in the constitution of the family. This peculiarity of the old Accadian law is so much the more worthy of attention, not only because we find nothing similar in the Semitic world, but because it is directly opposed to the spirit of some posterior Babylonish institutions as revolting to morality as they were degrading to womankind, yet consecrated by religion, and as far as I can see of Kushite origin. I refer to the sacred prostitution which was imposed once at least in a lifetime upon all women, even those who were free, and the marriage of young girls under the form of a public auction, thus rendering it an act of *mancipatio*, which made the wife the property of her husband.[1]

Have we not discovered in the affinities now established amongst the Accadians and the Altaic tribes whose nationality is incontestable, sufficient proofs to allow us to pass from what seemed at first "improbable" in the fact of a Turanian nation's having been the primary occupant of Chaldea, and the inventor of a system of writing according with the genius of its language, to the great Chaldaic-Babylonian civilization?[2]

---

[1] It is well known that positive monumental information has been found to confirm the writings of Herodotus, on the annual auction of young girls at Babylon; see my *Premières Civilisations*, Vol. II., p. 229.

[2] The reader who desires to follow up this subject cannot do better than read Herbert Spencer's *magnum opus*, *Descriptive Sociology*, Vol. V., "The Asiatic Nations;" Lubbock's *Origin of Civilization*; and Tylor's *Researches into the Early History of Mankind*. The collection of facts and the collocation of the deductions to be derived from them may be considered as imparting almost a prophetic sense to the student of Archaic history.—*Ed.*

APPENDIX.

Sumir and Accad.

IT is a matter of great regret to me to find that I differ from my learned master and friend M. Oppert on the subject of these two names, but the reasons on which he bases his opinion do not commend themselves to my judgment at all.[1] It is, however, a question of secondary importance, and I only return to it now because it cannot be ignored in such a work as the present, in addition to which I wish to correct what I have already said with respect to this subject on former occasions.[2] I will not now speak with polemical exactitude, but I want briefly to sum up the data which have been proved indisputably, many of them founded on new documents recently brought to light to settle debates. I dare say that this exposition will not as yet lead my readers to form a decided opinion; there are many sides of the question about which we are still in ignorance. But if I am not mistaken, the most

---

[1] See *Sumer ou Accad*, par Jules Oppert, Paris, 1876.
[2] In my *Etudes Accadiennes*, Vol. I., fasc. 3.

probable conclusion will be, that neither M. Oppert nor myself were absolutely correct in our discussion upon the names Sumir and Accad. I am now convinced that we digressed into subjects not cognate to our subject, and started from a point which was not then sufficiently proved, viz., the difference of race between Sumir and Accad. In proportion as our studies advance, and light begins to dawn upon the fundamental data of the question, it becomes, on the other hand, more probable that the two primitive nations designated by this name were of the same race, and that the distinction between them was entirely geographical. If that be the case, it matters little whether we call the ante-Semitic or Turanian language of Chaldea, Sumirian or Accadian, there is consistency in both names, they are equally correct and equally incomplete; the only grounds we have for giving a preference to the latter, are that this latter is generally used in science, and since it is not inexact, there is nothing to be gained by changing it, and further also it is consecrated by the usage of the Assyrians themselves.

I. The first point, which seems to me established beyond a doubt, is that the Assyrians themselves used the two terms Assur and Accad in opposition to each other, to express the linguistic dualism of the Semitic and Turanian idioms. We know that this clause appears at the end of a lexicographical tablet, in which the words of the two languages stand opposite to each other: *ki pî duppi u lamadi labiruti*—GABRI *Assur u Akkad*. Of this phrase "conformably with the tablets and ancient teaching of Assur and Accad," is evidently the meaning. The word *GAB-RI* is the only one doubtful. M. Oppert, whom I followed up to a certain point in this matter, considers it to be the plural of the Semitic *gabru* (גבר), and translates *gabri Assur u Akkad* "the masters of Assur and Accad." Even starting from this translation and accepting it as correct, the inference to be drawn from the passage is yet clear and incontestable. It does not prove, as the learned Professor supposes, an assimilation between the grammarians of Assur and Accad, but on the contrary, a fixed opposition corresponding with the opposition between the two languages facing each other in the document which finishes with this clause. Furthermore, I believe the translation to be incorrect. M. Schrader first pointed out,[1] and M. Friedrich Delitzsch has since finally proved beyond all doubt,[2] that *GABRI* is not a Semitic word written phonetically, but an allophonic word which must be written in the Assyrian as *maḥiru* (plural *maḥiruti*, in the passage we have quoted). The Accadian *gabri* is originally a compound verb, the original and etymological meaning of which is "to rise in opposition." Hence it is naturally the equivalent of the Assyrian verbs *mahar* and *sanan*, expressing ideas of opposition, rivalry, and comparison. The participle *gabria*, and by contraction simply *gabri*, means then substantively "rival," and adjectively in another acceptation "compared, assimilated." This confirms

---

[1] *Ienüer Literaturzeitung*, 1874, p. 200.
[2] *Assyrische Studien*, p. 3, 120, et seq.

the astronomical signification of the Accadian *gabri*. In such documents as these, it designates the star which rises on the horizon opposite to the spectator. Passing into the Assyrian, the word gave rise to *gabratuv*, "the apparition of the star upon the horizon." Thus in *W. A. I.*, Vol. III, 63 verso, l. 33, after a list of the phases of the planet Venus during the twelve months of the year, divided into as many sections as there are months, comes: *sanesrit kisruta gabratuv sa AN-NIN-ŠI-AN-NA GAB-RI Babili*, "twelve sections, apparition of the planet Venus on the Babylonian horizon." In the same way in *W. A. I.*, Vol. III, 64 verso, l. 32. After another astronomical table, we read: *kî pî IZ-LI-HU-SI-UM GAB-RI Babili*, "conformably with the manuscripts of the apparitions on the Babylonian horizon."

This meaning of *GABRI*, *mahiru*, once fairly established, so that we may no longer confuse it with the Semitic *gabri*, it remains that the only correct translation of *duppi labiruti mahiruti* is M. Schrader's, "the ancient tablets arranged in parallel columns," corresponding exactly with the order of the document at the end of which such a statement occurs.[1] There is yet another thing to be added which completes the proof: the bilingual legal tablet of *W. A. I.*, Vol. II., 10, has at the end these simple words *GAB-RI Assur*. If we translate with M.

[1] M. Fried. Delitzsch has answered the objection which might be made to the difference of order in the designation of a lexicon as "Assyrian-Accadian," and the arrangement of the columns where the Accadian comes before the Assyrian. Although the Accadian is in the first column, the lexicographical tablets are none the less the remains of an "Assyrian-Accadian" dictionary, since the arrangement is determined by the affinity of sound between the Assyrian and not the Accadian words.

Oppert, "the masters of Assyria," what could this strange note mean? It would have no sense at all. But let us read it more correctly as "opposite to the Assyrian," then everything is clear and natural; for we must mention that this tablet is one of that small number of tablets which are distinguished by having the Assyrian translation of the primitive Accadian text in a column opposite, instead of following the interlinear arrangement much more common in documents of this kind.

According to the old rendering the most that we could do would be to translate *duppi mahiruti* by "tablets compared to each other," instead of "tablets in parallel columns." This meaning seems to me the correct one in the final formula of W. A. I., Vol. III., 55, 2: *kî pî duppi u IZ-LI-ḪU-SI labiruti GAB-RI (mahiruti) Assur Sumer u Akkad*. Here it is not only Accad, but Sumir and Accad which constitute the opposition to Assur. But this opposition seems to me to be entirely geographical, and designating Babylonia in relation to Assyria; I do not think we have any ground for concluding with M. Schrader[1] that the Assyrians used indifferently "language of Sumir and Accad," or simply "language of Accad," to describe the old non-Semitic idiom. Indeed, the document in which this last formula occurs is not bilingual, but written exclusively in Assyrian. It is an astronomical table which may have been compiled from a comparison of Assyrian and Accadian documents, but the evidence of this is

[1] *Ist das Akkadische eine Sprache*, p. 46.

not strong enough to warrant our determining its linguistic value by the final clause.

To return to the lexicographical tablet. Whether we translate it "conformably with the ancient tablets and documents of instruction of Assur and Accad compared together," or "conformably with the ancient tablets and documents of instruction of Assur and Accad in parallel columns," the conclusion must be the same as that to which M. Oppert's translation would lead us: the final formula refers to a geographical opposition, which cannot correspond to the linguistic opposition exhibited in the document. Either it is a question of parallel columns of Assyrian and Accadian, or else a comparison of the Assyrian and Accadian documents was necessary in order to compile a lexicon of the two languages. In either case the Assyrians used the term Accadian to signify the dialect which was not Assyrian. Therefore we follow their example in naming this dialect Accadian.

II. There now remains another question, viz., Is the duality of Sumir and Accad ethnic or merely geographical?

I am quite convinced that these two names were understood in a geographical sense as the north and south of Babylonia. The geographical character of the name *Akkad* is particularly certain: it had a double sense, one wide, the other limited.

In the commonest acceptation, Accad was the general designation of the whole, and it consisted of Babylonia and Chaldea, in fact all the southern provinces watered by the Euphrates and Tigris from the frontier of Assyria to the Persian Gulf. When Accad had this meaning, the name of Assur was opposed to it as the second term of the parallelism,[1] and it was the opposition between Babylonia and Assyria both understood in that wide sense.

But in a stricter sense the term Accad is confined, as in the case of Sumir and Accad, to a fixed portion of this vast geographical whole. When Assurbanipal speaks " of the spoil of the country of the Sumirs, of the country of the Accadians and of Gan-Dunyas,"[2] it is evident he uses the two first expressions as names of provinces, since the third, *Gan-Dunyas*, as numerous examples bear witness, is a designation for the particular district of Babylon, called since the time of the Cissian dynasty the city of Kar-Dunyas. The book of Genesis[3] restricts the sense of Accad still more, for it seemed to make it the name of a town, of which acceptation there is no sign in the magic texts.

We have now to examine into the position of Accad in the sense of a particular province. It is defined very exactly in the prism of Sennacherib,[4] which describes the march of Elamite troops who had left their country to help the Babylonian insurgent Suzub. "They took" it says, "the road to Accad and came in the direction of Babylon as far as Suzub, the Chaldean king of Babylon," *uruḫ Akkad iṣbatunuvva ana Babili tebuni adi Suzubi Kalduai sar Babili*. The

---

[1] See amongst others the prism of Esarhaddon, col. 4, l. 45.
[2] Smith's *History of Assurbanipal*, p. 255. [3] Gen. x. 10.
[4] Col. 5, l. 39-41.

province of Accad was, therefore, situated on the route of an army coming from Elam to Babylon, to the south of this town and Babylonia, so it must have been the same as Chaldea, the lower part of Mesopotamia. This is the conclusion to be drawn from the passages of the tablet referring to the ancient political relations between Assyria and Babylonia; in this tablet to which English scholars have given the name *Synchronous History*, the Persian Gulf is called "the sea which is above Accad," *marrati sa elis Akkad;*[1] and we read further,[2] that whilst a prince sat on the throne of Kar-Dunyas (Babylon), his rebellious brother fortified himself in the country of Accad. I think we may safely affirm that this geographical name, taken in the strictest sense, when it designates not the whole of Babylonia but one province in particular, is synonymous with *Kaldu*, which did not appear till much later, towards the ninth century before our era,[3] and then gradually supplanted the old term in proportion as the tribe of Kaldu, which was at first very insignificant, increased in the region to which it finally gave its name, to the exclusion of any other designation. And at the time when this triumph was consummated, when the Sargons were governing Assyria, we find mention still made of Sumir and Accad as a relic of bygone times; the same geographical duality was expressed in a new way more

[1] *Trans. Soc. Bib. Arch.*, Vol. II., p. 130, l. 17; and *Records of the Past*, Vol. III., p. 25.

[2] *Ibid.*, p. 137, l. 20, 21.

[3] As I have already remarked above, the country of Chaldea is designated as part of the country of Accadia, in the inscriptions of Shalmaneser III.; on the obelisk of Samsi-Bin the two names seem to be identified.

suited to a later state of things, by the parallelism and opposition of the two names Babili and Kaldu, Babylonia and Chaldea.¹ In fact. directly we take Accad geographically, and in the limited sense as defining the south of Chaldea, we must regard Sumir as representing the other division, the north.² This refers us to an essential fact of the problem which I have already reiterated several times, and which M. Oppert combats in vain, namely the identity of Sumir with the Shinar of the Bible. שנער is certainly not a Semitic name, and it is impossible to find a satisfactory etymology for it in that family of languages. It is the Hebraic rendering of an Accadian name and the ע certainly replaces a *g* of the primitive form, as it appears in the appellation *Lagamar*, transcribed לעמר. This granted there is exactly the same difference between שנער and Sumir, as between the parallel forms *dingir* and *dimer* for the word "god," and *Gingir* and *Gimir* for a surname of the goddess Ishtar; they are

¹ See Finzi, *Ricerche per lo studio dell'antichita assira*, p. 164.
² Mr. Smith tried a little while ago to propagate an entirely different opinion, making Sumir the south and Accad the north of Babylonia, on the ground of an assimilation between the city south of Babylon itself, whose name every Assyriologist had read as Agane up to that time and the city of Accad spoken of in Genesis. The last sign in the orthography of the name Agane can indeed in its polyphony represent a dental, but it is always a *t* (in the Accadian a *dh*) and never a *d*. In that case we should have *Agate*, that is to say אגטע or אנטי, which could only be assimilated to Akkad, אבד, by a fantastic change of articulation, of which neither the Accadian nor the Assyrian allow. I therefore repudiate explicitly, as Prof. Sayce has already done, the identification thus suggested by the ingenious English Assyriologist.

I also object to his reading a dental in the last syllable. Indeed the reading Agane, which has the advantage of taking the sign there used in its original and most common acceptation, seems to me fully justified by its agreement with the Ἀγαμυνα of Ptolemy (V., 18, 7), which I also see in the אגמא of the Talmud of Babylon (*Baba mecia*, 86a; *Baba bathra*, 129a). This Agma or Agama is given as the neighbouring town to Pom-Beditha (Neubauer, *Geographie du Talmud*, p. 368), which refers it to the north of Babylon, situated on the Euphrates like the Agamna of the Greek geographer, and this position corresponds exactly with the description of Agane in the Cuneiform documents.

two forms of the same name, exhibiting a change (that of *ng* into *m*) peculiar to the Accadian, the existence of which in this language is incontestable.¹ And the tradition of this fact was preserved amongst the Syrians, since we still read in Abu-l-Faradj,² "Shinaar which is Samarrah." In the eleventh chapter of Genesis, Shinear, or Shinar, is used to designate expressly the plains around Babylon. It is used in the like manner also in the books of Isaiah³ and Jeremiah,⁴ where it certainly occurs as an obsolete name, but it is interesting to notice the meaning which Jewish tradition attached to it in their time. Both of these prophets applied the appellation of Shinar to Babylonia proper, and the Synagogue interpreted it in the same way, for in the Septuagint it is translated Βαβυλωνία and γῆ Βαβυλῶνος; the same interpretation occurs in the work of the Targumim. There is therefore, an identity of geographical position as well as a close philological relationship between *Sumir* and *Shinar*, which confirms our proposed identification still more. In Genesis x. 10, we must necessarily understand " in the land of Shinar," as applying exclusively to Calneh,⁵ rightly assimilated in the Talmud to the town of Nipur, which really belonged to Babylonia and not to Chaldea. By placing "Accad and Calneh in the

---

¹ If this assimilation were not admitted, the Biblical שנער would have no equivalent in the idigenous Babylonian and Assyrian documents, which would at least be strange.

² *Histor. dynast.*, p. 18, ed. Pococke. The same Abul-l-Faradj a few lines further on mentions a fabulous tradition, which is of real interest, in that it is the only trace left by the ancient people of the *Sumeri* in oriental recitals. It is the legend of Samirus, "with three eyes and two horns," the first king of Babylon after Nimrod, who invented weights and measures and the art of silk-weaving.

³ Isa. xi. 11.   ⁴ Jer. v. 11.   ⁵ *Yoma*, 10 a.

land of Shinar" side by side, the Biblical passage represents the opposition of Accad and Sumir in the historical texts, and that very faithfully. The argument is so perfect that we may well question whether Accad was really always the name of a town in this place, as in the text which we now possess, whether the latter is not incomplete, and whether some words did not get lost when the tradition of this ancient geography began to fade. For my part I am inclined to think so, and would willingly suppose that the primitive text ran something like this:

"The beginning of his empire was Babel, Erech, Ur[1] in the country of Accad, and Calneh in the land of Shinar."

Sumir is therefore the same thing as Shinar, the plain of Babylonia proper, whilst Accad in its limited sense is a more southern province, viz., Chaldea. But we must not go beyond this data. The fact which I admitted in common with M. Oppert, but from which I drew an opposite inference to his, that Sumir must have been the primitive name of Assyria was erroneous. It rested on an incorrect reading, which has since been rectified both by Mr. Smith and Friedrich Delitzsch. It is now plainly demonstrated that in the passage of the lexicographical

---

[1] Perhaps also *Surippak*. I have shown elsewhere the striking coincidence between the Biblical tetrapolis of Nimrod and the tetrapolis of Izdhubar or Dhubar in the Babylonian Epopee. The latter was composed of Babilu, Uruk, Surippak, and Nipur; Surippak corresponds with Accad in the book of Genesis. However, I prefer the restitution of אכד [ואור בארץ] (or else that the town of Ur is called Accad if anyone is unwilling to admit that the text is imperfect) on account of the passage in *W. A. I.* III., 70, l. 154: *uri* = (ideogr. of Accad) = *Akkadu*, and the passage finishes by referring the name of Accad to the south, the province of which Ur was the capital.

tablets upon which this opinion was founded, the original has *Surippakituv* instead of *Sumerituv*, and that the Accadian *MÂ-ZU*, thus explained, has no connection with *LIB-ZU*, one of the ideographic expressions of the name of the town of Assur.

III. These facts standing thus the reciprocal geographical position of Sumir and Accad seems to me, therefore, clearly defined. But these names really belonged to the people rather than to the provinces. This is proved by the fact that they almost always occur in the plural, *Sumeri u Akkadi*, when they are written phonetically, and even in the most ancient Semitic document that makes mention of them, the inscription of Hammuragas, in the Assyrian tongue, we find *nisi Sumeriv u Akkadiv*, "the men Sumirians and Accadians."[1] We must examine the origin and derivation of the expression, in order to discover if a difference of race or situation was primitively implied.

One thing seems to me very palpable; that neither of these names was Semitic or derived from any root of the Assyrian idiom; they belonged to another language, the earlier non-Semitic and Turanian idiom. The name of Accad is the only one of the two which we should be likely at first sight to refer to a Semitic origin, by derivation from the roots נכד or אכד (as the general opinion ran when this word was only known through the medium of the Bible), and its Accadian character and meaning in this language is now most clearly understood. *Akkad*, as Mr. Smith, Prof. Sayce, and myself, have shown, is a

[1] *W. A. I.* II., 46, l. 1, c, d.

word of the Accadian language meaning "mountain," with the suffix *u* taken under the form *akkadu*, in the plural *akkadi*. In one lexicographical tablet we find *akkad* translated by *matuv elituv*, "high country." This word *akkad* is evidently related to the verbal root, *aka*, "to raise, heap up." The particular ideogram which expresses it (and which is itself formed by doubling that of the verb *bur*, "to raise, tumify, swell,") gives so good an idea of "mountain," that we find it sometimes used to designate Ararat in Armenia,[1] in which use the Accadian reading would seem to have been *tilla*.[2]

The original meaning of *Sumeri* is more difficult to discover. To do so, we must refer to the equivalent constantly substituted for Sumir and Accad in the most ancient Accadian inscriptions. In my *Etudes accadiennes*, I disputed the parallelism between this expression and that of *Sumeri u Akkadi* in the Assyrian; but a passage from a new lexicographical tablet lately published by M. Friedrich Delitzsch,[3] has proved to me beyond a doubt that I was in error. The expression that I quoted occurs in the title of the kings of the ancient Chaldean empire, *ungal Kiengi ki Akkad*, and is the highest of all the titles applied to these monarchs; it implies a complete possession of the whole of Chaldea and Babylonia, while kings who governed one single town, like those of Uruk, did not make use of it. M. Schrader[4] proved that it must be translated "king

---

[1] Inscription of Khorsabad, l. 31; see H. Rawlinson in Vol. IV. of Canon Rawlinson's *Herodotus*, English edition, p. 250-254.
[2] *W. A. I.* II., 48, l. 13, c, d.   [3] *Assyrische Lesestücke*, p. 39.
[4] *Ist das akkadische eine Sprache?* p. 39.

of Kiengi with Accad," that is to say " Kiengi and Accad;" and indeed *kî* or *kîta*, " with," which are essentially postpositions in the Accadian, are sometimes used as conjunctions, like *ileh* in Turkish; *kiengi* is then the equivalent of the " land of Sumer."

But *kiengi* or *kingi*, is a well known substantive of the Accadian language, which is translated into Assyrian by *matuv*, " country," in the lexicographical tablet.[1] It has lost the final letters (as is so often the case in the Accadian[2]), and thus is an altered and contracted form of *kingina*, which is rendered elsewhere *irṣituv* " land;" and *kingina* itself is a compound, formed from *kî*, " land, country, place," and *gina* " existing, real, straight," in which the first *n* has no radical value; *ng* (which is one sound in the Accadian) should really be considered as a simple modification of the *g* placed between two similar vowels, a modification similar to one we see in the Accadian, when the Assyrian *nagû*, " district," is transformed into *nanga*, or *kî-kala* into *kankal*.[3]

Does *kiengi*, or *kingi*, whose meaning as a substantive is thus clear, apply to the country of Sumer, Babylonia proper, as being pre-eminently " the country "?

It is possible that M. Schrader may be right in his opinion. It seems to me though, that the opposition between *Kiengi* and *Akkad*, " the country " and " the mountain," implied rather the meaning of

---

[1] *W. A. I.* II., 39, l. 9, c, d; cf. its use in IV., 27, 4, l. 63.

[2] See my *Etude sur quelques parties des Syllabaires cunéiformes*, p. 72, et seq.; 102, et seq.

[3] *Ibid.*, p. 177.

"plain" in the first word, as in Assyrian, *matu*, "the country," is used in the sense of "plain," when it is opposed to *sadu*, "mountain." I think even that I have discovered the word *kingi* used in the sense of "plain," amongst a people speaking a language related to the Accadians, in the name of one of the provinces of Na'iri, *kingi Istilenzakhar*,[1] "the plain of Istilenzakhar." An idea of flatness analogous to that of a plain would result etymologically from the presence of the syllable *gina* in the compound *kingina*, contracted into *kingi*, and would give it a different meaning from the simple *ki*.

To return to *Sumeri*. This name designated the inhabitants of the country Kiengi, as Akkadi did the inhabitants of the country called Akkad, "the mountain," whence we must infer an identity of meaning between *sumer* = שנער and *kiengi*. Sumir is evidently a word formed by a suffix of derivation in *r*, other examples of which are now to be seen in the Accadian. But we do not yet know which was the earlier form, *sumer* or *sungir*, and consequently whether the root was *sum* or *suk*; both suppositions are equally allowable from a philological point of view, the first would give the meaning "low country," the second "watered country." All this leads us to the same conclusion with respect to *sumer*, as we came to in connection with *kiengi*, when it was opposed to Akkad: that it included the vast plain watered by the two great rivers in view of the high mountains, which bound it and tower above it on the eastern side. This

[1] Obelisk of Samsi-Bin (Shamas-Vul), col. 3, l. 53.

opinion is further confirmed by the unmistakeable traces, which we find in the geographical nomenclature of much later date, of a primitive extension of the name *Sumer* = שִׁנְעָר to the common valley of the Euphrates and the Tigris, from the source of the two rivers in the mountains of Armenia to their outlet in the Persian Gulf. In this vast extent of territory, which constitutes a clearly defined physical region, we find not only the Biblical Shinar, pre-eminently the plain, adjoining Babylon, but more to the north, between the Tigris and the Chaboras, the Singara of the classical writers,[1] the Sindjar of Arabian geographers,[2] with the chain of hills called by Ptolemy Σιγγάρων ὄρη,[3] which stretched from there to the Tigris, crossing the whole of western Assyria. The Egyptian monuments of the eighteenth dynasty mention frequently[4] a country of Sinker as situated alongside that of Assur, whilst they place Akati (Accad) some way to the south as compared with Nineveh.[5]

IV. The names Sumirians and Accadians meant then originally "the people of the plain" and "the mountaineers." These names take us back to a time long anterior to any of which we possess records, to a time when the two nations bearing these names dwelt, one on the banks of the two

---

[1] Ptol. V. 12, 9; Dio Casso, LXVIII. 22; Ammian. Marc. XVIII. 5, 20; Eckel, *Doctr. num. vet.*, Vol. III., p. 519; Ritter, *Erdkunde*, Vol. X., p. 118, 158, 247, 696, 718; Layard, *Nineveh and Babylon*, p. 249.

[2] Maracid, Vol. II., p. 57; Aboulfeda, p. 445; Qezovina, Vol. II., p. 262.

[3] V. 12, 2. Now the Sindjar mountains.

[4] Chabas, *Voyage d'un Egyptien*, p. 225.

[5] Maspéro, *De Carchemis oppidu situ*, p. 26; J. de Rougé, *Mélanges d'archeologie Egyptienne*, Vol. I., p. 46.

great rivers of Mesoptamia in the plain, the other amongst the eastern mountains, where, as we saw, some tribes called Chaldeans were to be found up to a very recent period. Later, a general migration took place which had not been historically recorded, and the place of abode and respective position of these two nations became changed without their undergoing any alteration of name, although the designations by which they were known no longer corresponded with the physical physiognomy of their then new resting places. This was often the case, however, with the names of nations which were given originally to mark some peculiarity of geographical position and were retained after an entire change of position, even when their etymological meaning was found to be quite at variance with the site occupied by the people who continued to use them or to whom they are even now still applied.

So although the Sumirians and Accadians retained the names which originally marked them as people of the plain and the mountain, both nations found themselves inhabitants of the plains bathed by the waters of the Euphrates and Tigris, the Sumirs in the north, in Babylonia, the Accadians in the south, in Chaldea; these mountaineers were thus the occupants of a country where there was not a single mountain to justify the use of their old title, which was continued, however, both from custom and tradition. And it is worthy of remark that the want of agreement, which resulted from the change of abode, between the meaning of the two names and the physical conditions of the countries henceforth inhabited by the nations to whom they were applied, contributed much (as we have proved was the case) to give to these designations the character of names of nations, used almost exclusively in the plural. The memory of the correct and original meaning of the two Accadian words, *sumer* and *akkad*, was vivid enough to lead to the use of the expression *mat Sumeri u mat Akkadi*, "the country of the Sumirs and the country of the Accadians," in speaking of Babylonia and Chaldea and not *Sumer u Akkad*, which would have meant indeed "the plain and the mountain," and have been both absurd and a violation of common sense, whilst the phrase that they did use was quite allowable "the country of the people of the plain, and the country of the mountaineers," referring to the original conditions and the point of departure of the dwellers in the two countries. It seems that *Akkadu* or *Akkad*, in the singular, as the name of a country and not of a people, did not come into use until much later during the Assyrian epoch, when the Accadian had become a dead language and the tradition of the real meaning of the word was consequently quite lost. And even at that time, the royal titles adopted by the Sargons when they made themselves masters of Babylon ran *sar Sumeri u Akkadi*, "king of the Sumirians and the Accadians," not "king of Sumir and Accad." In my opinion, all this tends to dispel any ethnical difference between the Sumirians and the Accadians. As the two names belonged to the Accadian language, it appears very probable, looking at the facts in the new light now thrown upon them, that they were of earlier date than the introduction of the Semitic or Kushito-Semitic element, that the two nations, whose respective geographical position they indicated, were two divisions of the non-Semitic or Turanian race, from whose language these names were taken. And when the Sumirians and Accadians had become the inhabitants of Babylonia and Chaldea, these two names continued to be used in this same sense after the introduction of the new ethnic element in either province; the distinction of race had nothing to do with it, the people of Babylonia, of whatever origin and language, were counted amongst the Sumirians, the people of Chaldea as Accadians.

If, as M. Schrader thinks, an example exists in which the Assyrians term the non-Semitic language of Chaldea as the language of the Sumirians and Accadians, the question would be definitely settled; we need look for no distinction of race under these two names. Unfortunately as I mentioned above, this decisive proof is still wanting. But in its absence I think we may arrive at the same conclusion by an argument of another kind.

Now that an indigenous document has shown us clearly that the title of the ancient kings of Ur, whose Accadian (or Sumer-Accadian) origin was testified by their proper names, *ungal Kiengi ki Akkad* was equivalent to "kings of the Sumirians and Accadians," part of M. Oppert's reasoning assumes great importance and we must assent to it. "In their title these kings place the equivalent of Sumir before Accad, so we may conclude that the Sumirians belonged to their race, for a sovereign does not generally call himself first king of a foreign race, he gives the priority to his own." But we cannot from this infer with the eminent philologist, that the Accadians represent the element speaking the Semitic language, since we noticed that the Assyrians compared Accad to Assur, when they wished to show the opposition between the non-Semitic and Semitic idioms. The only conclusion possible in the face of these facts, is that the Sumirians and Accadians belonged to the same race, that they were two divisions of the same blood; that it was no supposition of any ethnic distinction which prompted the awarding of the first rank, the place of honour to the Sumirians, but rather the peculiarly sacred character of their country, the important place taken by the plain of Shinar and Babylon, the principal sacred town in religious tradition.

V. Still the fact on which M. Oppert based his Sumirian theory remains. It raises a very difficult problem, which must I fear yet be left undecided. But the meaning of the fact seems to me too uncertain in itself, and too susceptible of diverse interpretations, for any good critic to make it the pivot on which all researches connected with the respective characters of the Sumirians and Accadians should turn.

In the inscriptions of the Assyrian period, the phonetic expression of the name of the Sumirians and the allophonic sign furnished by the old Accadian word *kiengi*, are frequently replaced by a complex ideographic group ▰▰▰ ▰▰, of which we have as yet found no earlier example.

The first sign of this complex group has the sure and only ideographic meaning, "language," therefore, the use of it would seem to indicate a difference of language between the Sumers and Accadians. This is the fact, and it is well to remark, that M. Oppert and I have been able with equal probability to make it the basis of two opposite theories.

The ideographic group, says M. Oppert, meant "language of worship," so it proves that the Sumirians were the original possessors of the non-Semitic idiom, which long remained as sacred to the Assyrians as it was to the Babylonians.

This reasoning is however by no means sure and unassailable, for two objections can be proved against it which seem instantly to destroy it.

1st. Nothing is less certain than the explanation and analysis of complex ideographic groups, when they are unaccompanied by any hints from the Assyrian grammarians themselves. Much prudence and forethought is necessary to prevent the student from being led away by his imagination, and an interpretation of this kind can rarely be taken as the foundation of an argument because it is so likely to be incorrect. Thus with regard to the case in point, no one can doubt that the first sign means "language," but the ideographic values ascribed to the second are various enough to make the meaning of the whole uncertain; three different translations at any rate are equally probable. That which runs "language of worship," is possible I own, but I consider it one of the least probable, for it ascribes to the second character a secondary and derivative sense which it seldom has, and which is only used as an extension of that of "service."

2nd. Even if this meaning were proved to be correct it does not follow that because the ideographic group was invented by the Assyrians, it must necessarily apply to the Turanian language, which we call *Accadian*. Indeed, it is far from clear that the Assyrians used this language as a "language of worship," that is, as a liturgical language. It had this character in Babylon, but I think we are quite at liberty to doubt whether it was ever so accepted in Assyria. The Assyrians searched out and studied the old Accadian books as sacred books, but though this was an indispensable foundation of all sacerdotal studies, it does not prove that their liturgy was in the Accadian. Such religious hymns as we possess in the Accadian tongue are directly connected with the worship of the principal sanctuaries of Babylonia and Chaldea; and we see that they were used in the ceremonies of the particular sanctuary which they mention. There is not a single one that seems to have been connected with the Assyrian temples. On the contrary, we now possess enough fragments of the liturgy of the Assyrians, properly so-called, both hymns and prayers, written only in Assyrian, to infer that in this country the "language of worship," the liturgical language, was the national language, and not the Accadian, in spite of the importance they continued to attach to the Accadian books as a means of religious instruction.

In my *Etudes Accadiennes* I thought I discovered in this same ideographic group the elements of an argument exactly contrary to that urged by M. Oppert. I observed, and so far I hold to my opinion, that the most common meaning of the second sign used in this group, 𒂍, would give "ordinary language," *lingua familiaris, lingua domestica*, instead of "language of worship;" and I therefore came to the conclusion that the Assyrians had invented this group in order to designate the Sumirians as the people who spoke the same language as themselves, in contrast with the Accadians. This would not be entirely opposed to my new opinion, that the names Sumirians and Accadians were originally applied to two divisions of the same non-Semitic race. Indeed the appellation of Sumirians was certainly afterwards used to designate the inhabitants of Babylonia as opposed to those of Chaldea, but without any definite ethnic idea being attached to it. Now it is historically certain, that the Turanian-Accadian element which was gradually supplanted by the Semitic-Assyrian, lost its supremacy and even died out altogether, much more quickly in the north than in the south, in Babylonia than in Chaldea. At the time that their national existence began and their external power arose, the Assyrians would have been quite right in considering the Sumirians, understood in the sense of inhabitants of Babylonia, as a population speaking the same language as themselves; but that teaches us nothing more about the ethnic value of this word than the use of the term *lingua Gallica* in modern Latin, to designate French, teaches us about the ancient language of the Gauls.[1] It would even be natural to think that they had the same reason for adopting the term "language of Accad," to designate the non-Semitic language which must have belonged to the primitive Sumirians as well as the Accadians, the country of Accad in its strictest sense being the place where it remained longest and where they saw it still a living language.

I would not, however, venture to assert that this interpretation, this way of looking at things, is perfectly certain; indeed that is a line I have never

[1] One fact at least is certain, that in consequence of more ancient ethnic changes of which Babylon was the scene, and of which we have tried to give an idea, founded partly on conjecture, the name of the people of this country, the Sumirians, early lost the exact individual meaning which the name of the Accadians retained much later; it assumed a vague character, and became one of those memories of the past which are used in royal titles even after they represent nothing substantial.

If the kings of Assyria, when they made themselves masters of Babylon, took the title of *Sar Sumeri u Akkadi*, it was a regular affectation of archaism, a revival of the ancient protocol which they thought gave an august character to their sovereignty. But we must not omit to notice that they took to it again after a period of suspension, or at least uncertainty as to its use, under the monarchs of the Cissian dynasty. In their Accadian inscriptions these kings reassume the ancient title *ungal Kiengi ki Akkad*, an entirely geographical title, together with those of *ungal Ká-dingira* or *ungal Karu-Dunyas* "king of Babylon," and *ungal Kassi* "king of the Kassi;" they even used it as an allophonic expression in some of their Assyrian inscriptions, *W. A. I.* IV., 41, col. 1, l. 30.

But when they substitute a phonetic expression for the allophonic expression of this title in the inscriptions in the same language, they do not write *sar Sumeri u Akkadi* but *sar Kassi u Akkadi* (see the inscription published in part in *W. A. I.* II., 38, 2, and more completely by Mr. Boscawen, *Trans. Soc. Bib. Arch.*, Vol. IV., p. 1; I can think also of two other examples). They replaced then *Sumeri* by *Kassi*, as a designation of the inhabitants of Babylonia, really because part of the nation of the Elamite Kassi, the people to whom these kings themselves belonged, had come and settled as conquerors in Babylonia. They are often mentioned in the precious document known as the *Synchronous History* in connection with events which happened under the later Cissian kings, and even under the first princes of the Assyrian dynasty which followed them. The Kassi seem to have been at that time a conquering and ruling people in Babylonia, triumphing over the old inhabitants who still retained their own language however, something in the same way that the Turks now rule most of their European provinces.

adopted.¹ I only suggest it as at least as possible a conclusion as M. Oppert's, or perhaps as even more probable. My chief reason for repeating it is to show how uncertain in the question of Sumir and Accad any argument is which rests on one particular interpretation of an ideographic expression of doubtful meaning, capable of many explanations and all of equal value, and how imprudent it is therefore to build up a theory about the ethnic character of these nations on such a fragile basis. And owing to the number of ideographic meanings attached to the second character of the group under consideration, a third explanation might be propounded with quite as much show of reason as the two that have already been given, and like them founded on unquestionable instances of the use of the character in this sense; the translation in this case would be "language of those sitting"² (no doubt in contradistinction to the nomadic tribes), which would suggest an entirely new train of thought.

Let us suppose for a minute what is not possible, without considering that our point of view would be completely changed, and imagine that we could prove from some example as yet unknown to us (which is by no means impossible), that the complex ideographic expression ▶︎▣ ▣ is not of Assyrian origin, but attributable to some earlier date. Then the difference of language which it seems to imply between the Sumirians and Accadians, would become

---

¹ See the same terms which I used in my *Etudes accadiennes*, Vol. I., 3, p. 91.

² The sign ▣ has the meaning "to put, place," intransitively "to sit," at least as often as that of "serve," and this rendering is much more usual than "adoration, worship."

a simple variation of the same, a purely dialectivc difference, instead of the regular opposition existing between a Semitic and Turanian language. That a variety of dialects of the ante-Semitic language did exist in the lower basin of the Tigris and Euphrates no one can doubt. The lexicographical tablets bear witness to the fact. They often contain certain words belonging to a dialect closely related to the Accadian, properly so-called, but differing from it in certain phonetic peculiarities, one of the most striking of which is the tendency to substitute *m* for *b*.[1] The words borrowed from this dialect are always distinguished from the pure Accadian words by the addition of an ideographic expression which shows them to be of some peculiar idiom, ⌞𒅴⌟ ⌞𒊩⌟ ; this expression seems to mean "language of women" (unless it means something quite different, which is still doubtful, for we are sure of the translation "language"), but in any case we should not omit to notice the close connection between it and the group used to designate the Sumirians in the Assyrian texts.

I must add that an inscription of Sennacherib's mentions in Babylonia, as side by side with the country of the Sumirians, designated by the expression ⌞𒅴⌟ ⌞𒆳⌟, not the country of the Accadians, or at least not one of the expressions generally used for it, but a country designated by an ideographic group so formed as to be a counterpart to it, and giving also an idea of language, ⌞𒅴⌟ ⌞𒂊𒈨𒂊⌟.[2]

What is the meaning of this last expression? It

[1] *W. A. I.* III., 4, 4.

[2] M. Oppert translates "country of the language of the slaves," but I do not know from what information.

would be bold to pretend to solve it. But that is one proof more of the obscurity in which these indications touching a diversity of language between certain tribes of Babylonia or Chaldea are still wrapped, and showing how dangerous it is to isolate one and draw from it inferences which are by no means indisputable.

The ideographic expression for the name of Sumirians, in the inscriptions of the Assyrian kings, suggests then a problem which is not yet resolved, and which it is not possible to resolve in the present state of the science; it must stand aside until we can obtain the necessary proofs from new documents. I repeat that the answer to the question is not to be found in an ideographic expression of doubtful meaning, which has been interpreted in two opposite ways and might be interpreted differently again; it needs other data like those we have been trying to bring forward.

The reader will perhaps think that the use of these data has not led me to any certain result, and that I now speak doubtfully on a subject on which I was formerly sure, and on which M. Oppert continues to be quite certain, though taking a view diametrically opposed to mine. But in science it is a step gained to admit that we are no longer certain on a point which in a hasty moment we were too ready to suppose was incontestable. Besides, amidst all the uncertainty which still exists there are two points which become daily clearer: the legitimacy of the name *Accadian language*, for which we have a precedent in the custom of the Assyrians, although it is probable that this language was not peculiar to the Accadians, at least not originally; the increasing probability that the names Sumirians and Accadians did not express the distinction between the Semitic or Kushito-Semitic race and the Turanian or Altaic race.

This latter point now renders useless all discussions about the choice between the appellations *Sumerian* or *Accadian* for the idiom which must have belonged both to the Sumirians and Accadians.

[77]

INDEX.

AAHLA. The Egyptian "Plains of Peace" 86
ABAMMON. His conference with Porphyry 75
ABU SHAREIN. The modern name of the ancient Eridu . . 28
ABYDENUS. His account of the resting-place of the Ark of Noah . 159
ACCAD.
   In later times called Kaldi . . 335
   The territory described by Sennacherib 393
ACCAD or SUMIR. MM. Oppert and Lenormant upon these terms . 387
ACCADIAN and EGYPTIAN MAGIC. Contrasts between . . . 107
ACCADIAN and FINNISH MYTHOLOGY. Their differences . . . 250
ACCADIAN and IRANIAN DEITIES of the three zones . . . 230
ACCADIAN MAGIC BOOKS. Various questions arising from the study of 198
ACCADIAN MAGICAL HYMNS. Many valuable ones only exist in an Assyrian version . . . 15
ACCADIAN LANGUAGE.
   A dead language in the time of Assurbanipal . . . 2
   Allied to the Mantchoo . . 295
   Assurbanipal tries to restore it . 369
   Differences between it and the Altaic languages . . . 283
   Examined in detail . . . 263
   Four fundamental principles relating to 268
   Generally used by the Assyrians for magical purposes . . 264
   How influenced under the Sargonides 329
   Its agglutinative character . . 296
   Its Altaic affinities . . 292, 299
   Its formation of derivatives . . 272
   Its incapsulations 297
   Its negative conjugations . . 281
   Its peculiar formation of the plural and dual numbers . . . 276
   Its periphrastic constructions . 291
   Its phonology 309
   Its postpositive conjugations . 280
   Its pronouns identical with those of the Altaic languages . . 278
   Its stages of development with regard to the pronominal subject of the verb 293
   Its three classes of vowels . . 271
   Its Turanian affinities . . . 270
   Its use of verbal forms instead of conjunctions 281

ACCADIAN LANGUAGE. (*Continued.*)
   No distinction between the two genders 277
   Peculiarities in its formation of adverbs 282
   Peculiarities in its use of particles 280
   Peculiarities in its use of postpositions 281
   Peculiarities in the formation of its roots 277
   Peculiarities of its adjectival forms 285
   Peculiar use of particles in its verbal voices 290
   Possesses few prefixes of derivation 283
   Preference for prepositive conjugations in 286
ACCADIANS, The.
   Believed in lucky and unlucky months 7
   Ignorant of the Assyrians in early times 333
   Probably came from Armenia . 361
   Their archaic legislation . . 378
   Their first writing hieroglyphic in character 363
   Their horror of darkness . . 178
   Their priority in Chaldea . . 350
ACHÆMENIDES. Their support of the Persian religion 220
ADAM. Deceived by the she-demon Lilith 38
ADAR.
   An Assyrian deity of strength, analogous to Nindar and Hercules. The god of the planet Saturn . . . 17, 55, 118
   Was both the husband and son of Belit 118
ADAR SAMDAN. Called the Sun of the South 131
ADONIS MYTH. Its Egyptian analogues 84
ADRA-KHASIS. See Khasisatra . 354
ÆON. Anu properly an Æon . 133
ÆSCHYLUS. Describes the Babylonians as a mixed crowd . 331
AGANE.
   Its monarchs of Kushito-Semitic origin 326
   The Agama of Ptolemy and the Babylonian Talmud . . 395
   The seat of the dynasty of the Sargonides 126
AGIEL. The intelligence of Saturn . 26
AGMA or AGAMA. The same as Agane 395
AGNI.
   An Aryan fire god, the analogue of the Accadian fire deity . . 27

AGNI. (*Continued.*)
  His analogue the fire god Bil-gi . 185
  His interchangeable character . 131
AHRIMAN. *See* Angromainyus.
AHTO. The Finnish king of the ocean 252
AHURAMAZDA.
  Confides the world to Darius Hystaspes 219
  His connection with Zarvana-akarana 229
  His cultus tinctured with Babylonian ideas 196
  His name unknown to Herodotus . 224
  Made into a triad with Mithra and Anahita 235
  Sublime titles of 199
AKAR. The proper name of the Egyptian hell 86
AKHKHARU. The Assyrian vampire . 37
AKU. The type of royalty, and the first divine monarch who reigned upon earth 208
AKU or PAKU. An Accadian deity . 206
ALAL.
  A wicked demon so called . 8, 16
  Causes chest diseases . . . 36
  Charms against 17
ALAP. The winged bull of the Assyrians considered as a protecting demon 24
ALEXANDRIA. The Neoplatonists of Alexandria described . . . 75
ALLAT, The goddess. Called Ningis-zida 140
ALTAIC AFFINITIES. Of the Accadian language examined . . . 292
ALTAIC DIALECTS. Their importance in the study of Accadian philology 268
ALU. The Assyrian analogues of the Alal 24
AMARUD. Identified with Marduk by M. Grival 10
AMAR-UTUKI. An Accadian name of Marduk 132
AMEN-KHEM. The Ithyphallic Horus 98
AMEN-RA.
  Invoked in an Egyptian incantation 101
  The analogue of Jupiter . . 78
AMENTI. The abode of the Egyptian gods 86
AMESTRIS. Sacrifices seven children to the god of darkness . . . 231
AM-KAHOU-EF. A mystical evil serpent assailing the bodies of the dead 93
AMSHASPANDS. Their Accadian analogues 200
ANA, The god.
  Called Zi-ana, Spirit of the Heavens 149
  His analogy to Ukko the god of the Finns 247
  His consort the goddess Nana . 149
  Not identical with Oannes . . 202
ANAHITA. Associated with Mithra and Ahuramazda 235
ANATA. An Egypto-Semitic goddess of war and revenge . . . 99
ANGELS. Of the planets . . . 26

ANGROMAINYUS.
  His connection with Zarvana-akarana 229
  Worshipped by the Magi . . 231
ANHUR. An Egyptian deity, his character and offices . . . 96
ANKH-USKH-SENH. The meaning of the formula 101
ANNA. The Accadian name of the god Anu 4
ANNEDOTUS.
  A fish deity, a form of Hea . . 157
  Origin of the name . . . 203
ANTHROPOMORPHISM. Early introduced into Egyptian theology . 82
ANU.
  Analogous with Eschmun, Marna, Baal-haldim, and Audh . . 134
  At the desire of Ishtar creates a bull to punish Izdubar . . 57
  Really an Æon, or heaven, earth, and time 133
  The father of Martu, the West . 120
  Worshipped at Urukh . . . 323
ANUBIS. How distinguished from Set 83
ANUNNAGE. Accadian deity called the Archangel of the Abyss. He was a form of Hea 164
ANUNNA-GE. The Accadian gods of the earth 17
ANUNNA-IRTSITI. The Assyrian spirits of the earth . . . 17
'Aός. Greek form of the god Hea . 115
APAP. *See* Apophis.
APHRODITE and MITHRA. Origin of the erroneous identification of, by Herodotus 234
APOLLO. His analogue in Horus-Ra 78
APOLLO PYTHIAS. Allusion to the sacred intoxication of his priestess 255
APOLLODORUS. His version of Berosus' account of the Annedoti . 157
APOPHIS. The great serpent of evil, originally a nature deity . . 83
APSU. The goddess of the Abyss . 113
ARABIA.
  Characteristics of its early religions 128
  Southern Arabia called the land of Pount 106
  The starting place of the Semitic nations 341
ARALLI. A mystical country rich in gold 152
ARDUSIN. An early Babylonian monarch 127
ARIA. An Accadian river deity . 183
ARK OF KHASISATRA. Its construction as described in the Deluge Tablet 160
ARK OF KHONSU. Sent into Bakhtan to cure the Princess Bintreschit . 33
ARK OF THE DELUGE. Rested on the Gordyœan mountains of Armenia 159, 362
ARMENIA. Origin of the Accadians in 361
ARPHAXAD. A Semitic chief . 339
ARROWS OF FATE. Represented in the hands of Marduk . . . 238

AU — 3 — BE

ARSAPHES. A form of Horus the Avenger 99
ARTAXERXES MNEMON. His inscription at Susa associates other deities with Ahuramazda . . . 235
ARYAN DEITIES. Turned into demons by the Vedic writers . . . 77
ARYAN SORCERY. Its Chaldean analogies 60
ASAAJAT. A class of Finnish magicians 243
ASAKKU. The Assyrian name of the Idpa demon 36
ASAPHIM. Were the Chaldean Theosophists 14
ASMUN. A Chaldean deity . 120
ASSESSORS. The forty-two assessors of Osiris 106
ASSOROS. Analogue of the god Assur 123
ASSUR. The first seat of civilization. Meaning of the name. Now called Kalah-Shergat 334
ASSURBAN-IBILA. An uncertain Chaldean(?) monarch . . . 370
ASSURBANIPAL.
  Had at least 30,000 magical tablets in his library 9
  Had the Accadian tablets copied into Assyrian . . . 2
  His conquest of Mongolian races . 347
  Tries to restore the sacred, i.e., Accadian language . . . 369
ASSYRIA. Prayer for the king of . 34
ASSYRIAN LANGUAGE. How influenced under the Sargonides . . 329
ASSYRIAN SCRIBES. Added phonetic commentaries on the lexicographical tablets 313
ASSYRIAN VERSION. Of the Accadian tablets not always literal . 3
ASSYRIANS. Originally called the Gutium 333
ASTROLOGERS, Chaldean. The Kasdim of Daniel . . . 14
ASTYAGES. Connected with serpent worship 233
ASURAS. The Aryan Asuras changed into the devils of the Vedas . 77
ATEF CROWN. Its nature and significance 95
ATHARVA VEDA. Its analogue in Accadian magical treatises. Formulæ 12
ATHRAVA. The Persian religion . 220
ATROPATENE.
  A second Ecbatana, surrounded with seven mystical walls . 227
  The early seat of fire worship . 197
ATYS MYTH. Its Egyptian analogies . 84
AUDH. An Arabian deity analogous with Anu 134
AUH-NARU. The Egyptian abode or heaven of Osiris . . . 86
AUSAR. An early deity after whom the town of Assur was named . 334
AUV KINUV. A primordial deity of the Chaldeans 113
AVESTA, The.
  Citations from . . . 223

AVESTA, The. *Continued.*
  Probably influenced by Babylonian theology 196
AZAZEL. Reference to the Jewish scapegoat of Azazel . . . 261

BA. The soul so called in Egyptian 84
BAAL. The general deity of the Semitic nations . . . 83
BAAL-HALDIM. An analogue of Anu 134
BAB-ILU. The original form of the name of Babel 114
BABYLON.
  Extreme antiquity of the great temple at 322
  Probably called Tin-tir . . 193
  Sacred prostitution at . . 386
  The tomb of Marduk at . . 132
BABYLONIA.
  Anciently called Ka-Dingira . 353
  Independent of Assyria till 800 B.C. 324
  The two ethnic elements in . 331
BABYLONIA and CHALDEA. Temporarily conquered by the Kushites 320
BABYLONIAN CITIES. Had generally two names, one Accadian, one Assyrian 353
BABYLONIAN ETHNOLOGICAL TYPES. M. Hamy's account of . . 348
BABYLONIAN GODS. Invoked seriatim to work evil on the Caillou Michaux 68
BACCHUS DIONYSUS. Probable origin of his title 17
BAGDAD. The Caillou Michaux found in the environs of . . . 68
BAH. A name of the deity Hapi-moui 104
BAHRAM-GOUR. Another form of the name of Varahran V. . . 227
BAHU or BOHU. A Phenician analogue of Dav-cina . . . 124
BAKHTAN. A country in Mesopotamia 32
BAKSY. The Kirghis sorcerers . 212
BAR. Another name of the god Bilgi 189
BARIS. The name of the bark of Osiris 83
BARKS of the gods. Their names in Egyptian mythology . . . 83
BASCHKIR KALMUKS. Their superstitions 212
BAT-ANA. The ancient name of the town of Diru 326
BAU. The Chaldean goddess of Chaos 120
BEDS of the Assyrians. Always stood on a platform . . 8
BEHISTUN INSCRIPTION. Refers to the suppression of the Magi . 219
BEIWA. The solar deity of the Laps 249
BEL. See Baal.
  An Assyrian deity, analogous to the Mul-ge of the Accadians . 16
  Worshipped at Nipur . . . 323
BELIT.
  An Assyrian goddess, analogous to the Accadian Nin-gelal . . 16
  Her functions and characteristics . 116
  The wife of Bel, and as Beltis the Assyrian goddess of war . . 68
BELLONA. Her analogue in Anaitis or Anata 99

28*

BEL-MARDUK. Accadian demiurge . 53
BENNU. A kind of heron used to symbolise the solar year . . 84
BEROSUS.
His account of the Annedoti . . 157
His Chaldean cosmogony examined in detail by Professor Sayce . 123
Source of his theogony . . . 53
BESA. The analogue of Mars . . 78
BIL-GI.
His various titles 186
Regarded by the Assyrians rather as a personification than a deity 188
The Accadian god of fire . . 184
The same as Izdhubar . . . 188
BIN.
Another name of the god Vul or Rimmon 117, 182
The Assyrian god of the atmosphere, and the Biblical Rimmon 17
BINTRESCHIT or BENT-RASH. A princess afflicted by a demon . 33
BIRCH, Dr. Translates the Stele of the Possessed Princess . . 34
BISEBA. An Accadian name of the sun 249
BIT-NUR. Amulet tablet of . . 46
BLACK RACES. Early distinguished in Accadian theology . . . 193
BODIN, Jean. A mediæval writer on demonology 23
BORSIPPA.
Astral significance of its seven terraced tower 227
Extreme antiquity of the great temple at 322
Various temples at . . . 193
BOSCAWEN, Mr. W. Translates a Hymn to the Mountain of the World . 126
BOTTA, M. Discovers small statuettes of the Assyrian gods at Khorsabad 47
BRAHMA. The Hindu creator . . 115
BROWN and WHITE RACES. Chaldean account of their origin . 336
BRUGSCH, HEINRICH. Translates the Romance of Setnau . . . 102
BUDDHA. Analogues between his Tchakra and the disk of Hea . 162
BUDDHISTS.
Of Ceylon term the Hindu gods demons 77
Use figures of demons to cure the diseases caused by them . . 51
BULL OF HADES. Engendered by the god Ungal-turda . . . 171
BULLS OF HADES. Their number and offices 170
BUNSEN, Chevalier. Has examined the Egyptian myth of the Meskem 88
BURNA-BURYAS. One of the last to use the Accadian language . . 369

CABBALA. The angels, spirits, and intelligences of 26
CAILLOU MICHAUX. A Babylonian boundary stone protected by curses 68
CAMBYSES. State of Persia during the absence of Cambyses . . 219

CANIDRA. The witch, resembled an Accadian magician . . . 5
CEPHENES. Meaning of the appellation. Synonymous with Ethiopians 337
CEPHEUS. Early Babylonian monarch 338
CEYLON. Triumph of Buddhism there 77
CHABAS, F. His translation of a magical talisman quoted . . 92
CHABORAS. Active volcanoes near . 10
CHÆREMON. Wrote a work upon Egyptian magic 101
CHAKAMIN. The term given by Daniel to the Chaldean physicians 14
CHALDÆO-BABYLONIAN RELIGION. Its doctrines examined . . . 111
CHALDEA.
Called a part of Accadia in the inscriptions of Shalmaneser III. . 394
To be distinguished from Babylonia 324
CHALDEA and BABYLONIA. Temporarily conquered by the Kushites . 320
CHALDEAN and Egyptian magic contrasted 78
CHALDEAN AMULETS. And their uses 39
CHALDEAN CIVILIZATION. Sumirian influence in 356
CHALDEAN COSMOGONY. Its origin 336
CHALDEAN DEITIES.
Also called Zi 148
Named by numbers . . . 25
Their eponymous character . . 127
CHALDEAN DEMONOLOGY. Its influence on the book of Enoch . 30
CHALDEAN DYNASTY. Reigned immediately after the Flood . . 339
CHALDEAN FAITH. Influenced by the Kushites 367
CHALDEAN GODS. Indicated by a star 155
CHALDEAN MAGICAL TABLETS. Monotonous style of the conjurations 15
CHALDEAN MATHEMATICS. Its cycles and systems 366
CHALDEAN MYTHOLOGY. Its development 125
CHALDEAN SORCERERS. Their supposed terrible powers . . . 61
CHALDEAN THEOLOGY. Its pantheistic nature 129
CHALDEAN VEDA. M. Lenormant's name for a collection of Accadian hymns 319
CHALDEANS. Had properly no physicians 35
CHALDEES or KALDU. Their growth under Assurnazirhabel and Salmanasar III. 340
CHAMAEL. The angel of Mars . 26
CHANGE OF PERSON. A common feature in Oriental composition . 16
CHANG-TI. The Chinese heaven deity 154
CHEDORLAOMER. Properly the Elamite conqueror Kudur-Lagamar . 120
CHIEF or Manager of Slaves. Accadian laws to restrain . . . 383
COCHABIEL. The spirit of Mercury 26
CONCUBINAGE. Accadian laws respecting 385

CONIFEROUS TREE. Used in enchantments 28
CONJURORS, Chaldean. The Khartumim of Daniel 14
CORN CROPS. Enchantments to prosper the 42
CORY, J. P. Value of his *Ancient Fragments* 119
COSMO-GEOGRAPHY of the Chaldeans. Examined in detail . . . 151
COSMOGONY of Berosus. Examined in detail by Rev. A. H. Sayce . 123
COSMOGONY of the Chaldeans. Pedigree of 115
COSMOGONY of the Phoenicians. Examined by Ewald and Sayce . 124
Cox. Identifies Ouranos and Varuna 134
CRAOSCHA, The archangel. His analogy to Silik-mulu-khi . . 195
CREATION TABLET. Discovered by George Smith . . . 113
CREMATION. Its origin among the Turanian races . . . 220
CUNEIFORM WRITING. Invented by the Turanians 371
CUPS. Assyrian magical drinking . 46
CUTHA. Sacred to the god Kanissura 120
CYBELE and ATYS. Egyptian origin of the Myth of . . . 84
CYRUS. Reason of his regard for the God of the Jews . . 223

DACCA. The Hindus of Dacca invent a goddess of small pox . 36
DAGON. A form of Oannes or Hea 157
DAHAKA. A terrible serpent in Zendic mythology . . . 233
DAHILLA. The Accadian river of the dead 258
DAMASCIUS.
 His description of the Chaldean trinity 115
 His version of the Accadian theogony 202
 Source of his theogony . . 53
DAMIETTA. Elephantiasis peculiar to 20
DAMKINA.
 Goes with Hea into his magic ark 160
 The wife of Hea . . . 22
DANIEL. Refers to the Accadian astrologers and Magi . . 14
DANIEL, Book of. The present version textually later than the time of Alexander the Great . . 14
DANTE. The seven spheres of the Inferno a Chaldean analogue . 167
DAPINA. Another name of the god Dun-kun-uddu . . . 172
DARIUS HYSTASPES.
 Claims to have been given by Ahuramazda for the reformation of the world . . . 219
 His inscriptions at El Khargeh cited 144
 His opposition to the Magi . 218
DARKNESS. Accadian horror of . 179
DAV-CINA or DAVKE. The Accadian female earth 124
DAVKINA. Her character as a nature goddess 159

DEE, Dr. John. His revelations tinged with Babylonian ideas . 58
DELUGE TABLET. The hero Izdubar possibly a fire deity . . . 10
DEMONS.
 Chiefly inhabit the desert . . 31
 Five great classes of . . . 25
 Many figures or parts of figures of remaining 52
 Their subtle influences . . 30
DEMONS of the Finns. Inhabit Pohjolo 256
DE ROUGE. Translates the Stele of the Possessed Princess . . 34
DESERT. Chiefly inhabited by demons 31
DEUS AVERRUNCUS. The proper office of Hea 158
DHUBAR. The true name of the hero Izdhubar 188
DIADEM. Its varieties . . . 41
DIANA. Her analogue in Nepthys . 78
DIANNISU. Or "Judge of Men," an Assyrian title of the sun god . 17
DICE. Used in Magian magic . 238
DII MINORES. Their origin described 73
DIMMER EA. A title of the god Fire 186
DINGIRA. The Accadian name of Ilu 113
DIODORUS SICULUS.
 His account of the Chaldean Magi 12
 His statements as to the Chaldean views of heaven and earth . 150
DIRU. Its Patesi had Semitic names, and wrote in Assyrian . . 326
DISEASES.
 Caused by demons, enumerated . 4-6
 Sent from the infernal regions . 21
DISK OF HEA. Its terrible nature and effects 162
DIVINING RODS. Used by the Magi 237
DRAGON and SUN MYTH. Its Assyrian analogues . . . 208
DRANGA. The *lie* which deceived the Persians in the reign of Cambyses 219
DREAM of the King of Bakhtan . 34
DUALISM of the Accadian magical system 146
DUALISMS of the Chaldean deities . 117
DUAL NATURE of Chaldean sorcery 58
DUNGI.
 An early king of Ur . . . 318
 Used Assyrian for his official inscriptions 326
DUN-KUN-UDDU. A title of the planet Mercury 172
DUNSTAN, Saint. Considered a magician in a good sense . . 73
DURRI-GALZU. One of the last to use the Accadian language . . 369
DUZI or DUMUZI. The Syrian Tammuz, and the consort of Istar . 118
DVERGUES. Scandinavian genii . 249

EARTH, The.
 Chaldean idea of the shape of . 150
 Identified as the goddess Nin-ki-gal 17
EAST. Believed by the Egyptians to be the position of all evil . . 51
ECBATANA. Astral significance of its seven walls 227

ECKSTEIN, Baron. His remarks on the mythology of the Turanian races . 177
ECSTASY. Of the Finnish magicians 255
EGRES. Spirits of vegetation . . 250
EGYPTIAN and CHALDEAN MAGIC. Their rites compared . . . 70
EGYPTIAN and FINNISH MEDICINE. Their analogies 258
EGYPTIAN DEITIES. Their eponymous character 127
EGYPTIAN MAGIC. Limited to certain deities 78
EGYPTIANS, The. .
  Believed in demons causing local diseases 36
  Their real religion monotheistic . 80
EKIM. The Assyrian analogues of the Gigim 24
ELEMENTARY SPIRITS. Origin of their worship 70
ELEPHANTA. Its triad referred to . 115
ELEPHANTIASIS. Peculiar to Damietta 20
ELIMIEL. The intelligence of the moon 26
EL KHARGEH, Temple of. Inscriptions to the spirits of the elements at . 144
ELOHIM. Chaldean analogies of . 124
E-MAKH-TILA. A great temple at Borsippa 193
ENCHANTED DRINKS. Used by the Accadians 41
ENCI. The Accadian Ea . . 124
ENDEME. His knowledge of the mystical Zarvana-akarana . . 229
ENI-DAZARMA. Conjuration by . 139
ENI-KIGA. A title of Hea . . 149
ENI-ME-SARA. Sons of the lord of the infernal regions who dwell in the flame 170
ENIZUNA. His analogy to the Finnish moon god Kuu . . . 249
ENOCH, The Book of. Its strongly Chaldean nature 30
EN-ZUNA. The Accadian moon god (?), eldest son of Mulge . . . 17
ERECH.
  Conquered by the Kushites . . 320
  The great necropolis of Chaldea . 116
  The seat of a famous Accadian ecclesiastical college . . . 13
ERIDHU.
  Governed by a Patesi . . . 325
  The earliest seat of the worship of Hea 28
ERYTHREAN SEA. Appearance of the deity Oes or Aôs in . . . 202
E-SAGGADHU. The temple of Marduk at Babylon 193
E-SARA. The Chaldean firmament . 153
ESARHADDON. Protected his palace gates by enchanted figures . . 54
ESTHONIAN LANGUAGE. Its Accadian affinities . . . . . 300, etc.
ETHIOPIANS. Known to the Greeks as Cephenes 337
ETHNOLOGY. Of the Babylonian nation 331

EUAHANES. See Oannes . . . 203
EUPHRATES. Accadian charm to close the waters of . . . 10
EURIDICE. The myth of Euridice compared with that of Istar . . 166
EWALD, Dr. His account of the Phoenician cosmogony . . . 124
EZEKIEL. Chaldean analogues of his vision at Chebar . . . 122
E-ZIDA. A temple at Borsippa . 193

FATHER. Accadian laws respecting the repudiation of a . . . 382
FEMALE DISEASES. Caused by evil demons 5
FERVERS. Their Accadian analogues 199
FETICHISM. Its origin . . 70, 71
FEVER. Its special demon called Idpa 36
FILIAL OBEDIENCE. Accadian laws respecting 382-384
FINNISH and ACCADIAN MYTHOLOGY. Their differences 250
FINNISH DEMONOLOGY. Further examined 253
FINNISH LANGUAGE. Its Accadian affinities . . . . . 300 etc.
FINNO-TARTARIAN MAGIC. Fully described in the Kalevala . . 241
FINNS.
  Accadian analogues of their religion 251
  The character of their Paganism . 242
  Their only priests were magicians 243
FIRE.
  Incantation over the sacred flame 65
  Said to have been brought down from heaven by the Magi . . 238
  The Assyrian god of, was perhaps Izdubar 10
FIRE GOD. A hymn to . . . 185
FIRE WORSHIP. Essentially Turanian 197
FISH. The great fish of the Ocean, a form of Hea 157
FRAVISHIS. Their Accadian analogues 199
FURIES. Their analogues in Finnic mythology 257

GABRIEL. The angel of the moon . 26
GAL-KHANA-ABZU. A title of Hea . 157
GALLU, The.
  Assumed the forms of bulls . . 56
  The Assyrian analogues of the Telal 25
GANZAKH. The Gazaca of Classical writers. Its seven walls . . 227
GATES of Palaces. Protected by enchanted winged bulls . . 54
GATHA I. A citation from . . 223
GATHAS and FARGARDS, The. Period of their composition . . . 220
GATHAS, The. Their doctrines influenced by Chaldaism . . . 197
GAUTAMA. The false Smerdis, restores Magism 218
GAZACA. The Classical name of the town of Ganzakh 14
GAZRIM. Who they were . . 227
GE. The Assyrian name of the lower abyss 165

GELAL and KIEL GELAL. The Ac-
    cadian Lilith 38
GHEZ LANGUAGE. Its mixed nature 343
GIGIM.
    Analogous to the Assyrian Ekim . 24
    An evil demon afflicting the neck . 3
    Cause bowel diseases . . . 36
    Charms against the . . 16, 17
    Wander in the desert . . . 31
GITMALU. An epithet title of Izdubar 189
GNOSTIC GEMS. Their Chaldean origin 52
GNOSTICISM and SABAISM. Their
    differentiations 137
GOETIA. Certain coarse and ancient
    rites of 238
GOOD and EVIL PRINCIPLES. Alike
    adored by the Magi . . . 231
GORDYENOI. Their Accadian origin
    or affinity 361
GORDYŒAN MOUNTAINS. The resting-
    place of the ark of Xisuthrus 159, 362
GRAPHAEL. The intelligence of Mars 26
GRIVAL, Joseph. Identifies Amarud
    with Marduk and Silik-mulu-khi . 10
GULA. A triform goddess . . 117
GUTIUM. The early appellation of
    the Assyrians 333

HADES.
    Its entrance guarded by human-
        headed bulls 170
    Its porter the god Negab . . 168
    Its seven spheres 167
    Its various titles 165
    Situated beyond the Ocean . . 169
    The Egyptian Hades described . 86
HAGIEL. The intelligence of Venus 26
HAK. A wine imported from Syria
    and used in magical rites . . 93
HALEVY, Joseph. His statements as
    to the Accadian language refuted 266
"HALL OF THE TWO TRUTHS." Its
    character 86
HALTIA. The local genius of the Finns 249
HAMIEL. The angel of Venus . 26
HAMITIC and SEMITIC RACES. Their
    connections and differentiations 342, 343
HAMITIC RACES. Confounded with
    the Semites 343
HAMMURABI.
    The Chaldean religion under . 111
    The first of the Kassite kings . 369
HAMY, M. Distinguishes two Baby-
    lonian types 348
HAPI or HAPIMOUI. The god of the
    Nile 104
HAOMA. Its use in the sacrificial
    rites of the Magi 231
HARRIS PAPYRUS. Contains magical
    formulæ 96
HARSHEFT, "Terrible face." A name
    of Horus the Warrior . . . 99
HARTATEF. Discovers a mystical
    chapter and talisman at Sesennou 90
HARUPUKA - KA - SHARU - SHABAU. A
    Nubian name of Osiris . . . 106
HATHORS. The seven mystical cows
    or Hathors of the Egyptians . . 56

HEA.
    Assumed the form of a fish . . 157
    Awful power of his mystical name 42
    Called also Nukimmut . . . 207
    Called En-ci by the Accadians . 124
    Called Lord of the Earth by Silik-
        mulu-khi 64
    Called Zikia, i.e., Spirit of the
        Earth 149
    Could not cause evil by himself . 181
    Directs Silikmulukhi to cure the
        diseased 21
    First worshipped at Eridu . . 28
    Has an ark wherein he and the
        deities sail 160
    His birth of a water goddess . 156
    His disk or Tchakra described . 162
    His great resemblance to Wäinä-
        möinen 247
    His six sons 184
    His weapon and regalia adored . 161
    The god of the Ocean. Father of
        Silik-mulu-khi 11
    The protector of Khasisatra . . 159
HEA and OANNES. Examination of
    the relationship between . . 201
HEABANI. His contest with the bull
    of Ishtar 57
HECATE. A form of the moon . . 117
HEJMOLAINEN. The servant of the
    evil giant Hiisi 257
HELIOPOLIS. A sacred residence of
    the god Tum 95
HELKA. Finnish goddess of health(?) 261
HELLADIUS. His account of the fish
    god Oes 202
HELLANICUS. His account of the
    Cephenes 337
HERACLEOPOLITE NOME. Sacred to
    Horus Harsheft 99
HERBED. A Parsee priest . . 222
HERCULES.
    His Accadian analogies . . 17
    His analogue in Onouris . . 78
HERMETIC BOOKS. Fragments of, in
    the Harris Papyrus . . . 96
HERMOPOLIS. A chapter of the
    Ritual found there in the reign of
    Mycerinus 90
HERODOTUS.
    Contrasts the Chaldean and Grecian
        medical systems . . . 35
    His account of the Persians . . 224
    His confused account of the Persian
        religion 225
    His equations of the Grecian and
        Egyptian divinities . . . 78
    His error with regard to the cha-
        racters of Mithra and Aphrodite 234
HERPETIC or CUTANEOUS DISEASES.
    Familiar to the Accadians . . 6
HES, The Land of. A mystical,
    possibly Arabian, country . . 106
HIEROGLYPHIC CHARACTER of the
    early Accadian syllabary . . 364
HIIDEN KISSA. The evil cat of Hiisi 257
HIIDEN-LINTU. The evil bird of the
    giant Hiisi 257

HIIDEN RUUNA. The evil horse of
   Hiisi 257
HIIDEN VAIKI. The Finnish furies . 257
HIISI. The Finnish evil giant. His
   family 257
HILLEWO. The goddess of the otters 252
HILTAAINEN. A Finnish deity of the
   woods 251
HIMYARITIC LANGUAGE. Its affinities 343
HINDUS.
   Great believers in amulets . . 39
   Their deities termed demons by the
      Budhists 77
HOBAL. Another name of the deity
   Baal Haldim 134
HOMER. Chaldean analogies of his
   cosmogony 152
HORRACK, P. J. De. Publishes the
   Lamentations of Isis and Nephthys 84
HORUS.
   An incantation in the name and
      power of 98
   The Egyptian Apollo . . . 78
HORUS MYTHS. Of the temple of
   Edfu described 83
HUMAN-HEADED BULLS. Guard the
   gates of Hades 170
HUMAN SACRIFICES. Introduced into
   Zoroastrianism by the Magi . . 231
HUNGARIANS. Their position as a
   Turanian race 373
HUSBAND. Accadian law respecting
   the repudiation of 382

IAMBLICUS. His account of the an-
   cient magicians 76
IBN KHALDUN. His account of Na-
   bathean sorcery 63
IDADU. An early Babylonian monarch 326
IDEDE. Spirits residing in heaven . 148
IDPA. The Chaldean demon of the
   plague 36
IGILI. Chaldean celestial spirits . 122
IHUARINEN. The divine smith of the
   Finns 253
IJIM. The wild beasts of the island 31
ILINOS. The Greek form of the name
   of the god Anu 115
ILMARINEN.
   His analogy to Mulge . . . 247
   The third of the great gods of the
      Finns, and the god of earth
      and of metals 247
ILU.
   Often confounded with Anu . . 114
   The Chaldean supreme being . 113
ILU-MUTABIL. An early Patesi of
   Diru 326
IMAGES of demons. Talismanic use of 179
IMAGES of the gods. Placed under
   the thresholds of the Babylonian
   palaces 47
IMAGES of wax. Used by the Chal-
   dean sorcerers 62
IMI or MERMER. The Accadian god
   of the wind 182
IMMORTALITY OF THE SOUL. First
   defended by the Egyptians . . 80

IMPRECATIONS. On the Caillou
   Michaux described . . . 68
INCANTATIONAL LITANIES. Their
   late date in Accadian magic . . 141
INCAPSULATIONS. Of the Accadian
   language 297
INCUBUS. Known to the Accadians. 38
INDIAN CYCLES. Their Babylonian
   affinities 366
INDRA. The great god of the Vedas 131
INHERITANCE. Accadian laws of . 384
INNIN. A species of nocturnal demon
   so called 9
INTELLIGENCES. Of the planets . 26
INTERPENETRATION of the Soul. An
   Assyro-Egyptian dogma . . 3
IRANIANS. Effects of their conquest
   of Media 232
IRON and COPPER. Their relative uses
   among the Accadians and Finns . 254
ISAIAH. Implies the possession of
   the desert by demons . . . 31
ISBAGGI-HEA. An early Chaldean city 325
ISIS and NEPHTHYS. Their Lamen-
   tations referred to 84
ISLAMISM. Not wholly destructive
   of civilisation 373
ISTAR.
   Astronomical origin of the double
      Ishtar 118
   Crosses the Ocean on her journey
      to Hades 169
   Delivered from Hades by the name
      of Hea 43
   Her descent into Hades . . 11
   Her Descent into Hades quoted from 165
   Sends a bull to punish Izdubar . 57
   The goddess of the planet Venus
      Possibly the analogue of Tiskhu 17
   The sister of Ninkigal . . . 11
ISTILENZAKHAR. A country so named 401
IZDHUBAR.
   A solar form of the god Bilgi . 188
   Invocation to 189
IZDUBAR.
   His tetrapolis analogous with
      Nimrod's 397
   Meaning of his name, "Mass of
      Fire" 10
   Perhaps the Assyrian god of fire . 10
   Zodiacal character of his twelve
      adventures 133
IZDUBAR and HEABANI. Their con-
   test with the bull of Ishtar . . 57

JEWS. Reasons for the sympathy of
   the Persians with the Jews . . 223
JOULU. A Finnish festival . . 249
JUOLITAR. The Finnish fisherman's
   deity 252
JUPITER.
   Herodotus states that the Persians
      worshipped Jupiter . . . 225
   His analogue in Amen-Ra . . 78
JUPITER, The Planet.
   Identified by the Assyrians with
      the god Marduk . . . 19
   Its angel, intelligence, and spirit . 26

KA-DINGIRA. An ancient name of Babylon 353
KÄITÖS. Finnish deities . . . 252
KAKAMA. An Accadian word used to signify "Amen" at the close of the magical tablets . . . 15
KÄKRI. Finnish pastoral deities . 252
KALAH SHERGAT. The modern name of the ruins of Assur . . . 334
KALDI.
Their chiefs bore Assyrian names. 368
The later name of Accad . . 335
KALEVALA.
Abounds in spells and magical rites 244
The great Finno-Tartarian epic . 241
Various incantations from the . 260
KALMUKS. Their superstitions . 212
KÄMULÄINEN. A Finnish earth and mining deity 253
KANISSURA. The god of Cutha . 120
KARDOUCHOI. Their Accadian origin 361
KASDIM, The. Who they were . 14
KASSI, The.
Their conquest of Chaldea . . 327
Who they were 410
KEIJUISET. Winged spirits in Finnish mythology 250
KER-NETER. The Egyptian underworld 86
KHARTUMIM. The Accadian conjurors 14
KHASISATRA.
Called Ubara-tutu . . . 354
The Noah of the Deluge Tablet .. 159
KHEPER. The name of the sun as a creator 81
KHI-TIM-KUR-KU or KHILUNKURKU. An Accadian spirit called the daughter of the ocean . . 140, 184
KHNUM. The soul of the gods, and maker of gods and men . . 103
KHONSU. An Egyptian fire deity . 33
KHORSABAD.
Arrangement of the beds in the palace of 8
Its seven storied tower . . . 227
Statuettes of the Assyrian gods discovered at 47
KHUSBI-KURU. The wife of Namtar 140
KIEL-GELAL. The Accadian Lilith . 38
KIENGI. Its relation to Sumiri . 401
KI-KURU-NIR. The consort of the river god Aria 183
KING. A prayer to the sun for an invalid king 181
KIPŪMÄKI. The Hill of Pains in Finnish mythology . . . 258
KIRCHER, Athanasius. His list of the angels of the planets . . 26
KIVUTAR or KIPU-TYTÖ. The Finnish goddess of diseases . . . 259
KOLPIA. The Phoenician god of the wind 124
KUDURLAGAMAR. The Chedorlaomer of the Old Testament . . 120
KUFA. A kind of boat used on the Euphrates 151

KUSHITE MYTHOLOGY. Its influence in Chaldean faith . . . 367
KUSHITES.
Their connection with the Lemluns 347
Their temporary conquest of Chaldea 320
KUSHITES and ETHIOPIANS. Who they were 341
KUSHITO-SEMITIC RELIGION. Its origin and triumph . . . 318
KUU. The Finnish male god of the moon. His analogy to Enizuna . 249

LABARTU. The Assyrian phantom . 37
LABASSU. The Assyrian spectre . 37
LAGAMAR. An Elamite deity . . 120
LAGUDA. An Elamite deity worshipped at Kisik 120
LAKHMU and LAKHAMU. The primordial Chaldean deities . . . 123
LAMAS. Like Nirgal represented as a man-headed lion . . . 121
LAMMA or LAMAS, "Giant." A second order of Chaldean demons . 24
LANCRE, Pierre de. A late writer on demonology 23
LAPLAND WITCHES. Their practices analogous to those of the Chaldean sorcerers 62
LAPPONIC LANGUAGE. Its Accadian affinities . . . . . 300, etc.
LARSA. A seat of empire, and the sacred town of Samas . . . 127
LATONA. The analogue of Sekhet . 78
LAULAJAT. A class of Finnish magicians 243
LAYARD. Discovered the library of the palace of Kouyunjik . . 12
LAZ. The consort of Nergal . . 118
LEGISLATION. Of the Accadians . 378
LEMANAEL. The spirit of the moon 26
LEMLUNS. Their antiquity and origin 347
LEMMINKÄINEN. The effects of his song and sorcery 245
LEMURES, Accadian. Were called Innin 9
LÉOUZON-LEDUC, M. His valuable version of the Kalevala . . 241
LEXICOGRAPHICAL TABLETS. Properly Assyrian-Accadian . . 390
LIKBABI.
An early Accadian monarch . . 318
His name found on all the ancient Accadian temples . . . 321
The earliest of the Accadian or Chaldean monarchs . . . 322
LILITH. A Cabalistic demon, the deceiver of Adam 38
LOUHIATAR. The Finnish demon of diseases 258

MAFEKH. The name of the bark of Pthah 83
MAFKA. The Egyptian name of turquoise 176
MAGI, The.
Adored both the good and evil principles alike . . . 231

MAGI. (*Continued.*)
  Became masters of the Persian
    empire under Gaumata . . 218
  Change of signification in the
    appellation 221
  Pretended to draw down fire from
    heaven 238
  The account of the Chaldean
    Magi given by Diodorus Siculus 12
  Their human sacrifices . . . 231
  Their treatment of the dead . 229
  Their use of the divining rod . 237
  Their worship of the elements . 225
MAGIC.
  Forbidden by Mazdeism . . 237
  Of the Ritual of the Dead examined 90
  Originally no distinction between
    good and evil magic . . . 72
MAGIC KNOTS. Used by the Ac-
  cadians to cure diseases . . 41
MAGICAL TABLET. An early magical
  litany first published by Rawlinson
  and Norris 1
MAGICAL TABLETS. At least 30,000
  were in the library of Assur-
  banipal 9
MAGICAL TEXTS. Iterations at the
  conclusion of 46
MAGISM.
  Handed down in the rites of the
    Yezidis 233
  Identical with the theology of the
    Babylonian tablets . . . 197
MAGOPHONIA, The. Origin of the
  festival 219
MAGYAR LANGUAGE. Its Accadian
  affinities . . . . 300, etc.
MAKAN. A country near Elam
  abounding in copper . . . 176
MAKO. A mystical crocodile called
  the son of Set 97
MATHEMATICAL IDEAS of the Chal-
  deans 25
MAMIT. The Assyrian talisman . 44
MAMUREMUKABABU. A mystical
  name of Osiris 105
MANTCHOO. Its Accadian analogies 295
MANTRAS. Learnt by the Hindus to
  avert dangers 40
MANU. The Chaldean god of fate . 120
MARDUK.
  Analogies with Silik-mulu-khi
    further examined . . . 195
  His contest with Tihamat . . 53
  His temple at Babylon called
    E-saggadhu 193
  His tomb in a pyramid at Babylon 132
  Holds the arrows of fate . . 238
  Often represented holding a pine
    cone 28
  The god of the planet Jupiter 19, 118
  The same as the Accadian Silik-
    mulu-khi 10
MARNA. A great deity of Gaza
  analogous to Anu 134
MARRIAGE. Accadian laws of . 384
MARRIED WOMEN. Allowed by the
  Accadians to be freeholders . . 384

MARS.
  His analogue in Besa . . 78
MARS, The Planet.
  Identified as the god Nergal . 118
  The angel, intelligence, and spirit
    of 26
MARTU. The Chaldean god of the
  west, and the son of Anu . . 120
MARUDUK-IDIN-AKHE. An early
  Babylonian semi-Mongolic king . 368
MARUTS, The. The Vedic gods of
  the wind 182
MAS. "Warrior."
  An Accadian order of demons of
    the first rank 24
  Dwelt on the heights . . . 31
MASKIM.
  A species of evil demon . . 8
  Called in Assyrian *Rabits* . . 25
  Charms against 17
  Were seven subterraneous demons 18
MASTERS. The "Twelve Masters"
  of the Chaldean astronomical
  system 119
MATERNAL PRIORITY. In Accadian
  and Finnish legislation . . . 385
MAT-LA-TAYARTI. *I.e.*, "the land
  of No-return," an Assyrian name
  of Hades 165
MAURY, M. A.
  His account of the Baschkir
    Kalmuks 212
  His account of the Turanian
    magicians 211
  His theory of the origin of magic . 70
MAZDEAN DOCTRINE. Essentially
  spiritualistic 222
MAZDEISM.
  Early corrupted by Median magism 196
  Temporarily restored by the Sas-
    sanian princes 221
MEDIAN MYTHOLOGY. Compared
  with the Chaldean 216
MEDICINE. Chaldean medicine a
  branch of magic 35
MELANIAN ELEMENT. In Chaldea
  and Babylonia 346
MEMRA, The.
  Development of the dogma of the
    Memra 104
  Its Chaldæo-Jewish analogies . 44
MEN. An androgynous lunar deity 133
MENTU. The Egyptian god of war,
  and the solar deity of Hermonthis 97
MERCURY, The Planet.
  His two phases made into two
    deities, Nebo and Nusku . . 118
  The angel, intelligence, and spirit
    of 26
MERMER.
  His part in the war of the seven
    evil spirits 205-7
  The Accadian god of the atmo-
    sphere. The analogue of the
    Assyrian Bin, or Vul, or Ramanu 17
  The Accadian god of the winds,
    in after times identified with
    Ramanu 182

MESKEM. The name of the Egyptian metempsychosis 88
METEMPSYCHOSIS. The nature of the Egyptian 88
MICHAEL. The angel of Mercury . 26
MICHAUX. The Caillou Michaux described 68
MIDNIGHT SUN. Accadian Hymn to 178
MILTON. His belief in invisible spirits 144
MINERVA. Her analogue in Neith . 78
MITHRA.
  Analogies between Mithra and Silik-mulu-khi 195
  His analogy to Silik-mulu-khi . 236
  Identified by Herodotus with Venus Mylitta 225
  Made one of a triad with Ahuramazda and Anahita . . . 236
  Origin of Herodotus' erroneous identification of Mithra with Aphrodite 234
  Origin of the two divine Mithras . 236
MITHRAIC MYSTERIES. Probably of Babylonian origin 56
MOBED. A Parsee priest . . . 222
MODINIEL. The spirit of Mars . 26
MONGOLIAN RACES. Seen on the bas-reliefs of Sennacherib and Assurbanipal 347
MONGOL ORIGIN. Of the Kaldi . 368
MONOTHEISM. The ancient principle of the Egyptian faith . . . 79
MONSTROSITIES. Fondness of the Babylonians for 53
MOON, The.
  The angel, intelligence, and spirit of 26
  War of the seven evil spirits against 204
MORDVINIAN LANGUAGE. Its Accadian affinities . . . 300, etc.
MOSLEM INCANTATIONS. As practised in modern Egypt by magicians . 77
MÛT. A Phoenician nature deity sometimes called Ulâmos . . 124
MOTHER. Accadian law respecting the repudiation of a . . . 382
MOUMIS or MAMI. A Chaldean water deity 123
MOUNTAIN OF MUL-GELAL. Near the entrance of Hades . . . 168
MOUNTAIN OF THE WORLD. An Accadian hymn to, translated by Mr. Boscawen 126
MUGHEIR. Inferences from the ruins of 328
MUL. A name of the fixed stars . 151
MUL-GE.
  An Accadian deity, the analogue of the Assyrian Bel 16
  His analogy to Ilmarinen . . 247
  Nature of his gloomy empire in Hades 174
MUL-GELAL. Hymn to Mul-gelal and other deities 172
MUMMY, The. Why it was always preserved intact 85

MUNU-AHGE. The companion of the gods in the ark of Hea . . . 160
MYCERINUS. A mystical tablet discovered at Sesennou in his reign . 90
MYLITTA. A form of Venus worshipped by the Persians . . 225
MYSTIC NAME OF HEA. Its awful power 42

NA. A form of Anu 124
NABATHEAN SORCERY. Description of the rites of 63
NABU-NADU. Meaning of the name 370
NADAK. The mystical goose, mother of Seb 104
NAGIEL. The intelligence of the sun 26
NAHASI. The Negroid races of Southern Arabia 106
NAKCH-I-RAJAB. Pehlevi inscription of, cited 221
NAMARBILI, The.
  A work in seventy tablets . . 365
  Composed of three distinct books on demonology 13
  The extent of the formulæ contained in 12
NAMARBILI OF SARGON. Its date cir. 2000 B.C. 333
NAMES OF THE CHALDEAN GODS. A tablet at Nineveh contains the names of nearly 1000 deities . 122
NAMES OF THE GODS. The magical importance of . . . 42, 104
NAMTAR.
  His consort named Khusbi-kuru . 140
  Is the servant of Allat, Queen of Hades 36
  The Chaldean demon of the plague 36
  The favorite son of Mul-ge by Nin-ki-gal 173
NANA.
  The wife of Ana 149
  Worshipped at Urukh . . . 323
NARAMSIN. The successor of Sargon I. 127
NARUDI. An Accadian deity . . 48
NATTIG. Represented as eagleheaded men 122
NAVILLE, Edouard. Publishes the myth of Horus 83
NEBO.
  Called the supreme intelligence on the Caillou Michaux . . 69
  Made into two deities, Nebo and Nusku 118
NEBUCHADNEZZAR.
  Restores the temple of Borsippa . 227
  Worshipped the goddess Tiamat . 113
NEGAB. The porter of Hades . . 168
NEITH. The analogue of Minerva . 78
NEMMA. The scaffold of torture in Hades 86
NEOPLATONISTS. Their theurgical system 74
NEPHTHYS.
  Her analogue in Diana . . . 78
  Said by Plutarch to have been the companion of Set . . . 83
NER. A cycle of 600 years . . 366

NERGAL.
  His image used to protect the
    enclosures of palaces . . 48
  Represented as a man-headed lion 121
  The Babylonian Mars . . . 55
  The god of the planet Mars . . 118
NERGALSAROSSOR. Restores the
    sacred pyramid of Babylon . 47
NILE, The.
  Adored as a god under the names
    of Hapimoui and Bah . . 104
  Why employed in Egyptian
    mythology 82
NIMROD.
  Came from or out of Assur . . 334
  His contest with Tihamat . . 53
  His tetrapolis analogous to Izdhu-
    bar's 397
  Meaning of the name . . . 338
NIN-AKHA-QUDDU. An uncertain
    goddess 29
NIN-A-ZU.
  An Accadian water deity . . 10
  The Accadian god of Hades, and
    husband of Ninkigal . . . 11
NINDAR. An Accadian deity, the
    analogue of the Assyrian Adar . 17
NINDARA.
  A son of Mulge, and the deity of
    the midnight sun . . . 175
  Came from the copper countries of
    Elam 176
NIN-DAZARMA. Conjuration by . 139
NINEVEH. Possibly the goddess
    Ninuah 140
NIN-GAR.
  Called also Nin-si-gar . . . 161
  The pilot of the ark of Hea . . 160
NIN-GELAL. An Accadian goddess,
    the analogue of the Assyrian
    Belit 16
NIN-GIS-ZIDA. A title of the goddess
    Allat 140
NIN-KA-SI. Another name of the
    goddess Nana 149
NIN-KI-GAL.
  Identified with the earth itself . 17
  Her analogue in Louhiatar, the old
    lady of Pohjola 258
  The sister of Ishtar, and Queen of
    Hades. Identified with Allat . 11
NIN-NUK, The consort of the god
    Ztak 11
NIN-SI-ANA. A name of the planet
    Venus 140
NIN-SI-GAR. Another name of Nin-
    gar, the pilot of Hea . . . 161
NINUAH. A doubtful goddess, the
    daughter of Hea 140
NIRBA. The Assyrian god of harvests 45
NIRGALLU. The Assyrian name of
    the winged lions 24
NOAH. His analogue in Khasisatra 159
NOGUEL. The spirit of the planet Venus 26
NOIJAT.
  Expelled diseases by enchantment 244
  The Finnish sorcerers . . . 243
NUAB. Title of an Assyrian viceroy 325

NUBIAN NAMES in the Ritual of the
    Dead. Used by the Egyptians
    for mystical purposes . . . 106
NU-KIMMUT. A title of Hea . . 207
NUN. A nature god, water . . 82
NUSKU.
  A form of the god Nebo as a phase
    of Mercury 118
  An Accadian deity, the messenger
    of Mul-ge 17
  Sent to tell Hea of the war of the
    seven evil spirits . . . 207

OANNES.
  And Hea identical 157
  First civilizes Chaldea . . . 350
  His five early theophanes . . 203
  His relationship with Hea examined 202
OES. A mystical fish-man deity . 202
OM. Its supposed mystical virtues
    among the Budhists . . . 29
ONE. A god so called from his
    number 25
ONOURIS.
  The Egyptian Hercules . . 78
  The same as Shu and Anhur . 96
OPPERT, Dr.
  His early translations of the
    magical tablets 2
  His use of the term Sumerian 387, etc.
OSIRIAN, The. Why the deceased
    was so called 89
OSIRIS.
  His name not to be uttered . . 43
  His numerous magical titles . . 103
  Origin of the myth of Osiris and
    Apophis 83
  The untranslatable mystical names
    of 105
  Why called Unnefer . . . 87
OSMANLI LANGUAGE. Its Accadian
    affinities . . . . 300, etc.
OSTHANES. Writes a book upon
    magic 238
OSTIAC LANGUAGE. Its Accadian
    affinities . . . . 300, etc.
OTAVA. The Finnish god of the
    constellation ursa major . . 249
OURANOS and VARUNA. Their
    analogues 134

PAIWA. The solar deity of the
    Finns 249
PANTHEISM. Of the Chaldean mytho-
    logy and theology 129
PAPSUKUL. The messenger of the
    Chaldean gods 120
PARENTAL RIGHTS. Accadian laws
    respecting 384
PARSOUDOS. The same as Perseus . 337
PATESI. The viceroys of the Chal-
    dean monarchs 325
PERSEPHONE. The analogy of the
    myths of Persephone and Ishtar . 166
PERSEUS. A Babylonian origin of
    the name 337
PERSIAN GULF. Its relation to the
    country of the Accadians . . 394

PERSIAN MONARCHS. Why they sympathized with the Jews . . 223
PERSIANS.
  Their iconoclastic fury . . . 224
  Their peculiar treatment of the dead 228
PERSONAL GENII. Converted by sorcery from good into evil ones to the person to whom they were attached 64
PHŒNICIAN COSMOGONY. Examined by Ewald and Sayce . . . 124
PHŒNIX MYTH. Its Egyptian origin 84
PHYLACTERIES, Jewish. Their Chaldean origin 45
PHYLACTERY. An Egyptian phylactery cited 99
PHYSICIANS. Unknown in Chaldea 35
PHYSICIANS, Chaldean. The Chakamim of Daniel 14
PICTET. His account of Aryan sorcery 60
PIERRET, Paul. His *Dictionnaire d'Archéologie* quoted . . . 83
PIG, The. Sometimes the abode of the soul of a wicked man . . 88
PINE CONE. Its mystical significance 28
PLACE, Victor. His great work *Nineve et l'Assyrie* cited . . 8
PLAGUE, The. Its special demon called Namtar 36
PLANETS. The Chaldean gods of . 118
PLANETS, Seven. Temples with seven walls having reference to the seven planets 227
PLUTARCH.
  His account of the Osiris myth . 83
  His account of the sacrifices of the Magi 231
PLUTO. His analogy with the Accadian deity Nin-a-zu . . . 11
POHJOLA. The Finnic Hades, or rather Hell 245
PORPHYRY.
  His *De Abstinentia* quoted . . 75
  Why he was displeased with the Egyptian magicians . . . 101
POSSESSED PRINCESS. Stele of, described 32, 33
POUNT. The land of Southern Arabia 106
PRAMANTHA. The fire wheel, or arani of the Aryans . . . 185
PRIEST and MAGICIAN. Where the two characters blended . . . 72
PRIVATE SANCTUARIES. Accadian laws respecting 384
PROCLUS. His *Elements of Theology* cited 75
PROTO-MEDIC PEOPLE. Their mythology examined 217
PSALM CXLVII. An Assyrian analogue to 192
PTHAH. Originally a nature deity . 82
PURGATORY. The Egyptian purgatory described 87
PYLONS. The pylons of Hades described 87

QEDESCHIN. Infamous magical rites practised by the Accadians . . 4

RA.
  Considered by the Egyptians as a prototype of man . . . 81
  His analogy to Nindara . . 175
  His mysterious birth, like that of Hea 156
  The creative virtues of his sweat . 247
RABITS. The Assyrian name of the Maskim 25
RACE, A. Five things required to constitute 379
RAGHA. An early seat of the Medic faith 220
RAMANU. See Rimmon.
RAMANU or RIMMON. Identified with the Accadian Mermer . . 182
RAMESES II. Introduced the worship of Anaitis into Egypt . . . 99
RAMESES XII.
  Marries a princess of Mesopotamia 32
  Sends the ark of Khonsu to cure the princess Bintreschit . . 33
RANEFERU. The wife of Rameses XII. 32
RAPGANMEA. The Accadian spectre 37
RAPGANMEKHAB. The Accadian vampire 37
RAPHAEL. The angel of the sun . 26
RATA. The Greek name of the town of Eridu 28
RAUTA-REKHI. The Finnish god of iron 254
RAWLINSON, Sir H.
  Favours M. Lenormant with advance sheets of *W.A.I.* IV., . 13
  His opinion as to the age of Likbabi 322
  His translation of the name of Izdubar 10
  His views on a hymn addressed to the bulls of Hades . . . 170
  His views on the origin of fire-worship 197
  Together with Edwin Norris publishes one of the first magic formulæ 1
RELIGION and MAGIC. Period of their fusion in Chaldea . . . 110
RENAN, M.
  His five constituents of a race examined 379
  His views on the origin of the cuneiform writing . . . 371
REPUDIATION. Accadian laws respecting 382
REPUDIATION OF A FATHER. Accadian punishment of . . 382
REPUDIATION OF A MOTHER. Accadian punishment of . . . 382
RESURRECTION.
  A fundamental Egyptian dogma . 84
  Chaldean views of 167
RIMMON or RAMANU. The Assyrian god of the atmosphere, and the analogue of the Accadian Mermer 17

RIMSIN. An early Babylonian monarch 127
RITUAL OF THE DEAD. Its magic examined in detail . . 89
ROBERTS. *Oriental Illustrations* quoted 39
RUNES, The. Their awful power . 248
RUSTA, The. A dwelling of Osiris . 87

SABAISM and ANTHROPOMORPHISM. Their fusion in Egyptian mythology 82
SABATHIEL. The spirit of Saturn . 26
SABBATIC REST, The. Originated with the Accadians . . . 124
SABUV. An early king of Agane . 326
SACERDOTAL SCHOOLS, The. Their theopolitical influence . . . 330
SACRED PROSTITUTION. Kushite origin of 386
SAGBA. The Accadian name of the Mamit 44
SAK, "Officer." Use of the term . 354
SAK-MIGA. A dark race of men so called by the Accadians . . 193
SALA. The consort of Bin . . 117
SAMARRAH. Identified with Shinar by Abul Faradj 396
SAMAS.
  His pre-eminence at Larsa . . 127
  The Assyrian god of the sun, and the analogue of the Accadian Udu 17
  Worshipped at Larsa . . . 323
SAMILA. A Chaldean deity . . 120
SAMIRUS. A mythical king of Babylon 396
SANCTUARIES. Accadian laws respecting 384
SARGON I.
  A high state of civilization introduced by 328
  Best period of Chaldæo-Babylonian religion 111
  Date of his great astrological collection 333
  Extent of his empire . . . 369
  Succeeded by Naramsin . . 127
  Unites the two races of Sumir and Accad 327
SARTURDA. Another form of the name of the Zu-god Ungal-turda 171
SASSANIAN PRINCES. Endeavoured to restore Mazdeism . . . 221
SATURN, The Planet.
  Identified with the god Adar . 118
  Nindar, or Adar the god of the planet 17
  The angel, intelligence, and spirit of 26
SAYCE, Rev. Prof.
  Gives a list of Accadian lucky and unlucky months . . . 7
  His letter on the Creation Tablet quoted 123
  His translation of an early Accadian magical tablet compared 3
  Translates an Accadian hymn describing the weapons of Hea . 163

SAZI. The son of the river god Aria 183
SCALP DISEASES. Charms against . 20
SCARABÆI EGYPTIAN. Their characteristics 46
SCEPTRE OF SILIK-MULU-KHI. Its symbolical office . . . 190
SCHRADER, Prof. E. His account of the origin of the Semitic nations . 342
SEB. The child of the mystical goose Nadak 104
SED, "Genius."
  An Assyrian order of demons of the first rank corresponding to the Accadian Mas . . . 24
  A species of benevolent dæmon . 24
SEHEM. The Chaldean term for the divine name 44
SEIDR. A Scandinavian magical rite 243
SEKHET. Perhaps an analogue of Latona 78
SEKHU. The name of the bark of Khonsu 83
SEMITIC. The term erroneously applied to Hamitic races . . 342
SEMITIC NATIONS. Started first from Arabia 341
SEMITIC TONGUES. Prevailed in Northern Chaldea . . . 334
SENNACHERIB. His conquest of Mongolian races 347
SERAKH. The Accadian name of the god of harvests . . . 45
SERPENT DEITIES. Their worship common to the Turanian nations . 232
SERRAKH. The god of Kis . . 120
SERUA. The consort of Assur . . 123
SESENNOU. A name of Hermopolis 90
SET.
  An Egyptian incantation against . 95
  The two phases of his cultus . 83
SET or SUTEKH. The analogue of Baal 83
SETI I. His sarcophagus in the Soane Museum 88
SETNAU, Romance of. Its curious magical character . . . 102
SEVEN EVIL SPIRITS.
  Their war with heaven described on the Chaldean tablets . 13
  Translation of the tablet relating their war against the moon . 204
SEVEN SPHERES. Of the Assyrian Hades 167
SEXAGESIMAL NUMERATION. Introduced into Chaldea . . . 366
SHAFRA. Opens the copper mines of Wady Magarah . . . 176
SHAITAN-KURIAZI. The evil being of the Baschkir Calmuks . . 212
SHAMANS, The. Turanian sorcerers 213
SHEOL and HADES. Inhabited by demon Larvæ 37
SHESHA SERPENT. Its analogue in the serpent like sword of Hea . 163
SHINAR.
  Called the land of Samarrah by Abul Faradj 396

SHINAR. (*Continued.*)
Is it identical with Sumir? . . 395
SHU. Sometimes the same as Anhur
  or Anouris 96
SIDEREAL DEITIES. Their place in
  Accadian Magic 137
SIGÉ. The primitive substance of
  the Universe 123
SILIK-KURU. Another rendering of
  the name of Silik-mulu-khi . . 190
SILIK-MULU-DUG. Another rendering
  of the name of Silik-mulu-khi . 19
SILIK-MULU-KHI.
  A hymn in praise of his benevolent
  offices 192
  And Mithra compared . . . 195
  Equated with the Assyrian Marduk 10
  His analogies with Mithra . . 237
  His counteracting influence against
  personal genii 64
  His symbolical sceptre . . . 190
  Invoked on an early Accadian
  tablet 10
  Restores the dead to life . . 167
  Rides in the ark of Hea . . 160
  Sent by Hea to cure diseases . 21
  Sent by Hea to relieve the god
  Aku 207
SILIK-RI-MULU. Another name of
  Silik-mulu-khi 190
SIN.
  An early Babylonian dynasty
  named after 127
  His pre-eminence at Ur . . 127
  The Assyrian moon-god, probably
  the analogue of the Accadian
  En-zuna 17
SINAI. Copper mines worked by the
  Egyptians at the foot of . . 176
SINGARA, The Country of. Its situation 402
SIRGILLA. A town of southern
  Chaldea 325
SIRIUS. The Egyptian Sothis . 97
SISITHRUS. *See* Khasisatra.
SIVA. The Hindu destroyer . . 115
SLAVES.
  Accadian laws respecting . . 383
  Accadian treatment of . . . 385
SMALL POX. A Hindu goddess of . 36
SMELIEL. The spirit of the sun . 26
SMITH, George. Discovers the Crea-
  tion Tablets 113
SMU. The punisher of the wicked,
  a form of Set 86
SON. Accadian law respecting the
  repudiation of a 382
SONG OF LEMMINKÄINEN. Its terrible
  effects 245
SOPHIEL. The intelligence of the
  planet Jupiter 26
SOSS. A cycle of 60 years . . 366
SOTHIS. The star Sirius invoked in
  an incantation 97
SOUL, The. Its return to the mummy
  a frequent subject on Egyptian
  papyri 85
SOURY, J. His views on the Syrian
  theology 131

SOUTH-WEST WIND. Why regarded
  as a demon by the Assyrians . 52
SPHERES OF HADES. Seven in number 167
SPHERES OF THE HEAVENS. The
  Chaldean spheres described . . 153
SPIRITS OF THE ELEMENTS. Common
  both to Egyptian and Accadian
  mythology 144
SPIRITS OF THE PLANETS. Accord-
  ing to the Cabbala . . . 26
SPIRITS OF THE STARS. Invocations
  to 138, 139
SPRENGER, Jacques. A mediæval
  writer on demonology . . . 23
SQEB-HU. *I.e.*, "Place of freedom,"
  an Egyptian designation of the
  tomb 165
STARS, The. Their worship in Median
  magic 226
SUCCUBUS, The. Known to the Ac-
  cadians 38
SUMER or SUMERI. Its relation to
  Kiengi 401
SUMIR. How the term was employed
  by the Assyrians 390
SUMIR AND ACCAD. Controversy
  between MM. Lenormant and
  Oppert upon these terms . . 387
SUMIRIAN INFLUENCE. In Chaldean
  civilization 356
SUN, The.
  Accadian incantation to . . 49
  Mystical names of the enemies of 105
  The angel, intelligence, and spirit
  of 26
SUN AND DRAGON MYTH. Its Ac-
  cadian or Assyrian origin . . 208
SUN IN TAURUS. Its probable con-
  nection with the Assyrian winged
  bulls 56
SUOMI. The old man of . . . 248
SUONETAR. A healing goddess in
  Finnish mythology . . . 262
SURIPPAK. Possibly the Ur of
  Genesis 397
SUSINKA. An Elamite deity . . 120
SUTEKH. The analogue of Baal . 83
SUVETAR. A Finnish pastoral deity 252
SWORD OF HEA. Its attributes
  described 162
SYLVESTER, Pope. A magician in a
  good sense 73
SYROPHŒNICIAN NATIONS. Their
  religious dualisms 117

TAHTI. The Finnish gods of the
  stars 249
TALBOT, H. Fox.
  His translation of an Accadian
  magical litany cited . . . 8
  His translation of the Creation
  Tablets given at length . . 122
  His translation of the Descent
  of Ishtar into Hades referred to 11
  His translation of the War of the
  Seven Evil Spirits referred to . 13
TALISMANIC FIGURES. Of demons
  employed to scare them away . 50

TALISMANS. Used by the Accadian
  magicians 8
TAMMUZ. The Chaldean Duzi, the
  husband of Ishtar 118
TAPIO. A Finnish wood deity . . 251
TASMIT. The consort of Nebo . 118
TAUTHE.
  The analogue of the goddess
    Tihamtu 123
  The same as Tihamat . . . 53
TCHAKRA OF BUDDHA. Compared
  with the disk of Hea . . . 162
TCHEMEN. A Tchuvache demon . 213
TCHEREMISSIAN LANGUAGE. Its Accadian affinities . . . 300, etc.
TCHOUVACHE LANGUAGE. Its Accadian affinities . . . 300
TELAL.
  Analogous to the Assyrian Gallu . 25
  Assumed the form of a bull . . 56
  A wicked demon . . . 8
  Cause diseases of the hand . . 36
  Charms against 17
  Steal into towns 31
TETEMHEBI. An Egyptian scribe
  priest 33
TETRAGRAMMATON, The. Its Chaldean
  analogies 29
TETRAPOLIS. Of Izdhubar and Nimrod analogous 397
THAVATH-OMOROCA. The same as
  Tihamat 53
THEOCRITUS. His *Pharmaceutria* referred to 65
THEOGONY OF THE CHALDEANS.
  Damascius's account of, again
  cited 202
THEOPHANIES OF OANNES. Five,
  between the creation and the
  deluge 203
THEOSOPHISTS, the Chaldean. Were
  the Asaphim of Daniel . . 14
THEURGICAL SYSTEM. Of the Neoplatonists 74
THIAN. An early Chinese heaven
  deity 154
THOUERIS. The devourer of souls . 86
THOTH.
  Evils which follow the theft of his
    magic book 102
  Reveals the mystical formulæ to
    deceased souls . . . 94
  The author of the Hermetic books 96
THOTHMES II. and III. Reopen the
  copper mines of Wady Magarah . 176
THRAETONA. Conquers the serpent
  Dahaka 233
TIAMAT or TIHAMAT. The goddess
  of the primordial sea . . 113
TIETAJAT.
  A class of Finnish magicians . 243
  Expelled diseases by enchantment 244
TIHAMAT. The goddess of the primordial sea 53
TIN-TIR.
  An Accadian town . . . 325
  Probably a name of the city of
    Babylon 193
TIRIEL. The intelligence of Mercury 26
TISKHU.
  An Accadian warlike goddess . 17
  Conjuration by 139
  Takes the throne of heaven jointly
    with Ana 206
TONTTU. The house gnome of the
  Finns 249
TRIADS OF THE CHALDEANS. Their
  respective zones . . . 153, 154
TRIMURTI, The Hindu. Its Chaldean
  analogues 115
TRINITIES. The three Chaldean
  trinities 117
TRINITY, The. Of the Chaldeans
  described 114
TRITA. The Zendic analogues of the
  myth of 233
TULLA INTOON. The ecstasy of the
  Finnish magicians . . . 255
TUM.
  A form of the midnight sun . . 81
  Invoked to repel the power of Set 95
  Ra as the midnight sun, an analogue of Nindara . . . 175
TUMOURS. Carefully described by
  the Accadian magicians . . 21
TUONELA. The river of the country
  of the dead in Finnish mythology 258
TUONI. The father of the Finnish
  goddess of diseases . . . 259
TURANIAN NATIONS. Their magic
  and religions examined . . . 210
TURANIAN RACES.
  Their veneration for earth deities . 177
  The Turks and Hungarians compared 373
TURANIAN TONGUES. Prevailed in
  Southern Chaldea . . . 334
TURANIANS.
  Invented the cuneiform writing . 371
TURKS.
  Really a great race . . . 372
  Their belief of and reverence to
    genii and spirits 144
TUR-TANU or TUR-DAN. Meaning of
  the name 354
TYLOR, E. B. His *Primitive Culture*
  referred to 59
TYPHON. The analogue of Sutekh 83

U-BARA-TUTU. A possible name of
  Khasisatra 354
UDU. An Accadian deity, possibly
  the analogue of the Assyrian Samas 17
UJGUR LANGUAGE. Its Accadian
  affinities 300
UKKO.
  An invocation to 262
  His analogy to Hea . . . 247
  The chief of the gods of the Finns,
    the god of heaven . . . 246
ULÁMOS. A Phoenician cosmic deity 124
UL-GANA. A lower zone in the
  heavens 153
ULOM. Another name of the deity
  Eschmun 134
UL-SARA. A name of the god Serakh 171

UM-URUK. A title of the goddess
    Belit 116
UNDERWORLD. The mythology of
    the underworld examined . . 177
UNGAL-ABA. The Accadian king
    of the wave 184
UNGAL-A-ABBA. The Accadian king
    of the sea 184
UNGAL-ARIADA. The Accadian king
    of the river 184
UNGAL-TURDA.
    A mystical deity of Hades . . 171
    His metamorphosis into the Zu bird 171
UNLUCKY MONTHS. Accadian re-
    ference to 7
UNNEFER. A title of Osiris as the
    "Good Being" 87
UR.
    Policy of the dynasty of . . 127
    Possibly the same as Surippak . 397
    The most Turanian of all the
        ancient Chaldean cities . . 339
URU-ÊA. Title of the god Bil-gi . 186
URUKU.
    An evil demon 3
    Many species of 10
URU SUKHAR. Title of the god Bil-gi 186
USTUR, The. Represented as human
    beings 121
USU. A Chaldean deity . . . 120
UTU. His analogy to Paiwa the
    Finnish god of the sun . . 249
UTUQ.
    A general term for all demons . 24
    Causes diseases of the forehead . 36
    Inhabit the deserts . . . 31
UUA. The name of the bark of the
    sun 83

VAMPYRES. Accadian demons of a
    like nature to 9
VARAHRAN V. Builds a palace to the
    seven planets 227
VARUNA. His indefinite character . 131
VAYU. The Vedic god of the wind . 182
VEDAS.
    The Atharva and Rig Veda com-
        pared with the Chaldean . . 319
    The gods of the Vedas compared
        with the Syrian deities . . 131
VEDIC WRITERS. Their opposition
    to the early Aryans . . . 77
VENUS.
    Called Nin-si-ana 140
    The angel, intelligence and spirit
        of 26
VENUS AND ADONIS. Perhaps ori-
    ginally an Egyptian myth . . 84
VENUS URANIA. The same as Venus
    Mylitta 225
VIRGIL. The charm in his VIIIth
    Eclogue referred to . . . 65
VISHNU. The Hindu preserver . 115
VOGÜÉ, Compte de. His views on
    Syro-Palestinian theology . . 128
VOGUL LANGUAGE. Its Accadian
    affinities . . . . 300, etc.
VOLCANOES. Near the river Chaboras 10

VOWELS. Of the Accadian and Altaic
    languages 271

WADY MAGARAH. The copper and
    turquoise mines of . . . 176
WÄINÄMÖINEN.
    Creative virtues of his sweat . 247
    His analogy to Hea . . . 247
    His wound cured by the goddess
        Helka 261
    The second of the gods of the
        Finns, the god of water and of
        the atmosphere 246
    Wounded by the axe of Pohja . 248
WARKA. Nature of the civilisation of 328
WATCH DOG. An Egyptian incanta-
    tion to give vigilance to . . 99
WAXEN FIGURES. Used for evil pur-
    poses by the Accadian magicians . 5
WEEK, The. Originated with the
    Accadians 124
WEIGHING OF SOULS. Took place
    in the Egyptian Hades . . . 86
WESI-HIISI. One of the servants of
    the evil giant Hiisi . . . 257
WEST, The. The Egyptians believed
    all good to proceed from . . 51
WIERUS, or PISCINARIUS. A mediæval
    writer on witchcraft . . . 23
WIFE. Accadian laws respecting the
    repudiation of a 382
WITCHCRAFT. Mediæval writers upon 23
WIZARD, or SORCERER. An incanta-
    tion against 61
WIZARDS and WITCHES. Their
    influence in Chaldea . . . 59
WOLF. The blood of a wolf used in
    the sacrificial rites of the Magi . 231
WOUNDING A SLAVE. Accadian law
    respecting 383
WUORIN VÄKI, The. The Finnish
    genii of the rocks and mines . 253

XERXES. Cruel sacrifice by his wife
    Amestris 231
XISISTHRUS. His ark rested on the
    Gordyan Mountains . . . 362
XISUTHRUS. The great analogue of
    Khasisatra 159

YACNA XXXVI. A citation from . 223
YAKUT LANGUAGE. Its Accadian
    affinities . . . . . 300 ·
YATUM. The religion of the enemies
    of Zoroaster 219
YAZATAS, The. Their Accadian ana-
    logues 201
YEZIDIS. Their rites derived from
    Magism 233

ZACHALIOS. An ancient writer upon
    magical gems 176
ZADAKIEL. The spirit of the planet
    Jupiter 26
ZADYKIEL. The angel of the planet
    Jupiter 26
ZALMAT-QAQQADI. The Assyrian name
    of the black races 193

ZAPKIEL. The angel of Saturn . 26
ZARPANIT. The consort of Marduk 118
ZARVANA-AKARANA. The common origin of both Ahuramazda and Angromainyus 229
ZARVANIANS, The. Their peculiar heresy 229
ZENDAVESTA.
  Changes in its theological ideas . 221
  The worship of the stars referred to in it, an interpolation . . 226
ZI.
  A common title of the Chaldean deities, considered as spirits . 148
  The origin of the myth of . . 143
ZIANA. A title of Ana . . . 149
ZIGARA. The same as Sigê, and the goddess of heaven . . . 123

ZIGGURRAT. Of Khorsabad described 227
ZIIM. The wild beasts of the desert 31
ZIKIA. A title of Hea . . . 149
ZIKU. The same as the Egyptian Nu 140
ZONES OF THE DEITIES. Their situation 154
ZOROASTER.
  His system of dualisms . . 145
  Probably influenced by Babylonian mythology 196
ZTAK. Supposed to be the god of the river Tigris . . . 11, 120
ZU (bird). A metamorphosis of the god Ungal-turda 171
ZYRIANIAN LANGUAGE. Its Accadian affinities . . . . 300, etc.

www.ingramcontent.com/pod-product-compliance
Lightning Source LLC
Chambersburg PA
CBHW020528300426
44111CB00008B/587